Assessing and Managing Problematic Sexual Interests

Assessing and Managing Problematic Sexual Interests: A Practitioner's Guide provides a thorough review of atypical sexual interests and offers various ways through which they can be measured and controlled, including compassion-focused and psychoanalytic approaches.

This unique guide presents a detailed analysis of deviant sexual interest. Part I, 'Assessment', overviews the range of sexual interests and fantasies in men and women. Part II, 'Management', investigates the cutting-edge tools, approaches, interventions, and treatment advances used in a variety of settings to control deviant sexual interest. In Part III, 'Approaches to assessment and management', the authors consider how females with sexual convictions can be assessed and how offence paralleling behaviour can be used for assessment and treatment. Throughout, *Assessing and Managing Problematic Sexual Interests* offers necessary perspectives and emerging research from international experts at the forefront of this field.

With a thorough assessment of current research and a critical overview of treatment advances for problematic sexual interests, *Assessing and Managing Problematic Sexual Interests* is an essential resource for clinical and forensic psychologists, probation officers, academics, students working in the field, and members of allied professional fields.

Geraldine Akerman is a Chartered and Registered Forensic Psychologist and Therapy Manager at HMP Grendon. She is a Visiting Lecturer at the University of Birmingham, UK, and Honorary Professor of Cardiff Metropolitan University, UK, and Chair Elect of the Division of Forensic Psychology.

Derek Perkins is a Registered and Chartered Clinical and Forensic Psychologist, Professor of Forensic Psychology at Royal Holloway University of London, and Co-Director of the onlineProtect research group on internet-related sexual offending. He has published on forensic assessment, sexual offending, sexual homicide, and child sexual exploitation, and regularly serves as an expert witness in Criminal and Family Court proceedings.

Ross M. Bartels is a Senior Lecturer in Forensic Psychology and leader of the Forensic and Clinical Research Group at the University of Lincoln, UK.

Issues in Forensic Psychology

Series editors: Richard Shuker and Geraldine Akerman

Research in Practice for Forensic Professionals
Edited by Kerry Sheldon, Jason Davies & Kevin Howells

Secure Recovery
Approaches to Recovery in Forensic Mental Health Settings
Edited by Gerard Drennan & Deborah Alred

Managing Clinical Risk
A Guide to Effective Practice
Edited by Caroline Logan & Lorraine Johnstone

Handbook on the Study of Multiple Perpetrator Rape
A Multidisciplinary Response to an International Problem
Edited by Miranda A. H. Horvath & Jessica Woodhams

Forensic Practice in the Community
Edited by Zoe Ashmore & Richard Shuker

Supervision for Forensic Practitioners
Edited by Jason Davies

Transforming Environments and Rehabilitation
A Guide for Practitioners in Forensic Settings and Criminal Justice
Edited by Geraldine Akerman, Adrian Needs & Claire Bainbridge

The Psychology of Criminal Investigation
From Theory to Practice
Edited by Andy Griffiths & Rebecca Milne

Assessing and Managing Problematic Sexual Interests
A Practitioner's Guide
Edited by Geraldine Akerman, Derek Perkins & Ross M. Bartels

For more information about this series, please visit:
www.routledge.com/Issues-in-Forensic-Psychology/book-series/IFP

Assessing and Managing Problematic Sexual Interests

A Practitioner's Guide

Edited by
Geraldine Akerman, Derek Perkins
and Ross M. Bartels

Routledge
Taylor & Francis Group

LONDON AND NEW YORK

First published 2021
by Routledge
2 Park Square, Milton Park, Abingdon, Oxon OX14 4RN

and by Routledge
52 Vanderbilt Avenue, New York, NY 10017

Routledge is an imprint of the Taylor & Francis Group, an informa business

British Library Cataloguing-in-Publication Data
A catalogue record for this book is available from the British Library

Library of Congress Cataloging-in-Publication Data
A catalog record has been requested for this book

ISBN: 978-0-367-25417-9 (hbk)
ISBN: 978-0-367-25418-6 (pbk)
ISBN: 978-0-429-28769-5 (ebk)

Typeset in Minion Pro
by Swales & Willis, Exeter, Devon, UK

Contents

Contributors

Geraldine Akerman is a Chartered and Registered Forensic Psychologist and Therapy Manager at HMP Grendon. She is a Visiting Lecturer at the University of Birmingham, UK and Honorary Professor of Cardiff Metropolitan University, UK and Chair Elect of the Division of Forensic Psychology.

Ross M. Bartels is a Senior Lecturer in Forensic Psychology and leader of the Forensic and Clinical Research Group at the University of Lincoln, UK.

Nicholas Blagden is an Associate Professor in Forensic Psychology, a co-founder and trustee of the Safer Living Foundation, Chartered Psychologist, and Head of the Sexual Offences Crime and Misconduct Research Unit (SOCAMRU). He has worked and researched within criminal justice and prison settings for over 10 years. His work has been funded by the Her Majesty's Prison and Probation Service (HMPPS) and he is currently engaged in numerous collaborative forensic projects with NTU, HMPPS, Institute for Mental Health, Canada and Correctional Services Australia. He sits on NOTA's policy and practice committee.

Sébastien Brouillette-Alarie (PhD) is the Scientific Coordinator of the Canadian Practitioners Network for the Prevention of Radicalization and Extremist Violence (CPN-PREV) and a lecturer in criminology at the Université de Montréal. He has published peer-reviewed articles on the risk assessment of criminal recidivism, the latent structure of risk scales for sexual offenders, the aetiology of risk in sexual offenders, online radicalisation, sexual sadism, the offending process of hebephiles, and psychopathy among women.

Meagan Donaldson is currently a Senior Psychologist in Sex and Violent Offender Therapeutic Programs, Corrective Services New South Wales, Australia. She has worked with sexual offenders for the past fifteen years, primarily in the delivery of treatment for incarcerated sexual offenders within a therapeutic environment.

Paul M. Hamilton, PhD earned his MA in Psychology from the University of Houston in 1977 and his PhD in Clinical Psychology from the Fielding Institute of Graduate Studies in 1996. Dr Hamilton is licensed in Texas as a

Licensed Psychologist, Licensed Specialist in School Psychology (LSSP) and Licensed Sex Offender Treatment Provider (LSOTP). He is Certified as an EEG Senior Fellow Emeritus in the Biofeedback Certification International Alliance (BCIA) and is an Emeritus Registrant with the National Register of Health Service Providers in Psychology. At the University of Houston, Victoria, he served as a Clinical Assistant Professor and program director for the schools Master's Degree program in Forensic Psychology.

Jennifer Hardy is a Lecturer in Psychology at the University of Chester, where she teaches on a number of forensic psychology modules. She gained her Bachelor's degree in Psychology at the University of Nottingham in 2012 and her Master's degree in Forensic Psychology at Nottingham Trent University in 2013. In 2013 she was awarded a PhD scholarship by Sheffield Hallam University. Jenny is currently lecturing at the University of Chester across a number of undergraduate and postgraduate modules. Her main research interests are in offender resettlement and treatment and women in the Criminal Justice System.

Kerensa Hocken is a registered Forensic Psychologist. In 2016 she was the winner of the prestigious Butler Trust award for excellence in correctional services, presented by Princess Anne. Kerensa is a trustee and co-founder of the Safer Living Foundation (SLF), a member of the Compassionate Mind Foundation, and cofounder of the CFT forensic special interest group.

Todd E. Hogue is a registered Forensic and Clinical Psychologist. His PhD research focused on the development of a self-report measure of denial in sexual offenders. During the early SOTP training he became interested staff attitudes and developed the Attitudes Towards Sexual Offenders (ATS) scale which is still actively being used. In 2006 he moved to an academic role at the University of Lincoln and is currently Professor of Forensic Psychology and Director of Research for the College of Social Science.

Lawrence Jones is a Forensic and Clinical Psychologist whose career has included working in the community, at HMP Wormwood Scrubs and at Rampton High Secure Hospital, UK. He is a former Chair of the Division of Forensic Psychology and teaches on the Sheffield and Leicester Clinical Psychology doctorate courses and the Nottingham Forensic Psychology Doctorate.

Emma Marshall is a PhD student and Hourly Paid Lecturer at Nottingham Trent University. She is part of the Sexual Offences, Crime and Misconduct Research Unit (SOCAMRU). Emma is currently undertaking a mixed methods PhD research project evaluating the effectiveness of medication to manage problematic sexual arousal (MMPSA) and improve well-being in a community setting. The research project has been designed to assess the impact and effectiveness of MMPSA in reducing problematic levels of sexual compulsivity and improving well-being for individuals who have recently been released from a custodial sentence.

Danielle Matsuo is the Director State-wide Programs, Corrective Services NSW. She has over 15 years' experience as a psychologist in a correctional environment, after completing her Master's degree in Forensic Psychology at the University of New South Wales. Danielle is responsible for the development, co-ordination and ongoing integrity of offender programs addressing the criminogenic needs of sexual, violent and general offenders in NSW.

Christine Norman is a Senior Lecturer in psychology at Nottingham Trent University. Her teaching and research are in biological psychology, psychopharmacology, forensic psychology and mental health. Current research interests are in overcontrolled personality type in relation to offending, the use of medication to manage problematic sexual arousal, sexual addiction and the implications of polyvagal theory in mental health.

Sarah Paquette (PhD) works as a Specialist Sexual Offending in the Internet Child Exploitation (ICE) unit of the provincial police of Quebec, Canada. She completed her PhD in psychology and is currently a lecturer in criminology at the University of Montreal. Her research focuses on the factors associated with online and contact sexual offending against children. She currently coordinates and leads the PRESEL research project that aims to help develop best police practices in order prevent child exploitation and to elaborate efficient intervention strategies and systematic case prioritisation tools.

Marek Páv, PhD is a psychiatrist and sexologist working in Bohnice Psychiatric Hospital as a Consultant and Medical Director and as Assistant Professor at the 1st Medical Faculty of Charles University. He is currently involved in the reform of the forensic care system in the Czech Republic. His research projects include psychiatric rehabilitation, assessment of cost of care, somatic care in SMI, risk assessment systems and sexology.

Derek Perkins is a Registered and Chartered Clinical and Forensic Psychologist, Professor of Forensic Psychology at Royal Holloway University of London, and Co-Director of the onlineProtect research group on internet-related sexual offending. He has published on forensic assessment, sexual offending, sexual homicide, and child sexual exploitation, and regularly serves as an expert witness in Criminal and Family Court proceedings.

Pekka Santtila is Professor of Applied Psychology at the Åbo Akademi University in Turku, Finland. He has published widely in the area of legal and forensic psychology with a focus on different aspects of child sexual abuse and its investigation. He has also led an Academy of Finland funded research project on implicit measurement of sexual interest in children.

Alexander Schmidt is a clinical psychologist and Professor of Forensic Psychology at Hamburg School of Medicine. With his colleague Prof Rainer Banse he developed and validated the EISIP in a number of settings.

Petra Skřivánková is a psychologist at Psychiatric Hospital Bohnice in Prague in the Czech Republic. She received her doctorate in Clinical Psychology from the Charles University. Her current research interests include high-risk assessment of offenders. She is currently completing a standardisation of a high-risk assessment tool for adolescents SAVRY in the Czech Republic.

Jamie Walton is a National Specialist Lead in HM Prison and Probation Service. He is a Registered Practitioner Psychologist (Forensic) with the Health and Care Professions Council (HCPC), a Chartered Psychologist and an Associate Fellow of the British Psychological Society (AFBPsS). Since 2006, Jamie has worked in prison and healthcare settings predominantly supporting individuals with convictions for sexual offending to lead crime-free lives. His research interests are primarily in the causes of paraphilia and the design and evaluation of therapeutic interventions designed to support safer living with paraphilia.

Jayson Ware is currently the Group Director, Offender Services and Programs, Corrective Services New South Wales, Australia. He has researched or worked with sexual offenders for the past twenty years and has authored 35 journal articles or book chapters primarily relating to the treatment of sexual offenders. He has particular research interests in offender denial, group work, enhancing treatment effectiveness, and therapeutic communities.

Charlotte Wesson is currently a PhD student at the University of Lincoln. Her PhD research centres on measurement of sexual preference using a variety of established and emerging measures. Though this research is mainly developed with 'typical' samples, there is scope to extrapolate this to forensic populations.

Belinda Winder is a Professor in Forensic Psychology and Research Director of the Centre for Crime, Offending, Prevention and Engagement at Nottingham Trent University. She is also part of the Sexual Offences, Crime and Misconduct Research Unit (SOCAMRU) in the Department of Psychology at Nottingham Trent University. Belinda is a co-founder, trustee, Vice Chair and Head of Research and Evaluation for the Safer Living Foundation. She received a Butler Trust Certificate for her work in prisoner rehabilitation in 2016, the Robin Corbett Award for Prisoner Rehabilitation in 2015, and the Guardian University Award for Social and Community Impact in 2016.

Rachel Worthington is a Consultant Psychologist, a Chartered Psychologist, and a full member of the Division of Forensic Psychology, including holding Associate Fellow status. She is also a Chartered Scientist and is fully registered with the HCPC. She is a Senior Lecturer at the University of Central Lancashire teaching on the Masters in Forensic Psychology and is also an accredited therapist in eye movement desensitisation and reprocessing (EMDR) for the treatment of trauma.

Jessica Yakeley is a Consultant Psychiatrist in Forensic Psychotherapy and Director of the Portman Clinic, and Director of Medical Education, Tavistock and Portman NHS Foundation Trust. She is also a Fellow of the British Psychoanalytic Society and Editor of the journal Psychoanalytic Psychotherapy. She is Research Lead for the Royal College of Psychiatrists Psychotherapy Faculty and for the British Psychoanalytic Council. She is currently leading the national development and implementation of new services for a multi-site randomised-controlled trial of mentalisation-based treatment for antisocial personality disorder as part of the UK Government's National Personality Disorder Offender Pathways Strategy.

Angelo Zappalà is a psychologist, clinical criminologist and cognitive behaviour therapist. He was awarded his PhD in Psychology at Åbo Akademi University. He teaches Psychology of Deviance at IUSTO (Pontifical Salesian University of Turin, Italy). In the same University he is the director of the CRIMELAB. He is also the director of Cognitive Behavioral Therapy School, the CBT.ACADEMY (approved by the Italian Ministry of the University and scientific research) and the director of the Italian Festival of Criminology of Turin.

This volume is dedicated to Dr Ruth Mann.
Ruth's kind, gentle and inspiring presence, both as a valued colleague and much loved friend, over many years will never be forgotten. It was always a pleasure to be in her company, to learn from her modestly of-fered wisdom and to have so many happy memories of times spent with her.

Series foreword

From its origins as a British Psychological Society journal, the *Issues in Forensic Psychology* series has had two central aspirations. The first has been to promote novel, innovative and relevant ideas within forensic psychology into a wider academic and professional domain, beyond that inhibited by Forensic Psychologists themselves. The series has always intended to make the forensic psychology open, accessible and available to practitioners in associated fields in other professional backgrounds. The second aspiration of the series has been to identify areas where gaps in research and practice were becoming apparent and for editions within the series to identify and respond to areas of emerging need and interest. *Issues in Forensic Psychology* has also wanted to approach traditional themes in the field from fresh perspectives as developments in the field take new directions. This was evident from the first edition of the book series which took a critical view of some of the well-established and perhaps well-worn ideas in the risk assessment literature, revising and developing concepts within the field of risk management and clinical formulation. Later editions such as the edition on secure recovery came to be influential in establishing new directions in forensic service development. This examined the accepted concepts of patient 'illness' arguing how therapeutic arrangements enabling a patient's involvement and engagement were key in personal recovery. Some of these ideas became expanded and developed in the more recent edition on transformative environments and rehabilitation which made a powerful argument for an empowering social climate as the portal for personal and therapeutic change. Developing applied practice has been emphasised throughout the series. The edition on forensic research opened up a broad range of research methodologies to a wider audience, making a compelling case for their utility and value. A later volume on supervision skills and practice brought supervision to life, making a strong argument for its utility and value for all those working in the forensic field. A volume on forensic practice in the community was commissioned in response to literature being disproportionately weighted towards those working in closed conditions despite the reality that the vast majority of forensic service users are likely to be under supervision, risk management or treatment within the community. Other editions have provided in-depth focus on areas where understanding

of offending needs to be improved, made evident in an edition on multi-
perpetrator rape which expanded knowledge in a neglected area.

This current volume, *Assessing and Managing Problematic Sexual Interests*,
edited by Akerman, Perkins and Bartels, provides a long-overdue, much-
anticipated and timely addition to the book series. As noted by Tony Beech and
by many of the contributors, recent developments in the field make it apparent
there is a clear need for a contribution to the field which provides an informed,
comprehensive and in-depth analysis of the area of deviant sexual interest.
The contributors certainly fulfil this objective. Part I provides a focussed,
nuanced, concise and in-depth analysis of developments, challenges, innovations and limitations of what is known about the assessment of sexual interest.
These chapters explore what is known about the measurement of interests
with specific populations such as those who have offended against children
and men who have committed sexual and non-sexual violent offences. The
developments in contrasting assessment technologies, including self-report
and physiological, are considered through the sharing of research and practice across different cultures and countries. Exciting and innovative research
is also covered in this section, drawing on the most recent developments in
implicit measures of attitude and sexual interest, providing an important contribution to an area which has significant potential. Other novel and valuable
developments in assessment practice are also considered. A chapter on Rapid
Serial Visual Presentation makes a strong case for the utility of this method
whilst reflecting on directions required for expanding its use. This theme is
expanded upon in a chapter reviewing eye related measures providing new
perspectives and contributions to the literature. Part I concludes by examining the relationship between sexual fantasy and deviant interest and provides
a novel angle and perspective of relevance to practitioners.

Part II explores the area of management and treatment from novel, varied
and contrasting approaches. The importance of contextual or process issues
in building an optimal therapeutic for the treatment of sexual deviancy is
emphasised; the role and utility of compassion and acceptance and how this
can provide an evidence-based and effective intervention enhancing the therapeutic relationship is also strongly made. The contribution of psychoanalytic
approaches is then made in an accessible and thought-provoking way. The
role and contribution of medication, is also considered and its relevance and
its relevance clearly highlighted.

In Part III the book concludes with two chapters that provide an overview
of two current therapeutic approaches. One is an exploration of assessment
and treatment approaches with females who have committed sexual offences,
the other exploring the mechanisms linking trauma and risk describing how

offence paralleling behaviour can be used to monitor ongoing offence-related sexual interest.

Together, this collection of chapters comprises an important and valuable contribution to the series which will be welcomed by all practitioners and academics with an interest in forensic practice.

Richard Shuker and Geraldine Akerman
Series Editors

Foreword

Probably one of the first to scientifically describe atypical sexual interests was Friedrich Salomon Krauss (1859–1938), who used the term 'paraphilia'[1] to describe *inverted erotic interests* (Beech, Miner & Thornton, 2016). John Money (1986) probably did the most to popularise the term 'paraphilia', which he described as 'a sexuoerotic embellishment of, or alternative to the official, ideological norm' (p. 139). As the most recent definition of deviant sexual interests as paraphilias,[2] Blanchard (2010) (chair of the Paraphilias Subworkgroup for the Diagnostic and Statistical Manual for Mental Disorders, Version 5 (DSM-5) Work Group on Sexual and Gender Identity Disorders), suggested this should be: 'any powerful and persistent sexual interest other than sexual interest in copulatory or pre-copulatory behavior with phenotypically normal, consenting adult human partners' (p. 367). DSM-5 also makes a distinction between aberrant sexual interests that are: (1) *anomalous sexual preferences*, such as: (1a) *courtship disorders* such as rape, exhibitionism, frotteurism, telephone scatologia (obscene phone calling), and voyeurism; (1b) *algolagnic disorders*, where sexual arousal is dependent on pain and suffering; and (2) *anomalous target preferences*, such as having a sexual interest in children. This type of offending is described in detail in Chapter 1, where research is described that examines paraphilic/non-paraphilic interest in those who have committed sexual offences against children). In Chapter 2 comparisons are made between sexual interests of violent men (both sexually and non-sexually violent).

It is not my intention to pick apart the book chapter by chapter, but to note that given the emerging themes in the field, the time has certainly come for a book that offers up-to-date information on the issues around deviant sexual interests, whether they be theoretical, research-informed or treatment-focussed. I would note that in my years being involved in forensic research, in relation to understanding why sexual offenders do what they do, and having an input into the treatment of such individuals, it has been my privilege to know the editors of this book, and to read their work. I also would note that those who have contributed chapters are at the forefront of work that attempts to assess, understand and provide treatment for those who sexually offend. Therefore, I am delighted that I can provide this foreword.

I would also note that the book itself is very wide-ranging and provides a useful resource around assessment and treatment of (deviant) sexual interests. Hence the reader will certainly find a wealth of important information contained within these pages.

Anthony Beech
Professor Emeritus
January 2020

Notes

1. This term is still in use today particularly in the psychiatric world (see Beech et al., 2016) although in this volume, where chapters are mainly written by psychologists, the preferred term used is 'deviant sexual interests'.
2. Just as an aside the actual number of unsual/paraphilic interests, as counted by Aggrawal (2008) number at least 547 (see: en.wikipedia.org/wiki/List_of_paraphilias). However, in truth, there are probably many more, as there is little limit to the human imagination, as the human sexual drive is a strong, primal motivator.

References

Beech, A. R., Miner, M., & Thornton, D. (2016, April). Paraphilias in DSM-5. *The Annual Review of Clinical Psychology, 12,* 13.1–13.24.

Blanchard, R. (2010). The DSM diagnostic criteria for transvestic fetishism. *Archives of Sexual Behavior, 239,* 363–372.

Money, J. (1986). *Lovemaps: Clinical concepts of sexual/erotic health and pathology, paraphilia, and gender transposition in childhood, adolescence, and maturity.* New York: Irvington.

Part I

Assessment

How do sexual interests cluster and relate to sexual offending behaviours against children?

1

Sarah Paquette and Sébastien Brouillette-Alarie

Introduction

Sexual interest, whether *normophilic* or *paraphilic*, is important for understanding human sexual behaviour as there are strong links between one's sexual interest and behaviour (Kafka & Hennen, 1999, 2002; Långstrom & Hanson, 2006). According to the DSM-5, a normophilic sexual interest refers to an 'interest in genital stimulation or preparatory fondling with phenotypically normal, physically mature, consenting human partners'; all other intense and persistent sexual interests are understood to be paraphilias (APA, 2013, p. 685). Paraphilias are not illegal per se but acting on some of them may constitute a criminal offence. An example of a legal sexual behaviour derived from a paraphilic interest would be to use an inanimate object, such as a shoe, to masturbate in a private room. Examples of illegal sexual behaviours are committing an act of bestiality driven by zoophilic interests, having sexual contact with a child driven by paedophilic interests, or displaying indecent behaviour in a public space. Individuals who commit sexual offences, including those who commit offences against children, may exhibit one or many paraphilias (Abel, Becker, Cunningham-Rathner, Mittelman, & Rouleau, 1988).

To contribute to knowledge on this topic, this chapter briefly reviews the scientific literature on the variety of sexual interests found among people who have committed sexual offences against children, followed by an analysis of the organizational patterns of these interests as well as their links to sexual offending behaviours. A discussion on the implications for assessment, treatment, and research concludes the chapter.

Sexual interests of men who have committed sexual offences

Paraphilic sexual interests are included in all contemporary multifactorial theories of sexual offending (e.g. Finkelhor, 1984; Hall & Hirschman, 1992; Ward & Beech, 2006, 2017; Ward & Siegert, 2002) and in a number of single factor theories (e.g. Kafka, 1997, 2003; Laws & Marshall, 1990; McGuire, Carlisle, & Young, 1965). McGuire et al. (1965) suggest that deviant sexual preferences are acquired through operant conditioning by masturbating to fantasies derived from early sexual experiences (i.e., the initial stimulus). Deviant sexual fantasies are reinforced by the pleasure procured from masturbation and non-deviant preferences are gradually extinguished when they are no longer used in masturbation scenarios. Sexual fantasies are also thought to play a role in the maintenance of sexual preferences. Laws and Marshall (1990) add that sexual preferences can disappear if negative reinforcement (e.g. punishment for acting on deviant sexual interests) occurs. These explanations for sexual preferences, drawn from conditioning and social learning theories, suggest that individuals with paedophilia who sexually offend against children develop and condition their sexual interests in children based on deviant early experiences that are later 'relived' as fantasies and used during masturbatory activities.

Links between paraphilic sexual interests and engaging and maintaining sexual offending behaviours have been well established (e.g. Baur, Forsman, Santtila, Johansson, Sandnabba, & Långström, 2017; Hanson & Morton-Bourgon, 2005; Mann, Hanson, & Thornton, 2010; Stephens, Cantor, Goodwill, & Seto, 2017). However, it appears that some specific types of sexual interests are better predictors of specific types of sexual offending; for example, paedophilia is a better predictor than sexual sadism of sexual offending against children (e.g. Mann et al., 2010).

Paedophilia

Paedophilia is defined as sexual interest in prepubescent children. This interest can be directed towards boys, girls, or both, and occur inside (incest) or outside (extrafamilial) the family, or both. It can be exclusive or not to children (APA, 2013). Although its precise prevalence is unknown in the general population, it is estimated to be between 1% and 3% among males and much lower among females (APA, 2013; Seto, 2013). Paedophilia appears to be the most documented sexual interest among individuals who commit sexual offences against children. While strongly associated with such offending behaviours (Hanson & Morton-Bourgon, 2005; Mann et al., 2010), it is not the only explanation, as only approximately half the men known to have committed contact sexual offences against children meet the diagnostic criteria for paedophilia (Seto, 2008). Paedophilia appears to be more common among men who consume child sexual exploitation material (CSEM) over the internet than among those who have committed contact sexual offences against children and even less common among those who use the internet to solicit children (Babchishin, Hanson, & Hermann, 2011; Babchishin, Hanson, & VanZuylen, 2015; Seto, Wood, Babchishin, & Flynn, 2012). Men who sexually solicit children over the internet are more frequently diagnosed with *hebephilia*; that is, a sexual interest in pubescent children (Brouillette-Alarie & Proulx, 2014; Seto et al., 2012).

In terms of offending behaviours, men with paedophilia tend to vary in the severity of their crimes, the number of victims, and recidivism risk level. Men who are sexually attracted to boys tend to have more contact victims than those who are sexually attracted to girls, while those who commit sexual offences against extrafamilial victims tend to have more victims than incestuous men (Abel, Becker, Mittelman, Cunningham-Rathner, Rouleau, & Murphy, 1987). Offences of incestuous men more frequently involve sexual intercourse – as opposed to fondling and genital contact – than those of extrafamilial offending men (Abel et al., 1987). In terms of risk of reoffending, sexual interests in boys, evidenced either by sexual contact with male children or consuming CSEM depicting boys, is associated with a higher risk of sexual recidivism and targeting extrafamilial victims (Hanson & Morton-Bourgon, 2005; Seto & Eke, 2015). These results show that paedophilia can manifest itself in different ways, leading to variation in sexual offending behaviours. The presence of other types of sexual interests in addition to paedophilia tends to increase the risk of reoffending among sexual offenders (Mann et al., 2010).

Other interests

A diversity of deviant sexual interests other than paedophilia are often observed among men who sexually offend. For example, among a sample of 221 men convicted of sexual offences against children, Smallbone and Wortley (2004) found that almost one-third reported sexual interests in voyeurism (32%), with lower prevalences found for exhibitionism (9%), public masturbation (7%), frotteurism (6%), telephone scatalogia (5%), fetishism (4%), masochism (4%), transvestic fetishim (3%), sadism (3%), and zoophilia (1%). Interestingly, while none of these sexual interests were associated with sexual offending behaviours, some of them – voyeurism, frotteurism, telephone scatalogia, masochism, and sadism – were significantly associated with nonsexual offending. In a sample of 30 men who had sexually offended against children and 28 who had sexually offended against adolescents, Sea and Beauregard

(2018) found evidence of sexual interest in sadism, voyeurism, and exhibitionism, but not of fetishism, public masturbation, frotteurism, masochism, telephone scatologia, necrophilia, or zoophilia. In a study comparing the sexual interests of men who had committed contact sexual offences against children, CSEM users, and mixed offenders (i.e., those who had committed both online and contact sexual offences), Sheldon and Howitt (2008) found that the fantasies most frequently reported by participants were normophilic. Paraphilias involving humiliation, violence, coercion, and death were all extremely rare and sometimes never reported. They also found that men who had consumed CSEM reported greater numbers of sexual fantasies involving female children but did not find any differences in sexual fantasies involving male children, humiliation, force, homo/heterosexual adults, non-contact sexual behaviours, and bestiality.

Men who consumed CSEM also displayed some paraphilic interests in the pornographic material used. Although pornographic material may be considered only a proxy for sexual interests, Eke and Seto (2017) found correlates between the preferences of men who use CSEM in terms of age/gender and the characteristics of victims depicted into their material, suggesting an association between sexual interests and the pornographic content viewed. A variety of pornographic content was found in CSEM users' collections. In a sample of 231 men arrested for CSEM-related offences, Endrass and colleagues (2009) found that 47% had pornography involving brutality, 45% involving excrement, and 44% involving animals. In a comparison of men who had committed online, contact, and mixed sexual offences against children, Paquette and Cortoni (2017) found that CSEM users reported significantly more consumption of pornography involving bondage, homosexual males, heterosexual adults, sex in groups, bestiality, and rape than those with contact offences. They did not find differences in terms of consumption of pornography depicting homosexual females but found that consumption of bestial pornography was positively associated with online sexual offending behaviours. No other type of pornographic content was associated with sexual offending behaviours against children.

Multiple paraphilias

Initial conceptualizations of paraphilia considered it to be a unidimensional construct: one was either sexually deviant or not (see Heil & Simons, 2008). Such conceptualizations failed to acknowledge various types of sexual interests or the coexistence of both normophilic and paraphilic interests. An early study by Abel and colleagues (1988), conducted among a community sample of 561 men diagnosed with paraphilias, refutes this conceptualization,

showing that very few (10%) of these men exhibited only one paraphilic interest. They also found that some paraphilias were less likely to be co-morbid
than others. For example, 52% of the men diagnosed with transsexualism had
no other paraphilia, while all men diagnosed with either bestiality, fetishism,
sadism, masochism, or coprophilia had at least one other deviant sexual interest. Among those sexually interested in children, 72% to 96% had multiple
paraphilias – up to 10 different kinds.

Having multiple paraphilias has been established as a risk factor for sexual recidivism (e.g. Brouillette-Alarie, Proulx, & Hanson, 2018; Mann et al.,
2010), but studies generally remain vague about the nature of this relationship,
neglecting to examine, for example, whether certain combinations of paraphilias are more frequent than others, which are most risk-relevant, or how
many are necessary for risk to increase. Preliminary investigations suggest that
some combinations of sexual paraphilias are more common than others. For
example, a Finnish population-based study examined the co-occurrence of
paraphilias among 5990 male and female participants and found that sadism
was more strongly associated with masochism but less strongly associated
with exhibitionism (Baur et al., 2017). Exhibitionism appeared to be more
strongly related to voyeurism, and some paraphilias were more strongly associated with sexually coercive behaviour (e.g. sadism vs transvestic fetishism).
The co-occurrence of paraphilias was a better predictor of sexual offending
than any paraphilia taken individually.

The current study

The scientific literature not only shows that paraphilic sexual interests are
associated with sexual offending behaviour, but also that: (1) certain types of
interest are better predictors of offending behaviour than others, and (2) the
presence of multiple paraphilias are associated with a greater risk of reoffending than having only one. However, although it has been shown that some
sexual paraphilias are more frequently found together, it remains unclear
whether certain combinations are associated with particular types of sexual
offending behaviour. The purpose of the current study was therefore to examine whether there are links between clusters of sexual interests and sexual
offending behaviours in a sample of men who had committed either online
and contact sexual offences against children or both.

While normophilic and paraphilic interests have been found to be characteristic of men who sexually offend against children, other research has found
evidence of atypical sexual interests among non-offending samples. A recent survey conducted among the general population in Canada revealed that both men
and women report sexual fantasies involving a variety of paraphilic behaviours

(Joyal & Carpentier, 2016). Men reported fantasies involving voyeurism (60%), fetishism (40%), exhibitionism (35%), frotteurism (34%), and masochism (19%), with less interest in sadism (10%), transvestism (7%), and paedophilia (1%). Given this finding, the scope of the current study was extended to include a sample of men with nonsexual offences in order to examine possible similarities or differences concerning normophilic and paraphilic interests.

Method

Participants

A total of 221 men convicted of either sexual or non-sexual offences took part in this study; all were incarcerated or under community supervision by the Correctional Service of the Province of Quebec, Canada. The mean age of participants was 41.05 years old ($SD = 13.05$; range = 19 to 78). Almost two-thirds of the sample ($n = 147$) had committed sexual offences against children; the other third ($n = 74$) had committed general or violent offences only. On average, the group that had committed sexual offences had .77 convictions for child pornography offences ($SD = 1.35$; range = 0 to 7); .50 convictions for child luring offences ($SD = 2.19$; range = 0 to 20); 1.01 convictions for contact sexual offences against children ($SD = 1.49$; range= 0 to 12); 1.97 convictions for general offences ($SD = 4.45$; range = 0 to 24); .57 convictions for violent offences ($SD = 1.46$; range = 0 to 11); and .86 convictions for breaches of probation restrictions ($SD = 2.66$; range = 0 to 24).

Men with non-sexual offences had an average of 7.62 convictions for general offences ($SD = 8.95$; range = 0 to 43), 1.51 for violent offences ($SD = 3.05$; range = 0 to 20); and 1.91 for breaches of probation restrictions ($SD = 2.80$; range = 0 to 13). Two participants were excluded from the analyses because of missing data.

Measures

SEXUAL INTEREST CARDSORT QUESTIONNAIRE

Participants completed the Sexual Interest Cardsort Questionnaire (SICQ; Abel & Becker, 1979), a 75-item self-report questionnaire designed to measure normophilic and paraphilic sexual interests. The SICQ is composed of 15 scales that deal, using clinical vignettes, with adult homosexuality, adult heterosexuality, voyeurism, exhibitionism, frotteurism, extrafamilial molestation of girls, incestuous molestation of girls, extrafamilial molestation of boys, incestuous molestation of boys, rape of adult females, sadism, masochism, male gender identity, female gender identity, and transvestic fetishism.

Examples of vignettes include 'I'm holding a burning cigarette butt against the big tits of a 30-year-old brunette. She's screaming for me to stop', measuring interest in sadism, or 'My son is curled up beside me in bed. I'm gently rubbing his small penis; he is getting an erection', measuring interest in incestuous molestation of boys. Each vignette is scored on seven-point Likert items ranging from 'extreme sexual repulsion' to 'extreme interest' (–3 to +3). Each scale ranges from –15 to +15. The questionnaire was validated on a sample of 371 men seeking assessment or treatment for sexual offending behaviours or interests. The internal consistency of the scales ranged from .71 to .97 (Holland, Zolondek, Abel, Jordan, & Becker, 2000).

Because extrafamilial molestation of girls and incestuous molestation of girls were collinear ($r = .87$), they were merged together into 'child molestation of girls'. The same was done for extrafamilial molestation of boys and incestuous molestation of boys, which were merged into 'child molestation of boys' ($r = .93$).

SEXUAL OFFENDING BEHAVIOURS AGAINST CHILDREN

The range and severity of sexual offending behaviours against children was operationalized in a 4-category ordinal variable: '0' meant that the individual never committed a sexual offence against children; '1' that he committed at least one online sexual offence, but no contact offence; '2' that he committed at least one contact sexual offence against children, but no online offence; and '3' that he committed both online and contact sexual offences against children. Criminal offences were obtained from participants' institutional files.

Analyses

Factor analysis

Exploratory factor analysis using MPlus v6.12 (Muthén & Muthén, 2010) was applied to the SICQ in order to identify clusters of sexual interests. Since the objective was to examine how sexual interests cluster rather than to validate the factor structure of the SICQ, factor analysis was applied directly to SICQ scales rather than to individual items.

Factor extraction and rotation

Factors were extracted using the weighted least square means- and variance-adjusted (WLSMV) method (Muthén & Muthén, 2010). Because the resulting factors were expected to be correlated, an oblique rotation method (geomin) was also used.

Factor retention

Four criteria were used to determine the number of factors retained in the final model: Kaiser's criterion (i.e., eigenvalues > 1.00; Kaiser, 1960), the scree plot (Cattell, 1966), parallel analysis (Horn, 1965), and Velicer's minimum average partial test (MAP test; Velicer, 1976). Each factor retention method has advantages and disadvantages, and therefore using multiple factor retention methods is preferred (Henson & Roberts, 2006). We acquired results that showed agreement among the different methods.

Factor structure fit

Factor structure fit was assessed using three indices. The root mean square error of approximation (RMSEA) assessed the lack of fit in a factor structure relative to a perfect factor structure (Tabachnick & Fidell, 2013); ideally, an RMSEA should not exceed .06 (Hu & Bentler, 1999). The comparative fit index (CFI) assessed the factor structure fit relative to a baseline model where there are no relationship between items (Brown, 2006); ideally, a CFI of .90 or greater indicates a good fit, but .95 is preferable (Hu & Bentler, 1999). Finally, the Tucker-Lewis Index (TLI) assessed the factor structure fit relative to a baseline model while taking into account the number of parameters (Tucker & Lewis, 1973); a TLI of .90 or greater indicates a good fit, .95 being preferable (Hu & Bentler, 1999).

Criteria for factor inclusion

The chosen criterion for the inclusion of items in factors was factor loadings of at least .40 (Stevens, 1992).

Ordinal regression

Ordinal regression (McCullagh, 1980) was used to assess the links between clusters of sexual interests resulting from the factor analysis and sexual offending behaviours. Ordinal regression is a type of regression adapted for ordinal dependent variables and was computed using SPSS 23.

Results

Factor analysis

Exploratory factor analysis was performed on SICQ scales to identify clusters of sexual interests. The convergence of results from the various factor retention

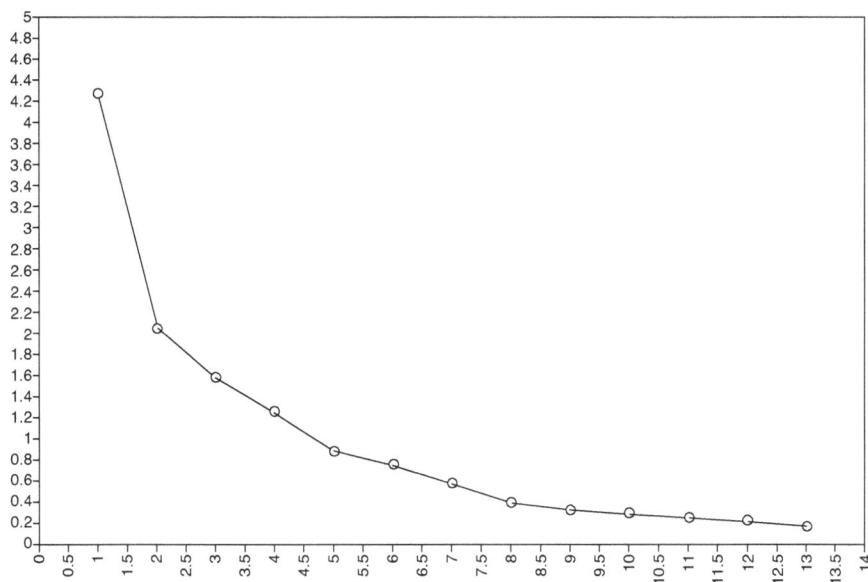

Figure 1.1 Scree plot.

criteria indicated a structure of four factors. Kaiser's criterion suggested four factors (those above 1 on the *y*-axis in Figure 1.1), as did parallel analysis. The scree plot (Figure 1.1) suggested four factors, as the point of inflection occurred at the fifth factor and it is agreed that only factors located above this point should be retained (Cattell, 1966; Field, 2013). The MAP test favoured a three-factor solution. Fit indices suggested a five-factor solution but contained a Heywood case – a factor loading greater than 1.00 (Heywood, 1931). Heywood cases, known to occur when sample size is too small or when too many factors are extracted, make a factor solution inadmissible (Minitab Inc., 2017). We therefore chose to retain the four-factor solution, as it was the most consensual.

The goodness-of-fit of the four-factor solution was underwhelming, with a RMSEA of .114 [90% CI = .093 – .135], a CFI of .93, and a TLI of .83. However, the four-factor solution was more theoretically intuitive than the five-factor one, and, more importantly, did not contain a Heywood case.

Factor loadings are presented in Table 1.1. Nearly all SICQ scales loaded on at least one factor, except male gender identity. Two scales loaded on two factors: voyeurism and rape of adult females.

The first factor was composed of five scales. In decreasing order of loading, these were exhibitionism, frotteurism, voyeurism, child molestation of girls, and rape of adult females. We labelled this factor *Atypical Sex towards Females*. The second factor was composed of four scales: adult heterosexuality,

Table 1.1 Factor analysis of the Sexual Interest Cardsort Questionnaire ($n = 219$).

Items	Factor 1 *Atypical Sex towards Women*	Factor 2 *Adult Heterosexuality*	Factor 3 *Agonistic Continuum*	Factor 4 *Gender Swapping*
	Factor loadings: λ			
Adult homosexuality	−.01	**−.48**	−.03	.28
Adult heterosexuality	.31	**.70**	−.01	−.05
Voyeurism	**.64**	**.46**	−.06	.10
Exhibitionism	**.81**	−.09	.13	.04
Frotteurism	**.80**	.07	.28	.01
Child molestation of girls	**.59**	−.31	−.03	−.03
Child molestation of boys	.08	**−.61**	−.03	.10
Rape of adult females	**.40**	−.03	**.70**	−.05
Sadism	.05	−.03	**.87**	.02
Masochism	−.06	.27	**.59**	.21
Male gender identity	.01	.19	−.09	.28
Female gender identity	.01	.03	−.02	**.90**
Transvestic fetishism	.15	−.09	.08	**.73**

Note. Factor loadings equal or superior to .40 are shown in **bold** typeface.

child molestation of boys (negative loading), adult homosexuality (negative loading), and voyeurism. This cluster of interests was labelled *Adult Heterosexuality*. The third factor was composed of three scales – sadism, rape of adult females, and masochism – and was labelled *Agonistic Continuum*. Finally, the fourth factor was composed of two scales: female gender identity and transvestic fetishism. This cluster was labelled *Gender Swapping*.

For associations between clusters of sexual interests, *Atypical Sex towards Females* was correlated at −.13 with *Adult Heterosexuality*, .23 with *Agonistic Continuum*, and .46 with *Gender Swapping*. *Adult Heterosexuality* had a correlation of −.14 with *Agonistic Continuum* and −.08 with *Gender Swapping*. Finally, *Agonistic Continuum* had a correlation of .18 with *Gender Swapping*.

Ordinal regression

To test the predictive validity of sexual interest clusters, factor scores equal to the sum of the variables constituting each factor were computed for each cluster. For example, the *Agonistic Continuum* was equal to the sum of sadism, rape of adult females, and masochism, while *Adult Heterosexuality* was equal to the sum of adult heterosexuality, voyeurism, child molestation of boys (inverted), and adult homosexuality (inverted).

Predictive validity analyses can be found in Table 1.2. The model was statistically significant, with the proposed model improving upon the null model ($\chi^2 = 23.52$, $df = 4$, $p < .001$). Goodness of fit indices were non-significant (Pearson $\chi^2 = 627.98$, $df = 620$, $p = .403$), which is the desired outcome for these statistics. According to the Nagelkerke's R^2, the model explained 11% of the variance of the sexual offending behaviour (dependent variable).

Table 1.2 shows that *Atypical Sex towards Females* was positively associated with sexual offending behaviours against children. That is, the higher participants were on this factor, the more likely they were to have committed multiple types of sexual offences against children, both online and offline. The *Agonistic Continuum* cluster was negatively associated with sexual offending behaviours. Thus, higher scores on the agonistic continuum were associated with fewer sexual offending behaviours against children. Both the *Adult Heterosexuality* and *Gender Swapping* clusters were not significantly associated with sexual offending against children.

Discussion

This chapter investigates how typical and atypical sexual interests cluster and examines the links such clusters have with sexual offending behaviours against children. Results from the factor analysis of SICQ scales suggest four clusters of sexual interests: *Atypical Sex towards Females, Agonistic Continuum, Adult Heterosexuality*, and *Gender Swapping*. Moreover, results from the regression analysis showed associations between *Atypical Sex towards Females* and *Agonistic Continuum* with sexual offending behaviours against children. Overall,

Table 1.2 Ordinal regression of sexual interest clusters predicting sexual offending behaviours[1] ($n = 219$).

Estimate [95% CI]	Standard error	Wald	Statistical significance
.15 [.08 to .22]	.04	17.78	<.001
−.03 [−.09 to .03]	.03	.86	.353
−.12 [−.20 to −.03]	.04	6.97	.008
−.00 [−.06 to .06]	.03	.00	.96

Note. Statistically significant estimates are shown in bold.

[1] Ordinal variable with four categories: 0 = no sexual offending behaviour, 1 = online sexual offences only, 2 = contact sexual offences only, 3 = online and contact sexual offences.

these results support the hypothesis that sexual interests are better represented as being multidimensional than unidimensional.

Atypical Sex towards Females

The first cluster of sexual interests, *Atypical Sex towards Females*, includes a variety of paraphilias, some of which were directed towards women (i.e., child molestation of girls, rape of adult women). There was no evidence of sexual interest in either men or boys, suggesting that this cluster was centred around only females. Sexual interests included in this cluster were atypical and also illegal. Thus, it is not surprising to find a positive association with sexual offending behaviours against children: the higher participants were on this cluster, the more likely they were to have committed multiple types of sexual offending behaviours against children. This is consistent with results from meta-analyses showing that men with mixed sexual offences against children tend to exhibit higher levels of atypical sexual interests than men who had committed either only online or only contact sexual offences against children (Babchishin et al., 2011, 2015).

Furthermore, this cluster united paraphilias initially conceptualized as manifestations of courtship disorder – voyeurism, exhibitionism, frotteurism, and rape-prone interests. This cluster supports Freund and Blanchard's (1986) hypothesis that some men sexually interested in *tactile* interactions may not differ significantly from those sexually interested only in *pretactile* interactions. The association between sexual interests in both tactile and pretactile behaviours, in addition to their links with multiple sexual offending behaviours against children, may be partly explained by the fact that sexual offenders in this sample include online offenders who had committed both non tactile sexual offences (i.e., consuming online child exploitation material or sexually communicating with children over the internet) and tactile ones (i.e., contact sexual abuse of children).

Previous studies found that men interested in voyeurism, exhibitionism, and frotteurism are usually not interested in sexual violence (e.g. Gebhard, Gagnon, Pomeroy, & Christensen, 1965). Thus, the presence of sexual interest in the molestation of girls and the rape of adult women in the *Atypical Sex towards Females* cluster, coupled with the absence of specific interest in sexual sadism, might be understood as a general interest in any form of sexuality, without regard for the other partner's consent, rather than as a specific interest in sexual violence or coercion. In that context, this cluster could reflect a broader construct of hypersexuality that would be consistent with past studies showing that multiple paraphilias were associated with high sex drive as well as sexual offending behaviours and use of pornography (e.g. Knight & Cerce, 1999; Knight, Prentky, & Cerce, 1994).

Agonistic Continuum

The *Agonistic Continuum* cluster contained SICQ scales related to sexual sadism, rape of adult women, and masochism. Reflecting the fact that current theories posit that sexual sadism is a continuum in which both coercive and sadistic sexual interests coexist (Longpré, Guay, Knight, & Benbouriche, 2018; Longpré, Sims-Knight, Thornton, Neumann, Guay, & Knight, 2018), this cluster was labelled the *Agonistic Continuum* – a term proposed by Knight, Sims-Knight, and Guay (2013) to describe this phenomenon. The presence of masochism in this sexual interest cluster echoes the ICD-10 classification, which places masochism and sadism at opposite ends of the same spectrum (World Health Organization, 2016). However, that proposition remains to be empirically validated especially since the ICD-11 removed masochism from the sadism spectrum (World Health Organization, 2018).

The *Agonistic Continuum* was negatively related to sexual offending behaviours towards children. In other words, the more interest participants reported in coercive behaviours, the less likely they were to have committed sexual offences against children. This negative association could be due to the absence of participants with adult victims in our sample. Because participants with high scores on the dependant variable had one or more child victims and those with scores of 0 had none, it is possible that sexual interests of the latter group – violent or not – mainly involved adult women, which was echoed by the high factor loading of interest toward the rape of adult women. This would mean, in the context of our sample, that the negative link between the *Agonistic Continuum* and sexual offending behaviours does not indicate that sexual sadism is a protective factor but rather that participants who offended against children happened to have lower interests in sexual coercion than those who had no child victims. This would fit with research that indicates that sexual sadism is more often found in those whose victims are women rather than children (Brouillette-Alarie & Proulx, 2018; Longpré, Guay, & Knight, 2016).

Sexual interest clusters unrelated to sexual offending against children

Adult Heterosexuality and *Gender Swapping* were found to be *not* associated with sexual offending behaviours against children. *Adult Heterosexuality* unites consensual sexual interests towards women and voyeurism, and covaries negatively with two scales measuring sexual interests in males (adult homosexuality and child molestation of boys), suggesting that it captures a gender preference for females. Given the presence of sexual interests in consensual activities, as well as negative links with child molestation of boys, it is not surprising to see an absence of association with offending behaviours.

Even though voyeurism was included in the cluster, its overall pull towards criminal sexual activities was possibly negated by consensual interests. Furthermore, some paraphilias – voyeurism in the current case – may be less criminogenic than others. This is consistent with studies that found high rates of voyeurism among the general population, including male young adults and college students (e.g. Joyal & Carpentier, 2016). It should be noted, however, that there is an important distinction between sexual interests and willingness to act on such interests (Joyal & Carpentier, 2016; Joyal, Cossette, & Lapierre, 2015). This distinction is captured in a study in which about two-thirds of a sample of non-offending men admitted they would commit a voyeuristic act if it was not illegal (Rye & Meaney, 2007).

Similarly, the *Gender Swapping* cluster of sexual interests was not linked with sexual offending against children, again suggesting that some paraphilia clusters may be more associated with sexual offending than others. This cluster included sexual interests in female gender identity and transvestic fetishism. It should be noted that, in the current study, the only sexual interest that did not load on to a cluster was 'interest in male gender identity', possibly due to the fact that all participants were male. Sexual interest in opposite-sex behaviours appear to be rare, not only among sexual offenders but also in the general population (Abel et al., 1987; Joyal & Carpentier, 2016; Långstrom & Zucker, 2005; Sea & Beauregard, 2018). Its association with offending behaviours remains unclear as a previous study found that transvestic fetishism was linked with sexual coercive behaviours, but only when this paraphilia co-occurred with other paraphilias (Baur et al., 2017). Thus, the absence of an association with offending against children is not surprising and may suggest that this type of interest is not specific to sexual offending behaviours against children.

Implications

Implications emerging from this study concern assessment and investigation. First, our findings contribute to a better understanding of the sexual interests of men who sexually offend against children, indicating that a multidimensional representation of these interests may be preferable to a unidimensional one. In addition, some clusters of sexual interests were found to be more strongly associated with sexual offending behaviours than others, suggesting that some clusters may be more risk relevant. If this is the case, multiple risk scales that integrate measures of sexual deviance could benefit from differentiating between risk-relevant paraphilias and those that are not risk relevant. While previous studies have found that the presence of multiple paraphilias is a better predictor of sexual offending than single ones, our results suggest that it is important not only to measure paraphilias quantitatively but also to consider their nature.

Second, our findings could ultimately contribute to identifying factors that can be used to predict when men using the internet to sexually exploit children are susceptible to switching to offline (contact) offending against children – a major concern when assessing an online sexual offending population. Future research should therefore examine whether some clusters of sexual interests can predict contact sexual offending among men who engage in online illegal sexual behaviours. From a law enforcement perspective, this could help investigators prioritize their caseloads and could be particularly relevant in child pornography cases, where investigators usually do not know the suspect's identity as they are dealing with pornographic images found in an online account. Eke and Seto (2017) found correlates between the content of pornographic material and the sexual interests of CSEM viewers, suggesting that prioritization of police cases might be partly informed by the pornographic material used by suspects. However, additional research using prospective data will be needed to determine such associations.

Limitations

The current study is not without limitations. First, because no participant in our sample had committed a sexual offence against adults, it was not possible to examine the association between clusters of sexual interests and coercive sexual behaviours towards women. If the sample had been changed to include such individuals, a different factor structure might have been found for both sexual offending subgroups in the sample, and similarly, different results concerning the *Agonistic Continuum* might have been obtained in relation to offending behaviours. Additionally, since previous studies have found that atypical sexual interests were common among non-offending individuals, future research should also include participants from the general population to examine group differences with regard to clusters of sexual interests.

Second, although our factor model makes theoretical sense, its overall fit was low, meaning that it did not accurately reproduce the values in our dataset. This has important implications, namely that the obtained factor structure may not hold in future research. Readers should therefore be cautious about making inferences from the sexual interest clusters presented in this chapter. Our factor analysis procedure, however, was particularly strict. For example, many authors do not report the fit indices of their factor solutions, nor do they use multiple factor retention criteria or adapted extraction/rotation parameters (Brouillette-Alarie, Babchishin, Hanson, & Helmus, 2016). We nevertheless urge caution concerning our factor structure, which is tentative, at least for the moment.

Third, using the SICQ to measure sexual interests comes with numerous limitations. For example, the SICQ does not cover all paraphilic interests;

some of those that are not included into the questionnaire, such as bestiality, have previously been found to be associated with online sexual offending (Paquette & Cortoni, 2017). Also, because the questionnaire uses very explicit clinical vignettes, it is possible that our participants were reluctant to reveal their interest in certain behaviours (as was the case for Holland et al., 2000). Social desirability, combined with the self-reveal nature of the questionnaire, may have restricted the range of answers obtained on SICQ scales. Future research could include other measures of typical and atypical sexual interests, such as phallometric indices or crime-scene proxies.

Conclusion

The current chapter is a review of the literature on paraphilias among CSEM users and men who commit contact sexual offences against children. The literature indicates that individuals in these groups display a number of different paraphilias and rarely exhibit only one paraphilia. Although certain paraphilias are more risk-relevant than others, it is unclear how clusters of paraphilias more commonly found together are related to the risk of sexual offending. To answer that question, we proposed a factor analysis of the SICQ to obtain a picture of how sexual interests, deviant or not, tend to cluster. We then linked the resulting clusters to a scale of sexual offending behaviours against children that ranged from no sexual offending behaviours to online and contact offences against children. Results indicate that a cluster of deviant sexual interests towards females, akin to those found in courtship disorder, are associated with online and offline offending. Inversely, a cluster composed of sexual sadism and coercion towards women was negatively related to offending. However, this result may be a by-product of the absence of men with sexual abuse against women in our sample. Our results have implications for the risk assessment and investigation of CSEM users and men with contact sexual offences against children and suggest that all paraphilias are not created equal with regard to their risk relevance.

References

Abel, G. G., & Becker, J. V. (1979). *The sexual interest card sort*. Unpublished manuscript.

Abel, G. G., Becker, J. V., Cunningham-Rathner, J., Mittelman, M., & Rouleau, J. L. (1988). Multiple paraphilic diagnoses among sex offenders. *The Bulletin of the American Academy of Psychiatry and the Law, 16*, 153–168.

Abel, G. G., Becker, J. V., Mittelman, M., Cunningham-Rathner, J., Rouleau, J. L., & Murphy, W. D. (1987). Self-reported sex crimes of nonincarcerated paraphiliacs. *Journal of Interpersonal Violence, 2*, 3–25. doi:10.1177/088626087002001001

American Psychiatric Association. (2013). *Diagnostic and statistical manual of mental disorders* (5th ed.). Arlington, VA: Author.

Babchishin, K. M., Hanson, R. K., & Hermann, C. A. (2011). The characteristics of online sex offenders: A meta-analysis. *Sexual Abuse, 23*, 92–123. doi:10.1177/1079063210370708

Babchishin, K. M., Hanson, R. K., & VanZuylen, H. (2015). Online child pornography offenders are different: A meta-analysis of the characteristics of online and offline sex offenders against children. *Archives of Sexual Behaviour, 44*, 45–66. doi:10.1007/s10508-014-0270-x

Baur, E., Forsman, M., Santtila, P., Johansson, A., Sandnabba, K., & Långström, N. (2017). Paraphilic sexual interests and sexually coercive behavior: A population-based twin study. *Archives of Sexual Behavior, 45*, 1163–1172. doi:10.1007/s10508-015-0674-2

Brouillette-Alarie, S., Babchishin, K. M., Hanson, R. K., & Helmus, L.-M. (2016). Latent constructs of the Static-99R and Static-2002R: A three-factor solution. *Assessment, 23*, 96–111. doi:10.1177/1073191114568114

Brouillette-Alarie, S., & Proulx, J. (2014). An exploratory analysis of the offending process of extrafamilial sexual aggressors against adolescents. In J. Proulx, E. Beauregard, P. Lussier, & B. Leclerc (Eds.), *Pathways to sexual aggression* (pp. 179–199). Abingdon, UK: Routledge.

Brouillette-Alarie, S., & Proulx, J. (2018). The etiology of risk in sexual offenders: A preliminary model. *Sexual Abuse*. Advance online publication. doi: 10.1177/1079063218759325.

Brouillette-Alarie, S., Proulx, J., & Hanson, R. K. (2018). Three central dimensions of sexual recidivism risk: Understanding the latent constructs of Static-99R and Static-2002R. *Sexual Abuse, 30*, 676–704. doi:10.1177/1079063217691965

Brown, T. A. (2006). *Confirmatory factor analysis for applied research*. New York, NY: Guilford Press.

Cattell, R. B. (1966). The scree test for the number of factors. *Multivariate Behavioral Research, 1*, 245–276. doi:10.1207/s15327906mbr0102_10

Eke, A. W., & Seto, M. C. (2017, October). Child pornography collection characteristics: Similarities with child victims. In S. Paquette (Chair), *Pedophilia: Taxometric properties, other atypical interests and links between child pornography and child victims*. Symposium presented at the 36th Annual Research and Treatment Conference of the Association for the Treatment of Sexual Abusers, Kansas City, United States.

Endrass, J., Urbaniok, F., Hammermeister, L. C., Benz, C., Elbert, T., Laubacher, A., & Rossegger, A. (2009). The consumption of Internet child pornography and violent and sex offending. *BMC Psychiatry, 9*. doi:10.1186/1471-244X-9-43

Field, A. (2013). *Discovering statistics using IBM SPSS statistics* (4th ed.). Thousand Oaks, CA: SAGE.

Finkelhor, D. (1984). *Child sexual aggression: New theory and research*. New York, NY: Free Press.

Freund, K., & Blanchard, R. (1986). The concept of courtship disorder. *Journal of Sex & Marital Therapy, 12*, 72–92. doi:10.1080/00926238608415397

Gebhard, P. H., Gagnon, J. H., Pomeroy, W. B., & Christensen, C. V. (1965). *Sex offenders*. New York, NY: Harper & Row.

Hall, G. C. N., & Hirschman, R. (1992). Sexual aggression against children: A conceptual perspective of etiology. *Criminal Justice and Behavior, 19*, 8–23. doi:10.1177/0093854892019001003

Hanson, R. K., & Morton-Bourgon, K. E. (2005). The characteristics of persistent sexual offenders: A meta-analysis of recidivism studies. *Journal of Consulting and Clinical Psychology, 73*, 1154–1163. doi:10.1037/0022-006X.73.6.1154

Heil, P., & Simons, D. (2008). Multiple paraphilias: Prevalence, etiology, assessment, and treatment. In D. R. Laws & W. T. O'Donohue (Eds.), *Sexual deviance: Theory, assessment, and treatment* (2nd ed., pp. 527–556). New York, NY: Guilford Press.

Henson, R. K., & Roberts, J. K. (2006). Use of exploratory factor analysis in published research. *Educational and Psychological Measurement, 66*, 393–416. doi:10.1177/0013164405282485

Heywood, H. B. (1931). On finite sequences of real numbers. *Proceedings of the Royal Society of London. Series A, Containing Papers of a Mathematical and Physical Character, 134*, 486–501. doi:10.1098/rspa.1931.0209

Holland, L. A., Zolondek, S. C., Abel, G. G., Jordan, A. D., & Becker, J. V. (2000). Psychometric analysis of the sexual interest cardsort questionnaire. *Sexual Abuse, 12*, 107–122. doi:10.1177/107906320001200203

Horn, J. L. (1965). A rationale and test for the number of factors in factor analysis. *Psychometrika, 30*, 179–185. doi:10.1007/BF02289447

Hu, L. T., & Bentler, P. M. (1999). Cutoff criteria for fit indexes in covariance structure analysis: Conventional criteria versus new alternatives. *Structural Equation Modeling: A Multidisciplinary Journal, 6*, 1–55. doi:10.1080/10705519909540118

Joyal, C., & Carpentier, J. (2016). The prevalence of paraphilic interests and behaviors in the general population: A provincial survey. *The Journal of Sex Research, 54*, 161–171. doi:10.1080/00224499.2016.1139034

Joyal, C. C., Cossette, A., & Lapierre, V. (2015). What exactly is an unusual sexual fantasy? *Journal of Sexual Medicine, 12*, 328–340. doi:10.1111/jsm.12734

Kafka, M. P. (1997). A monoamine hypothesis for the pathophysiology of paraphilic disorders. *Archives of Sexual Behavior, 26*, 337–352. doi:10.1023/A:1024535201089

Kafka, M. P. (2003). The monoamine hypothesis for the pathophysiology of paraphilic disorders: An update. *Annals New York Academy of Sciences, 989*, 86–94. doi:10.1111/j.1749-6632.2003. tb07295.x

Kafka, M. P., & Hennen, J. (1999). The paraphilia-related disorders: An empirical investigation of nonparaphilic hypersexuality disorders in outpatient males. *Journal of Sex & Marital Therapy, 25*, 305–319. doi:10.1080/00926239908404008

Kafka, M. P., & Hennen, J. (2002). A DSM-IV axis I comorbidity study of males (n = 120) with paraphilias and paraphilia-related disorders. *Sexual Abuse, 14*, 349–366. doi:10.1177/107906320201400405

Kaiser, H. F. (1960). The application of electronic computers to factor analysis. *Educational and Psychological Measurement, 20*, 141–151. doi:10.1177/001316446002000116

Knight, R. A., & Cerce, D. D. (1999). Validation and revision of the multidimensional assessment of sex and aggression. *Psychologica Belgica, 39*, 135–161.

Knight, R. A., Prentky, R. A., & Cerce, D. A. (1994). The development, reliability, and validity of the multidimensional assessment of sex and aggression. *Criminal Justice and Behavior, 21*, 72–94. doi:10.1177/0093854894021001006

Knight, R. A., Sims-Knight, J., & Guay, J. P. (2013). Is a separate diagnostic category defensible for paraphilic coercion? *Journal of Criminal Justice, 41*, 90–99. doi:10.1016/j.jcrimjus.2012.11.002

Långstrom, N., & Hanson, K. R. (2006). High rates of sexual behaviour in the general population: Correlates and predictors. *Archives of Sexual Behavior, 35*, 37–52. doi:10.1007/s10508-006-8993-y

Långstrom, N., & Zucker, K. J. (2005). Transvestic fetishism in the general population. *Journal of Sex & Marital Therapy, 31*, 87–95. doi:10.1080/00926230590477934

Laws, D. R., & Marshall, W. L. (1990). A conditioning theory of the etiology and maintenance of deviant sexual preferences and behavior. In W. L. Marshall, D. R. Laws, & H. E. Barbaree (Eds.), *Handbook of sexual assault: Issues, theories, and treatment of the offender* (pp. 209–229). New York, NY: Plenum Press.

Longpré, N., Guay, J.-P., & Knight, R. A. (2016, November). Is severe sexual sadist behavior exclusive to rapists? An examination of sadistic behavior among sexual offenders. *Poster presented at the annual meeting of the Association for the Treatment of Sexual Abusers*, Orlando, FL.

Longpré, N., Guay, J. P., Knight, R. A., & Benbouriche, M. (2018). Sadistic offender or sexual sadism? Taxometric evidence for a dimensional structure of sexual sadism. *Archives of Sexual Behaviors, 47,* 403–416. Online first, 2017 10.1007/s10508-017-1068-4.

Longpré, N., Sims-Knight, J. E., Thornton, D., Neumann, C., Guay, J. P., & Knight, R. A. (under review). *Is paraphilic coercion a different construct from sadism or simply the lower end of an agonistic continuum?* (pp. 1–37).

Mann, R. E., Hanson, R. K., & Thornton, D. (2010). Assessing risk for sexual recidivism: Some proposals on the nature of psychologically meaningful risk factors. *Sexual Abuse, 22,* 191–217. doi:10.1177/1079063210366039

McCullagh, P. (1980). Regression models for ordinal data. *Journal of the Royal Statistical Society, 42,* 109–142.

McGuire, R. J., Carlisle, J. M., & Young, B. G. (1965). Sexual deviations as conditioned behaviour: A hypothesis. *Behaviour Research and Therapy, 3,* 185–190. doi:10.1016/0005-7967(64)90014-2

Minitab Inc. (2017). *What is a Heywood case?* Retrieved from https://support.minitab.com/en-us/minitab/18/help-and-how-to/modeling-statistics/multivariate/supporting-topics/principal-components-and-factor-analysis/what-is-a-heywood-case/

Muthén, L. K., & Muthén, B. O. (2010). *Mplus user's guide.* Los Angeles, CA: Authors.

Paquette, S., & Cortoni, F. (2017, October). Pornography use, paraphilic interests and online sexual offending: An exploratory analysis. In S. Paquette (Chair), *Pedophilia: Taxometric properties, other atypical interests and links between child pornography and child victims.* Symposium presented at the 36th Annual Research and Treatment Conference of the Association for the Treatment of Sexual Abusers, Kansas City, United-States.

Paquette, S., & Cortoni, F. (under review). Offense-supportive cognitions, atypical sexuality, problematic self-regulation, and the perceived anonymity among online and contact sexual offenders against children. *Archives of Sexual Behavior.*

Rye, B. J., & Meaney, B. A. (2007). Voyeurism. *International Journal of Sexual Health, 19,* 47–56. doi:10.1300/J514v19n01_06

Sea, J., & Beauregard, E. (2018). The hebephiliac: Pedophile or teleiophiliac? *International Journal of Offender Therapy and Comparative Criminology, 62,* 2507–2526. doi:10.1177/0306624X17723627

Seto, M. C. (2008). *Pedophilia and sexual offending against children: Theory, assessment, and intervention.* Washington, DC: American Psychological Association.

Seto, M. C. (2013). *Internet sex offenders.* Washington, DC: American Psychological Association.

Seto, M. C., & Eke, A. W. (2015). Predicting recidivism among adult male child pornography offenders: Development of the Child Pornography Offender Risk Tool (CPORT). *Law and Human Behavior, 39,* 416–429. doi:10.1037/lhb0000128

Seto, M. C., Wood, J. M., Babchishin, K. M., & Flynn, S. (2012). Online solicitation offenders are different from child pornography offenders and lower risk contact sexual offenders. *American Psychological Association, 36,* 320–330. doi:10.1037/h0093925

Sheldon, K., & Howitt, D. (2008). Sexual fantasy in paedophile offenders: Can any model explain satisfactorily new findings from a study of Internet and contact sexual offenders? *Legal and Criminological Psychology, 13,* 137–158. doi:10.1348/135532506X173045

Smallbone, S. W., & Wortley, R. K. (2004). Criminal diversity and paraphilic interests among adult males convicted of sexual offenses against children. *International Journal of Offender Therapy and Comparative Criminology, 48,* 175–188. doi:10.1177/0306624X03258477

Stephens, S., Cantor, J. M., Goodwill, A. M., & Seto, M. C. (2017). Multiple indicators of sexual interest in prepubescent or pubescent children as predictors of sexual recidivism. *Journal of Consulting and Clinical Psychology, 85,* 585–595. doi:10.1037/ccp0000194

Stevens, J. P. (1992). *Applied multivariate statistics for the social sciences* (2nd ed.). Hillsdale, NJ: Erlbaum.

Tabachnick, B. G., & Fidell, L. S. (2013). *Using multivariate statistics* (6th ed.). Boston, MA: Pearson Education.

Tucker, L. R., & Lewis, C. (1973). A reliability coefficient for maximum likelihood factor analysis. *Psychometrika, 38,* 1–10. doi:10.1007/BF02291170

Velicer, W. F. (1976). Determining the number of components from the matrix of partial correlations. *Psychometrika, 41,* 321–327. doi:10.1007/BF02293557

Ward, T., & Beech, A. (2006). An integrated theory of sexual offending. *Aggression and Violent Behavior, 11,* 44–63. doi:10.1016/j.avb.2005.05.002

Ward, T., & Beech, A. (2017). An integrated theory of sexual offending – Revised: A multifield-perspective. In D. P. Boer, A. R. Beech, & T. Ward (Eds.), *The Wiley Handbook on the theories, assessment and treatment of sexual offending – Section I: Current multifactorial theories* (pp. 123–137). Chichester, UK: Wiley.

Ward, T., & Siegert, R. J. (2002). Ward and Siegert's pathways model. In T. Ward, D. L. L. Polaschek, & A. R. Beech (Eds.), *Theories of sexual offending* (pp. 61–77). Chichester, UK: Wiley.

World Health Organization. (2016). *ICD-10 Version:2016.* Retrieved from http://apps.who.int/classifications/icd10/browse/2016/en

World Health Organization. (2018). *ICD-11 for mortality and morbidity statistics.* Retrieved from https://icd.who.int/browse11/l-m/en

Exploring and assessing the current sexual interest of men who have committed sexual and non-sexual violent offences

2

Geraldine Akerman, Jennifer Hardy and Paul Hamilton

Introduction

Assessing current sexual interest in men who have committed sexual offence can be somewhat problematic, particularly in relation to those who are serving probation, where disclosing offence-related sexual interest may lead to a serious penalty (e.g. incarceration). This chapter describes the Current Sexual Interest Measure (CSIM; Akerman, 2015) and how it was used to assess men serving their sentence in the community in Texas, USA; comparing them to two groups of men in custody in the United Kingdom. Those serving their sentence in the UK included a group of men who had been convicted of sexual offences, as well as a group of men convicted of violent offences to provide contrasting data. Both groups of men were participating in therapy in a prison-based therapeutic community and so possible effects on the data are considered. In addition, data were collected from men in a lower-security prison to provide further contrast.

The chapter discusses use of the CSIM as a means of disclosing sexual interests in an open manner and further developments of the measure to include additional items relating to appropriate sexual interests. The similarities and differences in the sentencing and management of those who have offended in Texas and the UK are also discussed. The Texas cohort showed less diverse and lower levels of offence-related sexual interest compared to those in custody. Thought was given to how able they may have felt to disclose should they have such sexual interests. Arguably, if the men could discuss their current sexual interests and gain help to manage them, they would be less likely to re-offend. We then discuss the revision of the CSIM in light of the findings. This involved the addition of items that relate to what was deemed more common sexual practices, providing a measure that is less weighted towards paraphilias and that allows demonstration of treatment progression.

Background

Research relating to sexual interests

A great deal of research into sexual offending is carried out on men who are incarcerated for such offences (Duwe, 2012). Duwe suggested that those in custody can be a useful group of potential participants, because any data collected on them can be used to help understand first time offending and prevent recidivism. Furthermore, those in custody can then be targeted for treatment to prevent further offending. However, it could be argued that the most important group of men to carry out research on are those in the community, as they are in a much better position (in terms of opportunity) to re-offend. That said, measuring the risk of recidivism could prove difficult, because gaining accurate crime rates is problematic. Pepper, Petrie, and Sullivan (2009) discuss difficulties associated with gathering accurate rates of offending. They highlight that there are a number of chances for error in recording crime, including measurement error (e.g. individuals are not likely to accurately report their own offending) and administrative error in recording data.

Helmus, Hanson, Thornton, Babchishin, and Harris (2012) discussed the difficulties in predicting absolute re-offending in a group of those who had sexually offended previously and identified the trend in lower rates of offending. While more recent data supports this, indicating a reduction in sexual offending against women (Planty, Langton, Krebs, Berzofsky, & Smiley-McDonald, 2013), there has been a recent increase in the reporting of historical sexual offences, and the downloading and or distributing Child Sexual Exploitation Material (CSEM; Merdian, Perkins, Dustagheer, & Glorney, 2018). While it is not clear what is contributing to this apparent reduction in some forms of sexual re-offending, Finkelhor and Jones (2006) attribute the reduction in sexual offending against children to a diverse range of factors, including the legalization of abortion, economic growth, more social welfare, and the psychiatric use of medication, some/all of which may impact on sexual violence towards women. In addition, those who have been convicted of sexual offences face increased monitoring and registration, and more access to treatment, which should reduce the likelihood of further offending.

Repeat sexual offending understandably causes great concern and so identifying who will and will not offend is the focus of much research (Duwe, 2012). Craig, Beech, and Cortoni (2013) highlighted that deviant sexual interest is one of the strongest predictors of sexual recidivism. Kahr (2007) hypothesized that those who had been sexually abused, or experienced other traumas, unconsciously incorporated these experiences into their fantasy world. That is, the distress they once experienced is converted into pleasure. Many of those in Kahr's study had developed intricate and specific sexual fantasies and interests without awareness of the link between the abuse and the fantasy. So, while there is evidence that many fantasize about diverse sexual interests, it is not clear why some go on to offend and others do not.

While various researchers (e.g. Hanson, Morton-Bourgon, Helmus, & Hodgson, 2009; Ward & Beech, 2008) underscore sexual deviancy, sexual pre-occupation, poor self-control, grievance thinking, and lack of meaningful intimate relationships with adults as being the most important treatment targets, they do not discuss the aetiology of the sexual interest. Seto (2008) notes that paraphilic interests tend to co-occur, and that those who are sexually attracted to children are more likely than men in the general population to engage in other paraphilic behaviours, for example sadism. Furthermore, meta-analyses have shown that a sexual interest in/preference for sex with children is the strongest predictor of future offending (Hanson & Bussiere, 1998; Hanson & Morton-Bourgon, 2005; Mann, Hanson, & Thornton, 2010). Therefore, sexual interests are important to consider, including their interaction with other risk-related factors. That said, Schmidt, Mokros, and Banse (2013) and Seto (2008) noted that only 25% to 50% of those who have offended against children exhibit deviant sexual preferences for children, suggesting that the behaviour alone is not enough to suggest the presence of paedophilia. The above literature indicates that deviant sexual interest is a complex phenomenon, requiring a range of approaches to be accurately measured. Moreover, it requires a willingness on the behalf of the client to be open, in addition to them having insight into their own sexual predilections.

Management of those who have offended

The differences in sentencing policies between the UK and various states in the USA mean that men could serve their sentence in prison in the UK and in the community in the USA for the same offence. Parole is used in the USA (and UK) as a means of community supervision, applied when released from prison before the sentence has expired. There is also wide variation between US states. Thus, this chapter will concentrate on the state of Texas, where these data were collected. Lieb, Kemshall, and Thomas (2011) discuss the ways of managing those who have committed sexual offences and have been released into the community. They report that a broad range of policies are used in the USA, while those used in the UK are more aimed at the specific offence committed. Both use other means of management, such as polygraph, electronic monitoring, and protection orders to prevent further offending.

Sex offender treatment programme, Texas

One group of men taking part in the study reported in this chapter were on probation in Texas. Treatment providers on the programme require participants to admit to their offence in group (unless they pass an instant offence polygraph stating it did not happen). They use that admission to build their understanding of how their thoughts and behaviour led to their offence and how to avoid that in the future. Treatment then proceeds, even with a polygraph sustaining a claim of innocence, as this allows such men to still comply with their court-ordered treatment. Those who pass the polygraph while claiming innocence have their treatment adapted to their circumstances. Treatment is likely to be shorter, and since the programme is designed to build skills through psycho-educational/cognitive-behavioural techniques, they receive much of the same treatment as those on alternative programmes.

There is some variety in the work that each treatment provider undertakes with their probationers. However, they should comply with the standards set by the statutory body whose job it is to manage those who provide treatment and reduce recidivism of sex offences as well as enhance public safety (Council on Sex Offender Treatment, 2011). This document explains terms, the qualifications required to provide treatment, and quantifies the number of hours required on each aspect of treatment (e.g. assessment, sexual assault victim related training, use of polygraph and PPG). It does not, however, describe what the treatment would involve in detail. Therefore, the work undertaken is reliant on those providing the intervention. The majority of licensed treatment providers hold a Master's degree and are counsellors (LPCs), rather than doctoral-level psychologists. In order to work with those who have committed sexual offences, practitioners are required to hold another mental health license and to be a Licensed Sex Offender Treatment Provider (LSOTP) in order to work with probationers around sex offences. Recent findings indicate that programmes are more effective if qualified staff are fully involved in them (Gannon, Olver, Mallion, & James, 2019).

Texas's Council on Sex Offender Treatment (CSOT) suggests the use of cognitive-behavioural techniques that are 'based on empirical research with regard to favourable treatment outcomes and are professionally accepted in the field of sex offender treatment and the treatment of juveniles with sexual behaviour problems'. The CSOT requires that treatment providers obtain training in order to provide services to specialized populations, such as juveniles, women or those with learning difficulties. They describe offence-specific treatment as a 'long-term comprehensive set of planned treatment experiences and interventions that modify sexually deviant thoughts, fantasies, and behaviour and that utilize specific strategies to promote change and to reduce the chance of re-offending' (p. 7). This contrasts with the UK, where those in treatment may undertake some bespoke one-to-one work but the programmes are accredited and run along much the same lines throughout the prison and community settings. The typical probationer in the treatment facility where the Texas population came from is managed in collaboration with the 'containment team' (composed of treatment staff, probation staff, police and so forth). Initially, the probationer undertakes a period of pre-treatment assessment, whereas other treatment providers in Texas may rely on interview alone.

Following assessment, the probationers begin treatment in an Orientation Group, which lasts about two months. This enables acclimatization to groups and how the groups function. Probationers learn the terminology of the treatment programme, as well as the rules and procedures. This orientation component helps probationers to begin the process of acknowledging that they have been convicted of a sexual offence or have pleaded guilty to a sexual offence. This is a mind-set that is often difficult for recently adjudicated probationers and is the beginning stage for them to accept their need for treatment. Following the completion of Orientation Group assignments, probationers are transferred to the Core Group. The probationer may stay in Core Group anywhere from two to five years, depending on their needs and their ability to make good progress in the treatment programme. The Core Group members meet weekly and go through a maturation process. This provides the opportunity to be with others who have made the same mistakes and discuss the problems associated with being on probation, to talk about their offences, and to reflect on and understand their actions. The treatment model uses cognitive-behavioural techniques and discussion on healthy sexuality, using ideas from Ferrara (2009) among others. Orientation and Core Groups are weekly groups with between four and ten group members attending.

There are three levels of transitional groups that the clients may move into, once Core Group is completed, so that the clients can be transitioned from weekly support to bi-monthly, monthly, to quarterly support, before being released from treatment, probation, or deferred adjudication. The probationer is subject to polygraph testing, testing for HIV/AIDS and must provide Deoxyribonucleic Acid (DNA) samples. Should they not participate (e.g. miss sessions, not complete homework, etc.), their Probation Officer will be informed. After two to three years, they will progress to alternate weeks and then finally to monthly groups in order to help them transition from a highly structured environment to the unstructured situation they will face once they have completed probation.

Whereas in the UK, much thought is given to the 'over-treatment' of probationers, such that they would not be given excessive treatment, the Texas model functions as a psycho-educational one. State board rules for Licensed Sex Offender Treatment Providers specify that a sexual offender would not be deemed 'cured', and all work is in collaboration with the supervising officer and judge as a containment team until the end of their sentence. In UK, low risk men (as assessed on Risk Matrix 2000, Thornton et al., 2003) would not be given such high doses of treatment.

A quick word about those convicted in Texas

The Texas Legislature passed a law for certain felony offences in 2007 that limits the options for those convicted of sexual offences. These are referred to as 3G offences, referring to Article 42.12, Section 3(g) of the Texas Code of Criminal Procedure. This statute covers the following sexual offences: Indecency with a Child by contact; Aggravated Sexual Assault; Sexual Assault; Sexual Performance by a child under 18; Compelling Prostitution, if the victim is under age 18; and Trafficking of Persons. A number of other felonies are also covered, but the above are the ones that we are concerned with in sex offender treatment. This relatively recent law prohibits a judge from accepting a plea agreement for straight probation. The judge may accept a plea agreement for deferred adjudication as long as the underlying sentence is for less than 10 years. If the offender chooses to go to trial, then only the jury can give a probated sentence, not the judge. If the individual is sentenced to jail, he cannot earn 'good time' credit to help him achieve parole as early as if he did not commit a 3G offence. He must serve at least half of his sentence in prison before being considered eligible for parole.

One result of this law is that there is an increase in people accused of 3G felonies who plead guilty in order to get deferred adjudication. Probation seems to be an unlikely event, should the defendant decide to gamble with a criminal trial. Thus, there are a few instances in which the programme must work with a person who is convicted but may actually be innocent of his charges. All probationers undergo an Instant Offence polygraph to assist with reducing the minimization and denial that often accompanies the probationers into treatment. There is the rare occasion when the probationer will pass an instant offence polygraph stating it did not happen. Treatment will proceed even with a polygraph sustaining a claim of innocence, so the probationers can still comply with court-ordered treatment. Those probationers who pass the polygraph while claiming innocence have their treatment adapted to their circumstances. Treatment is likely to be shorter, and since the programme is designed to build skills through psycho-educational/cognitive-behavioural techniques, it is much like the standard programme.

Now that the details of the Texas programme has been fully described, and its differences/similarities with UK programmes, the chapter will continue with the CSIM and its construction, presenting data from the UK and USA, before explaining the aim of the study using Texas and UK samples.

Development of the current sexual interest measure

The CSIM was developed in response to a need (observed in clinical practice) to assess sexual interest following an intervention (Akerman, 2008). That is, existing measures are not sensitive to change following treatment as they tend to ask, 'Have you …?' rather than 'Do you …?'. Following a systematic review (Akerman & Beech, 2011), the CSIM was developed using views from a range of perspectives; namely, those convicted of offences in the UK and USA, as well as experts working in this arena. Focus groups and the Delphi method were used to collect the views of practitioners who have experience of working with men who have committed sexual offences (Akerman, 2015). The psycho-metric measure was developed, and practitioners were asked to comment on its content, with resulting revisions made.

Thought was given to the role of attitudes, behaviour, and fantasy related to sexual interest, along with socially desirable responding. The wording of items (in terms of being sexually explicit) and appropriate timescale (in terms of the sexual interest being deemed 'current') were carefully consid-ered. Thought was also given to the need for the inclusion of items relating to more appropriate sexual interests and fantasies so as to provide a scale that did not relate to deviant sexual interest alone. This would allow the option of agreeing to more generally acceptable sexual interests, enabling the measure to be used to assess change following treatment. Responses col-lected on the CSIM were analysed using Principal Component Analysis and preliminary components were proposed, as described below. Cronbach's coefficient of reliability was .79. In terms of validity, the CSIM components 'Sexual preoccupation' and 'Sexual Interests in children' correlated with the Multiphasic Sex Inventory (Nichols & Molinder, 1984) 'Obsessive' subscale (−.54 & −.53 respectively). The final version of the CSIM was composed of 23 items.

We will now discuss the results of our research that explored whether men serving probation in the community in Texas reported similar or different CSIM scores compared to those in custody in the UK.

Our *a priori* hypotheses, based on the existing literature, were as follows:

1. Those who have committed a sexual offence against a child would have sexual interests in children.
2. Men who have offended against children would have more diverse sexual interests than men offending against adults.

3. Those who have been sexually abused would have more diverse sexual interests.
4. Men serving their sentence in the community would have less deviant sexual interests than those in custody.
5. Those who have committed sexual offences would have more deviant or diverse sexual interests than those who have committed other violent offences.

Method

Participants

The current study included four groups; one composed of men serving community sentences for sexual assaults (on adults and/or children) in Texas; two composed of men serving custodial sentences in the UK for sexual offences; and one composed of men who had committed other violent offences. The samples are described below.

Texas group

There were 53 respondents in the Texas sample whose ages were recorded in ranges; two aged under 21 (4%), 11 aged 21–30 (21%), 16 aged 31–40 (31%), 13 aged 41–50 (25%), and 11 aged 51 and over (21%). The group consisted of men whose offences included Indecency with a child (49%), sexual assault (24%), aggravated sexual assault (8%), possession of child abuse images (4%), indecent exposure to a child (7%), and aggravated sexual assault on a child (8%). This sample is referred to as 'US sexual offence group' in the results.

UK groups who had been convicted of sexual offences

Men in a prison-based therapeutic community

UK residents in a prison-based therapeutic community were invited to participate in the study. There were 49 respondents who had committed sexual offences whose ages ranged from 26 to 69 ($M = 44$ SD $= 10.23$). Their offences included: rape or attempted rape (30%), sexual assault (14%), murder with a sexual element (8%), murder (14%), robbery (8%), possessing sexual images (6%), attempted murder (2%), aggravated burglary (2%), manslaughter (2%), kidnap (2%) kidnap with sexual intent (2%), and wounding with sexual intent (2%), arson, (6%) grievous bodily harm, GBH (2%). They are referred to in the results as 'UK sex offences Group 1'.

Men residing in C category prison

Residents in a prison housing men who had committed sexual offences were approached and asked to complete the CSIM. A total of 111 residents completed and returned the measure, of which 106 met the inclusion criteria. Inclusion criteria were: having indicated full consent; no abusive responses; and having been in custody more than six months. The latter was crucial as this chapter compares those in custody in the UK with those in the community in the USA. Thus, it was important to ensure the responses referred to their time in custody. The data relies on accurate self-report, which can be problematic when questions are left unanswered.

Approximately half of the respondents were aged 51 or older (n = 42, 52%), whereas those aged 41–50 was the second largest group (n = 16, 20%), 13 (16%) individuals were aged 31–40, eight (10%) were aged 21–30 and only two respondents (2%) were aged under 21. This is representative of the prison population convicted for sexual offences, who are older on average than other prisoners.

Fifty-six men (69%) indicated having committed sexual offences prior to their index offence. Many individuals indicated having committed a combination of offence types- (e.g. both contact and non-contact sexual offences against both genders or against both adult and child victims). Twenty-nine men (36%) detailed having possessed indecent images of children. Index offences reported included: contact sexual offences against a child victim (n = 36; 44%), non-contact sexual offences against a child victim (n = 21, 26%), contact sexual offences against an adult victim (n = 29; 36%), non-contact sexual offences against an adult victim (n = 4; 5%), violent offences (n = 3; 4%), recall (n = 2; 2%) or a non-sexual crime (n = 2; 2%). Contact sexual offences included making indecent images, indecent assault, rape, and attempted rape, non-contact offences included offending concerning the use of a webcam and paying for sexual services. Non-contact offences included exposure, voyeurism, internet offences, and possession and distribution of indecent images. Respondents were also asked about past violent offences. Four (5%) had adult male victims of violence (ranging from 1–10 victims), five (6%) had male victims aged Under 16 (range = 1–2 victims), 16 (20%) reported having adult female victims of violence (range = 1–5 victims) and five (6%) had committed violent offences against female victims under 16 years old (range = 1–6 victims). They are referred to in the results as 'UK sex offences Group 2'.

UK group convicted of violent offences in the prison-based therapeutic community

Twenty-four men convicted of non-sexual violent offences formed a comparison group. They were comparable in that they had committed serious crimes and were participating in a therapeutic community but did not have any convictions for sexual offences. The offences committed included murder (39%), robbery (18%), aggravated burglary (9%), arson (9%), attempted murder (4%), GBH (4%), firearms (4%), wounding with intent (8%), and conspiracy to murder (4%). The age range of the men in this group was 24 to 51 ($M = 35$, $SD = 7.16$). They will be referred to as the 'UK Violent offence group'.

Procedure

Men who were in treatment in Texas were approached as to their willingness to participate in the research developing the CSIM. Data were collected by a research assistant who was not involved in their treatment to encourage open responding and all data were completely anonymized. They were given the CSIM while attending for treatment so as not to impede on their time unduly.

For the UK sample residing in a lower security (Category C) prison, a CSIM booklet was collated within a sealed envelope (consisting of an information sheet, consent form, the CSIM itself, and a debrief form). This booklet was distributed to all 840 inmates in the establishment by those collaborating in the research, with the help of wing staff. Distributing the questionnaires to each cell allowed them to be completed voluntarily and confidentially. The questionnaires were collected from the wing comments boxes, the psychology department, and wing staff.

For the other two UK samples both were undergoing treatment in a prison-based therapeutic community, either for a sexual offence or a violent offence, men were invited to participate at individual community meetings. Those who volunteered provided demographic information and completed the CSIM, before receiving debrief information.

Principal component analysis

Before testing the core hypotheses, participants' responses to the CSIM were first analysed using principal component analysis. This revealed three clear components and one less clear component indicative of disinterest in deviant sex. Component 1 contained items indicating a focus on sex and sexual thoughts in general and so was labelled 'Sexual Preoccupation'. For Component 2, the highest loading items related to children and teenagers, as well as about having intrusive thoughts. It was labelled as 'Sexual Interest in Children', with 'children' referring to both prepubescent and postpubescent targets. Although the term 'teenager' was used, we argue that respondents would associate this term with younger teenagers, rather than 18/19-year-olds. The highest loading items for Component 3 related to being aroused by hurting/frightening/humiliating/others (including past victims) using accessories and thoughts that the respondent is uncomfortable with. This component was labelled as 'Being Aroused by Sexual Thoughts of Hurting Others'. Component 4 contained items of interest, but at this stage it is not clear whether they form a clinically-sound subscale. Moreover, the items loaded negatively. Thus, they were related to *not* being sexually aroused by, for example, being kidnapped for sexual reasons or being sexually attacked. As the scale is newly developed, further analysis may well indicate whether this component is sound or is merely an artefact of the remaining items. At this point in time, this component was labelled as 'Disinterest in Deviant Sex.'

Results

Texas group

Table 2.1 shows correlations between having a conviction for sexually abusing a child (under 16 years old) and each CSIM component. The pattern of results arguably falls in line with Hypothesis 1 ('Those who have committed a sexual offence against a child would have sexual interests in children'). That is, having a conviction for a sexual offence against children under 16 positively correlated with the Sexual Interest in Children, Hurting Others, and Disinterest in Deviant Sex components. However, these correlations were weak and were not statistically significant. The pattern of correlations also fall

Table 2.1 Correlations between having sexually offended against a child and each CSIM component.

CSIM Component	Committed an offence against child under 16	p
Sexual preoccupation	.04	.73
Sexual Interest in Children	.01	.96
Hurting Others	.03	.84
Disinterest in Deviant Sex	.06	.63

Note: τ [a] Kendall's Tau was used for the correlation due to the small sample size.

in line with Hypothesis 2, which stated that 'Men who have offended against children would have more diverse sexual interests'. Caution is strongly warranted here, however, as these positive relationships were very small in size and non-significant.

There was a significant relationship between having been physically abused and having been sexually abused ($r = .68$, $p < .05$). Having experienced sexual abuse was not correlated with any of the components, neither was having experienced physical abuse (see Table 2.2). Thus, this did not support Hypothesis 3 ('Those who have been sexually abused would have more diverse sexual interests').

Comparison of groups

Table 2.3 shows the mean scores for each CSIM component for all four groups (i.e. the two UK sexual offence group, the UK violent offence group, and the US sexual offence sample).

Table 2.2 Correlation between each CSIM component and having experienced sexual and physical abuse (p-value in brackets).

CSIM Components	Sexual abuse	Physical abuse
Sexual Preoccupation	−.09 (.47)	−.11(.35)
Sexual Interest in Children	−.07 (.60)	−.06 (.61)
Hurting Others	−.04 (.49)	.11 (.40)
Disinterest in Deviant Sex	−.01 (.93)	−.07 (.60)

Note. ι ˮ Kendall's Tau was used for the correlations due to small sample sizes.

Table 2.3 Mean scores (standard deviations) on the CSIM for across all four groups.

Group	Sexual Preoccupation M (SD)	Sexual Interest in Children M (SD)	Aroused by Hurting Others M (SD)	Disinterest in Deviant Sex M (SD)
UK sexual offences: Group 1 (n = 49)	13.10 (8.38)	2.12 (3.17)	2.10 (2.90)	1.86 (2.66)
UK violent offences (n = 24)	13.54 (9.77)	1.43 (2.79)	1.42 (2.60)	1.29 (2.20)
US sexual offences (n = 53)	6.26 (6.34)	1.28 (1.80)	0.89 (1.220	1.08 (1.76)
UK sexual offences: Group 2 (n = 106)	9.17 (8.71)	2.57 (4.11)	1.90 (3.37)	1.72 (2.75)

An examination of these means shows that the two UK sexual offence groups had greater scores on this component relative to the US group and the non-sexual violent UK group. The violent UK group also scored higher on this component relative to the US sexual offence group.

Due to the Levene's test for homogeneity of variance being significant, the non-parametric Kruskal Wallis test was carried out to compare groups on CSIM scores (see Table 2.4). The only significant effect was for the Sexual Preoccupation component (see Table 2.4). Therefore, while the two UK sexual offence groups scored higher than the US and violent UK sample on the deviant sexual interest components, the difference did not reach significance. Therefore, the Hypothesis 4 ('Those who have committed sexual offences would have more deviant or diverse sexual interests than those who have committed other violent offences') was not supported. These results suggest that the UK sample had equivalent levels of current sexual interests as the other groups, but that their sexual preoccupation levels still remained high.

Finally, while not statistically significant, the data were in line with Hypothesis 5 ('Men serving their sentence in the community would have less deviant sexual interests to those in custody'). That is, men serving a community sentence for a sexual offence against a child (US sample) scored much lower on the deviant sexual interest components than those serving custodial sentence (see Table 2.3). It should be noted also that the community (US) group did not score higher on the 'Disinterest in Deviant Sex' component.

Discussion and consideration for best practice

The aim of this chapter was to explore the current sexual interests of those in custody in the UK compared to those serving a community sentence in Texas. This was done using the Current Sexual Interests Measure (CSIM). It was expected that those serving their sentence in the community would have less deviant and diverse sexual interests than those in custody. This hypothesis

Table 2.4 Analysis of variance between scores as assessed by Kruskal Wallis.

CSIM Components	Significance (p) value
Sexual preoccupation	.01
Sexual Interest in Children	.38
Hurting Others	.15
Disinterest in Deviant Sex	.27

was based on the assumption that those serving a sentence in custody would have committed more serious sexual offences, which would be reflected in their sexual interests. There was a trend supporting this hypothesis, as those in the Texas community sample had lower mean scores on all four CSIM components relative to those with custodial sentences, with a significant effect found for Sexual Preoccupation.

The lack of a significant effect for the sexual interest-specific components may have been a result of their conviction, or because they felt less able to be open about their sexual interests. If this were the case, it would be disappointing but may not be surprising given their circumstances. Part of the purpose of the development of the CSIM was to aid service-users to disclose and discuss their sexual interest to gain help with its management, should that be required. Therefore, the low level of reporting of sexual interests was a concern, especially given that every effort was made to enable open disclosure (e.g. use of research assistant not involved in treatment and informing participants that their responses would not impact on their treatment or perceived level of risk). Alternatively, participants may in fact have had less diverse or deviant current sexual interests, perhaps as a result of engaging in treatment. Alternatively, perhaps the shock of conviction for a sexual offence, and the on-going consequences, had affected their sexual interest levels.

While the expected group comparison findings did not reach significance, those in the Texas sample who had committed an offence against a child under 16 did report some sexual interest in children on the CSIM and reported some diversity in their sexual interests. Again, given the low response rate, these findings should be viewed with caution. It is noted that 51% of the UK sex offences group reported having a child victim as well as adult victims, potentially indicating diverse sexual interests and possible motives for offending. Although the men in the community in USA were deemed to be low risk in terms of re-offending, they have the easiest access to do so, and therefore every effort should be made to enable them to talk about their problematic sexual thoughts and fantasies. It is hoped that the CSIM provides such a platform, highlighting the importance of further research.

Those who self-reported having been sexually abused also indicated that they had more diverse sexual interests, as their scores correlated with Sexual Interests in Children, Hurting Others, and Disinterest in Deviant Sex. This finding requires further investigation in order to understand the link between having been sexually abused and its impact on sexual interest. Especially in light of Kahr's (2007) assertion that uncomfortable sexual experiences can be unconsciously integrated into sexual fantasy so as to make them pleasurable and tolerable.

Limitations of the findings

Within two of the groups (the US and second UK sexual offender sample), participants provided demographic information, whereas for the other two groups, this was collected by researchers. This use of self-report led to there being some missing data in the former two samples. In order to overcome this problem, missing values were replaced with mean values, as deleting pairwise would not have provided sufficient data for analysis. It should therefore be acknowledged that this procedure lowers the standard deviation and so could lead to significant results, which may otherwise not be significant (Field, 2005). Furthermore, all the men in the sample were in or had been in treatment, so they may be responding in a different manner from those who had not gained insight into their sexual interests or offending behaviour.

Further directions include collecting more data in order to complete follow-up Principal Component Analyses to verify the current structure of the CSIM. Also, we aim to collect of data from those who are known to not have offended in order to have a more diverse sample with which to provide normative data. It would be useful to assess past sexual interest (as per most existing measures) and compare the scores to current sexual interest using the CSIM. This will potentially indicate whether any changes in sexual interest (perhaps via treatment) have occurred. It would also potentially explain the lack of correlation with sexual offending behaviour and deviant sexual interest that was found in this study.

In conclusion, the development of a scale measuring current sexual interest is challenging but has been possible here to some extent. The CSIM provides a platform from which to discuss this very personal issue within treatment settings. It is also flexible so that further items can be added to cover the diverse sexual interests that people can have. Further, the CSIM has the potential to demonstrate change over time and, although it relies upon the openness of the client, the CSIM provides an applicable and useful tool for those working in treatment.

References

Akerman, G. (2008). The development of a fantasy modification programme for a prison-based therapeutic community. *International Journal of Therapeutic Communities*, *29*, 180–188.

Akerman, G. & Beech A. (2011). A systematic review of measures of deviant sexual interest and arousal. *Psychiatry, Psychology and Law*, *19*, 118–143. doi: http://dx.doi.org/10.1080/132187 19.2010.547161

Akerman, G. (2015). *The development and validation of a psychometric measure of current sexual interest*. PhD Thesis, Birmingham: University of Birmingham.

Council on Sex Offender Treatment. (2011). *Title 3, Occupations Code, Chapter 110 Title 22.* Examining Boards Chapter 810.

Craig, L. A., Beech, A. R., & Cortoni, F. (2013). What work as in assessing risk in sexual and violent offenders. In L. A. Craig, L. Dixon, & T. A. Gannon (Eds.), *What works in offender rehabilitation: An evidence-based approach in assessment and treatment* (pp. 94–114). Chichester: Wiley. doi:10.1002/9781118320655.ch5

Duwe, G. (2012). Predicting first-time sexual offending among prisoners without a prior sex offense history. The Minnesota Sexual Criminal Offending Risk Estimate (MnSCORE). *Criminal Justice and Behaviour, 39,* 1436–1456. doi:10.1177/0093854812453911

Ferrara, M. (2009). *Pathways to healthy sexuality.* ISBN: 978-1439268407. USA: BookSurge Publishing.

Field, A. (2005). *Discovering statistics using SPSS* (2nd ed.). London: Sage.

Finkelhor, D., & Jones, L. (2006). Why have child maltreatment and child victimization declined? *Journal of Social Issues, 62,* 685–716. doi:10.1111/j.1540-4560.2006.00483.x

Gannon, T. A., Olver, M. E., Mallion, J. S., & James, M. (2019). *Does specialized psychological treatment for offending reduce recidivism? A meta-analysis examining staff and program variables as predictors of treatment effectiveness.* Manuscript submitted for publication.

Hanson, K. R., Bourgon, G., Helmus, L., & Hodgson, S. (2009). The principles of effective correctional treatment also apply to sexual offenders: A meta-analysis. *Criminal Justice and Behavior, 36,* 865–891.

Hanson, K. R., & Bussiere, M. T. (1998). Predicting relapse: A meta-analysis of sexual offender recidivism studies. *Journal of Consulting and Clinical Psychology, 66,* 348–362.

Hanson, R. K., & Morton-Bourgon, K. E. (2005). The characteristics of persistent sexual offenders: A meta-analysis of recidivism studies. *Journal of Consulting and Clinical Psychology, 73,* 1154–1163. doi:10.1037/0022-006X.73.6.1154

Helmus, L., Hanson, R. K., Thornton, D., Babchishin, K. M., & Harris, A. J. R. (2012). Absolute recidivism rates predicted by Static-99R and Static-2002R sex offender risk assessment tools vary across samples: A meta-analysis. *Criminal Justice and Behavior, 9,* 1148–1171. doi:10.1177/0093854812443648

Kahr, B. (2007). *Sex and the psyche: The truth about our most secret fantasies.* UK: Penguin.

Lieb, R., Kemshall, H., & Thomas, T. (2011). Post-release controls for sex offenders in the U.S. and UK. *International Journal of Law and Psychiatry, 34,* 226–232.

Mann, R. E., Hanson, K. R., & Thornton, D. (2010). Assessing risk for sexual recidivism: Some proposals on the nature of psychologically meaningful risk factors. *Sexual Abuse: A Journal of Research and Treatment, 22,* 191–217. doi:10.1177/1079063210366039

Merdian, H. L., Perkins, D. E., Dustagheer, E., & Glorney, E. (2018). Developments if a case formulation model for individuals who have viewed, distributed, and/or shared child sexual exploitation material. *International Journal of Offender Therapy and Comparative Criminology, 1–19.* doi:10.1177/0306624X17748067

Nichols, H.R., & Molinder, L. (1984). The multiphasic sex inventory manual. Retrieved from Nichols and Molinder, 437 Bowes Drive, Tacoma, WA, 98466.

Pepper, J. V., Petrie, C., & Sullivan, S. (2009). Measurement error in criminal justice data. In A. Piquero & D. Weisburd (Eds.), *Handbook of quantitative criminology* (pp. 353–374)). USA: Springer.

Planty, M., Langton, L., Krebs, C., Berzofsky, M., & Smiley-McDonald, H. U. S. and Department of Justice, Office of Justice Programs. (2013). *Female victims of sexual violence, 1994-2010 (NCJ-240655).* Retrieved from U.S Government Printing Office Website: http://bjs.gov/content/pub/pdf/fvsv9410.pdf.

Schmidt, A. F., Mokros, A., & Banse, R. (2013). Is pedophilic sexual preference continuous? A taxometric analysis based on direct and indirect measures. *Psychological Assessment, 25,* 1146–1153. doi:10.1037/a0033326

Seto, M. C. (2008). *Pedophilia and sexual offending against children: Theory, assessment, and intervention.* Washington, DC: American Psychological Association.

Thornton, D., Mann, R., Webster, S., Blud, L., Travers, R., Friendship, C., & Erikson, M. (2003). Distinguishing and combining risks for sexual and violent recidivism. In R. Prentky, E. Janus, M. Seto, & A. W. Burgess (Eds.), *Annals of the New York Academy of Sciences, 989,* (pp. 225–235).

Ward, T., & Beech, T. (2008). An integrated theory of sexual offending. In D. Laws & W. O'Donohue (Eds.), *Sexual deviance: Theory, assessment, and treatment* (2nd ed., pp. 21–36). New York: Guilford.

The role of PPG in sexological assessment and treatment of sexual offenders

3

A comparison of British and Czech practice

Derek Perkins, Marek Páv and Petra Skřivánková

Introduction

Phalopletysmographic examination (Czech Republic), also known as penile plethysmographic assessment (UK), was invented by Kurt Freund in 1957 in Prague when he measured volume changes in the penis during exposition of sexual and nonsexual stimuli (Freund, 1963). In the UK, PPG assessment was first introduced into the prison service and high secures forensic mental health services in the 1970s. In the Czech Republic, PPG use is deeply rooted in the practice of sexology diagnosis and treatment, further developed by Freund with his co-workers (Kolářský, Madlafousek, & Novotná, 1978).

The PPG is a laboratory procedure for assessing sexual preferences by penile tumescence measurement. PPG assessment involves the presentation of sexual stimuli to a male subject and the concomitant measurement of changes in the penis circumference, length, or volume. PPG findings are based on analyses of relative penile responses to different categories of stimuli – child vs. adult, consent vs. coercion etc. The PPG is used for both clinical and research purposes. Clinically, it is used to: assist with case formulation; risk management; treatment planning; evaluation of treatment effects and engaging offenders with case formulation and treatment (Dean & Perkins, 2008). The PPG provides an assessment of the man's current sexual arousal profile within the laboratory setting, from which it is posited that this profile may be indicative of his more general pattern of sexual interests, together with indications of whether he may have difficulty managing any offence-related arousal. Both findings can be relevant in planning treatment and managing risks.

If conducted sensitively and collaboratively, PPG assessments also provide a useful method for engaging subjects – offenders, patients, clients – in further relevant assessments and treatment interventions based on a shared understanding of any offence-related sexual interests that are identified. For example, a sexual preference for children, or for sexual violence, or any other problematic paraphilia, can begin to be addressed through an agreed understanding between patient and therapist, aided by the relevant PPG profiles. This is perhaps analogous, within the sphere of physical medicine, to patient and doctor reviewing X-rays or MRI scans, as part of the clinical decision-making and treatment planning process.

Materials and methods

Comparative analysis of PPG purposes and methodologies in the assessment of paraphilic sexual offenders was undertaken between Broadmoor Hospital UK, and Bohnice Hospital, Czech Republic. This was carried out within the broader context of national consensus in each country concerning PPG use, based on relevant literature, national guidelines and expert opinions.

Results

Sexual aggression in classifications systems DSM-5 and MKN-11

Only a minority of individuals who have sexually offended have a diagnosed paraphilia. Most sexual aggressions are committed by men with histories of disrupted early lives and attachments (Ward, Hudson, & Marshall, 1996), personality disorder(s), alcohol and drug abuse histories or by people suffering other psychiatric disorders. The term paraphilia (from Greek *para-*, means out of, a *philia*, means love) is a biomedical term which was first used by I.F. Krause and introduced in sexology by W. Stekel (Weiss, 2010). The term *paraphilia* is in the *Diagnostic and Statistical Manual of Mental Disorders* (DSM-5) described as an intense and persistent sexual interest other than sexual interest in genital stimulation or preparatory fondling with phenotypically normal, physically mature, consenting human partners. In some circumstances, the criteria 'intense and persistent' may be difficult to apply, such as in the assessment of persons who are very old or medically ill and who may not have 'intense' sexual interests of any kind. In such circumstances, the term *paraphilia* may be defined as any sexual interest greater than or equal to normophilic sexual interests (American Psychiatric Association, 2013).

In preparation of the fifth DSM revision, discussions were held on the inclusion of the Paraphilic Coercive Disorder (PCD) in the DSM-5 classification to clarify the current diagnosis of the undetermined paraphilia (Quinsey, 2010). The proposed general diagnostic criteria were analogous to other paraphilia- present for at least six months, repeated sexual fantasies; the person is seriously distressed by these fantasies, or forced sexual stimulation or violent sex with at least three disagreeing partners has occurred (Stern, 2010). Clinical experience with men who repeatedly sexually offend led a number of authors to propose the inclusion of this subgroup of aggressors, different from typical sadists, into this separate diagnostic category (Quinsey, 2010; Stern, 2010; Thornton, 2010). Phallometric data support this by demonstrating that, while only 10% of non-rapists show responses to depictions of rape, 60% of men who have committed rape show equal or greater arousal (Lalumière, Quinsey, Harris, Rice, & Trautrimas, 2003). However, another group of authors argue that there is not enough evidence to confirm the stability of this diagnostic construct and nonexistence of the robust data for its introduction (Balon, 2013; Knight, 2010). PCD was not ultimately included as a DSM-V classification, and remains among the categorical units requiring further investigation and acquisition of additional data (Agalaryan & Rouleau, 2014).

Some authors, therefore, sought to define a new subgroup of patients with a sadistic disorder. Such individuals are focused on humiliating and dominating the victim, causing pain and suffering, sometimes causing injuries or death. However, the sadistic spectrum is quite broad, and, as a diagnostic unit, suffers by a weak consistency, so a dimensional classification of sadism is more appropriate, with dimensions of control and domination, aggression, humiliation, cruelty without sexuality, and torture (Longpré, Guay, Knight, & Benbouriche, 2018). Knight proposed sexual sadism as an 'agonistic continuum' (spectrum) ranging from mere fantasies (ideational sadism) to consensual sadistic (or complementary sadomasochistic) activities over sexually violent behaviour to clearly and explicitly expressed sexually sadistic behaviour (Knight, 2010; Knight, Sims-Knight, & Guay, 2013).

The World Health Organization (WHO) published the 11th revision of the ICD on 18 June 2018 to allow translation into national languages. It will be submitted for approval by the World Health Assembly 2019 and Member States will use it for statistical purposes from 2022. The expected ICD-11 category F65 – 'Sexual preference disorders' are renamed Paraphilic Disorders and would be limited to disorders that involve sexual arousal patterns that focus on non-consenting others or are associated with substantial distress or direct risk of injury or death. A person with paraphilia is strongly stressed by the nature of his sexual arousal, not only fear of rejection by others. The WGS-DSH Working Group on Classification of Sexual Disorders and Sexual Health (WGSDSH) took into account the needs of public health, health services and the legal tradition of the member countries (namely Brazil, India, South Africa, Lebanon, Mexico, Germany) and invited other experts to discuss (Kaplan & Krueger, 2012). It introduces ICD-10 as well-grounded with a well-needed new diagnosis in forensic sexology: Coercive Sexual Sadism Disorder, Sadistic Force Disorder, and Other Paraphilic Disorder Involving Non-Consenting Individuals, or Another Paraphilic Disorder involving Non-Conscious Individuals. Designed kernels to identify the sexual arousal that causes physical or psychological harm to reluctant or incompetent subjects. The reason for classifying new diagnoses is specific forensic applicability because this persistent pattern of sexual arousal has been found to be an important factor, for example, among individuals treated in forensic institutions (Briken, Bourget, & Dufour, 2014; Kaplan & Krueger, 2012). In contrast to DSM 5, ICD-11 postulates the persistence of paraphilia, not just 6 months of manifestation.

PPG – test or tool?

Dean and Perkins (2008) set out reasons why the PPG should be regarded as a *clinical tool* rather than a *psychological test*. To meet the criteria for a psychological test, it must be: standardized in application, and reliable and valid in predicting future behaviour. PPG assessments currently lack the degree of uniform stimuli and testing methods to meet these requirements. More important, however, is the question of whether PPGs are measuring stable traits, as in the case of intelligence for example, or whether relative levels of sexual arousal to different stimuli/situations are at least partly state-based. For example, if an individual's propensity to be aroused by sexual violence were dependent on feeling angry and alienated (e.g. see Yates, Barbaree, & Marshall, 1984), then the presence of such a state would be expected to influence findings at two time periods; one where the individual was angry/alienated and at the other where he was not. One of the authors carried out assessment with a male individual convicted of a sexual homicide (binding, rape and beating to death) where a sadistic PPG profile at initial testing ameliorated during a period when the individual was reportedly in love with another person; only to revert to the earlier sadistic profile after this loving emotional state had ended.

The implication is that, while for some individuals, PPG findings may be measuring a stable trait, for others it may be measuring a combination of state and trait factors, and hence the psychological test principle of *reliability* will not be achieved. While this would negate the PPG as meeting one important criterion for it to be viewed as a psychometric test, PPG can still be viewed as a useful clinical tool.

In relation to the final test criterion of *validity* in predicting future behaviour, while offence-related sexual interest has consistently been identified as a risk predictor for sexual offending against children (Hanson & Morton-Bourgon, 2005), such offences arise through a combination of interacting factors, notably sexual deviance (as above), offence-supportive attitudes and beliefs, and antisocial/psychopathic traits. Hence, not all deviant PPGs will predict reoffending in individual cases. For example, in the case of paedophilia, Finkelhor's (1984) Preconditions Model of child sexual abuse highlights that the motivation to offend (the first precondition) might be paedophilic sexual interest. However, it might alternatively, or additionally, be emotional congruence with children. Hence, not all men who have sexually abused a child will have a deviant PPG. Similarly, while men who use child sexual exploitation material (CSEM) (sometimes referred to as child pornography offenders) typically display higher levels of paedophilic sexual interest than those who commit contact sexual abuse against a child, the majority do not reoffend with CSEM offences and even fewer commit future contact sexual offences (Babchishin, Hanson, & VanZuylen, 2015; Seto, Lalumière, Harris, & Chivers, 2012;).

PPG examination description-methods

PPG examination is often used to investigate paraphilia and other offence-related sexual deviance and involves having a measurement device fitted around the penis, with penile tumescence measured in response to visual or auditory stimuli explicit stimuli (Dean & Perkins, 2008; Mackaronis, Byrne, & Strassberg, 2016). PPG assessment was initially undertaken by a volumetric method using an uncomfortable cylinder, which stimulated further development of alternative measurement methods, notably those using circumferential measures. Disadvantages of these alternatives are that they are less sensitive in measurement: comparison of both methods shows, that while the volumetric method is more movement prone, circumferential methods are less expensive, more user-friendly with clinically sufficient reliability (Laws, 2009).

Issues in PPG use

Dean and Perkins (2008) noted some practical challenges in PPG use: (a) achieving subject engagement with the procedure, as PPGs can be seen as invasive, embarrassing or anxiety provoking; (b) it is time-consuming, generally taking about two hours including preparation, carrying out the assessment and debriefing; and (c) it is costly to administer, due to the complex and demanding requirements of the laboratory procedure. As such, they argued that PPG assessment is unsuited to wide-scale application across the full spectrum of criminal justice and forensic mental health services.

PPG testing is not used in a number of countries because of 'ethical' issues (Babchishin, Nunes, & Hermann, 2013), and concerns have also been raised about: (a) a lack of procedural and stimulus standardization (Laws, 2009); (b) poor test–retest reliability (Renaud et al., 2010); and (c) the capacity of those undertaking PPGs to suppress their responses (Renaud et al., 2009).

Nevertheless, PPG assessment has for many years been the most commonly used method of assessing male sexual interest, and has been evaluated in comparative reviews as having the best combination of accuracy and robustness in the face of counter-measures (Akerman & Beech, 2012; Fromberger et al., 2013; Kalmus & Beech, 2005). While subjects' attempts at faking through response suppression need careful consideration, subjects who are unresponsive ('flat-lining') have not successfully 'faked' the results, which would be regarded as uninterpretable. To truly fake the test, a subject would need to consistently suppress sexual responses to the preferred stimulus (e.g. child) and generate a high response to a non-preferred stimulus (e.g. adult), arguably a complex and difficult feat to accomplish.

PPG in sexual aggression assessment in the Czech Republic

History

Based on courtship disorder postulated by Freund (1963), Czech investigators looked for deepened diagnostics distinguishing the reactions of exhibitionists, frotteurists, rapists, and sadists (Kolářský et al., 1978). They wanted to understand the essence of individual deviations based on PPG stimuli presentation. At the end of the 1960s, they distinguished the aggressors from the sadists otherwise deviant (Kolářský et al., 1978; Mellan, Nedoma, & Pondělíčková, 1972). These authors have highlighted hunting stereotypes, lack of pre-touch interaction with the victim, hitting, crashing, or attempting to penetrate or directly immobilize victims in numerous non-sadistic delinquents' cases. Such sudden attacks are unlike the sadistic offender's prolonged torture of the victim. Zvěřina with Pondělíčkova (Zvěřina & Pondělíčková, 1984) found highly aggressive rapists as well as attackers not targeting coitus. For those who have committed non-sadistic sexual aggression, the pleonastic term 'pathological sexual aggression' was chosen in the Czech Republic, although we do not know whether or not there is 'normal' sexual aggression in human eroticism. However, the term 'atypical aggressiveness' for men who repetitively assault women but do not rape them (Brichcín, 1969) has not been taken up.

There has always been a specific group of men who sexually aggress (so-called 'assault sadists') who commit the most serious acts, brutally attacking their victims, immobilizing and manipulating them frequently to achieve sexual satisfaction (Weiss, 2010). The existence of this small subgroup sui generis is not questioned, and diagnostics also do not usually face any significant difficulties. Kolářský and Brichcín (2000) also describe a combination of swift victim immobilization without victim torture. Such men perceive the victim as prey, having no sense of the victim as a human being with feelings and wishes.

The importance of PPG in sexology assessment of such offenders was realized from its beginning, using the volumetric method to measure penile responses to slides presenting various offence-relevant stimuli (Brichcín & Weiss, 1989). In forensic cases, phallometry is also used to assess the effect of complex sexology treatment, and as one of data sources in predicting the risk of recurrence. There was also research conducted on men with paraphilias, in which phallometry research also significantly contributed to appraising sexual motivation states theory (Kolářský et al., 1978). Sexual motivation state theory equally influenced practical PPG examination procedure, the order of stimuli and of course their form and aesthetics (Kolářský, Brichcín, & Hollý, 2001).

Current practice

Nowadays, in the Czech Republic, mainly photos are used as stimuli during the PPG assessment. The usual setting is that individual is seated in a chair and watches the photographic images presented on the monitor and his sexual response is measured by PPG. There is a consensus, that photos from the major categories should be presented (adult men, adult women, preadolescents of both sexes, photos of violent scenes, consensual partner interactions scenes), and there should be an adjustment in the stimuli in response to further information about specific behaviour in a given case. Some units alternatively also use audio stimuli. Some experts prefer sorting stimuli sequentially (e.g. according to convergence of lovers based on motivation state theory); some workplaces use random presentation. Usual exposition length varies from 5 to 60 seconds, with a neutral stimulus presentation in between. There is a call to use video presentation as sexual stimuli for individuals, but it is not used due to the criminality of child pornography video, and lack of artificial material suitable to use.

Evaluation of the record is nowadays computerized, widely used is Z-score calculation discriminating level of reactions in specific stimuli category. There is also consensus about the necessity of comparison of reactions to stimuli within category and comparison between categories. There is also consensus concerning post exposition reaction. Taking these reactions into consideration is widely accepted. A critical approach to result evaluation is essential, as the validity of an examination – dependent on actual arousal (Howes & Howes, 2017) – does not necessarily reflect long-term reactivity; this holds naturally also for negative findings. The whole context of the clinical case must be therefore taken into account and phallometric findings should be coupled with documented conduct (Marshall & Fernandez, 2001), results of the clinical examination and or other instrumental methods as implicit association Tests (IAT) or polygraphy (Wilcox, 2000).

Sexual aggression diagnostics

When meeting the general criteria for paraphilia and taking into account the specific features of the individual's behaviour and a proper analysis of the skipping in the perpetrator's motivation system, this subgroup of perpetrators is clinically well distinguishable and classifiable. In recognition of the disorder, the sexological anamnesis is a significant source of information such as often atypical manifestations in childhood, accelerated sexual development, difficulty in maintaining partner relationships, or the long-term presence of fantasy of victim abuse can point to an anomaly in sexuality. It is also worthwhile to identify the characteristics of the perpetrator's access to the victim, means of overcoming victim resistance and behaviour of the perpetrator after the committed offence. An important source of information is provided by a PPG examination recording the reactivity to conventional or atypical stimuli such as violent scenes (Seto et al., 2012). PPG is evident in distinguishing a subgroup of sadistic disorders in which also fMRI, when observing pain-display scenes, specifically activates both the areas responsible for sexual arousal (amygdala, hypothalamus, ventral striatum) and for the treatment of pain (anterior cingulum and insula) (Harenski, Thornton, Harenski, Decety, & Kiehl, 2012)

Case example, Czech Republic

A boy, aged 16, was convicted of sexual assault on his classmate – a girl aged 15. He said that the sexual assault was planned. Three hours before their meeting he was thinking about how to get her drunk and overpower her. He had no previous convictions, but he had a lot of physical conflicts with his father. His personality had dissocial traits, he felt no remorse, his empathy was very low, and he was very shy. After the assault, he did not know what happened, why he was sexually thrilled by overpowering the girl and by the violence. He was confused.

PPG assessment showed a clear sexual preference for non-sexual violence to young women (scenes of overpowering, punching, kicking and strangling women). After that, he was comprehensively sexologically examined and the result was that he suffers from paraphilic sexual sadism disorder. It was very hard for him and his family to deal with this fact but on the other hand, they felt relief that they know what is going on. The boy started to be treated within group therapies working on the origins of his sexual interests, intimacy difficulties and shame of talking to not only girls but also to peers, followed by one-to-one therapy with psychologists and sexologist.

PPGs in the UK

History

PPGs were first used within the UK prison and secure hospital services in the 1970s as part of the range of psychological assessments carried out with men who had sexually offended, for the purpose of assisting risk assessment and treatment planning. Interestingly, its use within the UK Prison Service was banned in the 1980s by the then Director of Prison Medical Services, on the basis that its use was excessively intrusive. However, with the emergence of evidence-based treatment programmes for men who had sexually offended, the UK's then Home Secretary set a policy direction in 1990 that saw PPGs reintroduced within some UK prisons as part of the pre- and post-sex offender treatment program (SOTP) assessment measures. At the time of writing, PPGs have ceased to be used within the UK prison system but continue to be used on an individualized referral basis within forensic psychiatric services.

Research on modifying offence-related sexual interests has yielded modest supportive evidence for both behavioural management techniques (Schmucker & Lösel, 2015) and anti-libidinal medication (Bradford & Harris, 2003). Other research has suggested that certain sexual preferences, notably paedophilia in the forensic context, has a sufficiently biological basis that attempting to reshape sexual interest is less likely to be successful than self-monitoring and self-management: see for example Bradford, Fedoroff, and Gulati (2013), Cantor (2015)[1] and Cantor (2015)[2] in response to Muller et al. (2014).

Current practice

PPGs in the UK are carried out in line with the British Psychological Society's (BPS) professional guidelines for their use (www1.bps.org.uk/content/penile-plethysmography-guidance-psychologists-1). This sets out, amongst other things, gaining informed consent, clearly specified assessment purposes, targeted and proportionate assessment stimuli, the legality and ethical appropriateness of stimuli, and the requirement that PPGs should only be carried out and interpreted in the context of a wider set of assessments. As described for CZ above, this typically includes file review, interview information, psychometric assessments and collateral behavioural observations. No decision should be made purely on the basis of PPG findings.

Case example

Mr A, aged 23, attacked a woman in a park at twilight, pushing her to the ground, punching her face and stealing her handbag. The woman said that, by the way he grabbed hold of her (i.e. touching her breasts and thighs), she thought she was going to be raped but Mr A denied that this was his intention. He had no previous convictions, but the social enquiry report said that he had been banned from visiting his aunt's house when he was 15 and she caught him masturbating in her bedroom. PPG assessment assessed his relative responses to consenting heterosexual sex, rape (scenes of overpowering and forcing sex on a woman), and non-sexual violence to women (scenes of overpowering, punching, kicking and strangling women). The PPG results indicated that Mr A responded least to violence but at a higher and similar level to consent and rape as a percentage of his maximum response (as diagrammatically illustrated in Figure 3.1)

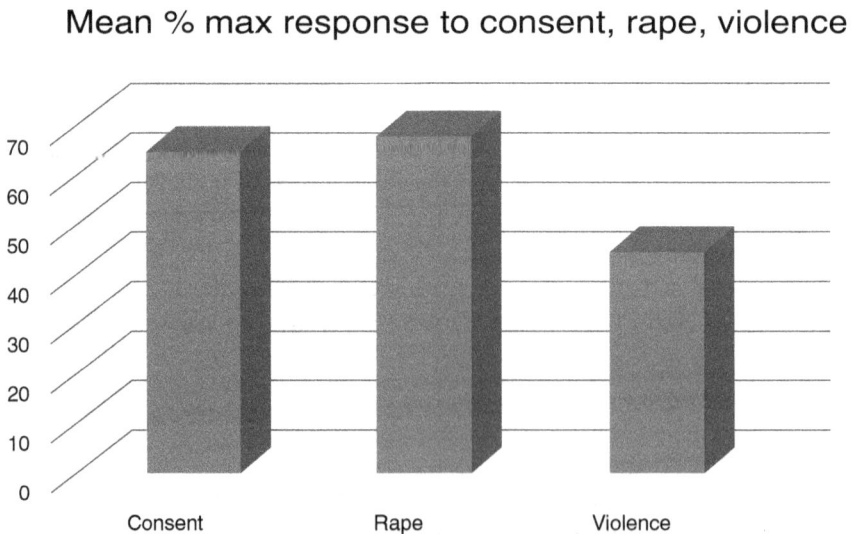

Figure 3.1 PPG results for Mr A as mean maximum responses for consent, rape and violence stimuli as percentages of maximum response obtained during the assessment.

PPG accelerations for consent, rape and violence

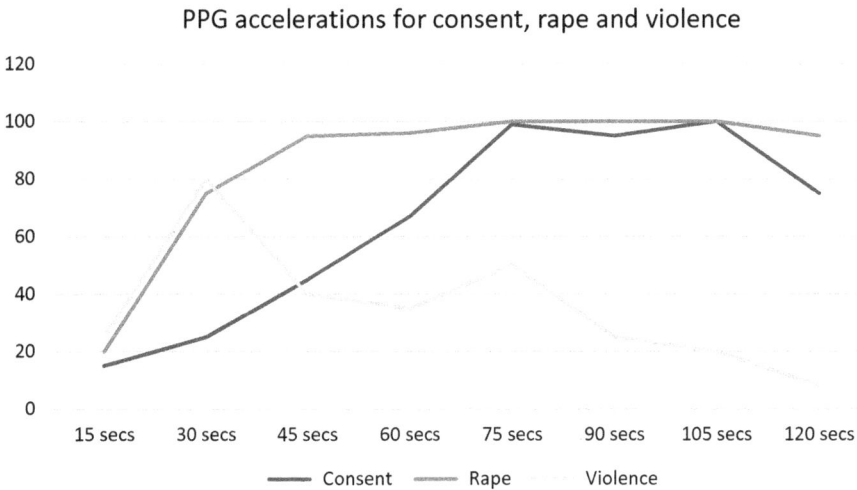

Figure 3.2 Mr A's PPG mean responses to consent, rape and violence stimuli over the duration of the stimulus presentations as percentages of maximum response obtained.

It was noted that he responded to initial scenes of overpowering women in both the rape and the violence scenes, and that this arousal declined as the violence scenes progressed but continued to rise in the rape scenes (as diagrammatically illustrated in Figure 3.2). This is consistent with a hypothesis that he was most sexually interested in overpowering and raping women (rape category) rather than in extreme violence such as kicking, punching and strangling (violence category). On the consent scenes, he responded most in the latter stages when sex was occurring, in contrast to the rape scenes where he responded to both the overpowering segments and the sex segments. He acknowledged in discussing the findings that they reflected his sexual interests, and it was possible, as in many such cases, to then move onto treatment planning more quickly and in a more informed way than would otherwise have been the case.

Discussion: comparison of both practice systems

Although the history of PPG is deeply rooted in the Czech Republic and although there are many experts in this field who use PPG, not only in forensic sex diagnosis and treatment diagnostics, it is still a method that is not standardized in the Czech Republic and its value is therefore potentially underestimated by some experts. There is no uniform approach in the sexodiagnostic examination in the Czech Republic and PPG examination is not always included.

PPG assessment also has a long history in the UK, dating back to the 1970s, but again standardization of procedures, stimulus and interpretations is not uniform. There are, however, some UK professional practice guidelines which have proved very helpful, and a number of these principles are also mirrored in Czech practice. After the 11th revision of the ICD comes into use, it will be possible to code paraphilic violence into separate diagnostic categories: namely, Coercive sexual sadism disorder and sui generis diagnosis Other Paraphilic Disorder Involving Non-Consenting Individuals. This latter subgroup is different from the subgroup of individuals who have sexually offended and have sadistic disorders and, of course, from all other people who commit sexual violence for reasons other than a paraphilic motivation (e.g. due to intoxication, personality disorder or other mental disorder); in other words, without the presence of paraphilia. Although motivation state theory is more descriptive than causal, it still gives a solid explanatory frame to sexodiagnostic differentiation between these two subgroups of individuals who have sexually offended. PPG examination can, in most cases, contribute to differentiation not only between individuals who are paraphilic and nonparaphilic, but also between the above mentioned paraphilias. Responses of both types of paraphilia are typically different and PPG assessment can, thus, significantly contribute to determining correct diagnosis.

Evidence-based conclusions in differential diagnosis cannot be reached by the currently inconsistent approach in sexodiagnosis. It is important to find common ground also in the legal and clinical framework of sexodiagnostic examination because the lack of data (despite apparent clinical experience in this field) also inhibits the therapeutic advancement in this area. In this situation, PPG standardization in the near future seems to be the optimal and logical follow-up process. Some countries have already implemented this, such as the UK, from which Czech practice can draw relevant guidelines and practices, and with whom it can cooperate. We can help to increase the unification, transparency and validity of the sexodiagnostic examination not only for clinicians in this area but also for the law system, and to increase benefits to patients by achieving greater standardization, efficiency and ethical acceptability of PPG examination.

Conclusion

The aim of this chapter was to describe the development and individual approaches in the implementation of PPG examinations in the Czech Republic and the UK in case formulations, diagnoses and treatment of men who have sexually offended. For future practice, it is important to introduce more targeted and complex stimuli into routine PPG assessments. Despite the different sexological assessment and treatment backgrounds of the Czech Republic and the UK, we can hopefully learn from and enrich our clinical sexological practice from each other. In this, we aim to obtain evidence-based and standardized methods for more effective sexological assessment and diagnosis, and to inform better treatments to not only protect victims of sexual offending, but also offer effective treatments for men who sexually offend and who suffer from paraphilias.

References

Agalaryan, A., & Rouleau, J. L. (2014). Paraphilic coercive disorder: An unresolved issue. *Archives of Sexual Behavior, 43*, 1253–1256. doi:10.1007/s10508-014-0372-5

Akerman, G., & Beech, A. R. (2012). A systematic review of measures of deviant sexual interest and arousal. *Psychiatry, Psychology and Law, 19*, 118–143.

American Psychiatric Association. (2013). *Diagnostic and statistical manual of mental disorders (DSM-5)* (5th ed.). Washington, DC: American Psychiatric Association.

Babchishin, K. M., Hanson, R. K., & VanZuylen, H. (2015). Online child pornography offenders are different: A meta-analysis of the characteristics of online and offline sex offenders against children. *Archives of Sexual Behavior, 44*, 45–66. doi:10.1007/s10508-014-0270-x

Babchishin, K. M., Nunes, K. L., & Hermann, C. A. (2013). The validity of Implicit Association Test (IAT) measures of sexual attraction to children: A meta-analysis. *Archives Sexual Behavior, 42*, 487–499.

Balon, R. (2013). Controversies in the diagnosis and treatment of paraphilias. *Journal of Sex and Marital Therapy, 39*, 7–20. doi:10.1080/0092623X.2012.709219

Bradford, J., Fedoroff, P., & Gulati, S. (2013). Can sexual offenders be treated? *International Journal of Law and Psychiatry, 36*(3–4), May–August 2013, 235–240.

Bradford, J., & Harris, V. L. (2003). Psychopharmacological treatment of sex offenders. In Y. Monden (Ed.), *Practice of forensic psychiatry* (2nd ed.). New York: Taylor Francis.

Brichcín, S. (1969). Atypical sexual aggressiveness of 3 young deviants. *Ceskoslovenska Psychiatrie, 65*, 401–406.

Brichcín, S., & Weiss, P. (1989). Sexologic forensic expert evaluation of sex offenders. *Ceskoslovenská Psychiatrie, 85*, 408–413.

Briken, P., Bourget, D., & Dufour, M. (2014). Sexual sadism in sexual offenders and sexually motivated homicide. *Psychiatric Clinics, 37*(2), 215–230.

Cantor, J. (2015)[2]. Purported changes in pedophilia as statistical artefacts: Comment on Muller et al. (2014). *Archives of Sexual Behavior, 44*, 253–254. doi:10.1007/s10508-014-0343-x

Cantor, J. M. (2015)[1]. Milestones in sex research: What causes pedophilia? In J. S. Hyde, J. D. DeLamater, & E. S. Byers (Eds.), *Understanding human sexuality* (6th Canadian ed. ed., pp. 452–453). Toronto: McGraw-Hill Ryerson.

Dean, C., & Perkins, D. (2008) Penile plethysmography. *Prison Service Journal, 178*, July, 20–25.

Finkelhor, D. (1984). *Child sexual abuse: New theory and research*. New York: Free Press.

Freund, K. (1963). A laboratroy method for diagnosing predominance of homo- or heteroerotic interest in males. *Behaviour Research and Therapy, 1*, 85–93.

Fromberger, P., Jordan, K., Steinkrauss, H., von Herder, J., Stolpmann, G., Kröner-Herwig, B., & Müller, J. L. (2013). Eye movements in pedophiles: Automatic and controlled attentional processes while viewing prepubescent stimuli. *Journal of Abnormal Psychology, 122,* 587–599.

Hanson, R. K., & Morton-Bourgon, K. E. (2005). The characteristics of persistent sexual offenders: A meta-analysis of recidivism studies. *Journal of Consulting and Clinical Psychology, 73,* 1154–1163. doi:10.1037/002006X.73.6.1154

Harenski, C. L., Thornton, D. M., Harenski, K. A., Decety, J., & Kiehl, K. A. (2012). Increased frontotemporal activation during pain observation in sexual sadism: Preliminary findings. *Archives of General Psychiatry, 69,* 283–292.

Howes, R. J., & Howes, R. S. E. (2017). Sexual arousal as a function of stimulus mode: Implications for phallometric assessment. *Journal Forensic Research, 8,* 1–7. doi:10.4172/2157-7145.1000398

Kalmus, E., & Beech, A. R. (2005). Forensic assessment of sexual intterest: A review. *Aggression and Violent Behavior, 10,* 193–217.

Kaplan, M. S., & Krueger, R. B. (2012). Cognitive-behavioral treatment of the paraphilias. *Israel Journal of Psychiatry and Related Sciences, 49*(4).

Knight, R. A. (2010). Is a diagnostic category for paraphilic coercive disorder defensible? *Archives of Sexual Behavior, 39,* 419–426. doi:10.1007/s10508-009-9571-x

Knight, R. A., Sims-Knight, J., & Guay, J. P. (2013). Is a separate diagnostic category defensible for paraphilic coercion? *Journal of Criminal Justice, 41*(2), 90–99. doi:10.1016/j.jcrimjus.2012.11.002

Kolářský, A., & Brichcín, S. (2000). Nezávislá sexodiagnostika. *Psychiatrie, 4,* 97–111.

Kolářský, A., Brichcín, S., & Hollý, M. (2001). The significance of theory in the logic of sexodiagnostics. *Psychiatrie, 5,* 242–247.

Kolářský, A., Madlafousek, J., & Novotná, V. (1978). Stimuli eliciting sexual arousal in males who offend adult women: An experimental study. *Archives of Sexual Behavior, 7,* 79–87.

Lalumière, M. L., Quinsey, V. L., Harris, G. T., Rice, M. E., & Trautrimas, C. (2003). Are rapists differentially aroused by coercive sex in phallometric assessments? *Annals of the New York Academy of Sciences, 989,* 211–224.

Laws, D. R. (2009). Penile plethysmography: Strengths, limitations, innovations. In D. Thornton & D. R. Laws (Eds.), *Cognitive approaches to the assessment of sexual interest in sexual offenders* (pp. 7–29). Chichester, UK: Wiley.

Longpré, N., Guay, J. P., Knight, R. A., & Benbouriche, M. (2018). Sadistic offender or sexual sadism? Taxometric evidence for a dimensional structure of sexual sadism. *Archives of Sexual Behavior, 47,* 403–416. doi:10.1007/s10508-017-1068-4

Mackaronis, J. E., Byrne, P. M., & Strassberg, D. S. (2016). Assessing sexual interest in adolescents who have sexually offended. *Sexual Abuse, 28,* 96–115.

Marshall, W. L., & Fernandez, Y. M. (2001). Phallometry in forensic practice. *Journal of Forensic Psychology Practice, 1,* 77–87. doi:10.1300/J158v01n02_06

Mellan, J., Nedoma, K., & Pondělíčková, J. (1972). Forensic evaluation of sex offenders. *Ceskoslovenska Psychiatrie, 68,* 218–222.

Muller, K., Curry, S., Ranger, R., Briken, P., Bradford, J., & Fedoroff, J. P. (2014). Changes in sexual arousal as measured by penile plethysmography in men with pedophilic sexual interest. *Journal of Sexual Medicine, 11,* 1221–1229.

Quinsey, V. L. (2010). Coercive paraphilic disorder. *Archives of Sexual Behavior, 39,* 405–410. doi:10.1007/s10508-009-9547-x

Renaud, P., Chartier, S., Rouleau, J.-L., Proulx, J., Trottier, D., Bradford, J. P., … Bouchard, S. (2009). Gaze behaviour nonlinear dynamics assessed in virtual immersion as a diagnostic index of sexual deviancy: Preliminary results. *Journal of Virtual Reality and Broadcasting, 6.* doi:10.20385/1860-2037/6.2009.3

Renaud, P., Goyette, M., Zhornitski, S., Trottier, D., Rouleau, J.-L., Proulx, J., ... Bouchard, S. (2010). Using immersive virtual reality and ecological psychology to probe into child molesters' phenomenology. *Journal of Sexual Aggression, 19,* 102–120.

Schmucker, M., & Lösel, F. (2015). The effects of sexual offender treatment on recidivism: An international meta-analysis of sound quality evaluations. *Journal of Experimental Criminology, 11*(4), 597–630.

Seto, M. C., Lalumière, M. L., Harris, G. T., & Chivers, M. L. (2012). The sexual responses of sexual sadists. *Journal of Abnormal Psychology, 121,* 739–753. doi:10.1037/a0028714

Stern, P. (2010). Paraphilic coercive disorder in the DSM: The right diagnosis for the right reasons. *Archives of Sexual Behavior, 39,* 1443–1447. doi:10.1007/s10508-010-9645-9

Thornton, D. (2010). Evidence regarding the need for a diagnostic category for a coercive paraphilia. *Archives of Sexual Behavior, 39,* 411–418. doi:10.1007/s10508-009-9583-6

Ward, T., Hudson, S. M., & Marshall, W. L. (1996). Attachment style in sex offenders: A preliminary study. *The Journal of Sex Research, 33,* 17–26.

Weiss, P. (2010). *Sexuologie.* Prague: GRADA Publishing.

Wilcox, D. T. (2000). Application of the clinical polygraph examination to the assessment, treatment and monitoring of sex offenders. *Journal of Sexual Aggression, 5,* 134–152. doi:10.1080/13552600008413304

Yates, E., Barbaree, H. E., & Marshall, W. L. (1984). Anger and deviant sexual arousal. *Behavior Therapy, 15,* 287–294.

Zvěřina, J., & Pondělíčková, J. (1984). Psychopathological findings in sexual aggressors. *Ceskoslovenska Psychiatrie, 80,* 298–302.

Using the Explicit and Implicit Sexual Interest Profile in applied forensic or clinical contexts

4

Alexander F. Schmidt and Derek Perkins

Paraphilic interests in forensic contexts

The assessment of sexual interests is a crucial diagnostic task in forensic assessments of sexual offenders. Particularly, paraphilic sexual interest in non-normative sexual objects or activities (i.e. as a motivating factor) together with antisocial dispositions (i.e. as a facilitating factor) are discussed as major risk factors for sexual offending (Seto, 2019). Both constructs are among the core underlying factors in widely-used actuarial recidivism risk assessment instruments such as the Static-99R or Static 2002R (Brouillette-Alarie, Proulx, & Hanson, 2018). Paraphilic interests have been meta-analytically identified as among the most valid predictors of sexual reoffending (Mann, Hanson, & Thornton, 2010) and there are self-reported cross-sectional links to sexual victimization of children in community males (Dombert et al., 2016; Klein, Schmidt, Turner, & Briken, 2015).

Usually, in applied forensic and clinical contexts sexual interests are inferred from behavioural observations based on known offending behaviour (for an overview of recent advances see Lehmann, Dahle, & Schmidt, 2018) in combination with self- and other-reports (Kalmus & Beech, 2005). However, these approaches are limited in terms of validity as the offending behaviour-paraphilic interest link is equivocal and self-reports are problematic due to the associated legal and social repercussions for the respondent (Jahnke, 2018). Not every individual with paedophilic sexual interest is sexually victimizing children (Dombert et al., 2016; Seto, 2018) and the majority of child sexual abusers does not exhibit sexual preferences in the sense of a paedophilic disorder (Schmidt, Mokros, & Banse, 2013). Moreover, with roughly one out of three diagnoses of paedophilic disorder being invalid (Mokros, Habermeyer, & Küchenhoff, 2018), the diagnostic accuracy of routine care clinical paedophilia diagnoses falls short of the desired validity threshold for single case assessments informing decisions that need to balance civil freedom restrictions against public safety.

Indirect latency-based measures of sexual interest in children

In order to tackle the abovementioned problems with the more or less direct assessment of paraphilic interests in applied forensic and clinical contexts, particularly indirect latency-based measures of sexual interest in children have seen a growing body of research over the last two decades. Several (social-) cognitive psychology paradigms have been validated within sexual offender samples (for recent overviews see Bartels, Gray, & Snowden, 2017; Schmidt, Banse, & Imhoff, 2015). However, most of these measures are in relatively early validation stages based only on few studies at most with the exception of Viewing Time (VT; e.g. Harris, Rice, Quinsey, & Chaplin, 1996) measures and Implicit Association Tests (IAT; e.g. Gray, Brown, MacCulloch, Smith, & Snowden, 2005) for which cumulative meta-analyses exist.

For VT measures the average meta-analytic effect size for discriminating child sexual abusers (as a proxy measure for sexual interest in children) from controls (Schmidt, Babchishin, & Lehmann, 2017) is $d = 0.60$, $CI_{95\%}$ [0.51, 0.68], $n = 2,705$, $k = 14$. This increases once an optimal scoring algorithm based on a maximized sexual preference index for children over adults (described below) will be used ($d = 1.03$, $CI_{95\%}$ [0.82, 1.25], $n = 414$, $k = 7$). Moreover, VT measures are meaningfully associated with offence-behavioural indicators (Screening Scale for Pedophilic Interests [SSPI]; Seto & Lalumière, 2001), self-report, penile plethysmographic, and IAT measures of sexual interest in children (Schmidt et al., 2017) as well as other such indirect latency-based and oculomotoric measures (Ó Ciardha, Attard-Johnson, & Bindemann, 2018). Furthermore, it has been shown that a VT measure of sexual interest in children predicts sexual recidivism over a 15-year follow-up interval (Harrel's $c = .68$; Gray et al., 2015). For IAT measures of sexual preferences for children over adults meta-analytic results show a similar average effect in discriminating child sexual abusers from controls ($d = 0.63$, $CI_{95\%}$ [0.42, 0.83], $n = 707$, $k = 12$). However, predictive validity for sexual preference IATs remains untested to date. Notably, for comparison, penile plethysmographic measures for sexual interest in children yield similar meta-analytic validity estimates for contrasting sexual offenders against children from controls ($d = 0.67$, $CI_{95\%}$ [0.50, 0.84], $n = 6,734$, $k = 32$) increasing to $d = 1.01$, $CI_{95\%}$ [0.64, 1.37], $n = 3,116$, $k = 13$, if based on a z-standardized preference index and a mean predictive validity of $d = 0.44$, $CI_{95\%}$ [0.32, 0.57], $n = 1,961$, $k = 16$ (McPhail et al., 2019).

The explicit and implicit sexual interest profile

From a psychometric perspective it is a fact that any single measure is amenable to personal and situational moderators. Therefore, resting diagnostic single-case decisions solely on single measures is suboptimal. A solution to this problem lies in the general diagnostic principle of convergence according to which diagnostic conclusions can be drawn with greater confidence if they are derived from several conceptually different, valid, and convergent measures. Based on this notion, we combined the empirically most promising indirect latency-based measures as well as a self-report questionnaire into a computer-based test battery of sexual interests in children and adults – the *Explicit and Implicit Sexual Interest Profile* (EISIP; Banse, Schmidt, & Clarbour, 2010; note also the yet not forensically validated EISIP variant tapping into interests in sexual coercion; Larue et al., 2014). In the following we will describe the different EISIP measures in the order as they occur during assessment.

Viewing time measures

The VT measure consists of 80 (plus four practice trials) pictures of semi-nude White Caucasian male and female persons in bathing clothes presented in a prefixed random-order. All stimuli are computer-manipulated pictures from the Not-Real People picture set (Pacific Psychological Assessment Corporation, 2004) depicting non-existing humans. Stimuli are grouped into male and female stimuli with each eight exemplars across five sexual maturity stages (Tanner stages; Tanner, 1973; see Figure 4.1). Tanner stages are based on the physical development of primary and secondary sexual organs (shape, size, colour) and must not be mapped onto specific age bands due to individual differences in onset and course of pubertal development. Conventionally, Tanner stages are grouped into prepubescent (Tanner 1), peripubescent (Tanner 2, 3), and postpubescent (Tanner 4, 5) classes dovetailing with paedophilic, hebephilic, and teleiophilic sexual interests, respectively. Respondents are asked to rate the subjective sexual attractiveness of the target stimuli on a five-point Likert scale ranging from 1 ('sexually unexciting') to 5 ('sexually very exciting') without time constraints while VT is unobtrusively recorded.

MEASUREMENT RATIONALE

The original idea of using viewing times as a measure related to sexual interest is based on Rosenzweig (1942) although the first application of a VT measure in the sense described here dates back to Zamansky (1956). It is a robust

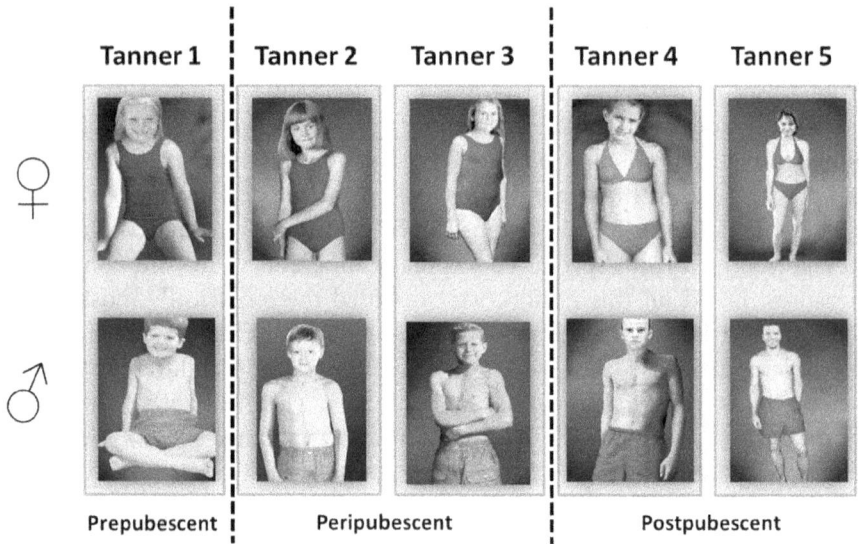

Figure 4.1 Illustration of Tanner stages with exemplary pictures from the Not-Real People picture set (Pacific Psychological Assessment Corporation, 2004).

finding that the more sexually attractive stimuli are, the longer it takes to reach a rating decision in terms of their subjective sexual attractivity (Imhoff et al., 2010; Schmidt et al., 2017). Notably, these decision latencies are not caused by attentional engagement or holding effects (Imhoff, Barker, & Schmidt, 2019) as often supposed in the literature (Imhoff et al., 2010) but are the result of an experimentally corroborated feature checking process (Imhoff, Schmidt, Weiß, Young, & Banse, 2012). According to this notion, in order to decide whether a stimulus is sexually attractive, one needs to check a set of idiosyncratic features such as, for example, age, gender, and attractivity. Once one of these features can be ruled out, the rating process ends (i.e. a relatively faster process) whereas as long as features cannot be rejected, the decision process will need to take further features into account (i.e. a relatively slower process). Importantly, from this psychological process it follows that it is not the stimuli features that drive VT effects but rather the set of features that determine subjective sexual attractiveness. The latter set ultimately is a function of the rating task (Imhoff et al., 2012). From an applied perspective, this task-driven effect poses an important potential diagnostic validity threat to VT paradigms: Only as long as participants comply with the instructions to rate targets' sexual attractiveness from their own personal perspective the measure produces meaningful results. On the contrary, whenever participants perform rating tasks not relevant to their own sexual perspective (e.g. rating stimuli from a vicarious perspective or determining exclusively a single stimulus property such as age or hair colour), latency patterns in standard VT paradigms become invalid (Imhoff et al., 2012; Pohl, Wolters, & Ponseti, 2016).

SCORING

For diagnostic purposes, VT latencies (in milliseconds) are aggregated into 2 (Target Gender) x 5 (Tanner Stages) subscales indicating *absolute sexual interest levels*. Absolute measures have the advantage to illustrate absolute sexual interest differences across all target categories. Subtracting the maximum adult category (Tanner 4, 5) from the maximum child category (Tanner 1, 2, 3) irrespective of target gender results in a *relative sexual preference index*[1] that is independent of sexual orientation (i.e. sexual gender preferences). It indicates to what extent children are sexually preferred over adults. Relative preference indexes, however, *must not* be interpreted in absolute terms (i.e. they are not informative whether the identified sexual preference or non-preference is due to high or low absolute levels of sexual interest in the underlying target categories). As laid out above – and similar to PPG assessments (McPhail et al., 2019) – this preference index is the most valid measure when it comes to criterion group differentiation (Schmidt et al., 2017).

Implicit association tests

The EISIP consist of three different sexual preference IATs: a Men–Women IAT, a Girls–Women IAT, and a Boys–Men IAT. The first IAT assesses sexual preferences between adult females and males (i.e. sexual orientation) whereas the latter IATs tap into sexual age preferences for adults over children within both gender categories, respectively. Each IAT follows the original five-block order as described in Greenwald, McGhee, and Schwartz (1998) but with an increased number of trials. All blocks were presented in the same prefixed random order as described in the following utilizing pictorial stimuli from the VT measure. The first block of 40 trials is a categorization task of ten words (i.e. attribute categories) that have to be classified as sexually exciting (erotic, exciting, lustful, sensual, orgasm) or unexciting (dull, bland, indifferent, unexciting, boring) by pressing a left or right response key. In the second 40-trial block, ten pictures have to be assigned to the target categories man versus woman (girl vs. woman, boy vs. man, respectively in the other two IATs). In the third block, both tasks are mixed in alternating order. Four practice trials precede 80 test trials. The left response key has to be pressed for items belonging to the categories man or sexually unexciting as opposed to the right response key for items indicating woman or sexual excitement. The fourth block of 40 trials is similar to the second, but the key assignment is reversed. Finally, in the fifth block 80 of test trials (plus four practice trials), both tasks are again combined, however, with reversed target categories: Now the left response key has to be pressed for items relating to the categories man or sexually exciting, and the right response key for woman or sexually unexciting attributes (similarly adapted for the Boys–Men and Girls–Women IATs). Incorrect responses are indicated by an error message to the participant throughout all blocks without requiring a further correct response.

MEASUREMENT RATIONALE

The IAT was originally developed by Greenwald et al. (1998). It is a latency-based measure that serves as an indicator of the strengths of implicit associations between attribute and target categories each arranged on bipolar dimensions. As laid out above, respondents classify word or picture stimuli that each represent one of these four categories (e.g. men vs. women as target categories and words representing sexual excitement vs. no excitement) using two response keys, each assigned to the crosswise combined target and attribute categories. In this double discrimination task, classifications are relatively faster (i.e. cognitively easier) if two closely associated target and attribute concepts share the same response key (compared to trials in which they are assigned to different response keys). The underlying psychological process is most likely an effect of response interference if two non-associated concepts share the same response key (Gawronski, Deutsch, & Banse, 2011).

SCORING

The IATs are scored by calculating the difference between the mean response latencies of the critical third and fifth block, divided by the pooled standard deviation of response latencies (D-measure; Greenwald, Nosek, & Banaji, 2003). Only correct trials are included into the analysis. This standardized individual effect size measure – similar to Cohen's d – reflects relative sexual preferences for one target category over the other and controls for individual differences in executive functioning abilities (De Houwer, Teige-Mocigemba, Spruyt, & Moors, 2009). In the EISIP higher sexual preference scores represent the magnitude of atypical or paraphilic preferences for men over women, girls over women, and boys over men, respectively.

Explicit Sexual Interest Questionnaire (ESIQ)

The *Explicit Sexual Interest Questionnaire* (ESIQ; Banse et al., 2010; see Table 4.1 for the slightly modified item set that differs from the originally

Table 4.1 Item overview of the revised Explicit Sexual Interest Questionnaire (ESIQ; Banse et al., 2010).

Behaviour	I have enjoyed orally stimulating X.
	I have tongue kissed X.
	I have enjoyed getting my private parts touched by X.
	I have sexually caressed X.
	I have had sexual intercourse with X.
Fantasy	I find it erotic if I see X's beautiful chest.
	I have daydreamed of having sex with X.
	I find it erotic to see X's body through the clothes.
	I find it erotic to see X's beautiful bottom.
	I get excited when I imagine that X stimulates me.

Note. The original ESIQ items from Banse et al. (2010) have been slightly modified to better fit prototypical sexual behaviours that are shown across all target groups – both items mentioning penetrative acts have been replaced with the 'I have tongue kissed' and 'I have had sexual intercourse' items. 'X' refers to four different groups of stimuli and has to be replaced with 'a young girl', 'a young boy', 'a woman', 'a man', respectively.

published items and is currently in use) was purpose-designed in order to be able to compute absolute measures of sexual interest in children and adults (i.e. indicators of how sexually attractive certain target categories are that can be compared with the absolute indicators from the VT assessments) and relative sexual preference indexes (i.e. indicators of how much more children are sexually preferred over adults that comparable with the IAT results and the VT sexual preference index).

SCORING

The 40-item ESIQ consists of each five self-report items tapping into basic (a) sexual behaviours and (b) sexual fantasies. Moreover, each of these items is assessed relating to four sexual target categories: (1) young girls, (2) young boys, (3) women, (4) men. All items refer to life-time prevalences starting from when respondents' were 18 years old and are rated on a binary forced-choice (yes/no) scale, thus, indicating the rate of scale items acknowledged. Child categories are referring to prepubescent stimuli younger than 12 years as defined in the general instructions. Mean scales scores can be aggregated into 2 (Behaviours or Fantasies) × 4 (Target categories) subscales or – on a higher level – into the four sexual target categories only.

Psychometric properties

CRITERION VALIDITY

Due to the fact that at present a psychometrically flawless criterion for sexual interest in children is missing, validation attempts for such measures need to be tested against several possible proxy criteria of these paraphilic interests (Schmidt et al., 2017).[2] The EISIP has been shown to validly discriminate between multiple proxy criteria of sexual interest in children and adults: It distinguishes convicted child sexual abusers from various offender and non-offender control groups (Banse et al., 2010) including different groups of sexual offenders against children (i.e. extrafamilial child sexual abusers show more paedohebephilic sexual preferences than intrafamilial offenders; Schmidt, Gykiere, Vanhoeck, Mann, & Banse, 2014). Aggregated EISIP scores and the underlying single measures were meaningfully associated with clinicians' diagnoses of paedophilic disorder (Schmidt, Bonus, & Banse, 2010), a phallometrically validated offence-behavioural measure (SSPI, Seto & Lalumière, 2001) and static actuarial risk assessment measures (as shown in Banse et al., 2010; Schmidt et al., 2014). Moreover, taxometric analyses among men with and without sexual interests in children have revealed a taxonic structure of paedohebephilic interests based on the EISIP – as well as only its latency-based measures – with roughly every fourth child sexual abuser exhibiting relatively marked paedohebephilic preferences as compared to non-paedohebephilic men (Schmidt et al., 2013). Notably, EISIP indirect latency-based measures are incrementally valid above and beyond self-report measures of sexual interest in children and adults as shown for selected non-denying (Banse et al., 2010) vs. routine care (i.e. containing a larger amount of denying child sexual abusers; Schmidt et al., 2010) samples of sexual offenders against children. Also, these studies revealed that the VT measures outperformed the IATs in multivariate group classifications based on the single EISIP measures (Banse et al., 2010; Schmidt et al., 2010, 2013).

Although, the EISIP seems to be unrelated to general socially desirable responding tendencies (Banse et al., 2010), it certainly can be wilfully altered – much like any psychological measure – if the underlying measurement rationale is known and the respondent has the cognitive abilities and the motivation to do so. Strikingly, among convicted contact child sexual abusers we have found that men who denied any sexual interest in children or any sexual behaviour involving minors on the ESIQ show decreased sexual preference indexes for children over adults on the EISIP indirect latency-based measures. This may look like corroborating the deliberate malleability of the EISIP. However, the SSPI scores of these paedophilic interest-denying sexual offenders against children were also lower than in the non-denying child sexual abusing controls (Figure 4.2). Taken together, this corroborates that deniers' offending

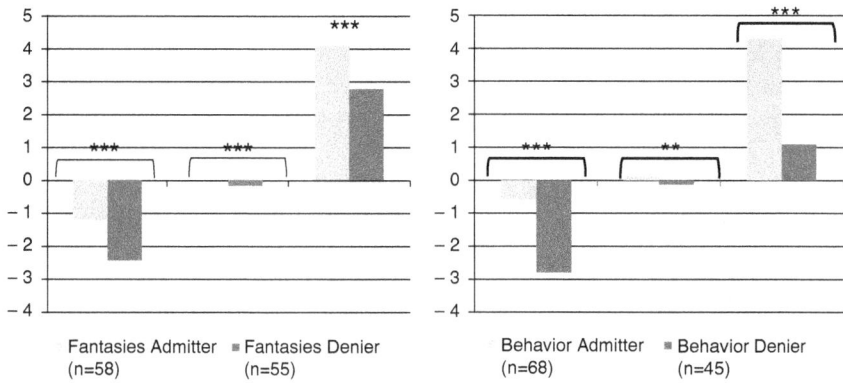

Figure 4.2 Indirect latency-based EISIP measures (sexual preference indexes) and Screening Scale for Pedophilic Interest (SSPI) scores in convicted contact child sexual abusers who admitted vs. denied sexual fantasies or sexual behaviours involving children on the Explicit Sexual Interest Questionnaire (ESIQ; unpublished data).

*** $p < .001$; ** $p < .01$.

behaviour (as an independent objective indicator) also indicated lesser sexual interest in children over adults underscoring the notion that their self-report is actually more valid than prototypically supposed in forensic (research) contexts.

RELIABILITY

In single case diagnostics – apart from a measure's validity – reliability is of crucial concern (in fact, reliability limits the validity of psychological measures according to classical test theory). While latency-based measures are notorious for low reliabilities (i.e. internal consistencies, test-retest correlations), the EISIP consistently yields remarkably good reliability coefficients. In terms of internal consistencies (Cronbach's αs), the ESIQ behaviour and fantasy subscales range from .86 (good) to .96 (excellent; Banse et al., 2010) and .88 to .97 for the aggregated ESIQ sexual interest scales (Banse et al., 2010; Schmidt et al., 2014). The absolute VT measures range between .77 and .85 in samples including sexual offenders, non-sexual offenders, and non-offenders (Banse et al., 2010) and from .90 to .95 in exclusive child sexual abuser samples (Schmidt et al., 2014). The relative sexual preference IATs ranged from .79 to .89 with the exception of the Boys-Man IAT that reached values of .61 and .65 (Banse et al., 2010; Schmidt et al., 2014). The low internal consistency of the Boys–Men IAT is highly likely a result of a sampling artefact due to a lack of gay men who were not child sexual abusers in the samples. Therefore, virtually all participants were either sexually attracted to men and boys or to neither of them. In consequence, the IAT as a relative measure of sexual preference for one target category over the other could not detect substantial individual differences in its Boy–Man version (i.e. mostly near-zero scores leading to low variability) and hence, reliability was low.

Last but not least, recent data (Welsch, Schmidt, Tuner, & Rettenberger, 2019) revealed that classical relative test-retest reliabilities for the EISIP sexual preference scores were surprisingly high over a 14-day interval that had been chosen to rule out spontaneous change of sexual preferences in convicted child sexual abusers and community controls. Intraclass correlation coefficients (ICCs) for sexual preference indexes ranged from satisfactory to excellent (.66 IAT, .78 VT, .87 ESIQ, and .90 full EISIP aggregate score). However, more sophisticated absolute test-retest reliability analyses based on Bland-Altman plots found that quite large effects from roughly a third to three quarters of a standardized mean difference unit will be needed to rule out artificial change induced by transient measurement error. This means the EISIP is a particularly well-suited measure in case repeated assessments seek to elucidate rank order stability of sexual preferences for children over adults over time. However, if the actual amount of individual change is the main research question one will need to show relatively larger differences between measurement times in order to be sure that genuine change in sexual preferences has taken place (for a detailed discussion see Welsch et al., 2019).

Testing single cases with the Explicit and Implicit Sexual Interest Profile

Single case assessments with the EISIP are fully computerized (i.e. standardized presentation and instructions are presented on a laptop during the assessment) and take about 30 minutes for the average participant. At present there are German, English, and Flemish/Dutch versions of the EISIP and further translations could be easily implemented. Respondents need basic reading and computer handling skills. The EISIP can be applied with prototypical (non-intellectually challenged) offender populations in forensic psychiatric and prison settings. Once the respondent has taken the assessment, there is a tool available that generates the EISIP profile directly from the assessment data (Figures 4.3 and 4.4).

Importantly, the EISIP is a measure that is designed to assess *sexual interests in children and adults*. Based on the outlined studies we can be quite certain that it is valid for this task, indeed. Moreover, it has been

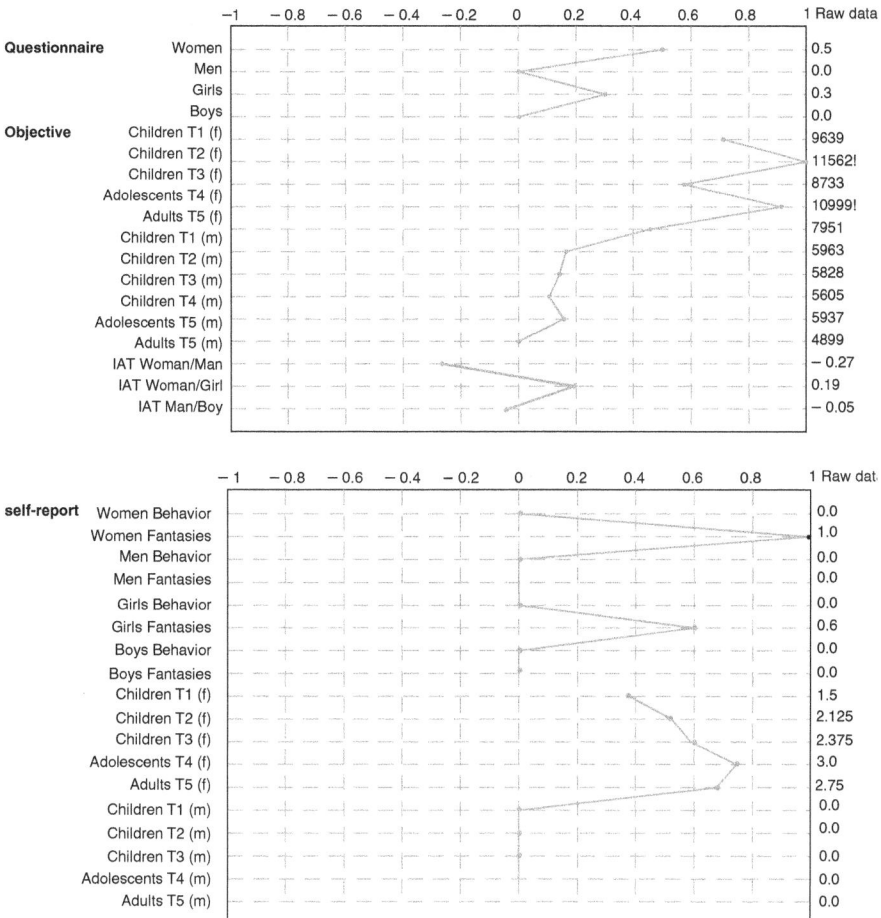

Figure 4.3 EISIP profiles from a convicted child sexual abuser with a diagnosis of paedophilic disorder who had victimized multiple partly prepubescent and partly extrafamilial girls (upper panel: aggregated ESIQ scales, absolute VT indexes, and IAT preference scores; lower panel: ESIQ subscales, explicit picture ratings in the EISIP).

shown that the EISIP measures of paedo-, hebe-, and teleiophilic interests are cross-sectionally associated with forensically relevant risk factors for reoffending (Schmidt et al., 2014) and a similar VT measure such as used in the EISIP has been prospectively linked to recidivism risk in forensic samples (Gray et al., 2015). Although in cross-sectional studies with community males self-reported paedohebephilic interest and sexual offending against children have been shown to be related (Bailey, Bernhard, & Hsu, 2016; Dombert et al., 2016; Klein et al., 2015), the causal relationship, however,

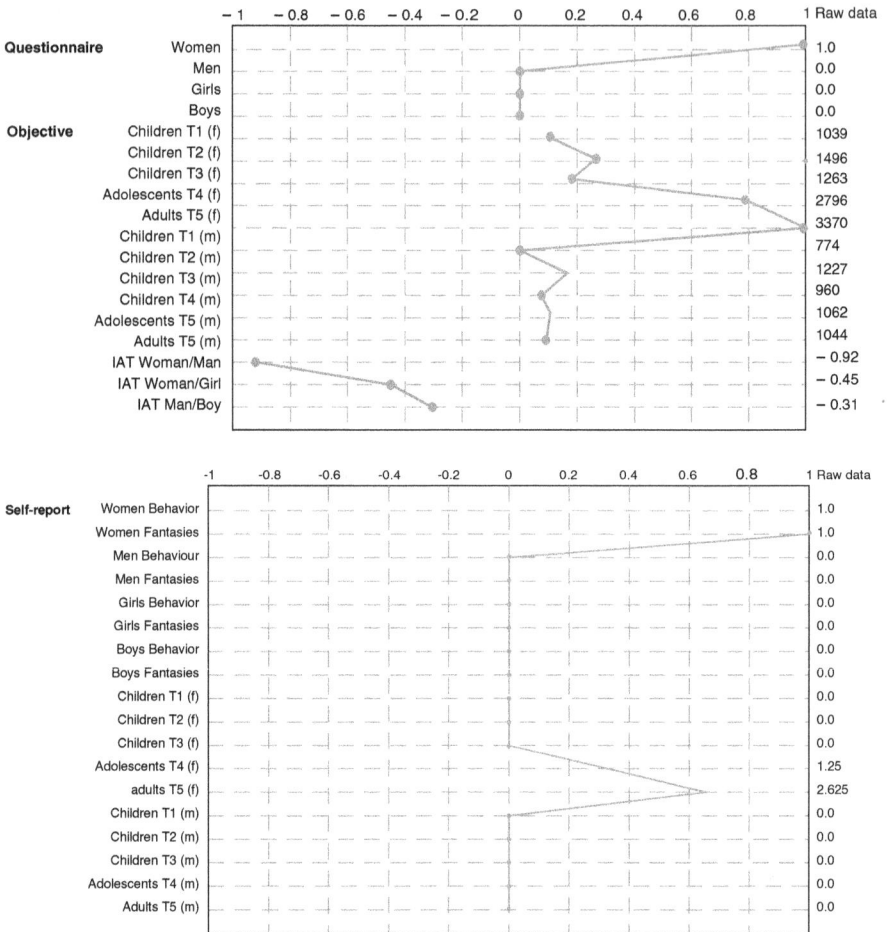

Figure 4.4 EISIP profiles from a convicted violent offender with no history of sexual offending (upper panel: aggregated ESIQ scales, absolute VT indexes, and IAT preference scores; lower panel: ESIQ subscales, explicit picture ratings in the EISIP).

of child sexual abuse and paedohebephilic interests remains inconclusive in non-forensic contexts. Hence, application of the EISIP as a screening measure in non-offending community samples needs to carefully take into account these validity restrictions (e.g. Turner, Hoyer, Schmidt, Klein, & Briken, 2016). Based on these findings, the EISIP *must not* be used to determine whether a) any respondent has sexually offended in the past or b) to determine a non-offending respondent's future risk for sexual victimization of children.[3]

Graphical assessment profile output

The graphical output of the assessment results can be generated via a simple computer program that allows to print and electronically store single case EISIP profiles in a standard graphic format. It produces two profiles on separate pages (Figures 4.3 and 4.4). On the left side margin the respective measurement categories are labelled whereas on the right side margin raw values for each measurement category are reported in order to give the diagnostician full transparency across the whole assessment outcomes. The metric used to graphically display the profile is arbitrary in case of the VT measure and must not be compared with the ESIQ and IAT profiles nor with different VT profiles from other cases.

Profile page 1 – aggregated self-report and indirect latency-based measures

The first profile on page one (upper panels of Figures 4.3 and 4.4) presents an overview of the ESIQ self-reports aggregated over behaviours and fantasies for the women, men, girls, and boys subscales, respectively. The section labelled 'Questionnaire' lists the rate of items per category that have been answered with 'yes' with scores varying between 0 and 1 (rates > 0.5 indicate that at least one sexual behaviour on this scales has necessarily been endorsed).

The first ten rows in the section labelled 'Objective' report the VT latencies across Tanner categories 1 to 5 for female and male stimuli. Raw mean latencies ≥ 10.000 ms will be indicated with an exclamation mark as in the validation studies all single latencies that exceed this threshold were truncated at 10.000 ms. However, in order for the diagnostician to get a more accurate overview of the assessment this has not been implemented in the graphical output. All VT categories are rescaled to a minimum category value of zero and a maximum of 1. The last three rows in the 'Objective' section outline the results from the sexual preference IAT assessments starting with the Woman/ Man IAT, followed by the Woman/Girl IAT and the Man/Boy IAT as indicated by the actual sexual preference D-scores. Higher values point to relatively stronger preferences for men over women (i.e. gay sexual orientation for male respondents), girls over women, and boys over men, respectively. The plotted range is restricted from –1 to 1, larger sexual preferences will be displayed as –1 or 1, respectively, and marked with a 'T' (i.e. truncated) in the right margin displaying the raw values. However, sexual preference D-scores $> |1|$ represent very large sexual preferences and are empirically rather seldom. Additionally, IAT mean error rates $\geq 35\%$ for the respective measures are indicated below the profile as these should be interpreted only with caution.

Profile page 2 – detailed self-reports

The second profile page (lower panels of Figures 4.3 and 4.4) displays all self-reported measures from the EISIP. It starts with the more detailed endorsement rates for the behaviour and fantasy ESIQ subscales for women, men, girls, and boys. These allow to assess dissociations of sexual behaviours and fantasies across sexual target categories. They are followed by the explicit mean picture ratings from the VT assessments, starting with female targets from Tanner 1 to Tanner 5 and followed by male targets in the same order. Raw values for rating plots range from zero to four and are rescaled from zero to one for the graphical output.

Interpreting assessments

The EISIP does not provide norms to compare assessment results against. Hence, profile interpretations need to be based on ipsative comparisons of high and low points in the sexual interest profile. These can be used as a reference frame or baseline of the subjectively least and most sexually interesting target categories within and across the EISIP measures. Note that the VT and ESIQ measures represent absolute sexual interest indicators for each target category whereas the IAT measures are relative sexual preference measures of one target category over the other that cannot be compared directly against each other. Absolute sexual interest measures are informative about how interesting single target categories are. In contrast, relative sexual preference measures reveal how much more sexually interesting a specific target category is than another comparison target category (see the section on VT scoring above). Also, it should be noted that VT measures consistently turn out as more valid than the IATs which needs to be taken into account when interpreting the EISIP profiles.

Case 1: paedophilic sexual offender against children

The assessment of the first case presented in Figure 4.2 stems from a convicted male child sexual abuser who had been diagnosed with a paedophilic disorder by the treating clinicians. He had offended against multiple female child victims including victims below twelve years of age and extrafamilial victims. His aggregated self-reported sexual interests (upper panel in Figure 4.2) indicate that women are his preferred sexual target category followed by somewhat lesser sexual interest in girls. Male targets have been identified as sexually unappealing. This is corroborated by the VT measures that show clearly decreased sexual interest levels for any male target category in comparison to any female target category. Moreover, Tanner 4 (i.e. postpubescent) females yield the second highest decision latencies (note that Tanner 4 and Tanner 2 females showed raw mean latencies ≥ 10.000 ms which are roughly twice as long as for the least interesting target category of Tanner 5 males). However, in contrast to the self-reported sexual interest maximum for women VT measures indicate a maximum interest level for Tanner 2 females. Also, note the sharp decline from Tanner 4 to Tanner 5 females. This sexual preference for girls over woman is backed up by the Woman/Girl IAT showing also a slight relative preference for girls over woman (with a D-score of 0.19 which can be interpreted similar to Cohen's d in terms of effect size conventions; Cohen, 1988). The sexual orientation Woman/Man IAT indicates heterosexual preferences among adult sexual targets. In line with this finding, there is no sexual preference for men over boys (D-score –0.05). Note that this does not necessarily mean that men and boys are sexually irrelevant as it could also be the case that both target categories are highly interesting to this respondent. Both cases of correspondingly high or low absolute sexual interests in the underlying target categories would result in a sexual preference score of zero. The VT results, however, corroborate the latter interpretation of generally low absolute sexual interest levels in any male target category.

This diagnostic picture is further elucidated taking into account the assessment results from the second profile page (lower panel in Figure 4.2). The explicit picture ratings also fit in with the former findings of a clear heterosexual orientation (as indicated by zero ratings for any male picture). Strikingly, the respondent acknowledges sexual attraction for any of the female pictures across the whole sexual maturity range (with an apparent linear increase from Tanner 1 to Tanner 5). This dissociation between the VT assessment and the self-reported indications might be explained by the fact that the ESIQ woman behaviour subscale shows no sexual experience with adult women at all as opposed to a maximum of sexual fantasies directed towards adult females. Clinically, this might indicate difficulties in engaging in intimate relationships with adults although considerable interest in sexual contacts with women might be present. This might be followed up in the post-assessment interview. Notably, the respondent also acknowledges sexual fantasies involving prepubescent girls but denies any sexual contacts with girls with the former clearly indicating paedophilic sexual interest but the latter contradicting his actual conviction for child sexual abuse (there might be meaningful reasons that explain this minimization of offending behaviour; e.g. Maruna & Mann, 2006).

Case 2: violent non-sexual offender

The second case presented in Figure 4.4 reports an EISIP profile from a male violent offender with no official history of sexual offending. The first profile page (upper panel in Figure 4.4) indicates exclusive sexual interest in adult

women in the aggregated ESIQ self-report matched by clear sexual preferences for women over men and women over girls in the IATs (*D*-scores −0.92
and −0.45, respectively). This is well corroborated by the VT profile showing
the prototypical 'normality spike' that indicates a strong heterosexual preference for postpubescent Tanner 4 and Tanner 5 females over any other sexual
target category. Finally, the Man/Boy IAT yields a mild preference of men over
boys which might be explained by the fact that the respondent exhibits stronger general implicit associations between adults and sex than for children and
sex although the VT measures and the ESIQ self-reports showed low absolute
sexual interest levels in any male sexual target category. The second profile
page fully underscores the outlined diagnostic pattern of exclusive sexual preferences for postpubescent females.

Feedbacking assessment results in therapeutic contexts

Particularly in therapeutic contexts, feedbacking the EISIP might be the most
central aspect of the sexual interest assessment as here a fundamental part of
the foundation for the following therapeutic interventions and working alliance will be laid. As usual in therapeutic contexts, the EISIP should be used
to foster a collaborative process and not as a 'truth detector' or psychological
'x-ray machine'. For therapeutic purposes it might be more important to get
a sense of what the respondent concludes for himself from the assessment.
Hence, the feedback should try to elicit the subjective meaning and hypotheses
that the assessed individual comes up with when given information what the
EISIP might indicate about his sexual interests from the view of the therapist.
In clinical contexts it might thus be helpful to start with sexually healthy or
unproblematic sexual interests as these might be used as therapeutic resources
for the following process of strengthening non-deviant sexual interests and/or
managing paedohebephilic interests (this shall not imply that it is impossible
in any case to change manifest paedohebephilic sexual preferences). It might
also be worthwhile to elucidate patterns of temporal stability for the given
sexual interest pattern and to explore boundary conditions or situational factors under which healthy and deviant sexual interests over the life course have
been increased or decreased. Moreover, possible early sexual victimization
experiences of the respondent himself should be explored in the sense of how
these might relate to the specific pattern of EISIP results.

Importantly, we advise against the direct use of the actual profile printout
when feedbacking the results as the raw values and profile labels might elicit
questions concerning the underlying measures. The actual names of underlying tasks nor the fact that latencies are recorded during the assessment must

not be mentioned as this unduly reveals the measurement rationale to the respondent and thus will prevent further use of the EISIP in applied contexts in the longer run. Moreover, one should never mention VT or the exact nature of the dependent variables used in the EISIP. It is bad enough that the DSM-5 (American Psychiatric Association, 2013) mentions VT as a valid diagnostic tool in the introductory section on paedophilic disorder giving away the rationale of these tasks. Note that although this might sound as if we were actively deceiving respondents neither do diagnosticians/clinicians (a) regularly reveal the actual scoring keys of any diagnostic interview or psychometric scale to the respondents in order to protect their assessments' future diagnostic potential, nor (b) is the EISIP assessment particularly deceptive on what it actually assesses. It is rather clear from the first trial on, what the assessment purpose of the EISIP is (namely, sexual interest in children and adults). Certainly – as with any other measure as well – every respondent is free to deny an EISIP assessment or stop taking part in it during the assessment process (as well as trying to get access to the published literature on any assessment he is interested in). An ethically satisficing way of explaining the underlying measurement rationale while at the same time protecting the EISIP's validity might be to refer to individual differences in information processing that are exhibited in classification and sorting tasks (without mentioning response latencies of course) as laid out in the next section on how to apply the EISIP in court.

Using the Explicit and Implicit Sexual Interest Profile in court

Forensic psychological assessments for Court proceedings (criminal or civil) and for other, quasi-judicial, processes such as Mental Health Review Tribunals and Prison Parole Boards require a comprehensive and multifaceted approach. It is recognized that no single type of assessment on its own is likely to be valid or robust against test counter measures in responding to the questions typically needing to be addressed. In much the same way that the EISIP comprises several elements from which a triangulation of findings can be achieved, using the EISIP in court and similar proceedings also requires this test to be used in combination with other assessments. These include a thorough file review, interviews with the person concerned (patient, prisoner, defendant etc.) and with relevant others (spouse, parents, friends etc.), together with findings from other modalities of assessment, such as psychometric, psychophysiological, or observed behavioural responses.

As noted earlier, the EISIP is designed for, and is successful in identifying patterns of sexual interest across different age groups and gender. On its own, it is unable to, and is therefore inappropriate for, explaining past sexual offending or assessing risks of future offending. However, given that paedophilic sexual interest is one of two major risk factors for sexual recidivism (Hanson & Morton-Bourgon, 2005; Seto, 2019) – the second being general antisociality – the EISIP, when combined with measures of other relevant factors, such as antisocial attitudes, patterns of socio-sexual behaviour, opportunities to offend and the absence of barriers to offending, can have a useful part to play within Court or similar proceedings. Issues to be addressed will typically include (a) psychological case formulation of the behaviour of concern – child sexual abuse, sexual violence against adults etc. – (b) assessment of likely future risk, (c) identification of treatment needs and (d) analysis of data on treatment progress. It is important that these assessments cover an appropriately wide range of domains, combine different assessment modalities and adopt a hypothesis-testing and hypothesis-generating approach. Within this context, information from EISIP assessments can be very helpful. The fact that an EISIP interpretation profile can be instantaneously produced, in a format that can be quickly interpreted by the assessor, can aid assessment by feeding back and discussing the findings, in the context of other information, within the assessment session.

In the second author's clinical and forensic experience, this process of testing, feedback and discussion often leads to disclosures and acknowledgements that can assist in clarifying risks, needs, and future offence risk management strategies. Where the findings from the EISIP's various subsections align – i.e. where self-report on the ESIQ, viewing time and IAT findings are all pointing in the same direction – this increases confidence in the results. Where this is not the case, differences in the sub-test findings can be discussed with the subject and this often provides information useful to the assessment – for example possible explanations for these differences or the generation of further hypotheses to be tested. It can of course also arise that the two objective measures align – for example to suggest sexual interest in pre-pubescent girls – but are discrepant from the subject's self-report – for example a sole sexual interest in women. This can in turn raise questions about the test subject's insight or test faking, for example. This would be particularly so if known past behaviours (such as a previous conviction for child sexual abuse or child sexual exploitation material) and fantasies (for example, child fantasies disclosed during previous assessments or in the subject's private writings) are not acknowledged in the ESIQ. In such cases, while it is not possible to categorically assert that the EISIP's objective measures 'prove' a subject's sexual interests, discrepancy between these and the ESIQ, especially where the ESIQ is also discrepant with known history, increases confidence in a hypothesis of minimization of sexual interest in children or denial of past behaviours. Again, while this does not itself help quantify risk, it both highlights areas for further exploration (such as motives for minimization: fear, shame, self-interest) and points to aspects that might be most pertinent in generating an offence formulation and, through this, identifying relative risks and needs.

The following two cases – anonymized by altering specific, potentially identifying features – illustrate some of these points in the incorporation of EISIP testing into wider psychological assessments for legal proceedings.

Case 1

Mr A, aged 28, was a named party in Family Court proceedings in which the two pre-pubescent children of his partner Ms X had been put at risk by Ms X's prior association with a convicted child sexual abuser who had targeted her online, seemingly to access her two young daughters. Mr A, who had entered the relationship with Ms X shortly after this, but before police and social care became involved, was therefore also subject to investigation. As part of this, his computer and mobile devices were subject to forensic analysis, revealing that he had accessed pornography, including 'teen' material recovered from his computer. There was concern that he too might be a risk to the children.

As part of the psychological evaluation of Mr A for the Court, file review and collateral interviews were carried out, Mr A undertook various interviews and psychometrics assessments, including the EISIP, and the full contents of his pornography collection were sought, obtained, and analysed. The question was whether his association with Ms X and her children, his minimizations of the risk her daughters had faced – in an apparent attempt to protect her from police scrutiny – and his possession of 'teen' material, meant that he too might be a risk to the girls.

On the ESIQ, he indicated only adult heterosexual behaviours and fantasies, which could of course be a faked response. On the EISIP's VT measure of sexual interest, his profile indicated an interest in post-pubescent females, but one which was higher for post-pubescent teenaged females than for adult females. On the implicit association test, his profile indicated preferences for women rather than girls.

Mr A's pornography collection, while containing some teen material, also contained other categories of sexual interest in adult females, such as 'lesbian', 'uniformed women', 'older females', which in total exceeded the quantity of teen material; he was not therefore exclusively focused on teens. There was no pre-pubescent material recovered, which was consistent with his own account and the EISIP findings. In relation to general antisociality (the second major dynamic risk factor for sexual offending; Hanson & Morton-Bourgon, 2005; Seto, 2019), he had only one conviction, for a driving offence, there were no indications of generalized antisocial behaviour. He appeared desperate to maintain his relationship with Ms X following past episodes of partners leaving him, because he was regarded as too passive and unassertive, qualities that Ms X appeared to value, and the Court accepted that this was the main but misguided reason he tried to minimize the risk to the girls. The couple successful undertook some individual and joint therapy to address aspects of the risk and need assessment, to which the EISIP had made a useful contribution.

Case 2

Mr B, aged 34, was a recently married man who had been involved in five previous adult heterosexual relationships. During a period of work stress and marital problems, he increasingly accessed adult pornography, seemingly to distract from, and soothe himself in response to his other problems. During this period, his pornography access drifted to younger female images. He was arrested for possessing illegal child material of girls in the range 12–16 years.

Mr B recalled early and very exciting sexual activity with a 14-year-old girl when he was aged 13, which he contrasted to the more awkward and less exciting sexual activity with his first 18-year-old girlfriend when he was 20. She left him for another man, which resulted in him being cautious about forming further relationships and he had a period of casual sexual encounters. He eventually entered a relationship with a young woman of his own age whom he met at work and they married.

His lifelong difficulties discussing his emotions appeared to have combined with his marital and work related problems and he recaptured earlier experiences of sexual excitement in viewing online adult pornography during which he was drawn to younger, teen images, which he said during assessment reminded him of his early sexual experiences at age 13.

Mr B took part in a psychological evaluation for the criminal court, in which a formulation of his offending and assessment of future offending risk were required. In addition to file review, interviews and psychometric testing of cognitive, personality and mental health functioning, he undertook the EISIP. On the ESIQ, he acknowledged some previous fantasies of girls in addition to his predominantly adult heterosexual fantasies and behaviour. He rated Tanner 4 teenaged girls as the most sexually exciting category. On the VT, he showed similar response to pubescent and post-pubescent females (Tanner 3 – Tanner 5), but not to pre-pubescent children. On the IATs, his sexual orientation was predominantly adult female.

In the assessment interviews, which included a review of his psychometric test results including the EISP, Mr B acknowledged a sexual interest in pubescent girls. He had justified to himself that accessing such images online 'did no harm' as the material was 'already out there'. He was very ashamed, fearful and contrite and responded well to psychoeducational sessions about the nature of, and harm created by the viewing of online indecent images of children or minors. He received a community disposal and he and his wife worked together to restore and enhance their relationship.

Case 3

Mr C, aged 56, was a married man whose wife was aged 62. They had been married for 15 years and there were no children of the marriage. Mr C had three previous convictions involving pre-pubescent boys. At 26, he was convicted of indecent assault of a 10-year-old boy, who was the son of family friends. Mr C was placed on probation and maintained that he was suffering from work-related stress and the breakup of a relationship at the time. He said that he had accepted that he had touched the boy but had only done so as he was advised that this would prevent a prison sentence. He said that he had no sexual interest or preoccupation with boys.

His second conviction, at the age of 41, was just before his marriage. He was convicted of sexually touching two boys, aged 9 and 10, while working at his church Sunday school. He maintained that these boys had heard of his previous conviction and had made up the story as they were jealous of his attention to other children in the group. He went to prison for 12 months; he was not eligible for sexual offender treatment, and he and his wife moved from the city to a new rural home upon release.

Mr and Mrs C ran a local shop and, fourteen years after moving there, two boys aged 10 and 11 made complaints that Mr C had touched them sexually while they were helping him with gardening and odd jobs at the shop: they had responded to an advertisement for this work. Mr C was arrested and his computer searched but there was nothing incriminating found on it. Enquiries suggested that other boys may have been assaulted and those continued while Mr C was being assessed prior to the trial.

Mr C completed a psychological assessment, which drew on the court papers, including witness statements and forensic evidence; interviews with Mr and Mrs C; and psychological testing, including the EISIP. On the ESIQ, Mr C acknowledged only adult heterosexual behaviour and fantasies, but the VT measure and the IATs indicated otherwise. On VT, his responses peaked at Tanner 2 and Tanner 3 males (this is, boys aged approximately 10–14 years old), with some elevation to Tanner 5 adult male. On the IATs, his result on the male dimension was skewed well over to boys rather than men. On the female dimension his score was in the middle.

The interpretation of the EISIP findings was that Mr C showed a strong interest in peri-pubescent males and this was fed back to him during the assessment for his comments. His response was less about whether this was correct than about how this would be seen in the context of his trial. As more evidence of other possible offences came to light, Mr C asked to review the EISIP findings again. He said that he had no adult homosexual interest but said that he had been abused as a boy and he wondered if that could be the cause of the adult male Tanner 5 elevation. Without mentioning his previous denials about his sexual interest in boys, he said that the male Tanner 2 and Tanner 3 findings seemed accurate and he asked if there was anything that could be done about that. He said that his wife confided that she too had been sexually abused as a girl and that she was uncomfortable with sex, which he had found acceptable. After lengthy discussion, and in the context of other findings, Mr C was keen to pursue antilibidinal medication as an option for managing his sexual interest in boys. He was disinclined to other forms of therapy, partly because of his age and partly because he just wanted not to be tempted to be offending against boys again. He received three years imprisonment, was released and he had his wife moved again, into sheltered accommodation, where he continued to take antilibidinal medication.

Conclusion

We hope that this chapter on the potential use of the EISIP in forensic contexts is instructive. In summary, we believe that the EISIP (Banse et al., 2010) is a viable diagnostic adjunct to penile plethysmographic assessment procedures – the only other valid objective measure of paraphilic sexual interest that is available in applied clinical (forensic) contexts (McPhail et al., 2019). We hope that this necessarily short introduction into the practical use of the EISIP may aid in underscoring the diagnostic potential (as well as its limitations) for single case applications of this easy to apply computerized assessment battery.

Notes

1. This means that sexual interest and sexual preference are not used interchangeably in this chapter. Sexual interests – the broader conception – refers to absolute interest levels independent of other target categories whereas sexual preference – the narrower conception – is the result of the comparison (i.e., the difference) of two different target categories (see Schmidt et al., 2017 for a more detailed description).
2. Given the fact that only a minority of convicted child sexual abusers show genuine paedophilic preferences (Schmidt et al., 2013; Seto, 2018), validity estimates based on sexual offending samples will be highly likely to underestimate criterion validity.
3. At the present stage of research, this does not imply that the EISIP must not be used to assess paedohebephilic preferences in non-offending populations as long as one does not draw any firm conclusions on whether these sexual inclinations are causally linked to a possible onset of future sexual offending.

References

American Psychiatric Association. (2013). *Diagnostic and statistical manual of mental disorders* (5th ed.). Arlington, VA: Author.

Bailey, J. M., Bernhard, P. A., & Hsu, K. J. (2016). An Internet study of men sexually attracted to children: Correlates of sexual offending against children. *Journal of Abnormal Psychology*, *125*(7), 989–1000.

Banse, R., Schmidt, A. F., & Clarbour, J. (2010). Indirect measures of sexual interest in child sex offenders: A multimethod approach. *Criminal Justice and Behavior*, *37*(3), 319–335.

Bartels, R. M., Gray, N. S., & Snowden, R. J. (2017). Indirect measures of deviant sexual interest. In L. A. Craig & M. Rettenberger (Eds.), *The Wiley handbook on the theories, assessment, and treatment of sexual offending – Volume II: Assessment* (pp. 965–993). Chichester, West Sussex, UK: Wiley-Blackwell.

Brouillette-Alarie, S., Proulx, J., & Hanson, R. K. (2018). Three central dimensions of sexual recidivism risk: Understanding the latent constructs of Static-99R and Static-2002R. *Sexual Abuse*, *30*(6), 676–704.

Cohen, J. (1988). *Statistical power analysis for the behavioral sciences* (2nd ed.). Hillsdale, NJ: Erlbaum.

De Houwer, J., Teige-Mocigemba, S., Spruyt, A., & Moors, A. (2009). Implicit measures: A normative analysis and review. *Psychological Bulletin*, *135*(3), 347–368.

Dombert, B., Schmidt, A. F., Banse, R., Briken, P., Hoyer, J., Neutze, J., & Osterheider, M. (2016). How common is men's self-reported sexual interest in prepubescent children? *The Journal of Sex Research*, *53*(2), 214–223.

Gawronski, B., Deutsch, R., & Banse, R. (2011). Response interference tasks as indirect measures of automatic associations. In K. C. Klauer, C. Stahl, & A. Voss (Eds.), *Cognitive methods in social psychology* (pp. 78–123). New York, NY: Guilford Press.

Gray, N. S., Brown, A. S., MacCulloch, M. J., Smith, J., & Snowden, R. J. (2005). An implicit test of the associations between children and sex in pedophiles. *Journal of Abnormal Psychology*, *114*(2), 304–308.

Gray, S. R., Abel, G. G., Jordan, A., Garby, T., Wiegel, M., & Harlow, N. (2015). Visual reaction time™ as a predictor of sexual offense recidivism. *Sexual Abuse: A Journal of Research and Treatment*, *27*(2), 173–188.

Greenwald, A. G., McGhee, D. E., & Schwartz, J. L. K. (1998). Measuring individual differences in implicit cognition: The implicit association test. *Journal of Personality and Social Psychology*, *74*(6), 1464–1480.

Greenwald, A. G., Nosek, B. A., & Banaji, M. R. (2003). Understanding and using the implicit association test: I. An improved scoring algorithm. *Journal of Personality and Social Psychology*, *85*(2), 197–216.

Hanson, R. K., & Morton-Bourgon, K. E. (2005). The characteristics of persistent sexual offenders: A meta-analysis of recidivism studies. *Journal of Consulting and Clinical Psychology*, *73*(6), 1154–1163.

Harris, G. T., Rice, M. E., Quinsey, V. L., & Chaplin, T. C. (1996). Viewing time as a measure of sexual interest among child molesters and normal heterosexual men. *Behaviour Research and Therapy*, *34*(4), 389–394.

Imhoff, R., Barker, P., & Schmidt, A. F. (2019). To what extent do erotic images elicit visuospatial versus cognitive attentional processes? Consistent support for a (non-spatial) Sexual Content-Induced Delay. *Archives of Sexual Behavior*. Advance online publication.

Imhoff, R., Schmidt, A. F., Nordsiek, U., Luzar, C., Young, A. W., & Banse, R. (2010). Viewing time effects revisited: Prolonged response latencies for sexually attractive targets under restricted task conditions. *Archives of Sexual Behavior*, *39*(6), 1275–1288.

Imhoff, R., Schmidt, A. F., Weiß, S., Young, A. W., & Banse, R. (2012). Vicarious viewing time: Prolonged response latencies for sexually attractive targets as a function of task- or stimulus-specific processing. *Archives of Sexual Behavior, 41*(6), 1389–1401.

Jahnke, S. (2018). The stigma of pedophilia: Clinical and forensic implications. *European Psychologist, 23*(2), 144–153.

Kalmus, E., & Beech, A. R. (2005). Forensic assessment of sexual interest: A review. *Aggression and Violent Behavior, 10*(2), 193–217.

Klein, V., Schmidt, A. F., Turner, D., & Briken, P. (2015). Are sex drive and hypersexuality associated with pedophilic interest and child sexual abuse in a male community sample? *PLoS One, 10*(7), e0129730.

Larue, D., Schmidt, A. F., Imhoff, R., Eggers, K., Schönbrodt, F. D., & Banse, R. (2014). Validation of direct and indirect measures of preference for sexualized violence. *Psychological Assessment, 26*(4), 1173–1183.

Lehmann, R. J. B., Dahle, K.-P., & Schmidt, A. F. (2018). Primer on the contribution of crime scene behavior to the forensic assessment of sexual offenders. *European Psychologist, 23*(2), 154–166.

Mann, R. E., Hanson, R. K., & Thornton, D. (2010). Assessing risk for sexual recidivism: Some proposals on the nature of psychologically meaningful risk factors. *Sexual Abuse, 22*(2), 191–217.

Maruna, S., & Mann, R. E. (2006). A fundamental attribution error? Rethinking cognitive distortions. *Legal and Criminological Psychology, 11*(2), 155–177.

McPhail, I. V., Hermann, C. A., Fernane, S., Fernandez, Y. M., Nunes, K. L., & Cantor, J. M. (2019). Validity in phallometric testing for sexual interests in children: A meta-analytic review. *Assessment, 26*(3), 535–551.

Mokros, A., Habermeyer, E., & Küchenhoff, H. (2018). The uncertainty of psychological and psychiatric diagnoses. *Psychological Assessment, 30*(4), 556–560.

Ó Ciardha, C., Attard-Johnson, J., & Bindemann, M. (2018). Latency-based and psychophysiological measures of sexual interest show convergent and concurrent validity. *Archives of Sexual Behavior, 47*(3), 637–649.

Pacific Psychological Assessment Cooperation. (2004). *The Not-Real People stimulus set for assessment of sexual interest.* Victoria, BC: Author.

Pohl, A., Wolters, A., & Ponseti, J. (2016). Investigating the task dependency of viewing time effects. *The Journal of Sex Research, 53*(8), 1027–1035.

Rosenzweig, S. (1942) The photoscope as an objective device for evaluating sexual interest. *Psychosomatic Medicine*, April 1942 - pp 150–158.

Schmidt, A. F., Babchishin, K. M., & Lehmann, R. J. (2017). A meta-analysis of viewing time measures of sexual interest in children. *Archives of Sexual Behavior, 46*(1), 287–300.

Schmidt, A. F., Banse, R., & Imhoff, R. (2015). Indirect measures in forensic contexts. In F. J. R. van de Vijver & T. Ortner (Eds.), *Behavior based assessment in personality, social, and applied psychology* (pp. 173–194). Göttingen: Hogrefe.

Schmidt, A. F., Bonus, P., & Banse, R. (2010, July). Indirect measures of sexual interest in child sex offenders: A multimethod approach and its clinical implications. *Paper presented at the international summer conference in forensic psychiatry*, Regensburg, Germany.

Schmidt, A. F., Gykiere, K., Vanhoeck, K., Mann, R. E., & Banse, R. (2014). Direct and indirect measures of sexual maturity preferences differentiate subtypes of child sexual abusers. *Sexual Abuse, 26*(2), 107–128.

Schmidt, A. F., Mokros, A., & Banse, R. (2013). Is pedophilic sexual preference continuous? A taxometric analysis based on direct and indirect measures. *Psychological Assessment, 25*(4), 1146–1153.

Seto, M. C. (2018). *Pedophilia and sexual offending against children: Theory, assessment, and intervention* (2nd ed.). Washington, DC: American Psychological Association.

Seto, M. C. (2019). The motivation-facilitation model of sexual offending. *Sexual Abuse, 31*(1), 3–24.

Seto, M. C., & Lalumière, M. L. (2001). A brief screening scale to identify pedophilic interests among child molesters. *Sexual Abuse: A Journal of Research and Treatment, 13*(1), 15–25.

Tanner, J. M. (1973). Growing up. *Scientific American, 229,* 34–43.

Turner, D., Hoyer, J., Schmidt, A. F., Klein, V., & Briken, P. (2016). Risk factors for sexual offending in men working with children – A community based survey. *Archives of Sexual Behavior, 45,* 1851–1861.

Welsch, R., Schmidt, A. F., Turner, D., & Rettenberger, M. (2019). *Test-retest reliability and temporal agreement of direct and indirect sexual interest measures.* Manuscript submitted for publication.

Zamansky, H. S. (1956). A technique for measuring homosexual tendencies. *Journal of Personality, 24,* 436–448.

Using the Rapid Serial Visual Presentation to detect sexual interest[1]

5

Angelo Zappalà and Pekka Santtila

Why it is important to detect deviant sexual interest and how to detect it

Deviant Sexual Interest (DSI) has been shown to be a crucial factor in sex offending (Thornton, 2002) as well as a strong predictor of sex offence recidivism (Hanson & Bussière, 1998; Hanson & Morton-Bourgon, 2004, 2005). Therefore, it would be useful to have a valid and reliable diagnostic tool for the assessment of DSI. Such an assessment tool would be useful in both legal decision-making and in evaluating treatment outcomes for those who have committed sexual offences.

At present, there are three main approaches to measuring DSI in forensic settings (see Akerman & Beech, 2011; Kalmus & Beech, 2005). These include: physical methods (e.g. penile plethysmography [PPG]); non-physical methods (e.g. questionnaires, clinical interviews); and attention-based measurement procedures (e.g. viewing time, information-processing paradigms).

Physical measures, like PPG, suffer from physical intrusiveness and the issue that not all participants show a sufficient penile response during the procedure (Looman, Abracen, Maillet, & Di Fazio, 1998), thus, decreasing their usefulness. Another problem in PPG assessments is the measurement's susceptibility to faking. Studies show that it is possible to alter responses in the PPG both through voluntary suppression and voluntary expression of penile arousal (e.g. Golde, Strassberg, Turner, & Lowe, 2000; Howes, 1995; Trottier, Rouleau, Renaud, & Goyette, 2014). Furthermore, it has been found that the use of alcohol and/or drugs can influence sexual functioning and erectile response, which means that substance abuse can also influence the validity of the PPG (Thornton, Finch, & Goeser, 2007).

Several psychometric tools are available for the assessment of those who have sexually offended. The most commonly used methods include measures of attitudes towards women, attitudes towards sexual offending, personality measures, and measures of general psychopathology. Even if some differences among offenders and non-offenders have been reported (see Drieschner & Lange, 1999, for an overview), one problem is the obvious risk for faking on self-reports of attitudes. Seto (2008, p. 477) concluded that, even if self-reports represent a potential source of information, problematic issues, like recall bias, remain unresolved. Moreover, in forensic settings, self-reports are prone to faking because the participants have an obvious interest to present themselves in a socially desirable way. Similarly, clinical interviews collect information regarding what a participant is willing to say or has the ability to say (i.e. if he suffers some memory loss or cognitive impairment). Therefore, clinical interviews suffer from subjectivity of the interviewer in interpreting the interviewee's responses, as well as from the possibly decreased willingness or ability of the interviewee to disclose thoughts and emotions.

In order to overcome the critical points mentioned above, a new generation of procedures have been developed over the past few years.

Attention-based measurement procedures

Attention-based measurement procedures to detect DSI work through discriminating between the relatively increased and the relatively decreased attention directed towards highly sexually relevant (hereafter, sexually relevant) or less sexually relevant (hereafter, sexually irrelevant) stimuli. This attention is often measured through performance on simple information-processing tasks presented simultaneously, prior, or after a sexually relevant or irrelevant stimulus. The ability to identify sexual interest is thought to stem from variations in information-processing capacity due to the simultaneous processing of stimuli that are either relevant or irrelevant according to the individual's sexual interest (Kalmus & Beech, 2005).

Attentional measures of DSI are, thus, based on an information-processing model of human sexuality (Everaerd, 1995; Geer, Lapour, & Jackson, 1993). Such information-processing models commonly suggest that the processing of sexually significant stimuli initially occurs at a pre-attentive level (Spiering & Everaerd, 2007), where attention is automatically drawn to the stimulus. This conceptual model makes a distinction between automatic (unconscious or pre-attentive) and controlled processing of sexual stimuli. Attentional-based measures of DSI rely on the following findings: 1) The first stage of sexual arousal can be thought of as an attention-increasing phase much like an emotion, and has been hypothesized and empirically supported to be a pre-attentive and automatic process (Hietanen & Nummenmaa, 2011; Jiang, Costello, Fang, Huang, & He, 2006; Schupp, Junghöfer, Weike, & Hamm, 2003); 2) Salient stimuli capture attention, leading to better performance and more accurate reporting for affectively arousing vs. non-arousing stimuli (Vuilleumier, 2005); 3) Sexually salient stimuli may lead to a conscious allocation of cognitive resources that would interfere with the performance in other simultaneous tasks (see Kahneman, 1973); and 4) There is a hesitancy in decision-making related to erotic material termed the Sexual Content Induced Delay (SCID; Geer & Bellard, 1996; Geer & Melton, 1997).

In recent years, it has been investigated if the Rapid Serial Visual Presentation procedure can be used as an attention-based measurement procedure to detect DSI.

Rapid Serial Visual Presentation procedure

Rapid Serial Visual Presentation (RSVP) was originally developed as a procedure to study memory, attention, and perception. In the RSVP, an array of stimuli are presented sequentially at the same spatial location. Each stimulus appears during a short time frame (usually for a fraction of a second, e.g. 100 ms), and participants are asked either to report all the stimuli presented (full report) or report only target item(s) and to not pay attention to the remaining distractor stimuli (partial report). If the participants are instructed to report just one target item, the procedure is called a 'single-target Rapid Serial Visual Presentation', whereas if they are instructed to report two targets, the procedure is called the 'dual-target Rapid Serial Visual Presentation' (dtRSVP). The underlying fundamental principle of the RSVP paradigm is that, due to the limits on temporal processing imposed by the procedure, researchers are able to evaluate the rate at which information is perceived, analysed, and encoded by the participants (Chun & Wolfe, 2001; Coltheart, 1999). In the array of stimuli presented, researchers insert target stimuli (usually indicated as T1 and T2) between distractor stimuli. T1 precedes T2 in the sequence of stimuli. The presentation time of each stimulus usually varies from 50 ms to 18 ms, and each stimulus can be followed by a blank picture (20–70 ms). T1 and T2 differ from the distractor stimuli regarding perceptual features (e.g. two red digits between white digits), semantic features (e.g. two letters between digits) or a 32 combination (e.g. two red letters between white digits). Each RSVP trial (i.e. each isolated presentation of a sequence of stimuli) starts with a fixation point (e.g. a fixation cross usually presented for 1000 ms in the centre of the display) that informs the participant that the sequence of stimuli is incoming. The fixation cross is followed by a rapid serial presentation of the stimuli. After the stimuli are presented, participants are required to report T2 and to ignore T1 (if the procedure is a single-target Rapid Serial Visual Presentation) or to report both T1 and T2 (if the procedure is a dual-target Rapid Serial Visual Presentation). Participants use the computer's keyboard to make their choices. The participants are not put under time pressure when making their choices and researchers do not usually measure the reaction times. If unsure, participants are asked to make their best guess. After each response, another trial starts after approximately 1000 ms.

The attentional blink phenomenon

Broadbent and Broadbent (1987) were the first to report a decrease in accuracy in the reporting of T2 when they presented participants with RSVP streams of words containing two targets defined by either category or letter case (in Dux & Marois, 2009). In one experiment by Weichselgartner and Sperling (1987), participants were presented with RSVP streams of digits at the rate of 100 ms/item and were required to report an outlined digit (T1). It was found that participants usually reported T1, the subsequent item, and the items that were shown 400 ms after T1 (i.e. participants usually did not report the third and the fourth stimulus). In four experiments, Raymond, Shapiro, and Arnell (1992) explored whether the causes of the post-target processing deficit are either attentional (i.e. due to a limit of cognitive resources) or sensory (i.e. due to characteristics of the perception system). In these experiments, RSVP arrays of black letter stimuli were shown at the rate of 100 ms, and participants were required to name the T1 stimulus (a single white letter) and detect the presence or absence of the letter 'X' (T2). While T1 targets were correctly identified, the T2 probes were poorly detected when they were presented during a 270 ms interval beginning 180 ms after the target. T2 probes shown immediately after the target or later in the RSVP stream were correctly detected. Researchers found that the temporary reduction in probe detection did not occur in conditions in which a short blank interval followed the target or in which participants were not asked to identify the target.

In sum, when observers attempt to detect and identify these two targets, identification of T2 is impaired when it follows T1 within approximately 500 ms because attentional resources cannot be adequately allocated to a subsequent second target stimulus (T2). Considering the results of the four experiments, Raymond and colleagues (1992) stated that the findings could be explained as an Attentional Blink (AB). From this study onwards, the phenomenon in which the identification of the T2 stimulus is impaired when it follows a T1 stimulus within approximately 500 ms in a dtRSVP has been called Attentional Blink (see Figure 5.1).

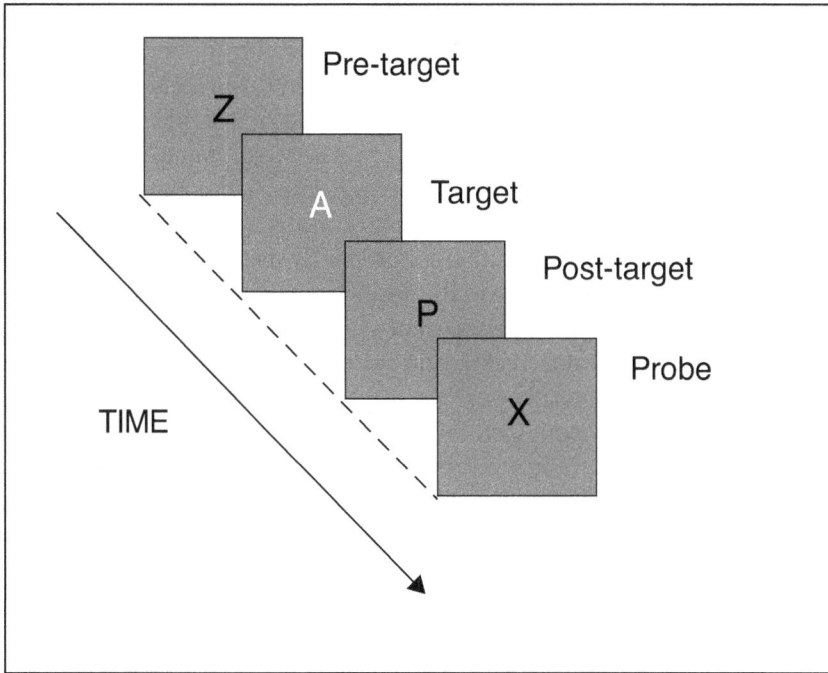

Figure 5.1 In a single-task Rapid Serial Visual Presentation, participants are required to detect the presence or absence of a letter (probe). The target is a white letter. Although targets are accurately detected, probes tend to be poorly detected when they are shown during a 270 ms interval beginning 180 ms after the target.

Dual-target Rapid Serial Visual Presentation (dtRSPV) as an attention-based measurement procedure to detect Deviant Sexual Interest (DSI)

Emotion and attentional blink

A few studies have found that, if T1 is emotionally arousing, it will receive preferential attention at the expense of attentional resources directed to process the following T2. In other words, the 'special attention' dedicated to the emotionally arousing T1 hampers the correct identification of T2. Research suggests that, irrespective of the valence of the emotionality of the stimulus (i.e. positive vs. negative), arousal value tends to be responsible for the AB (Anderson, 2005) and the effects of the processing of T1 on attention depends on the arousal caused by the emotionality of the stimulus itself (Schimmack & Derryberry,

2005). Most, Chun, Widders, and Zald (2005) concluded that 'attentional biases to emotional information induced a temporary inability to process stimuli that people actively sought' (p. 654). McHugo, Olatunji, and Zald (2013) named this phenomenon the 'Emotional Attentional Blink'. To explain the effects of emotional stimuli on the magnitude of the AB, Most, Wang, and colleagues suggested that emotional distractors cause an amplified competition for perceptual resources during the processing and consolidation of the target, rather than limiting awareness at the central bottleneck stage (Most & Wang, 2011; Wang & Most, 2012). According to this model, the emotional stimulus inhibits spatio-temporally adjacent goal-relevant stimulus representations (McHugo et al., 2013). Sexual stimuli (e.g. erotic pictures or sexual words) are generally rated as both emotionally positive and highly arousing by both men and women (Bradley, Codispoti, Cuthbert, & Lang, 2001) and can be considered evolutionarily valuable stimuli (e.g. they drive the attention to a potential mating opportunity). In a single-target Rapid Serial Visual Presentation, Most and his colleagues found that erotic stimuli induced spontaneous attentional blinks similar to those seen following negative pictures (Most et al., 2005). In their experiments, when participants searched for a target embedded in a RSVP stream of pictures, positively arousing emotional distractors captured and held attention to such a degree that they created deficits in processing the subsequent target. The authors coined these findings 'emotion-induced blindness' or 'attentional rubbernecking'. Ciesielski and colleagues (2010) found that at lag^2 2 (i.e. just one stimuli between the distractor and the target), erotic images induced the greatest deficits in subsequent target processing compared to other images, consistent with a large emotional attentional blink.

In the wake of these findings, a few studies were conducted to explore the possibility of using the magnitude of the AB in RSVP as an attention-based measurement procedure of Deviant Sexual Interest (DSI).

DSI and AB in dtRSVP procedure

The basic idea in using the AB to detect DSI is that, during the view of stream of visual stimuli in a dtRSVP, a participant's attention is captured by T1 stimuli that are emotionally arousing in terms of being sexually preferred. For example, participants who have a DSI in children will find pictures of a prepubescent individual more emotionally arousing than pictures of an adult. Therefore, an increased AB (i.e. a decrease in accuracy in the reporting of T2) would be expected when T2 follows a T1 depicting prepubescent children, compared to when T2 follows a T1 depicting an adult. In studies attempting to use the AB to measure sexual preferences, arrays of visual stimuli were shown and participants were required to report T1 and T2 stimuli according to a typical dtRSVP procedure. Several studies using the evaluation of AB in dtRSVP as an attention-based measurement procedure of DSI have been conducted.

Kalmus (2003) assessed the possibility of using the AB effect to differentiate between individuals belonging to two groups (36 individuals who had sexually offended against a child versus 20 non-offender participants). Kalmus used a sequence of images involving eight distractors and two target images. The T1 image of either a clothed child or an animal was closely followed by a T2 image of either a train or a chair. Participants were required to accurately report both targets. Kalmus found that a larger AB emerged in the offender sample when T2 was an image of a clothed child compared to when T1 was an image of an animal.

Beech, Kalmus, Tipper, Baudouin, Flak, and Humphreys (2008) used images of children and animals as T1 and investigated the differences between the effects of these two stimulus types on the AB in a sample of 35 men who had sexually abused a child (16 intrafamilial, 19 extrafamilial) and 17 non-sex offenders. The study consisted of two report conditions. In the first condition, T1 and T2 had to be reported (dtRSVP). That is, participants reported whether they saw a child or an animal (T1) and then whether they saw a train or a chair and its direction (oriented to the left or right). In the second condition, only T2 had to be reported (single-target Rapid Serial Visual Presentation). That is, participants reported whether they saw a train or a chair and its direction (left or right). In each trial, participants viewed a stream of 11 images. Two hundred and sixteen T1 stimuli were used (108 non-nude children or 108 animals) and 216 were used as T2 stimuli (trains and chairs, half facing left and half facing right). The T1 child category images (the age of the children varying from 6 to 11 years old) included facial, half-length, and full-length images of either a single child or groups of children in natural settings. Sex and ethnic group stimuli were used, with the weightings reflecting the recorded characteristics of the children who were molested. The T1 animal images included reptiles, birds, domestic and wild mammals. T2 stimuli consisted of 216 images (trains, chairs, half oriented to the left and half oriented to the right).

The researchers hypothesized that due to the AB: 1) those who had sexually abused a child, compared with the non sex offenders, would have a decrease in accuracy in the reporting of T2 following the explicit naming of a T1 image of sexual or emotional salience to the them, and; 2) the decrease in accuracy in the reporting of T2 following the explicit naming of T1 images of children will be particularly manifested in those with extrafamilial sex offences because of a hypothesized stronger sexual preference in children in the extrafamilial group compared with those committing incestuous offences. Regarding Hypothesis 1, researchers found that, compared with a control group of offenders who had not abused children, those who had abused a child in condition 1 (dtRSVP) showed a decreased in accuracy when reporting T2 stimuli following the explicit naming of a T1 image of sexual or non-sexual images of children. Significant differences were found between the control group and the intrafamilial group, and between the control group and the extrafamilial group, when comparing the accuracy in the reporting of T2 when T1 stimuli were pictures of animals or children. In condition 2, the researchers found that both samples of men who had abused a child were less accurate in reporting T2 when T1 was a picture of a child rather than a picture of an animal. The participants in the control group were less accurate in the reporting of T2 when T1 were animal stimuli. Regarding Hypothesis 2, no significant difference was found in the performance of those with intra- and extrafamilial offences.

Crooks, Rostill-Brooks, Beech, and Bickley (2009) evaluated the magnitude of AB among 20 adolescents with sex offence histories and 26 non-sex offenders using the RSVP. Their RSVP presented 216 ten-image sequences, composed of T1, T2, and eight neutral distractor images. Of the 216 T1 images, half were animals and half were children. Animals included domestic pets and wildlife animals. The child images were of clothed pre-adolescents of varying gender and ethnicity. Of the 216 T2 images, half displayed chairs and half displayed trains. One half of the trains and chairs were oriented to the left and the other half to the right. Each of the 10 images within a sequence was displayed for 100 ms. T1 was always followed by T2, but the interval between them could vary by a maximum of 300 ms. Participants were asked to report whether they had viewed an animal or a child (T1) and then a train or a chair, and whether they were oriented to the left or to the right (T2). For those who had sexually offended against children, a stronger AB effect was found after viewing child rather than animal images, but the expected differences between groups were not found. The authors hypothesized that their failure to produce similar results to Beech and colleagues (2008) could reflect the fluid nature of sexual preferences during the sexually formative years of adolescence.

Flak (2011) investigated whether the RSVP could detect sexual interest in child images using a sample of 14 men with a history of extrafamilial sex offences against children, 12 men with a history of intrafamilial child sex offences, 17 non-sexual offenders, and a control group. In the same study, Flak explored the potential bias of anxiety, social desirability, and IQ on RSVP performance. The stimuli were all drawn from 610 commercially available images. Of these, 216 were used as T1 stimuli, divided into 178 neutral images, 108 animals and 108 clothed child images. Of the remaining images, 216 were used as T2 stimuli, with 108 trains and 108 chairs (half facing left/half facing right). T1 child images portrayed children in natural settings, either full body or facial images of either a single child or children in groups. The age of the depicted children ranged between 6 and 11 years old. The T1 animal images included domestic and wild mammals, birds, and reptiles. Images were again facial, half-length or full-length pictures of single or groups of animals in natural settings. The procedure consisted of two conditions that were counterbalanced in order to control for order effects.

In Condition 1, the participants had to report T1 and T2 (dtRSVP), investigating whether an increase in error rate was detected in T2 when T1 was accurately reported. In Condition 2, the participants had to report T2 only in order to measure and control for the difficulty in reporting T2 when T1 did not have to be reported (single-target Rapid Serial Visual Presentation). Each trial consisted of 11 images, divided into 4 blocks (there was a short break in between each block), with 216 trials in total. In order to reduce the primacy and recency effect, images in each sequence were sequentially presented for 100 ms and the first and last image was neutral in every sequence. T1 images were always positioned between the second and the seventh position. T2 was always positioned between the third and ninth position, and it followed either immediately or immediately after the presentation of T1. The pictures assigned to the particular interval were counterbalanced across participants within each group. The analysis used T2 detection accuracy as a dependent variable for both conditions when T1 was also accurately identified in Condition 1. T2 stimuli had one of four separate responses (chair left, chair right, train left, train right). Therefore, the chance level for accurate detection was at 25%.

The analysis showed a significant interaction between image category and group, suggesting that image category had a differing effect across the three groups. This effect was due to the difference in performance of the groups, where men with extrafamilial offences displayed lower T2 accuracy when T1 was a child compared to when it was an animal. For men with intrafamilial offences, an opposite pattern was observed. A main effect of interval was also found. No significant interaction effects between anxiety or social desirability and T2 accuracy were found. This suggests that anxiety does not affect the magnitude of the AB and that social desirability did not exert a significant effect on T2 accuracy across all groups. Moreover, the results showed that participants' IQ affected the magnitude of the AB.

Zappalà, Antfolk, Dombert, Mokros, and Santtila (2016) investigated the possibility of using the dtRSVP to identify DSI in a forensic population of men with sexual offences. The sample consisted of 69 men who had sexually abused a child, 43 men who had committed other sex offences, 14 men with non-sexual offences, and 88 community controls. This study differed from the aforementioned studies in two ways: (1) besides evaluating the magnitude of the AB phenomenon, it also utilized the Pop Out Effect (POE) on both T1 and T2; and (2) it used computer-generated images (CGI) depicting humans in order to better control the variation in stimuli dimensions (gender, maturity level, and levels of sexual explicitness).[3]

POE refers to a phenomenon that occurs in visual search tasks, in which a unique visual target (e.g. a feature singleton) can be rapidly detected among a set of homogeneous distractors (Treisman & Souther, 1985; Wolfe, 1994). It has been found that AB is reduced (i.e. accurate reporting of T2 is relatively less decreased after the correct identification of T1) if T2 is particularly salient to the viewer (Arnell, Killman, & Fijavz, 2007; Anderson, 2005; Gantman & Van Bavel, 2014; Keil & Ihssen, 2004; Schwabe et al., 2011). It can be argued that the emotional valence of the stimulus represents dissociable target characteristics among homogeneous distractors. As such, the emotional arousing T2 breaks through and partially reduces the AB phenomenon in a dtRSVP procedure. Zappalà et al. argued that, even if the original formulation of POE was made in the domain of visual search paradigms that present several stimuli simultaneously in different spatial locations, the theory of POE can also contribute to explain the processing of the temporally presented stimuli in dtRSVP.

In this study, in each stream, two images (T1 and T2) were framed with a black frame. Both T1 and T2 could be an image of either a nude prepubescent (Tanner 1)[4] or an adult (Tanner 4/5) human. T1 and T2 always appeared with one distracter image between them. This image could not be of the same type as either T1 or T2. Also, the image after T2 could not be of the same type as T2. Of the 12 images in a stream, the two first images and the last image could not be a target image. T1 was, thus, presented between positions three and nine, and T2 between positions five and 11 (see Figure 5.2).

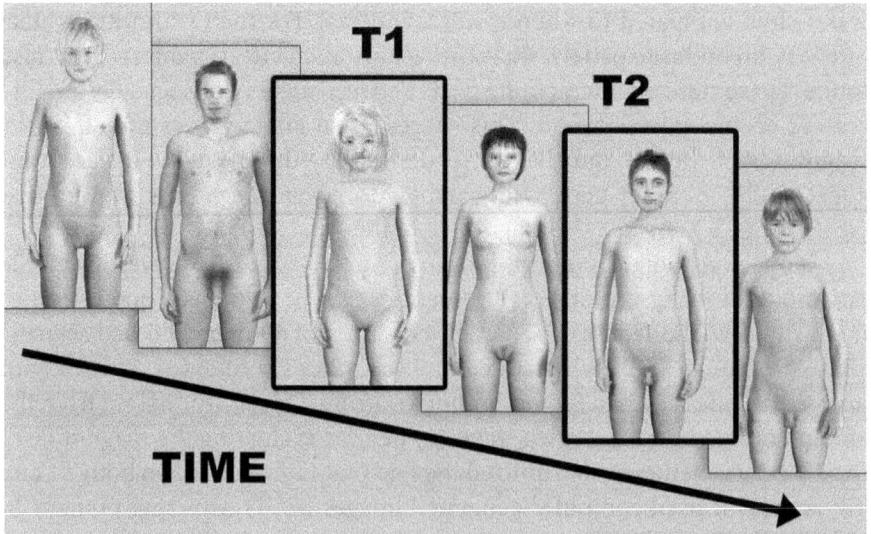

Figure 5.2 A schematic overview of the Rapid Serial Visual Presentation measurement procedure used. Twelve images were presented for 166ms each, and T1 could appear in positions 3–9 with T2 appearing with a one-stimulus interval.

After each trial, four response categories (pictorial images of nude child male, nude child female, nude adult male and nude adult female) were presented to the participants. The researchers hypothesized: (1) a Pop Out effect on T1 and T2 (i.e. the accuracy in reporting T1 and T2 would be relatively increased when these were of preferred gender and preferred maturity level compared to when they were not); and (2) an AB on the accuracy in reporting T2 (i.e. when correctly reported T1 were of preferred gender and maturity level the accuracy in reporting T2 would decrease in comparison to when T1 were not preferred).

Regarding Hypothesis 1, they found a better accuracy of reporting T1 and T2 when T1 and T2 were more sexually salient in terms of gender and maturity level. This means that when a participant viewed a sexually preferred image as a target, the encoding and/or reporting of this target was improved compared to when this target image was not sexually preferred. The secondary sexual characteristics depicted in the stimuli used could, therefore, be conceptualized as a feature that provokes a detectable POE. Regarding Hypothesis 2, they found the expected effect when the grouping of participants was based on the participant having or not having a score of three or more on the Screening Scale for Pedophilic Interests (SSPI; Seto & Lalumière, 2001).[5] The results also showed that paedophilic male participants processed sexual stimuli differently in comparison to non-paedophilic male participants, and that these differences were in the expected directions. Moreover, although they found group differences, individual indices based on detection rates did not allow for individual-level diagnostic categorization of participants ($AUC = .66$, $CI = .57$ to $.75$, $p = .01$).

Future directions

Several points could be considered in order to increase the efficacy of using the dtRSVP to detect DSI.

Improve the quality of stimuli

All the attention-based measurement procedures adapted to identify DSI, dtRSVP included, use the aesthetic response of the participants and work through discriminating the effect of increased attention towards sexually relevant stimuli upon information processing tasks. The aesthetic response depends not only on the shape of the body and/or quality of the texture of the skin, but also the attractiveness of the depicted individuals. Nakamura and Kawabata (2017) investigated the temporal modulation of visual attention induced by facial attractiveness and found that the identification of a second female target (T2) was impaired when a first target (T1) was attractive compared to neutral or unattractive. Therefore, considering that the visual stimuli play an important role to elicit the aesthetic response, the quality of stimuli ought to be further improved.

Participant's sexual desire level

It has been shown that the emotional state of participants affects the accessibility of highly valued or goal-relevant stimuli (Förster, Liberman, & Friedman, 2007), which may enhance perceptual awareness (Anderson, 2005; Anderson & Phelps, 2001; Bruner & Goodman, 1947; Vuilleumier, 2005). For example, food-related words are easier to recognize when one is hungry than when one is not (Radel & Clément-Guillotin, 2012; see also Balcetis, Dunning, & Granot, 2012) (in Gantman & Van Bavel, 2014). In addition, Conaglen (2004) found that individuals with lower levels of sexual desire responded more slowly to sexual stimuli than other participants, and rated sexual words as less familiar, less acceptable, and less positive emotional. These findings suggest that the information-processing of sexual information could be affected by sexual desire. Therefore, the 'wishful seeing' phenomenon and participants' sexual desire level should be investigated.

Mood traits and states

A few studies investigated the relation between the mood state of participants and the magnitude of the attentional blink in the RSVP procedure. Jefferies, Smilek, Eich, and Enns (2008) found that sadness (low arousal with negative affect) produced the highest levels of performance (i.e. a largest attentional blink), while anxiety (high arousal with negative affect) led to the lowest levels of performance. MacLean, Arnell, and Busseri (2010) found that higher levels of (self-reported) negative trait affect were associated with a greater attentional blink and that the magnitude of the attentional blink was negatively correlated with positive trait affect. MacLean et al. (2010) found a smaller attentional blink was associated with greater dispositional positive affect and that a larger attentional blink was associated with greater negative trait (similar findings were found by Rokke, Arnell, Koch, & Andrews, 2002 in relation to depression).

Kawahara and Sato (2013) also found that negative mood affected the magnitude of the attentional blink (i.e. negative mood was associated to a larger attentional blink). To explain this finding, they postulated that the attentional blink phenomenon could be due to a limitation in the resources available for consolidating the second target into working memory. Since negative mood states impair the encoding of events into working memory (e.g. Schoofs, Wolf, & Smeets, 2009), negative mood increases the magnitude of the attentional blink. In addition, it should be noted that it has been suggested that depression is associated with reduced attentional functioning (Hasher & Zacks, 1979). Rokke et al. (2002) observed that a large body of literature supports the proposition that depression is associated with limitations in the effortful processing of information on memory tasks. Overall, these findings suggest that the effect of participants' mood should be further investigated.

Faking

It would be necessary to investigate if the dtRSVP is resistant to faking and if the test's usefulness is maintained when the test-taker acquires knowledge about the test (Fiedler & Bluemke, 2005; Zappalà, Antfolk, Dombert, Mokros, & Santtila, 2013).

Participant stress

A couple of studies investigated the relation between the stress of the participants and the magnitude of the attentional blink in the RSVP procedure. Schwabe and Wolf (2010) found that stress had no effect on the attentional blink, while Kawahara and Sato (2013) found that stress manipulation increased the magnitude of the attentional blink deficit. The forensic setting, where the procedure could be applied, maybe anxiety-provoking and stressful. In light of these considerations, the effect of stress needs further investigation.

Test-retest

An objective assessment of the presence of DSI would allow evaluating the progress of treatment as well as confronting patients who are in denial about their sexual interests. In order to evaluate the efficacy of the treatment of individuals who have committed a sex offence against a child, it would be expected that the magnitude of the AB should be different before and after treatment. That is, before treatment, a greater magnitude of AB would be expected in comparison to after treatment. Consequently, the re-testability feature for RSVP is crucial. We reported positive findings of Flak's (2011) study that support the re-testability of RSVP. However, it should be noted that there are some studies that have investigated the possibility of eliminating the AB through repetitive practice (Braun, 1998; Maki & Padmanabhan, 1994; Taatgen, Juvina, Schipper, Borst, & Martens, 2009). Choi, Chang, Shibata, Sasaki, and Watanabe (2012) found that 'just 1hr of specific attentional training can completely eliminate AB, and that this effect is robust enough to persist for a few months after training' (p. 12242). Also, Tang, Badcock, and Visser (2014) found that 'whereas training may ameliorate the AB indirectly, the processing limits evidenced in the AB cannot be directly eliminated by brief exposure to the task' p. 406). These findings suggest that the issue of the test-retest should be further investigated.

Notes

1. This chapter is based on Angelo Zappalà's thesis summary "Separating Deviant and Non-Deviant Sexual Preferences with a Dual-Target Rapid Serial Visual Presentation Task" (Psychology Faculty of Arts, Psychology and Theology Åbo Akademi University Åbo, Finland, 2016).
2. The position of T2 with respect to T1 is indicated with the term 'lag'.
3. The use of visual stimuli depicting children in research and assessment concerning paedophilia necessitates a careful evaluation of the ethical and legal boundaries. Making pictures that depicts children is problematic, especially when the pictures will be used for identification of DSI. In fact, the children depicted neither can nor would give their informed consent for this use (Card & Olsen, 1996) and it could also be seen as problematic if parents or caregivers give their consent to produce suitable photographs of their children. Of course, for obvious reasons, it is also not possible to use child pornography materials from the web. For these reasons, Dombert et al. (2013) developed 108 computer-generated stimuli. The images vary in terms of gender (female/male), explicitness (naked/clothed), and physical maturity (prepubescent, pubescent, and adult) of the persons depicted. Dombert et al. state that this 'virtual people set' can be used as visual stimuli in implicit assessment of pedophilic sexual interest through viewing-time methods.
4. The Tanner stages describe physical development in children, adolescents and adults and was created by James Tanner, (Marshall & Tanner, 1969, 1970; Tanner, 1962). The scale defines physical measurements of development based on external primary and secondary sex characteristics, such as the size of the breast, genitalia, and development of pubic hair.
5. SSPI score varying from 0 (meaning no sexual attraction to prepubescent children interest) to 5 (maximum sexual attraction to prepubescent children interest).

References

Akerman, G., & Beech, A. (2011). A systematic review of measures of deviant sexual interest and arousal. *Psychiatry, Psychology and Law, 19*, 118–143.

Anderson, A. K. (2005). Affective influences on the attentional dynamics supporting awareness. *Journal of Experimental Psychology: General, 134*, 258–281.

Anderson, A. K., & Phelps, E. A. (2001). Lesions of the human amygdale impair enhanced perception of emotionally salient events. *Nature, 411*, 305–309.

Arnell, K. M., Killman, K. V., & Fijavz, D. (2007). Blinded by emotion: Target misses follow attention capture by arousing distractors in RSVP. *Emotion, 7*, 465–477.

Balcetis, E., Dunning, D., & Granot, Y. (2012). Subjective value determines initial dominance in binocular rivalry. *Journal of Experimental Social Psychology, 48*, 122–129.

Beech, A. R., Kalmus, E., Tipper, S. P., Baudouin, J., Flak, V., & Humphreys, G. W. (2008). Children induce enhanced an AB in child molesters. *Psychological Assessment, 20*, 397–402.

Bradley, P. J., Codispoti, M., Cuthbert, B., & Lang, P. J. (2001). Emotion and motivation I: Defensive and appetitive reactions in picture processing. *Emotion, 1*, 276–298.

Braun, J. (1998). Vision and attention: The role of training. *Nature, 393*, 424–425.

Broadbent, D. E., & Broadbent, M. H. P. (1987). From detection to identification: Response to multiple targets in Rapid Serial Visual Presentation. *Perception & Psychophysics, 42*, 105–113.

Bruner, J., & Goodman, C. (1947). Value and need as organizing factors in percepton. *Journal of Abnormal and Social Psychology, 42*, 33–44.

Card, R. D., & Olsen, S. E. (1996). Commentary: Visual plethysmograph stimuli involving children: Rethinking some quasi-logical issues. *Sexual Abuse, 8*, 267–271.

Chun, M. M., & Wolfe, J. M. (2001). Visual attention. In E. B. Goldstein (Ed.), *Blackwell's Handbook of perception* (Vol. Ch 9, pp. 272–310). Oxford, UK: Blackwell.

Ciesielski, K. T., Ahlfors, S. P., Bedrick, E. J., Kerwin, A. A., & Hamalainen, M. S. (2010). Top down control of MEG alphaband activity in children performing categorical N-Back Task. *Neuropsychologia, 48*, 3573–3579.

Choi, H., Chang, L. H., Shibata, K., Sasaki, Y., & Watanabe, T. (2012). Resetting capacity limitations revealed by long-lasting elimination of attentional blink through training. *Proceedings of the National Academy of Sciences, 109*(30), 12242–12247.

Coltheart, M. (1999). Modularity and cognition. *Trends in Cognitive Sciences, 3*, 115–120.

Conaglen, H. M. (2004). Sexual content induced delay: A reexamination investigating relation to sexual desire. *Archives of Sexual Behavior, 33*, 359–367.

Crooks, V. L., Rostill-Brookes, H., Beech, A. R., & Bickley, J. A. (2009). Applying Rapid Serial Visual Presentation to adolescent sexual offenders: Attentional bias as a measure of deviant sexual interest? *Sexual Abuse: A Journal of Research and Treatment, 21*, 135–148.

Drieschner, K., & Lange, A. (1999). A review of cognitive factors in the etiology of rape: Theories, empirical studies, and implications. *Clinical Psychology Review, 19*, 57–77.

Dux, P. E., & Marois, R. (2009). The attentional blink: A review of data and theory. *Attention, Perception & Psychophysics, 71*, 1683–1700.

Everaerd, W. (1995). Information processing approach and the sexual response in human studies. In J. Bancroft (Ed.), *The pharmacology of sexual function and dysfunction: Proceedings of the Esteve Foundation Symposium VI* (pp. 175–184). Amsterdam: Excerpta Medica.

Fiedler, K., & Bluemke, M. (2005). Faking the IAT: Aided and unaided response control on the Implicit Association Test. *Basis and Applied Social Psychology, 27*, 307–316.

Flak, V. E. (2011). Assessment of sexual interest in child sex offenders by the use of a computerized measure. *Unpublished doctoral thesis*, University of Birmingham, UK.

Förster, J., Liberman, N., & Friedman, R. S. (2007). Seven principles of goal activation: A systematic approach to distinguishing goal priming from priming of non-goal constructs. *Personality and Social Psychology Review, 11*, 211–233.

Gantman, A. P., & Van Bavel, J. J. (2014). The moral pop-out effect: Enhanced perceptual awareness of morally relevant stimuli. *Cognition, 132*, 22–29.

Geer, J. H., & Bellard, H. S. (1996). Sexual content induced delays in unprimed lexical decisions: Gender and context effects. *Archives of Sexual Behavior, 25*, 379–395.

Geer, J. H., Lapour, K. J., & Jackson, S. R. (1993). The information processing perspective to human sexuality. In N. Birbaumer & A. Ohman (Eds.), *The structure of emotion: Psychophysiological, cognitive and clinical aspects* (pp. 139–155). Toronto: Hogrefe – Huber.

Geer, J. H., & Melton, J. S. (1997). Sexual content-induced delay with double-entendreords. *Archives of Sexual Behavior, 26*, 295–316.

Golde, J. A., Strassberg, D. S., Turner, C. M., & Lowe, K. (2000). Attitudinal effects of degrading themes and sexual explicitness in video materials. *Sexual Abuse, 12*, 223–232.

Hanson, R. K., & Bussière, M. T. (1998). Predicting relapse: A meta-analysis of sexual offender recidivism studies. *Journal of Consulting and Clinical Psychology, 66*, 348–362.

Hanson, R. K., & Morton-Bourgon, K. (2004). Predictors of sexual recidivism: An updated meta-analysis (User report No. 2004-02). Ottawa, ON: Public Safety and Emergency Preparedness Canada.

Hanson, R. K., & Morton-Bourgon, K. E. (2005). The characteristics of persistent sexual offenders: A meta-analysis of recidivism studies. *Journal of Consulting and Clinical Psychology, 73*, 1154–1163.

Hasher, L., & Zacks, R. (1979). Automatic and effort full, processes in memory. *Journal of Experimental Psychology: General, 108*, 356–388.

Hietanen, J. K., & Nummenmaa, L. (2011). The naked truth: The face and body sensitive N170 response is enhanced for nude bodies. *PLoS ONE, 6*(11), e24408.

Howes, R. J. (1995). A survey of plethysmographic assessment in North America. *Sexual Abuse, 7*, 9–24.

Jefferies, L. N., Smilek, D., Eich, E., & Enns, J. T. (2008). Emotional valence and arousal interact in attentional control. *Psychological Science, 19*, 290–295.

Jiang, Y., Costello, P., Fang, F., Huang, M., & He, S. (2006). A gender- and sexual orientation dependent spatial attentional effect of invisible images. *PNAS, 103*, 17048–17052.

Kahneman, D. (1973). *Attention and effort.* Englewood Cliffs, NJ: Prentice-Hall.

Kalmus, E. (2003). Developing a computer-based assessment using Rapid Serial Visual Presentation and attentional phenomena: A new means of measuring sexual interest? *Unpublished doctoral thesis*, University of Birmingham, UK.

Kalmus, E., & Beech, A. R. (2005). Forensic assessment of sexual interest: A review. *Aggression and Violent Behavior, 10*, 193–217.

Kawahara, J., & Sato, H. (2013). The effect of fatigue on the attentional blink. *Attention, Perception, & Psychophysics, 75*, 1096–1102.

Keil, A., & Ihssen, N. (2004). Identification facilitation for emotionally arousing verbs during the AB. *Emotion, 4*, 23–35.

Looman, J., Abracen, J., Maillet, G., & Di Fazio, R. (1998). Phallometric non responding in sexual offenders. *Sexual Abuse: A Journal of Research and Treatment, 10*, 325–336.

MacLean, M. H., Arnell, K. M., & Busseri, M. A. (2010). Dispositional affect predicts temporal attention costs in the attentional blink paradigm. *Cognition and Emotion, 24*, 1431–1438.

Maki, W. S., & Padmanabhan, G. (1994). Transient suppression of processing during Rapid Serial Visual Presentation: Acquired distinctiveness of probes modulates the attentional blink. *Psychonomic Bulletin & Review, 1*, 499–504.

Marshall, W. A., & Tanner, J. M. (1969). Variations in pattern of pubertal changes in girls. *Archives of Disease in Childhood, 44*, 291–303.

Marshall, W. A., & Tanner, J. M. (1970). Variations in the pattern of pubertal changes in boys. *Archives of Disease in Childhood, London, 45*, 13–23.

McHugo, M., Olatunji, B. O., & Zald, D. H. (2013). The emotional attentional blink: What we know so far. *Frontiers in Human Neuroscience, 7*, 1–8.

Most, S. B., Chun, M. M., Widders, D. M., & Zald, D. H. (2005). Attentional rubbernecking: Cognitive control and personality in emotion induced blindness. *Psychonomic Bulletin & Review, 12*, 654–661.

Most, S. B., & Wang, L. (2011). Dissociating spatial attention and awareness in emotion-induced blindness. *Psychological Science, 22*, 300–305.

Nakamura, K., & Kawabata, H. (2017). Prioritized identification of attractive and romantic partner faces in Rapid Serial Visual Presentation. *Archives of Sexual Behavior, 46*, 2327–2338.

Radel, R., & Clément-Guillotin, C. (2012). Evidence of motivational influences in early visual perception hunger modulates conscious access. *Psychological Science, 23*, 232–234.

Raymond, J. E., Shapiro, K. L., & Arnell, K. M. (1992). Temporary suppression of visual processing in an RSVP task: An attentional blink? *Journal of Experimental Psychology: Human Perception and Performance, 18*, 849–860.

Rokke, P. D., Arnell, K. M., Koch, M. D., & Andrews, J. T. (2002). Dual-task attention deficits in dysphoric mood. *Journal of Abnormal Psychology, 111*, 370–379.

Schimmack, U., & Derryberry, D. (2005). Attentional interference effects of emotional pictures: Threat, negativity, or arousal? *Emotion, 5*, 55–66.

Schoofs, D., Wolf, O. T., & Smeets, T. (2009). Cold pressor stress impairs performance on working memory tasks requiring executive functions in healthy young men. *Behavioral Neuroscience, 123*, 1066–1075.

Schwabe, L., & Wolf, O. T. (2010). Emotional modulation of the attentional blink: Is there an effect of stress? *Emotion, 10*(2), 283–288. doi: https://doi.org/10.1037/a0017751

Schupp, H. T., Junghöfer, M., Weike, A. I., & Hamm, A. O. (2003). Attention and emotion: An ERP analysis of facilitated emotional stimulus processing. *Neuroreport, 14*, 1107–1110.

Schwabe, L., Merz, C. J., Walter, B., Vaiti, D., Wolf, O. T., & Stark, R. (2011). Emotional modulation of the attentional blink: The neural structures involved in capturing and holding attention. *Neuropsychologia, 49*, 416–425.

Seto, M. C. (2008). *Understanding pedophilia and sexual offending against children: Theory, assessment, and intervention.* Washington, DC: American Psychological Association.

Seto, M. C., & Lalumière, M. L. (2001). A brief screening scale to identify pedophilic interests among child molesters. *Sexual Abuse: A Journal of Research and Treatment, 13*, 15–25.

Spiering, M., & Everaerd, W. (2007). The unconscious sex. In E. Janssen (Ed.), *The psychophysiology of sex* (pp. 166–184). Bloomington, IN: Indiana University Press.

Taatgen, N. A., Juvina, I., Schipper, M., Borst, J. P., & Martens, S. (2009). Too much control can hurt: A threaded cognition model of the attentional blink. *Cognitive Psychology, 59*, 1–29.

Tang, M. F., Badcock, D. R., & Visser, T. A. W. (2014). Training and the attentional blink: Limits overcome or expectations raised? *Psychonomic Bulletin & Review, 21*, 406–411.

Tanner, J. M. (1962). *Growth of adolescents.* Oxford, UK: Blackwell.

Thornton, D. (2002). Constructing and testing a framework for dynamic risk assessment. *Sexual Abuse: A Journal of Research and Treatment, 14*, 139–153.

Thornton, D., Finch, K., & Goeser, L. (2007). Penile output and substance abuse history. *Paper presented at 26th annual association for the treatment of sexual abuse conference.* San Diego, CA, November 2007.

Treisman, A., & Souther, J. (1985). Search asymmetry: Adiagnostic for preattentive processing of separable features. *Journal of Experimental Psychology: General, 114*, 285–310.

Trottier, D., Rouleau, J. L., Renaud, P., & Goyette, M. (2014). Using eye tracking to identify faking attempts during penile plethysmography assessment. *Journal of Sex Research, 51*, 946–955.

Vuilleumier, P. (2005). How brains beware: Neural mechanisms of emotional attention. *Trends in Cognitive Sciences, 9*, 585–594.

Wang, L., & Most, S. B. (2012). Temporally dynamic changes in the emotion-induced spread of target suppression. *Journal of Vision, 12*, 3.

Weichselgartner, E., & Sperling, G. (1987). Dynamics of automatic and controlled visual attention. *Science, 238*, 778–780.

Wolfe, J. M. (1994). Guided search 2.0: A revised model of visual search. *Psychonomic Bulletin Review, 1*, 202–238.

Zappalà, A., Antfolk, J., Dombert, B., Mokros, A., & Santtila, P. (2013). Using a dual-target Rapid Serial Visual Presentation Task (RSVP) as an attention-based measurement procedure of sexual preference: Is it possible to fake? *Psychiatry, Psychology and Law, 20*, 73–90.

Zappalà, A., Antfolk, J., Dombert, D., Mokros, A., & Santtila, P. (2016). Identifying deviant sexual interest in a sex offender sample using dual-target Rapid Serial Visual Presentation task. *The Journal of Forensic Psychiatry and Psychology, 27*, 281–307.

Using eye-related measures to assess sexual interest

6

Charlotte Wesson and
Todd E. Hogue

There is an increasing tendency in the 21st century to turn to technology as a solution to a wide range of social and political problems. This predominance of addressing social issues through neuro-technical and robotic themes in the movies, mirrors the growth of neuropsychological research and the development of new methods of assessing and inferring psychological functioning. One area that has increased exponentially is the idea that you can follow where someone looks and infer from that gaze pattern what the individual is thinking.

Eye-tracking has advanced massively since its first inception. Early attempts to objectively measure eye movements date back to the late 19th century (Cognolato, Atzori, & Müller, 2018). However, the first eye-trackers were incredibly invasive, for instance using a 'cap' attached to a 'cocainized eye' (Li, Munn, & Pelz, 2008). By the beginning of the 20th century, recording of eye movements had become less invasive, and closer to the eye-tracking devices that we know today, by utilizing corneal reflection to track eye gaze (Cognolato et al., 2018). This area continued to develop and grow, with cameras being employed in conjunction with corneal reflection by the seventies. There was further progression in the area during the 1980s and 1990s in line with advancements in computer science and the development of electronic devices (Cognolato et al., 2018). Now, modern day video-based eye-trackers are either implemented using a PC (with or without a chin rest) or are wearable devices, such as head-mounted eye-trackers (e.g. EyeLink II), or even glasses (e.g. Tobii Pro Glasses 2). There are advantages and disadvantages to each type of eye-tracker, depending on what is required from them. Static eye-trackers may or may not have a chin rest in order to keep the participant's head stable during the image recording, however this restricts natural movement. Some eye-trackers have been developed in recent years that do not require a chin rest and therefore allow for free and naturalistic head movements. These have often been seen as superior as they work with numerous eye shapes, as well as contact lenses and spectacles (Hogue, Wesson, & Perkins, 2016). Head-mounted eye-trackers also allow for naturalistic head movements and can be easily used in real-world scenarios (Cognolato et al., 2018).

Present day eye-trackers have a variety of variables that they are able to measure. Eye movements that are typically measured by eye-trackers primarily include saccades (reflexive rapid eye movements) and fixations (stable dwellings on a specific characteristic) (Wenzlaff, Briken, & Dekker, 2016). However, many dependent variables can be recorded including (but not limited to): fixation/gaze/dwell time, number of fixations, time to first fixation, first fixation duration, total fixation/gaze/dwell time, and total number of fixations (Wenzlaff et al., 2016), as well as related measures such as pupil dilation.

Although eye-tracking has been around for many decades and applied to many areas of research such as: infant research (Hessels, Andersson, Hooge, Nyström, & Kemner, 2015), research into autism (Pierce, Marinero, Hazin, McKenna, Carter Barnes, & Malige, 2016), clinical research (Roux, Brunet-Gouet, Passerieux, & Ramus, 2016) and marketing research (Pieters, Erdem, & Martinovici, 2017), to name a few, it has only come to prominence in the area of sex research in the past decade or so (Wenzlaff et al., 2016). Eye-tracking can be very useful in the assessment of sexual interest for a number of reasons. It has been suggested that eye-tracking relates to Singer's (1984) first phase of sexual arousal – the 'aesthetic response' (Wenzlaff et al., 2016). As eye-tracking is based on the near-involuntary movement of the participant's eyes, eye-tracking is highly effective for measuring automatic and pre-attentive responses to a visual image. Moreover, as these eye movements are automatic, they should not be able to be overtly manipulated by individuals (Akhter, 2011). This makes it ideal for the accurate measurement of sexual preference, as individuals may be inclined to bias results to portray themselves in a socially desirable way, especially those who experience deviant sexual interests.

Previously used assessments for sexual preference

Eye-tracking has only recently become prominent in the field of sexual preference research. Prior to this, the main objective measure used was penile plethysmography (PPG) for men and vaginal photoplethysmography (VPP) for women. The premise of PPG is simple – a man's erection is seen to indicate his level of sexual arousal. Thus, the penile tumescence to various, normally sexual, stimuli is recorded (Merdian & Jones, 2011). There are two types of PPG – volumetric and circumferential. The former measures changes in air pressure in a glass cylinder that is placed over the penis (Kalmus & Beech, 2005), and the latter measures change in tumescence by a rubber or metal gauge that is placed around the penis, measuring the diameter of the penis (Merdian & Jones, 2011).

However, despite PPG being referred to as the 'gold standard' in sexual preference measurement (Trottier, Rouleau, Renaud, & Goyette, 2014), there are many limitations associated with this method. Firstly, PPG equates male erection with sexual arousal. Although genital response is evidently part of male sexual arousal, PPG may be putting too much importance on this physiological aspect. For instance, Janssen, McBride, Yarber, Hill., and Butler (2008) conducted a qualitative study and found that the importance of erection decreased with age. This suggests that, for some men, PPG would not be a valid measure. Similarly, another issue associated with PPG is the high rates of individuals who exhibit apparently no physical arousal to stimuli, whether this be because of intentional suppression, or an inability caused by anxiety (Kalmus & Beech, 2005). Moreover, apart from the aforementioned validity issues with PPG, there are also many others that call into question the utility of the measure. It is obviously invasive (Bailey et al., 2016), with the method being unavailable in many European countries due to the 'ethical concern' (Babchishin, Nunes, & Hermann, 2013).

Secondly, the procedures are not standardized between researchers or practitioners, which questions the reliability of the method (Laws & Gress, 2004). Another prominent issue in PPG is the presence of faking, whereby individuals exert voluntary control over their erections (Kalmus & Beech, 2005). Further, measures of genital arousal are not ideal for the comparative assessment of sexual preference between males and females. This is because different measurement processes are used for men and women (Huberman & Chivers, 2015). Women's genital vasocongestion is measured by a similar, yet non-identical method. This method uses a device that is inserted into the vagina. An incandescent light is then projected onto the vaginal wall, which is reflected back. The assumption is that a greater amount of light reflected back indicates more blood in the vessels of the vaginal wall, thus indicating greater arousal (Prause & Janssen, 2006). However, as PPG and VPP assess different aspects of vasocongestion (i.e. penile circumference/volume vs. change in blood flow in the vaginal canal, respectively), the results produced are non-comparable between men and women (Jones, 2013).

Eye-related measures are, therefore, thought to be a better option for assessing sexual interest compared to genital measures. It has also been said that individuals are less likely to decline an experiment that assesses eye-gaze (Rieger & Savin-Williams, 2012). Also, as the response is from the same organ (the eye) and physiologically identical across nearly all people, it allows directly comparable data for both sexes (Rieger & Savin-Williams, 2012). Moreover, Trottier et al. (2014) conducted a study using concurrent eye-tracking and PPG assessment in order to identify PPG faking attempts. They had two conditions: free-viewing non-preferred and preferred sexual stimuli, and intentionally suppressing their erectile responses to preferred sexual stimuli (i.e. they were instructed to use an aversive image that they were presented with as a cognitive strategy to suppress these responses). When comparing the

PPG data, they found that the men in their study were successful at suppressing their erectile responses to their preferred sexual stimuli when they were instructed to do so, with similar erectile responses observed in the 'inhibition' condition and the erectile responses to their non-preferred sexual stimuli. However, when looking at the eye-tracking data, the mean fixation duration remained the same in both the condition where they free-viewed preferred sexual stimuli and the condition where they had to intentionally suppress their erectile responses to preferred sexual stimuli. The authors concluded that using eye-tracking may help indicate the presence of cognitive strategies used to inhibit sexual arousal (Trottier et al., 2014).

Measuring sexual preference with eye-tracking

Non-deviant sexual interest

Lykins, Meana, and Kambe (2006) executed one of the first studies investigating sex differences in the visual processing of sexual stimuli (Akhter, 2011). They used erotic and non-erotic images of men and women to investigate human gaze behaviour. They found differences in attention to different body regions (e.g. both men and women spent more time looking at the bodies of the images, particularly when the image was erotic), and differences in attention to erotic and non-erotic images. Lykins et al. (2006) concluded that sexually salient stimuli are processed in a wholly different manner to non-erotic stimuli and that eye-tracking is a valid measure to capture the differences in the processing of both erotic and non-erotic stimuli at a visual level. Jiang, Costello, Fang, Huang, and He (2006) furthered this conclusion by investigating whether interocularly suppressed ('invisible') erotic images were able to direct the distribution of visual spatial attention. Both heterosexual males and females demonstrated an attentional bias towards their preferred sex (female nude pictures and male nude pictures, respectively). Jiang et al. (2006) concluded that, even when salient images are masked, the emotional system processes these images in a specific fashion, supporting the claim that erotic content is processed differently to non-erotic content. Similarly, Nummenmaa, Hietanen, Santtila, and Hyönä (2012) found that nude images attracted more fixations than clothed images, supporting the suggestion that erotic content is processed differently to non-erotic content.

Lykins, Meana, and Strauss (2008) extended Lykins et al.'s (2006) research and incorporated gender differences into their study. They utilized images of men and women performing acts of foreplay (and matched non-erotic images) to investigate eye-gaze behaviour. Lykins et al. (2008) found that men attended to their preferred sex, regardless of eroticism of the image, whereas women divided their attention more equally between the sexes, suggesting non-specificity in female sexual interest. Further work conducted by Hall, Hogue, and Guo (2011) instructed participants to view clothed images of different age groups (10-year-olds, 20–30-year-olds, and 40-year-olds). They found that the viewing patterns of men were linked to their sexual preference, with more attention being directed towards body areas that signalled fertility of the stimulus (e.g. waist–hip ratio) in stimuli that were appropriately aged. Fromberger et al. (2012a) conducted a study into the exploration of men's attentional engagement while presented with preferred (images of women) and non-preferred images (images of girls, boys, or men). They found that men demonstrated more first fixations (initial attention) and a higher percentage of cumulative fixations (controlled attention) to female stimuli than to male stimuli. Following from Fromberger et al. (2012a), a study by Dawson and Chivers (2016) looked at initial and controlled attention towards sexually preferred and non-preferred stimuli in both heterosexual men and heterosexual women. Similar to the abovementioned study, they found that men directed both their initial and controlled visual attention towards their preferred stimuli. Contrarily, however, heterosexual women only directed their *controlled* visual attention towards sexually preferred stimuli, whereas there were no significant differences between their initial attention towards both male and female sexual images (Dawson & Chivers, 2016).

To date, the studies mentioned have only used still images as stimuli. Tsujimura et al. (2008) were the first investigators to use videos in order to assess sexuality of heterosexual men and women using an eye-tracking methodology, with a view that they would find more detailed sex differences when moving images were used. To do this, they used sexually explicit videos. In the first clip, a naked male and female actor kissed and touched each other (but did not touch the genitals). In the second clip, these actors engaged in sexual intercourse. The authors found that men viewed the opposite sex longer and women viewed the same sex actor longer. Similarly, Dawson and Chivers (2018) looked at the effect of video stimuli on visual processing of sexual cues in heterosexual men and women. Video clips were without sound and depicted sexual activities (nude exercise, masturbation, coupled sex) and a variety of target combinations (lone male, lone female, male–male, female–female, and male–female). Akin to Tsujimura et al. (2009), they found that men's controlled visual attention was significantly greater for preferred sexual stimuli, whereas women attended significantly more to non-preferred stimuli (Dawson & Chivers, 2018).

In summary, when using eye-tracking to assess non-deviant sexual preference, erotic and non-erotic content are processed differently, and heterosexual women demonstrate a greater degree of non-category specificity in relation to their gaze behaviour. This means that heterosexual women are likely to divide their attention more evenly between images of men and women, while men are more likely to attend to their preferred sexual target.

Deviant sexual interest

The abovementioned studies used eye-tracking to study/assess only non-deviant sexual interest. In this next section, we explore the use of eye-tracking for deviant sexual preferences. A study by Fromberger et al. (2012b) assessed the diagnostic accuracy of using eye-movements to assess paedophilic sexual preferences. In their study, they found that paedophilic participants had longer relative fixation times to child stimuli compared to the controls. They concluded that the eye-tracking methodology can differentiate between paedophiles and non-paedophiles with high sensitivity and specificity. Hall, Hogue, and Guo (2015) also investigated gaze patterns to child images for individuals convicted of child sex offences. They found that individuals convicted of child sex offences had different gaze strategies, in that, they viewed the upper body of male and female children differently to non-offenders. Hall et al. (2015) suggested that their research should be used to inform future research on the utility of eye-tracking for sexual preference research.

Fromberger et al. (2013) used eye-tracking to assess automatic and controlled attention in paedophilic men when viewing prepubescent stimuli. They found that paedophilic men demonstrated shorter average entry times (i.e. early attentional processing) to child stimuli compared with adult stimuli. However, they had longer relative fixation times (i.e. controlled attention) to adult stimuli compared with child stimuli. They suggested that this latter result was either because: (a) the participants may have been trying to behave in a socially desirable way by directing their attention away from child stimuli; or (b) the images of adult stimuli in the study may have been more sexually arousing than the child stimuli (Fromberger et al., 2013). Furthering their investigation into automatic and controlled visual attention, Jordan, Fromberger, Laubinger, Dechent, and Müller (2014) looked at the potential change in visual processing of child stimuli in one paedophilic subject who had undergone antiandrogen therapy (ADT) to reduce sex drive and, thus, sexual recidivism. They found that, after ADT, the patient showed significantly higher relative fixation time for images of women, compared with images of prepubescent girls (whereas this was the opposite pre-ADT). This result suggests a difference in controlled attention. However, for early automatic attention, the results were unchanged to images of prepubescent girls, suggesting that automatic attention is still allocated to child stimuli after ADT. They suggested that the eye-tracking method may help uncover the variables that are (and are not) affected by treatment in order to determine its efficacy (Jordan et al., 2014).

Conversely, Jordan et al. (2016) examined whether a 'sexual distractor task' with concurrent eye-tracking could be used to assess sexual preference in paedophilic men. Regarding eye-tracking, they found that paedophilic men showed shorter fixation latencies (i.e. allocation of early attention) to all sexual distractors, independent of their age (child or adult). A further eye-tracking study by Jordan et al. (2018) examined whether individuals who were outpatients with a paedophilic sexual preference ('outpatients') and individuals who were forensic inpatients with a paedophilic sexual preference ('inpatients') differed from controls in relation to their visual attention to child and adult stimuli. They found that both the outpatients and inpatients differed significantly from the control group, in that, they viewed child stimuli quicker (i.e. early visual attention). As such, it appears that the first fixations (i.e. early allocation of attention) can be used with paedophilic individuals to assess their sexual preference.

In summary, studies that have used eye-tracking with paedophilic individuals suggest that eye-tracking is suitable for assessing age-preference. However, to do so, it seems most effective to look at early visual attention, rather than controlled visual attention.

Measuring sexual preference using pupil dilation

Apart from measuring fixation duration, number of fixations, and so on, pupillary responses can also be recorded by most eye-trackers as part of the eye-tracking process. This adds an interesting element because pupil dilation reflects people's interest, that is, individuals' pupils will dilate when viewing pleasant images and constrict when viewing unpleasant images (Hess & Polt, 1960). Pupil dilation is said to reflect automatic attention that is not under conscious control (Heaver & Hutton, 2011), Thus, it is unlikely that participants will be able to suppress or manipulate their pupillary responses, making it apt for sexual preference research (Rieger & Savin-Williams, 2012).

Non-deviant sexual preference

One initial study was conducted by Hess, Seltzer, and Shlien (1965), which investigated pupillary responses of hetero- and homosexual men to images of men and women. They found that pupil dilation patterns corroborated highly with sexual orientation. However, there were some limitations associated with this study. These included a small sample size ($n = 10$) and that the participants were associated with the experimenters.

Decades later, Rieger and Savin-Williams (2012) sought to conduct research into pupil dilation and sexual orientation using men and women who identified as heterosexual, homosexual, and bisexual. They found that pupil dilation was significantly related to participants' sexual orientation, with participants having greater pupil dilation to their preferred sex (apart from bisexual participants, whose pupils dilated equally to both sexes). They also found that pupil dilation patterns were significantly correlated with viewing time, self-reported sexual attraction, and self-reported sexual orientation (Rieger & Savin-Williams, 2012). Attard-Johnson and Bindemann (2017) conducted a study into whether pupillary responses for heterosexual men and women were different for dressed and naked images of adults. It was found that male participants' pupil size was larger when viewing female images, compared to male images. Similarly, female participants had greater pupil dilation when viewing male images, compared to female images. Positive correlations were also found between pupillary change and sexual appeal ratings for dressed and naked stimuli for male participants. However, this was not observed in female participants. Also, there was no difference between pupillary responses to dressed and naked preferred-sex stimuli. Attard-Johnson and Bindemann (2017), therefore, concluded that pupillary responses provide a sex-specific measure but are not sensitive to sexually explicit content.

Contrastingly, Watts, Holmes, Savin-Williams, and Rieger (2017) examined whether non-explicit sexual stimuli evoked the same pupillary response as explicit sexual stimuli. They found 'small to modest' correlations between pupil dilations to explicit stimuli and matching non-explicit sexual stimuli in both men and women. They also found sexual orientation differences for both explicit and non-explicit stimuli. However, some of these were only detected with explicit stimuli, and pupil dilation patterns were weaker with the non-explicit stimuli compared with the explicit stimuli.

Deviant sexual preference

Regarding age-preferences, an initial study was conducted by Atwood and Howell (1971) using 'female-aggressing paedophiles'. They found that images of child females produced pupil dilations in the majority of these participants, suggesting that pupil dilation can be used to assess age-specific sexual preferences. Since then, much work has been done by Attard-Johnson and colleagues around pupil dilation as a measure of sex- and age-preference. In one study, they looked at pupillary response as an age-specific measure of sexual preference (Attard-Johnson, Bindemann, & Ó Ciardha, 2016). Firstly, they found that men demonstrated less dilation (or more constriction) to images of men and had the most dilation to images of women (compared with images of men, boys, girls, and landscape scenes). For female participants, results were less clear. That is, images of women elicited more pupil dilation than the other categories. This is not unexpected, however, as women notably exhibit more non-category specific responding on sexual preference measures (Chivers, 2017). For both men and women, there was more pupil constriction to child images compared with adult images.

This study was extended by the same authors, this time looking at hetero-sexual, homosexual, and bisexual men's pupillary responses to images of adult and prepubescent males and females across two studies (Attard-Johnson, Bindemann, & Ó Ciardha, 2017). In their first study, they found that homo-sexual men demonstrated greater pupil dilation to images of men compared to heterosexual men, and heterosexual men demonstrated more pupil dilation to images of women compared with homosexual men. Bisexual men's pupils dilated during the viewing of women, but there was not a reliable change to images of men. Across all men, pupil constriction was seen for prepubescent images, consistent with their age-preferences (Attard-Johnson et al., 2017). Their second study involved asking participants to rate the sexual appeal of the stimuli while their pupillary responses were being recorded. Similar to the first study, Attard-Johnson et al. (2017) found that homosexual (and also bisexual) men exhibited larger pupils to male images, compared with hetero-sexual men. When viewing female stimuli, heterosexual men demonstrated larger pupils compared with homosexual and bisexual men. As with their first study, more pupil constriction was seen for prepubescent images (Attard-Johnson et al., 2017). They also found that there were positive correlations between pupil change and sexual appeal ratings, indicating corroborating results for objective and self-report data.

Limitations to eye-tracking

Despite the advantages to utilizing eye-tracking as a measure of sexual interest, especially in comparison to genital measures, it is not without its limitations. Eye-tracking research on sexual interest is still relatively new, and it has been suggested that the methodology is not yet fully optimized (Wenzlaff et al., 2016). Moreover, stationary eye-trackers are often not easily portable devices, which may be inconvenient, as well as costly (Kumar, 2006). Secondly, par-ticipants can be hyper-aware of the fact that their eye-gaze is being tracked and so may attempt to bias the results by responding in a way that portrays them in a favourable light. Risko and Kingstone (2011) found that wearing an eye-tracker (an implied social presence) led non-deviant individuals to avoid looking at provocative stimuli. This suggests that there is an 'eye-tracker awareness' bias, with participants being particularly sensitive to having their eye-gaze monitored (Risko & Kingstone, 2011). However, Nasiopoulos, Risko, Foulsham, and Kingstone (2015) found that this 'eye-tracker awareness' bias was abolished after around 10 minutes of using a wearable eye-tracker. Only when the participants had their attention drawn back to the eye-tracker was the effect reactivated. Moreover, one study looking at picture valence found that pupil diameter increased when pictures were both pleasant and unpleasant, suggesting that increased sympathetic activity mediates pupillary changes during affective picture viewing; not necessarily the valence of the image itself (Bradley, Miccoli, Escrig, & Lang, 2008).

Key conclusions and summary of recommendations for best practice

Eye-tracking technology has rapidly developed over the past 20 years, with eye-trackers becoming more portable, accessible, and easier for non-experts to use, all at significantly decreased costs. At the same time, there has been an increased interest in applying new technologies to address forensic practice questions. This is reflected in the development of a range of physiological and indirect measures. Eye-tracking is a promising area for such future development, as it potentially offers a less intrusive method of assessing sensitive topics, such as sexual and deviant sexual interests, while being resistant to intentional manipulation. There may be a temptation to quickly integrate such a methodology into forensic practice. However, it is important to recognize its limits within the current evidence base.

At present, the available research suggests that, when assessing non-deviant sexual interest, erotic and non-erotic content are processed differently, with men more likely to attend to their preferred sexual target and heterosexual women more likely to demonstrate a greater degree of non-category specificity in relation to their gaze behaviour. When assessing deviant sexual interest, or more specifically paedophilic sexual preference, there is evidence to suggest that eye-tracking is suitable for assessing age-preference and this is mainly related to the early visual attention to images. Other metrics available from the eye-tracking process, such as pupil dilation, are being developed to assess sexual interest. There is supportive recent research examining pupil dilation suggesting that it is a promising area for future development. A significant limitation across the area is that most of the research has focused on the assessment of paedophilic interest with virtually no research related to the use of eye-tracking to assess sexual interest to sexual aggression against adults and other deviant interests. Thus, while using eye-tracking as a possible way of assessing both normative and deviant sexual interest in forensic practice has an intuitive appeal, the evidence base to support this is limited (or restricted to the assessment of non-deviant sexual orientation or paedophilic interest). As such, the present evidence base is not sufficiently strong enough to support the applied use of eye-tracking in forensic practice. As such, eye-tracking remains a potentially rich area for future development and research and should be used as an adjunct to existing forensic practice in the area.

References

Akhter, S. (2011). *Visual attention to erotic stimuli in androphilic male-to-female transsexuals.* (Doctoral Thesis). University of Nevada, Las Vegas.

Attard-Johnson, J., & Bindemann, M. (2017). Sex-specific but not sexually explicit: Pupillary responses to dressed and naked adults. *Royal Society Open Science, 4,* 160963. doi:10.1098/rsos.160963.

Attard-Johnson, J., Bindemann, M., & Ó Ciardha, C. (2016). Pupillary response as an age-specific measure of sexual interest. *Archives of Sexual Behavior, 45,* 855–870. doi:10.1007/s10508-015-0681-3.

Attard-Johnson, J., Bindemann, M., & Ó Ciardha, C. (2017). Heterosexual, homosexual, and bisexual men's pupillary responses to persons at different stages of sexual development. *Journal of Sex Research, 54,* 1085–1096. doi:10.1080/00224499.2016.1241857

Atwood, R. W., & Howell, R. J. (1971). Pupillometric and personality test score differences of female aggressing pedophiliacs and normals. *Psychonomic Science, 22,* 115–116.

Babchishin, K., Nunes, K., & Hermann, C. (2013). The validity of the Implicit Association Test (IAT) measures of sexual attraction to children: A meta-analysis. *Archives of Sexual Behavior, 42,* 487–499.. doi:10.1007/s10508-012-0022-8.

Bailey, M., Vasey, P., Diamond, L., Breedlove, M., Vilain, E., & Epprecht, M. (2016). Sexual orientation, controversy and science. *Psychological Science in the Public Interest, 17,* 45–101. doi:10.1177/1529100616637616.

Bradley, M. M., Miccoli, L., Escrig, M. A., & Lang, P. J. (2008). The pupil as a measure of emotional arousal and autonomic activation. *Psychophysiology, 45,* 602–607. doi:10.1111/j.1469-8986.2008 00654.x.

Cognolato, M., Atzori, M., & Müller, H. (2018). Head-mounted eye gaze tracking devices: An overview of modern devices and recent advances. *Journal of Rehabilitation and Assistive Technologies Engineering, 5,* 1–13. doi:10.1177/2055668318773991

Chivers, M. L. (2017). The specificity of women's sexual response and its relationship with sexual orientations: A review and ten hypotheses. *Archives of Sexual Behavior, 46*(5), 1161–1179.

Dawson, S., & Chivers, M. (2016). Gender-specificity of initial and controlled visual attention to sexual stimuli in androphilic women and gynephilic men. *PLoS ONE, 11,* e0152785. doi:10.1371/journal.pone.0152785.

Dawson, S. J., & Chivers, M. L. (2018). The effect of static versus dynamic stimuli on visual processing of sexual cues in androphilic women and gynephilic men. *Royal Society Open Science, 5,* 172286. doi:10.1098/rsos.172286

Fromberger, P., Jordan, K., Steinkrauss, H., von Herder, J., Stolpmann, G., Kroner-Herwig, B., & Muller, J. (2013). Eye movements in pedophiles: Automatic and controlled attentional processes while viewing prepubescent stimuli. *Journal of Abnormal Psychology, 122,* 587–599. doi:10.1037/a0030659.

Fromberger, P., Jordan, K., von Herder, J., Steinkrauss, H., Nemetschek, R., Stolpmann, G., & Muller, J. (2012a). Initial orienting towards sexually relevant stimuli: Preliminary evidence from eye movement measures. *Archives of Sexual Behavior, 41*, 919–928. doi:10.1007/s10508-011-9816-3

Fromberger, P., Jordan, K., Steinkrauss, H., von Herder, J., Witzel, J., Stolpmann, G., … Muller, J. (2012b). Diagnostic accuracy of eye movements in assessing pedophilia. *Journal of Sex Med, 9*, 1868–1882. doi:10.1111/j.1743-6109.2012.02754.x.

Hall, C., Hogue, T., & Guo, K. (2011). Differential gaze behaviour towards sexually preferred and non-preferred human figures. *Journal of Sex Research, 48*, 1–9. doi:10.1080/00224499.2010.521899

Hall, C. L., Hogue, T. E., & Guo, K. (2015). Gaze patterns to child figures reflect deviant sexual preference in child sex offenders—a first glance. *Journal of Sexual Aggression, 21*, 303–317. doi:10.1080/13552600.2014.931475.

Heaver, B., & Hutton, S. B. (2011). Keeping an eye on the truth? Pupil size changes associated with recognition memory. *Memory, 19*, 398–405. doi:10.1080/09658211.2011.575788

Hess, E. H., & Polt, J. M. (1960). Pupil size as related to interest value of visual stimuli. *Science, 132*, 349–350. doi:10.1126/science.132.3423.349

Hess, E. H., Seltzer, A. L., & Shlien, J. M. (1965). Pupil response of hetero-and homosexual males to pictures of men and women: A pilot study. *Journal of Abnormal Psychology, 70*, 165. doi:10.1037/h0021978

Hessels, R. S., Andersson, R., Hooge, I. T., Nyström, M., & Kemner, C. (2015). Consequences of eye color, positioning, and head movement for eye-tracking data quality in infant research. *Infancy, 20*, 601–633. doi:10.1111/infa.12093

Hogue, T. E., Wesson, C., & Perkins, D. (2016). Eye-tracking and assessing sexual interest in forensic contexts. In D. Boer (Ed.), *The Wiley handbook on theories, assessment and treatment of sexual offending* (pp. 995–1014). Chichester, West Sussex: Wiley Blackwell.

Huberman, J., & Chivers, M. (2015). Examining gender specificity of sexual response with concurrent thermography and plethysmography. *Psychophysiology, 52*, 1382–1395. doi:10.1111/psyp.12466

Janssen, E., McBride, K., Yarber, W., Hill., B., & Butler, S. (2008). Factors that influence sexual arousal in men: A focus group study. *Archives of Sexual Behavior,37*, 252–265. doi:10.1007/s10508-007-9245-5.

Jiang, Y., Costello, P., Fang, F., Huang, M., & He, S. (2006). A gender- and sexual orientation- dependent spatial attentional effect of invisible images. *PNAS, 101*, 17048–17052. doi:10.10/3/pnas.06056/8103

Jones, S. (2013). *The impact of sexual arousal on the category specificity of women's visual attention to erotic stimuli* (Unpublished doctoral dissertation). University of Nevada, Las Vegas.

Jordan, K., Fromberger, P., Laubinger, H., Dechent, P., & Müller, J. (2014). Changed processing of visual sexual stimuli under GnRH-therapy – A single case study in pedophilia using eye tracking and fMRI. *BMC Psychiatry, 14*, 142–155. doi:10.1186/1471-244X-14-142

Jordan, K., Fromberger, P., Muller, I., Wernicke, M., Stolpmann, G., & Muller, J. (2018). Sexual interest and sexual self-control in men with self-reported sexual interest in children – A first eye tracking study. *Journal of Psychiatric Research, 96*, 138–144. doi:10.1016/j.jpsychires.2017.10.004

Jordan, K., Fromberger, P., von Herder, J., Steinkrauss, H., Nemetschek, R., Witzel, J., & Muller, J. (2016). Can we measure sexual interest in pedophiles using a sexual distractor task? *Journal of Forensic Psychology, 1*. doi:10.4172/JFPY.1000109.

Kalmus, E., & Beech, A. (2005). Forensic assessment of sexual interest: A review. *Aggression and Violent Behavior, 10*, 193–217. doi:10.1016/j.avb.2003.12.002.

Kumar, M. (2006). *Reducing the cost of eye tracking systems. GUIDe: Gaze-enhanced User Interface Design, Stanford*. Retrieved from: http://hci.stanford.edu/cstr/reports/2006-08.pdf

Laws, D., & Gress, C. (2004). Seeing things differently: The viewing time alternative to penile plethysmography. *Legal and Criminological Psychology, 9*, 183–196. doi:10.1348/1355325041719338

Li, F., Munn, S., & Pelz, J. (2008). A model-based approach to video-based eye tracking. *Journal of Modern Optics, 55*, 503–531. doi:10.1080/09500340701467827

Lykins, A., Meana, M., & Kambe, G. (2006). Detection of differential viewing patterns to erotic and non-erotic stimuli using eye-tracking methodology. *Archives of Sexual Behavior, 35*, 569–575.

Lykins, A., Meana, M., & Strauss, G. (2008). Sex differences in visual attention to erotic and non-erotic stimuli. *Archives of Sexual Behavior, 37*, 219–228.

Merdian, H., & Jones, D. (2011). Chapter Seven: Phallometric assessment of sexual arousal. In D. Boer, R. Eher, M. Miner, F. Pfäfflin, & L. Craig (Eds.), *International perspectives on the assessment and treatment of sexual offenders: Theory, practice and research* (pp. 141–169). Chichester: John Wiley and Sons.

Nasiopoulos, E., Risko, E. F., Foulsham, T., & Kingstone, A. (2015). Wearable computing: Will it make people prosocial? *British Journal of Psychology, 106*, 209–216. doi:10.1111/bjop.12080

Nummenmaa, L., Hietanen, J., Santtila, P., & Hyönä, J. (2012). Gender and visibility of sexual cues influence eye movements while viewing faces and bodies. *Archives of Sexual Behaviour, 41*, 1439–1451. doi:10.1007/s10508-012-9911-0

Pierce, K., Marinero, S., Hazin, R., McKenna, B., Barnes, C. C., & Malige, A. (2016). Eye tracking reveals abnormal visual preference for geometric images as an early biomarker of an autism spectrum disorder subtype associated with increased symptom severity. *Biological Psychiatry, 79*, 657–666. doi:10.1016/j.biopsych.2015.03.032

Pieters, R., Erdem, T., & Martinovici, A. (2017). Rapid evidence accumulation during brand choice: An eye-tracking analysis. In A. Gneezy, V. Griskevicius, & P. Williams (Eds.), *Advances in consumer research* (Vol. 45, pp. 286–290). Duluth, MN: Association for Consumer Research.

Prause, N., & Janssen, E. (2006). Blood flow: Vaginal photoplethysmography. In I. Goldstein, C. Meston, S. Davis, & A. Traish (Eds.), *Women's sexual function and dysfunction: Study, diagnosis and treatment* (pp. 359–367). Oxton: Taylor & Francis.

Rieger, G., & Savin-Williams, R. (2012). The eyes have it: Sex and sexual orientation differences in pupil dilation patterns. *PLoS ONE, 7*, e40256. doi:10.1371/journal.pone.0040256

Risko, E., & Kingstone, A. (2011). Eyes wide shut: Implied social presence, eye tracking and attention. *Attention, Perception, & Psychophysics, 73*, 291–296. doi:10.3758/s13414-010-0042-1

Roux, P., Brunet-Gouet, E., Passerieux, C., & Ramus, F. (2016). Eye-tracking reveals a slowdown of social context processing during intention attribution in patients with schizophrenia. *Journal of Psychiatry & Neuroscience: JPN, 41*, E13–E21. doi:10.1503/jpn.150045

Singer, B. (1984). Conceptualizing sexual arousal and attraction. *Journal of Sex Research, 20*, 230–240. doi:10.1080/00224498409551222

Trottier, D., Rouleau, J., Renaud, P., & Goyette, M. (2014). Using eye tracking to identify faking attempts during penile plethysmography assessment. *Journal of Sex Research, 51*, 946–955. doi:10.1080/00224499.2013.832133

Tsujimura, A., Miyagawa, Y., Takada, S., Matsuoka, Y., Takao, T., Hirai, T., … Okuyama, A. (2008). Sex differences in visual attention to sexually explicit videos: A preliminary study. *The Journal of Sexual Medicine, 6*, 1011–1017. doi:10.1111/j.1743-6109.2008.01031.x

Watts, T. M., Holmes, L., Savin-Williams, R. C., & Rieger, G. (2017). Pupil dilation to explicit and non-explicit sexual stimuli. *Archives of Sexual Behavior, 46*(1), 155–165. doi:10.1007/s10508-016-0801-8.

Wenzlaff, F., Briken, P., & Dekker, A. (2016). Video-based eye tracking in sex research: A systematic literature review. *The Journal of Sex Research, 53*, 1008–1019. doi:10.1080/00224499.2015.1107524

Sexual fantasy use as a proxy for assessing deviant sexual interest

7

Ross M. Bartels

Introduction

Sexual interest can be thought of as an evaluative construct regarding the sexual appeal of a particular target category (e.g. men, women, children) or behavioural category (e.g. dominance). If an example of one of these categories is thought of (internally) or observed (externally) in a sexual context, it can elicit a sexual response. Thus, subjective and objective sexual arousal can often be an indicator of one's sexual interest (Chivers, 2005). Within the forensic psychology domain, sexual interests that involve categories related to sexual offending behaviour (*offence-related sexual interests*) are a core factor in the assessment and treatment of individuals who have committed a sexual crime. Such interests would include a sexual interest in children (offence-related target) or non-consensual sex with an adult (offence-related-behaviour).

The idea that sexual interest can elicit a sexual response is a widely recognized notion, as genital arousal has long been used as a means to measure offence-related sexual interests (e.g. using penile plethysmography), while self-report measures have been used to assess subjective sexual arousal towards such interests (Akerman & Beech, 2012; Kalmus & Beech, 2005). However, sexual arousal is not the only means of assessing a sexual interest. As mentioned, people can internally envision a sexual target or behaviour in their mind's eye. This typically occurs in the form of a sexual fantasy, whereby the target or behaviour is contextualized in the form of an 'elaborate sexual scenario or script' (Bartels & Gannon, 2011, p. 553). Indeed, Chivers (2005) notes that sexual fantasies generally express a sexual interest. As such, many forensic researchers have used sexual fantasy measures as a way to assess offence-related sexual interests (Beggs & Grace, 2011; Gannon, Terriere, & Leader, 2012; Hudson, Wales, Bakker, & Ward, 2002). The aim of the present chapter is to examine this approach to sexual interest assessment.

Sexual fantasy versus sexual fantasizing

The most commonly cited definition of sexual fantasy is by Leitenberg and Henning (1995), who state that it is 'almost any mental imagery that is sexually arousing or erotic to the individual' (p. 470). This definition was based on Wilson's (1978) assertion that a sexual fantasy can be both fleeting and elaborate; both spontaneous and deliberate; both previously experienced and purely imagined; and both realistic and 'bizarre'. Thus, as noted by Bartels and Gannon (2011), Leitenberg and Henning (1995) offer an all-encompassing definition of sexual fantasies. However, this view is theoretically flawed and practically unhelpful. For example, the processes underlying fleeting sexual thoughts are very likely to differ from those that are deliberately engaged in and, as such, signal the need for two distinct assessment and treatment strategies (Bartels & Beech, 2016).

Another important issue with this definition is that it positions 'sexual fantasy' as a *noun* or a cognitive construct (e.g. 'My sexual fantasy is to be dominant with my partner'). Used in this way, the term 'sexual fantasy' is almost synonymous with the term 'sexual interest'.[1] As such, it only tells us whether a sexual fantasy (and possibly a sexual interest) is present or not; not the extent to which one engages with it. To exemplify this point further, imagine that Person A and Person B both have a sexual fantasy (noun) to rape somebody. This is concerning for obvious reasons. But then imagine that they are asked to state how often they *fantasize* (verb) about this sexual fantasy. Person A states every other day, while Person B states once a year. Thus, although they share the same fantasy, Person A uses it far more frequently. With that one extra piece of information, Person A has become more of a concern.

This highlights a crucial distinction between having a 'sexual fantasy' and the act of 'sexual fantasizing'. That is, although the two are interrelated (i.e. one can sexually fantasize about their sexual fantasy) and can involve the same content (e.g. non-consensual sex), they are two distinct psychological phenomena (Bartels & Beech, 2016). Of course, it can be useful to determine the presence of a sexual fantasy in an individual or sample. For example, it helps to determine prevalence rates of certain sexual fantasies in the population, and can also help demonstrate how sexual interests are represented in the mind's eye (e.g. some people with a sexual interest in dominance will have a fantasy that involves blindfolding and tying up a partner, while others will have a fantasy that involve more aggressive behaviours, such as whipping and spanking).

However, I argue that 'sexual fantasizing' (as a cognitive activity/process) is the more useful concept to focus on in forensic research and practice for a number of reasons. First, the distinction enables us to home in on a particular psychological phenomenon, rather than treating and addressing all manner of sexual thoughts as the same. For example, by arguing that sexual fantasizing is a deliberate cognitive activity, Bartels and Beech (2016) distinguished it from spontaneous sexual thoughts that pop into one's mind. Second, it is the act of sexual fantasizing that elicits sexual arousal; affects emotions; incites motivation; and creates behavioural sexual scripts (Bartels & Gannon, 2011). As such, sexual fantasizing is of more use to clinicians working with individuals who have sexually offended. Third, and central to this chapter, the focus on sexual fantasizing can provide an indication of how sexually appealing an individual finds a particular target or behaviour. In other words, assessing the frequency of sexual fantasizing provides an insight into the level of someone's sexual interest. For example, if a man very frequently fantasizes about children, it can be argued that he has a strong sexual interest in children.

The role of sexual fantasizing in sex offending

For many decades, sexual fantasy has remained a key factor in the aetiology and treatment of sexual offending (Abel & Blanchard, 1974). For example, in a study examining sexually sadistic behaviour, MacCulloch, Snowden, Wood, and Mills (1983) argued that sexual fantasizing can lead to the formation of a behavioural sequence that the individual may eventually wish to enact in real-life. Their findings supported this hypothesis, in that, 13 out of 16 of the participants had engaged in a number of 'behavioural try-outs' before the index offence was committed. In other words, the act of sexual fantasizing appeared to have had a direct influence on offending behaviour. Similarly, Pithers, Kashima, Cumming, Beal, and Buell (1988) argued that the recurrent use of offence-related sexual fantasies can lead to 'passive planning', whereby the modus operandi is cognitively refined until it is eventually carried out in the form of a sexual offence. This idea that sexual fantasizing can create an 'offence script' has also been noted by Tony Ward in his work on implicit planning (Ward & Hudson, 2000; see also Gee, Ward, & Eccleston, 2003) and 'expertise' in sex offending (e.g. Bourke, Ward, & Rose, 2012).

Over the years, theorists and researchers have proposed and identified many other ways in which sexual fantasy can influence sex offending behaviour. This is likely because sexual fantasies are a multifaceted phenomenon (Bartels & Gannon, 2011), meaning that sexual fantasizing can interact with many of the four core risk factors associated with sexual (re)offending. These four factors are dynamic in nature (i.e. relatively stable but changeable factors) and have been shown to predict sexual recidivism (Mann, Hanson, & Thornton, 2010). They include: *deviant sexual interest* (Domain 1), *offence-supportive beliefs and attitudes* (Domain 2), *socio-affective functioning* (Domain 3), and *self-management problems* (Domain 4). According to Beech and Ward (2004), offence-related sexual fantasies are 'triggering events' (or 'contextual risk factors') that can interact with these four dynamic risk factors. The nature of this interaction is likely to dictate the type of function that an offence-related sexual fantasy can serve. For example, individuals who have difficulty managing their negative moods due to self-management problems may use sexual fantasies as a way of regulating or escaping their negative affective state. Indeed, individuals who have sexually offended have reported using offence-related sexual fantasies to cope with or escape from life problems and regulate their emotional state (Gee et al., 2003).

Of particular importance to the present chapter, however, is the link between sexual fantasizing and 'deviant sexual interests' (Domain 1). In the 1960s and 1970s, this link was central to explaining and treating offence-related sexual interests (Davison, 1968; Marquis, 1970; Marshall, 1979), largely inspired by McGuire, Carlisle, and Young's (1965) conditioning theory of deviant sexual preferences. Later in Laws and Marshall (1990) developed these ideas further by offering a more comprehensive learning-based theory of deviant sexual interests. Across both theories, sexual fantasizing about a deviant theme (especially in conjunction with masturbation) is argued to induce and entrench sexual arousal responses towards that particular theme due to classical and operant conditioning processes. As a result, a sexual interest is formed, which is maintained by the reinforcement that is caused by further sexual fantasizing. Given its central role in these theories, sexual fantasizing was deemed a key factor to address in the treatment of deviant sexual interests (Abel & Blanchard, 1974) and still remains a key aspect of many sex offending theories (e.g. Ward & Beech, 2006). Moreover, in a recent meta-analysis, Gannon, Olver, Mallion, and James (2019) found that the inclusion of arousal reconditioning strategies increases the efficacy of sex offending treatment programmes.

Since offence-related sexual interest is regarded as an important factor in the aetiology of sexual offending (Ward & Beech, 2006) and has been shown to be one of the strongest predictors of sexual recidivism (Hanson & Morton-Bourgon, 2005), it is important that researchers and clinicians have effective methods for assessing sexual interest. Given that sexual interests are theorized to be influenced (i.e. strengthened and/or maintained) by the act of sexual fantasizing, sexual fantasy use is arguably one method for measuring the presence and strength of offence-related sexual interests. In the following section, various methods for assessing sexual fantasy use (and sexual interest by proxy) will be discussed.

Assessing sexual fantasy use

At present, there is no direct physiological measure for assessing the use of offence-related sexual fantasies. Instead, sexual fantasy use tends to be assessed using various self-report methods (Leitenberg & Henning, 1995). For example, 'fantasy diaries' or monitoring reports have been used with those who have committed a sexual offence, where the individual is required to record their use of sexual fantasies over a specific period of time (e.g. Looman, 1999; McKibben, Proulx, & Lusignan, 1994). This method provides real-time data on one's sexual fantasy use, as well as other relevant information occurring around the same time (e.g. triggers and emotions). For example, Looman (1999) asked men who had committed a sexual offence to monitor their sexual fantasy use and emotional states in an ongoing diary for 28 days and found that deviant fantasy use was positively associated with negative emotional states. The advantage of the diary method is that it is not confounded by recollection problems often associated with interviews and questionnaires (McKibben et al., 1994). Fantasy diaries are also used during treatment. This is done typically to establish a frequency of use baseline, so that any real-time changes during the treatment process can be monitored (see Marshall, 2006, 2007). This approach will provide an insight into the strength of one's sexual interest, with a greater frequency of fantasy use indicting a stronger level of sexual interest. However, researchers/clinicians would have to find a way to ensure that the task is being carried out, as the client may forget or not want to record all of the fantasies they experience (McCoy & Fremouw, 2010), or may even falsely report fantasy use due to feeling that they need to do so.

Other approaches include the use of clinical interviews, which allows researchers and clinicians to gather richer information about the use of sexual fantasy use. That is, in addition to frequency of use, other useful information can be gathered such as the factors that trigger the fantasy, the origin of the fantasy, the function of the fantasy, meta-appraisal or evaluation of the fantasy content, and so on (see Gee, Ward, Belofastov, & Beech, 2006; Kahr, 2007). As such, interviews allow the interviewer to uncover whether the sexual fantasy is reflective of an enduring sexual interest, or merely a transient flight of fancy. The issue here, however, is that the information provided by interviews are not quantifiable, meaning that the data gathered cannot be easily standardized. Also, it is difficult to ascertain the legitimacy of what the interviewee is disclosing, unless it can be corroborated via other means. This is particularly an issue when the interviewee believes that honest disclosure will have an adverse effect, such as being denied parole. Realizing this limitation, Swaffer, Hollin, Beech, Beckett, and Fisher (2000) suggest that researchers/clinicians using interviews should administer a social desirability scale to detect whether someone is likely to be dissimulating about their sexual fantasy use (although these measure can be very transparent themselves).

Another, less-discussed method for supposedly assessing sexual fantasy use is projective tests. Morgan and Murray (1935) published the 'Thematic Apperception Test' (TAT) – a psychoanalytically-based instrument designed to assess unconscious fantasies. The TAT comprises a set of ambiguous pictures and the respondent is required to think of a story for each picture. It is believed that the stories will reflect things about the respondent that they are not willing or able to tell (due to it being out of their conscious awareness). The TAT is highly controversial and can be summed up as being a 'clinician's delight and a statistician's nightmare' (Vane, 1981, p. 319). However, Schlesinger and Kutash (1981) noticed that certain TAT pictures elicited fantasy-related information for some violent offenders. This prompted them to develop the *Criminal Fantasy Technique* (CFT); a projective technique that focuses on eliciting various crime-related fantasies. The CFT is made up of 12 cards that depict hand-drawn pictures of various crimes that are either about to happen, are presently happening, or have just happened. The twelve depicted offences include drug dealing; arson; bank robbery; exhibitionism; break and entry; assault; embezzlement; sexual assault; child sexual abuse; organized crime; stealing; and a neutral picture depicting no offence. Participants are told that the pictures show various crimes and are instructed to create stories about each one. Seven prompting questions are also included, such as 'Why did he/she do it?' and 'What will the person gain?'

Schlesinger and Kutash (1981) tested the CFT on a mixed sample of 37 individuals who had committed a sexual offence and a sample of 13 individuals who had misused substances with no history of sexual offending. The stories were rated blindly by two independent psychologists as being either 'pathological' or 'not pathological'. A story was deemed pathological if it went beyond mere description of the scene by including compulsive motives and fantasies, and also if the plot was accompanied by a high intensity of affect. According to the authors, the CFT showed very high inter-rater reliability (0.96). Moreover, results showed that the pictures portraying sexual offences (i.e. exhibitionism, sexual assault, and child sexual abuse) elicited greater pathological stories in men who had committed a sexual offence compared to those who misuse substances. Interestingly, the 'break and entry' picture came out as being significantly pathological also. For instance, those who had committed a sexual offence tended to create sexual stories centring on the idea of stealing female underwear for sexual reasons or raping a woman. A similar finding emerged, to a lesser extent, for the neutral picture that showed no offence. The picture involves a man standing with one hand in his pocket, yet many of the participants who had committed a sexual offence created stories where the man had either just committed rape or was in the process of looking for someone to assault. The authors argue that the capability of the neutral picture to elicit such responses demonstrates the intensity of sexual fantasies in those who had sexually offended.

Very few studies have used the CFT. In one study, Deu and Edelmann (1997) compared the CFT stories of men who had committed a predatory sex offence, an opportunistic sex offence, and a nonsexual offence, as well as those who had never offended. In line with their hypotheses, those who had committed predatory sex offences created stories that were more organized than the three other groups and were more elaborate and planned than the stories of those who committed opportunistic sex offences. Based on these findings, the authors concluded that those who repeatedly commit 'organized' sex offences are driven by a rich sexual fantasy life.

An advantage that the CFT is that it may be able to (indirectly) reveal one's sexual fantasies without them having to explicitly admit to them (Deu & Edelmann, 1997). In other words, the pressure of social desirability is reduced. However, for this advantage to hold, one has to first assume that the created stories are a reliable reflection of the sexual fantasies used in real-life. It could be argued that they are simply a reflection of distorted thinking patterns or beliefs. If this is the case, the CFT may be susceptible to producing false positives (i.e. concluding that someone uses deviant sexual fantasies when they do not). In other words, it is not exactly clear what the CFT is measuring. If it truly reflects deviant sexual fantasy use (and by extension, a sexual interest), it may be a useful tool to use in practice. However, more research is needed to better understand the construct validity of the technique.

Probably the most common method for assessing offence-related sexual fantasies is the questionnaire. Sexual fantasy questionnaires typically include a list of items describing a sexual behaviour. Respondents are required to rate how often they fantasize about each behaviour. For example, on the item 'Having intercourse with a loved partner' on the Wilson Sex Fantasy Questionnaire (Wilson, 1978), respondents would indicate how often they fantasize about that behaviour using a scale ranging from, for example, Never (0) to Regularly (5). The sum of the ratings for all items provides an overall score that indicates how often one fantasizes in general (i.e. across a number of varying themes). Also, certain items tend to group together to form an overarching theme or subscale (e.g. romantic fantasies or sadomasochistic fantasies). The questionnaires that have been used to assess the use of offence-related sexual fantasies include those:

- designed to assess the use of deviant and non-deviant fantasies, such as the *Wilson Sex Fantasy Questionnaire* (Wilson, 1978);
- designed to specifically assess the use of deviant fantasies, such as the *Paraphilic Sexual Fantasy Questionnaire* (O'Donohue, Letourneau, & Dowling, 1997); and
- that assess sexual fantasy use as part of an overall assessment of sexual deviancy, such as the *Multiphasic Sex Inventory I and II* (Nichols & Molinder, 1984, 1996) and the *Explicit Sexual Interest Questionnaire* (Banse, Schmidt, & Clarbour, 2010).

Of these measures, the Wilson Sex Fantasy Questionnaire (WSFQ) has been the most widely used in research with both general and forensic populations. First appearing in Wilson's 1978 seminal book, *The Secrets of Sexual Fantasy*, the WSFQ was one of the first sexual fantasy questionnaires to be published. It is made up of 40 items that are rated on a 6-point Likert scale. These items can be categorized into four factor analytically-derived themes, which include: (1) *Exploratory* fantasies such as group sex and promiscuity; (2) *Intimate* fantasies such as kissing passionately and sex with a loved partner; (3) *Impersonal* fantasies such as sex with a stranger and watching others having sex; and (4) *Sadomasochistic* fantasies, such as hurting a partner and being forced to have sex.

A few studies have factor analysed the four WSFQ subscale scores provided by individuals who have sexually offended against children (ISOCs) and found that they load on to a single factor (Allan, Grace, Rutherford, & Hudson, 2007; Stevens, Tan, & Grace, 2016). In both studies, this factor was termed 'Sexual Interests' and was argued to measure the strength of the participants' sexual interest. Although this factor correlated with sexual recidivism, it does not indicate the specific sexual interest that the offenders harbour. Thus, if one is interested in determining the presence of a specific sexual interest, this factor (akin to the total WSFQ score) is not useful.

However, according to Wilson (1988), the Impersonal subscale reflects fetishistic fantasies, while the Sadomasochistic subscale reflects fantasies of dominance and submission. As such, Wilson argues that these subscales can be used to assess paraphilic sexual interests and discriminate paraphilic individuals from those with conventional sexual interests. Indeed, Gosselin and Wilson (1980) found that sexually variant men showed markedly higher scores on the Impersonal and Sadomasochistic fantasies. Moreover, higher scores on the Impersonal and Sadomasochistic subscales, relative to the Intimate and Exploratory subscales (referred to as the 'Variant Quotient'), have been shown to distinguish men with paraphilic interests from men with non-paraphilic interests (Rahman & Symeonides, 2008; Waismann, Fenwick, Wilson, Hewett, & Lumsden, 2003). However, Baumgartner, Scalora, and Huss (2002) found that, relative to non-sexual offenders, ISOCs scored higher on the Intimate and Exploratory subscales; not the Impersonal or Sadomasochistic subscales. Thus, these two subscales may be of little use for those who are likely to have a specific sexual interest (e.g. a sexual interest in children).

Again, this seems be because these two subscales only indicate the strength of one's *paraphilic* sexual interest; they are not specific to a particular sexual interest. The same goes for the other subscales. For example, Alleyne, Gannon, Ó Ciardha, and Wood (2014) found that scores on the Exploratory subscale were associated with an interest in committing multiple-perpetrator rape in non-offending participants. Although the authors noted that the item

'*Participating in an orgy*' is present in this subscale (which may be construed as reflecting a fantasy scenario similar to multiple-perpetrator rape), the subscale itself does not reflect this particular interest.

This suggests that specific WSFQ items may be more useful when attempting to assess the presence and strength of a specific sexual interest. For example, '*Forcing someone to do something*' may be useful for assessing an interest in sexual coercion; '*Watching others have sex*' may be useful for assessing voyeurism; and the '*Exposing yourself*' item could be used to assess exhibitionism. With regards to sexual interest in children, there are no specific items. However, Baumgartner et al. (2002) found that ISOCs showed higher scores on two specific WSFQ items that they deemed were closely related to sexual activity with children; namely, '*Seducing an "innocent"*' and '*Having sex with someone much younger than yourself*'. More recently, Bartels, Lehmann, and Thornton (2019) found that, in a sample of ISOCs, these two items were associated with the self-reported use of sexual fantasies about pre-pubescent children. Also, male ISOCs and community males with a self-reported sexual interest in children scored higher on these two items than community males with no sexual interest in children. However, the difference between ISOCs and community males with no sexual interest in children on the '*Having sex with someone much younger than yourself*' item was moderated by participant age. That is, the fantasy was used more often by ISOCs when the community controls were younger and used more often by the community males when they were older. This highlights an obvious issue with this item; namely, that it is ambiguous with respect to the actual age of the person in the fantasy. Thus, older males may simply think of a much younger adult. This ambiguity issue was addressed by Joyal, Cossette, and Lapierre (2015), who amended the WSFQ. For example, they changed the above item so that it clearly referred to a 'legal' young person, and they added in a fantasy item referring specifically to pre-pubescent children. Dyer and Olver (2016) factor-analysed Joyal et al.'s (2015) version and found a factor that was composed of paraphilic fantasy themes (i.e. items referring to children, force, animals, urination, and fetishes). While scores on this 'Paraphilias' subscale only provides information about the strength of one's paraphilic sexual interests more generally, some of the individual items are likely to be useful for assessing specific offence-related sexual interests.

O'Donohue et al. (1997) also noted that many of the WSFQ items are vague. Consequently, they devised and tested a sexual fantasy questionnaire aimed specifically at measuring paraphilic fantasies. Their Paraphilic Sexual Fantasy Questionnaire (PSFQ) consists of 155 items that are rated on a three-point scale (i.e. *Never, Sometimes, Always*), which can be categorized into seven subscales; (1) *Normal Scale*; (2) *Bondage Scale*; (3) *Sadism Scale*; (4) *Masochism Scale*; (5) *Rape Scale*; (6) *Child Scale*; and (7) *Other Paraphilias*

Scale. The items are much more specific, which is clearly evident with regards to the item asking about a child's age (e.g. *About how old is the child in this fantasy? 0–2 years old (baby); 3–5 years old (preschool age),* etc.). Further, with the exception of the Normal Scale items, the PSFQ clearly asks about deviant fantasies (e.g. *'Forcing my penis into the vagina of an unwilling woman'* and *'Thrusting my penis into a boy's rear end'*).

Using 37 ISOCs and 76 student controls, O'Donohue et al. (1997) subjected the measure and its subscales to various reliability tests. They found that the seven subscales had good internal consistencies (Cronbach's alphas ranging from 0.59 to 0.92), with five of the seven subscales falling within the very good range of 0.80 to 0.92. Test-retest reliability scores (using a one-week interval) were also good (*r*'s ranging from 0.72 to 0.94 for the full sample). Also, the PSFQ was found to have good criterion-related validity (i.e. ISOCs scored higher on the Child Scale than controls) and content-related validity (i.e. the PSFQ includes most offence-related paraphilic fantasies). Based on these results, the PSFQ appears to be an ideal tool for assessing the offence-related sexual interests (via the assessment of how often they are sexually fantasized about). However, to the author's knowledge, there have only been two published studies using the PSFQ since its introduction into the literature (Seifert, Boulas, Huss, & Scalora, 2017; Skovran, Huss, & Scalora, 2010). The reason for its lack of use may be because the items are rather graphic, which some may feel will distress respondents or increase the likelihood of socially desirable responding (see also the CSIM; Chapter 2 in this volume).

In summary, there are a number of approaches to measuring the use offence-related sexual fantasies, with some more well-known than others and more researched than others, but each with their own strengths and weaknesses. The most common and reliable method is sexual fantasy questionnaires. However, there are some issues that need to consider and addressed when using these methods (see below).

Issues and recommendations

When measuring the use of sexual fantasies, there are a number of issues that can impact on the validity and accuracy of the assessment outcome. In this section, the main issues are examined, along with recommendations for how they can be addressed in research and practice. First, many sexual fantasy studies and measures do not clearly state how sexual fantasy was defined or operationalized. Thus, when responding to sexual fantasy questionnaire items, it is not known whether participants are referring to the frequency of intrusive/spontaneous sexual thoughts, rather the deliberate act of sexual fantasizing about an elaborate sexual scenario. The same issue applies to measures that provide a broad, all-encompassing definition. For example, in their PSFQ, O'Donohue et al. (1997) state that 'Sexual fantasy was operationalized as *any* thought or daydream about something that is found to be sexually interesting' (p. 170, italics added).

As mentioned earlier, Bartels and Beech (2016) argue that spontaneous, fleeting sexual thoughts are conceptually distinct from deliberate, elaborate sexual fantasizing and, therefore, should be treated as distinct. This includes during their assessment. To exemplify this point, imagine that two people share a sexual interest in children. Person A frequently experiences spontaneous sexual thoughts about children (outside of their control), while Person B frequently engages in deliberate acts of sexual fantasizing. Without clearly operationalizing what is meant by sexual fantasy (noun) *and* sexual fantasizing (verb), both people would likely score high on an item asking about sexual fantasies related to children. This would obscure the possibility that Person B is more actively engaging with their offence-related sexual interest. Therefore, when assessing sexual fantasy use, researchers and clinicians should be more specific in their definition, making it clear what is meant by sexual fantasizing (as discussed above). It would also be useful to have two versions of a sexual fantasy questionnaire; one designed to assess spontaneous, fleeting thoughts about the sexual fantasy, and one to assess the deliberate envisioning of the sexual fantasy. This will allow one to determine if a client has more spontaneous sexual thoughts versus deliberate acts of sexual fantasizing, or vice versa.

A second point to consider is that, although sexual fantasies and sexual interests are linked, the disclosure of a sexual fantasy does not automatically mean it reflects an enduring sexual interest. As noted by Joyal (2015), 'although a given SF [sexual fantasy] might be arousing, it is not necessarily indicative of a sexual interest' (p. 329). Furthermore, if a sexual fantasy does reflect a sexual interest, its disclosure does not reveal anything about the strength of that sexual interest. To address this, assessors should focus on how often one uses a sexual fantasy, as this is more useful in determining sexual interest strength. That is, someone with a less strong sexual interest may only deliberately fantasize about it once or twice a year, while someone with stronger sexual interest may fantasize about it every day. Of course, to more firmly establish this, the assessment of other factors is required, since two individuals may have a similar level of sexual interest, but one may have better self-management skills than the other that consequently leads to more frequent sexual fantasizing.

A third point to note is that most sexual fantasy questionnaires contain behavioural items that do not specify the target. For example, an individual may score high on an intimate sexual fantasy item, as well as a sexually aggressive item. However, they may actually fantasize about the former with a female child as the target, and the latter with a female adult as the target. Thus, assessors should consider administering a sexual fantasy questionnaire (using behavioural items only) for each target of interest (e.g. once for children as the target and again with adults as the target). This would provide richer information about one's use of sexual fantasies, as well as how (or if) various sexual interests are combined within fantasy. This idea was advocated by Bartels and Harper (under review). In examining the factor structure of Gray, Watt, Hassan, and MacCulloch's (2003) Sexual Fantasy Questionnaire (using only the 87 behavioural items), Bartels and Harper identified six clear factors. Using the seven highest loading items on each factor, they created a 37-item revised short form version of the questionnaire. Bartels and Harper recommended that researchers and clinicians should consider using this short-form version separately for specific targets, so as to provide a Target x Behaviour assessment of sexual fantasy use.

Conclusion

The aim of this chapter was to examine measures of sexual fantasy use as a means to detect the presence and strength of a sexual interest(s). A contemporary view for conceptually understanding sexual fantasizing was offered, followed by an overview of the assessment methods for measuring sexual fantasy use. Taking account of the idea that sexual fantasizing is a cognitive act that is distinct from automatic sexual thoughts (and 'sexual fantasy' as a cognitive construct), various recommendations for more accurate assessment were then offered. It is hoped that the theoretical insights, critical comments, and practical recommendations will be of use to those who are involved in the assessment of offence-related sexual fantasies and interests.

Note

1. Or various interests if the fantasy contains a particular target, behaviour, and location, such as oral sex with a film star on the beach (Turner-Moore & Waterman, 2017).

References

Abel, G. G., & Blanchard, E. B. (1974). The role of fantasy in the treatment of sexual deviation. *Archives of General Psychiatry, 30*, 467–475. doi:10.1001/archpsyc.1974.01760100035007

Akerman, G., & Beech, A. R. (2012). A systematic review of measures of deviant sexual interest and arousal. *Psychiatry, Psychology and Law, 19*, 118–143. doi:10.1080/13218719.2010.547161

Allan, M., Grace, R. C., Rutherford, B., & Hudson, S. M. (2007). Psychometric assessment of dynamic risk factors for child molesters. *Sexual Abuse: A Journal of Research and Treatment, 19*, 347–367. doi:10.1177/107906320701900402

Alleyne, E., Gannon, T. A., Ciardha, C. Ó., & Wood, J. L. (2014). Community males show multi-ple-perpetrator rape proclivity: Development and preliminary validation of an interest scale. *Sexual Abuse, 26,* 82–104. doi:10.1177/1079063213480819

Banse, R., Schmidt, A. F., & Clarbour, J. (2010). Indirect measures of sexual interest in child sex offenders: A multimethod approach. *Criminal Justice and Behavior, 37,* 319–335. doi:10.1177/0093854809357598

Bartels, R. M., & Beech, A. R. (2016). Theories of deviant sexual fantasy. In *The Wiley handbook on the theories, assessment, & treatment of sexual offending,* (Ed.). D. P. Boer. *Volume I: Theo-ries,* (Ed) A. R. Beech, & T. Ward. John Wiley & Sons. doi:10.1002/9781118574003.wattso008.

Bartels, R. M., & Gannon, T. A. (2011). Understanding the sexual fantasies of sex offenders and their correlates. *Aggression and Violent Behavior, 16,* 551–561. doi:10.1016/j.avb.2011.08.002

Bartels, R. M., & Harper, C. A. (under review). *An exploration of the factor structure of Gray et al.'s Sexual Fantasy Questionnaire.* Manuscript under review.

Bartels, R. M., Lehmann, R. J. B., & Thornton, D. (2019). Validating the utility of the Wilson sex fantasy questionnaire with men who have sexually offended against children. *Frontiers in Psychiatry, 10,* 206.

Baumgartner, J. V., Scalora, M. J., & Huss, M. T. (2002). Assessment of the Wilson Sex Fan-tasy Questionnaire among child molesters and nonsexual forensic offenders. *Sexual Abuse, 14*(19–30). doi:10.1023/A:1013025410090

Beech, A. R., & Ward, T. (2004). The integration of etiology and risk in sexual offenders: A theo-retical framework. *Aggression and Violent Behavior, 10,* 31–63. doi:10.1016/j. avb.2003.08.002

Beggs, S., & Grace, R. C. (2011). Treatment gain for sexual offenders against children predicts reduced recidivism: A comparative validity. *Journal of Consulting and Clinical Psychology, 79,* 182–192. doi:10.1037/a0022900

Bourke, P., Ward, T., & Rose, C. (2012). Expertise and sexual offending: A preliminary empiri-cal model. *Journal of Interpersonal Violence, 27,* 2391–2414. doi:10.1177/0886260511433513

Chivers, M. L. (2005). A brief review and discussion of sex differences in the specificity of sexual arousal. *Sexual and Relationship Therapy, 20,* 377–390. doi:10.1080/14681990500238802

Davison, G. C. (1968). Elimination of a sadistic fantasy by a client-controlled countercondi-tioning technique: A case study. *Journal of Abnormal Psychology, 73,* 84–90. doi:10.1037/h0025440

Deu, N., & Edelmann, R. J. (1997). The role of criminal fantasy in predatory and opportunistic sex offending. *Journal of Interpersonal Violence, 12,* 18–29. doi:10.1177/088626097012001002

Dyer, T. J., & Olver, M. E. (2016). Self-reported psychopathy and its association with deviant sexual fantasy and sexual compulsivity in a nonclinical sample. *Sexual Offender Treatment, 11,* 1–18.

Gannon, T. A., Olver, M. E., Mallion, J. S., & James, M. (2019). Does specialized psychological treatment for offending reduce recidivism? A meta-analysis examining staff and program variables as predictors of treatment effectiveness. *Clinical Psychology Review,* 101752.

Gannon, T., Terriere, R., & Leader, T. (2012). Ward and Siegert's pathways model of child sexual offending: A cluster analysis evaluation. *Psychology, Crime, & Law, 18,* 129–153. doi:10.1080/10683160903535917

Gee, D. G., Ward, T., Belofastov, A., & Beech, A. R. (2006). The structural properties of sexual fantasies for sexual offenders: A preliminary model. *Journal of Sexual Aggression, 12,* 213–226. doi:10.1080/13552600601009956

Gee, D. G., Ward, T., & Eccleston, L. (2003). The function of sexual fantasies for sexual offend-ers: A preliminary model. *Behavior Change, 20,* 44–60. doi:10.1375/bech.20.1.44.24846

Gosselin, C., & Wilson, G. D. (1980). *Sexual variations: Fetishism, sadomasochism, and trans-vestism.* New York, NY: Simon & Schuster.

Gray, N. S., Watt, A., Hassan, S., & MacCulloch, M. J. (2003). Behavioral indicators of sadistic sexual murder predict the presence of sadistic sexual fantasy in a normative sample. *Journal of Interpersonal Violence, 18*, 1018–1034. doi:10.1177/0886260503254462

Hanson, R. K., & Morton-Bourgon, K. E. (2005). The characteristics of persistent sexual offenders: A meta-analysis of recidivism studies. *Journal of Consulting and Clinical Psychology, 73*, 1154–1163. doi:10.1037/0022-006X.73.6.1154

Hudson, S. M., Wales, D. S., Bakker, L., & Ward, T. (2002). Dynamic risk factors: The Kia Marama evaluation. *Sexual Abuse, 14*, 103–119. doi:10.1023/A:1014616113997

Joyal, C. C. (2015). Defining 'normophilic' and 'paraphilic' sexual fantasies in a population based sample: On the importance of considering subgroups. *Sexual Medicine, 3*, 321–330. doi:10.1002/sm2.96

Joyal, C. C., Cossette, A., & Lapierre, V. (2015). What exactly is an unusual sexual fantasy? *The Journal of Sexual Medicine, 12*, 328–340. doi:10.1111/jsm.12734

Kahr, B. (2007). *Sex and the psyche*. London: Allen Lane.

Kalmus, E., & Beech, A. R. (2005). Forensic assessment of sexual interest: A review. *Aggression and Violent Behavior, 10*, 193–217. doi:10.1016/j.avb.2003.12.002

Laws, D. R., & Marshall, W. L. (1990). A conditioning theory of the etiology and maintenance of deviant sexual preferences and behavior. In W. L. Marshall, D. R. Laws, & H. E. Barbaree (Eds.), *Handbook of sexual assault: Issues, theories, and treatment of the offender* (pp. 209–230). New York, NY: Plenum Press.

Leitenberg, H., & Henning, K. (1995). Sexual fantasy. *Psychological Bulletin, 117*, 469–496. doi:10.1037/0033-2909.117.3.469

Looman, J. (1999). Mood, conflict and deviant fantasies. In B. K. Schwartz (Ed.), *The sex offender: Theoretical advances treating special populations and legal developments* (pp. 1–11). Kingston, NJ: Civic Research Institute.

MacCulloch, M. J., Snowden, P. R., Wood, P. J. W., & Mills, H. E. (1983). Sadistic fantasy, sadistic behavior, and offending. *The British Journal of Psychiatry, 143*, 20–29. doi:10.1192/bjp.143.1.20

Mann, R. E., Hanson, K. R., & Thornton, D. (2010). Assessing risk for sexual recidivism: Some proposals on the nature of psychologically meaningful risk factors. *Sexual Abuse, 22*, 191–217. doi:10.1177/1079063210366039

Marquis, J. N. (1970). Orgasmic reconditioning: Changing sexual object choice through controlling masturbation fantasies. *Journal of Behavior Therapy and Experimental Psychiatry, 1*, 263–271. doi:10.1016/0005-7916(70)90050-9

Marshall, W. L. (1979). Satiation therapy: A procedure for reducing deviant sexual arousal. *Journal of Applied Behavior Analysis, 12*, 377–389. doi:10.1901/jaba.1979.12-377

Marshall, W. L. (2006). Olfactory aversion and directed masturbation in the modification of deviant preferences; A case study of a child molesters. *Clinical Case Studies, 5*, 3–14. doi:10.1177/1534650103259754

Marshall, W. L. (2007). Covert association: A case demonstration with a child molester. *Clinical Case Studies, 6*, 218–231. doi:10.1177/1534650105280329

McCoy, K., & Fremouw, W. (2010). The relation between negative affect and sexual offending: A critical review. *Clinical Psychology Review, 30*, 317–325. doi:10.1016/j.cpr.2009.12.006

McGuire, R. J., Carlisle, J. M., & Young, B. G. (1965). Sexual deviation as conditional behavior: A hypothesis. *Behavior Research and Therapy, 2*, 185–190.

McKibben, A., Proulx, J., & Lusignan, R. (1994). Relationships between conflict, affect and deviant sexual behaviors in rapists and paedophiles. *Behavior Research and Therapy, 32*, 571–575. doi:10.1016/0005-7967(64)90014-2

Morgan, C. D., & Murray, H. A. (1935). A method for investigating fantasies: The thematic apperception test. *Archives of Neurology & Psychiatry, 34*, 289–306. doi:10.1001/archneurpsyc.1935.02250200049005

Nichols, H. R., & Molinder, I. (1984). *Multiphasic Sex Inventory (MSI) manual.* Tacoma, WA: Author.

Nichols, H. R., & Molinder, I. (1996). *Multiphasic Sex Inventory II.* Tacoma, WA: Nichols and Molinder Assessments.

O'Donohue, W., Letourneau, E. J., & Dowling, H. (1997). Development and preliminary validation of a paraphilic sexual fantasy questionnaire. *Sexual Abuse, 9*, 167–178. doi:10.1007/BF02675062

Pithers, W. D., Kashima, K. M., Cumming, G. F., Beal, L. S., & Buell, M. M. (1988). Relapse prevention of sexual aggression. *Annals of the New York Academy of Sciences, 528*, 244–260. doi:10.1111/j.1749-6632.1988.tb50868.x

Rahman, Q., & Symeonides, D. J. (2008). Neurodevelopmental correlates of paraphilic sexual interests in men. *Archives of Sexual Behavior, 37*, 166–172. doi:10.1007/s10508-007-9255-3

Schlesinger, L. B., & Kutash, I. L. (1981). The criminal fantasy technique: A comparison of sex offenders and substance abusers. *Journal of Clinical Psychology, 37*, 210–218. doi:10.1002/1097-4679(198101)37:1<210::AID-JCLP2270370143>3.0.CO;2-O.

Seifert, K., Boulas, J., Huss, M. T., & Scalora, M. J. (2017). Response bias on self-report measures of sexual fantasies among sexual offenders. *International Journal of Offender Therapy and Comparative Criminology, 61*, 269–281. doi:10.1177/0306624X15593748

Skovran, L. C., Huss, M. T., & Scalora, M. J. (2010). Sexual fantasies and sensation seeking among psychopathic sexual offenders. *Psychology, Crime & Law, 16*, 617–629. doi:10.1080/10683160902998025

Stevens, C. D., Tan, L., & Grace, R. C. (2016). Socially desirable responding and psychometric assessment of dynamic risk in sexual offenders against children. *Psychology, Crime & Law, 22*, 420–434. doi:10.1080/1068316X.2015.1120868

Swaffer, T., Hollin, C., Beech, A., Beckett, R., & Fisher, D. (2000). An exploration of child sexual abusers' sexual fantasies before and after treatment. *Sexual Abuse, 12*, 61–68. doi:10.1177/107906320001200107

Turner-Moore, T., & Waterman, M. (2017). Men presenting with sexual thoughts of children or coercion: Flights of fancy or plans for crime? *The Journal of Sexual Medicine, 14*, 113–124. doi:10.1016/j.jsxm.2016.11.003

Vane, J. R. (1981). The thematic apperception test: A review. *Clinical Psychology Review, 1*, 319–336. doi:10.1016/0272-7358(81)90009-X

Waismann, R., Fenwick, P. B. C., Wilson, G. D., Hewett, T. D., & Lumsden, J. (2003). EEG responses to visual erotic stimuli in men with normal and paraphilic interests. *Archives of Sexual Behavior, 32*, 135–144. doi:10.1023/A:1022448308791

Ward, T., & Beech, A. R. (2006). An integrated theory of sexual offending. *Aggression and Violent Behavior, 11*, 44–63. doi:10.1016/j.avb.2005.05.002

Ward, T., & Hudson, S. M. (2000). Sexual offenders' implicit planning: A conceptual model. *Sexual Abuse, 12*, 189–202. doi:10.1023/A:1009534109157

Wilson, G. (1978). *The secrets of sexual fantasy.* London: J.M. Dent & Sons.

Wilson, G. (1988). Measurement of sex fantasy. *Sexual and Marital Therapy, 3*, 45–55. doi:10.1080/02674658808407692

Part II
Management

The treatment of sexual deviance within a therapeutic setting

8

Jayson Ware, Meagan Donaldson and Danielle Matsuo

Introduction

There is no doubt that individuals convicted of a sexual offence require assistance with their sexual functioning. Deviant sexual interests, sexual preoccupation, and sexual entitlement have all been found to robustly relate to risk of recidivism (see Mann, Hanson, & Thornton, 2010). It is, therefore, somewhat surprising that sexual interests (including healthy sexuality) is often not adequately addressed in treatment programmes (Marshall, Hall, & Woo, 2017) or, if it is addressed, there is often an absence of clarity regarding treatment targets and technique (Marshall, Marshall, Serran, & O'Brien, 2011). Further there seems to be a distinct lack of robust research into the validity and reliability of these techniques, at least within the sex offender-specific literature, in comparison to other psychological areas such as sexual dysfunction.

This chapter will describe treatment targets, concepts, and techniques used with adult individuals convicted of a sexual offence within an Australian jurisdiction (Corrective Services New South Wales). These treatment concepts are used, with small adjustments, interchangeably with those convicted of rape, child molestation, and individuals convicted of non-contact sexual offences. Similarly these are used with heterosexual as well as homosexual offenders. Importantly, these same treatment concepts are used for healthy sexual functioning, deviant sexual thoughts and behaviours, and sexual preoccupation depending upon our formulation of the individual offender's treatment needs. While individuals within our programmes may be referred for pharmacological interventions, we do not describe their use within this chapter (see instead Ware & Allnutt, 2010; see Chapter 11 in this volume for a description of their use).

We will initially describe our treatment philosophy which reflects a theoretical move away from the specific behavioural techniques used to change deviant sexual interests towards a treatment approach using more generic and simpler techniques derived, in part, from the sexual dysfunctions and relationships areas. Our approach is to use fewer techniques and to keep these consistent with the skills the offender needs to use in all areas of his life. This smaller number of techniques are then learnt and practiced across time and context – both within the prison environment and upon release. This, in effect, sets the scene for our description of what treatment techniques we use. We will also focus on the important *process* issues relating to the delivery of these techniques. Specifically, we describe the therapeutic settings and therapist characteristics that we believe are essential to assisting individuals with their sexual functioning. At this point, we describe a small number of techniques we use specific to sexual deviance organized under physiological arousal, cognitions, and behavioural headings. We conclude by providing a brief case study as an illustration of our approach.

Treatment philosophy

Our general philosophy is that the reduction of deviant sexual thoughts, fantasies, or arousal occurs within a broader focus on healthy sexual functioning. We note that many individuals have offended in very specific circumstances or contexts and therefore we do not assume that an explicit focus on techniques to reduce deviant sexual thoughts or fantasies is always needed. Our view is that if many of those in custody were to develop the attitudes, skills, and confidence to function effectively in adult prosocial sexual relationships, then deviant sexual interests are no longer required to compensate for these deficiencies (see also Mann & Marshall, 2009; Marshall, 1997). In support of this theoretical position, Marshall and Fernandez (2003) have noted that not all individuals convicted of a sexual offence are assessed as having enduring deviant sexual thoughts or feelings. There are individuals, however, that have high levels of deviant sexual thoughts and arousal such as those with sexual preoccupation and, for these people, we espouse the limited use of a number of explicitly focused behavioural approaches despite their limitations.

Broader focus

Any effort to modify an individual's sexual interest should occur within the broader context of treatment. It should not be seen, in our view, as a standalone treatment module. We agree with Marshall, O'Brien, and Marshall (2009) who argued that efforts to modify sexual interests should be embedded within the context of all other relevant issues addressed in the sex offender treatment program. As we will go on to outline, discussions relevant to sexual functioning should occur repeatedly over the course of the treatment programme or programmes and the environmental context within which treatment takes place needs to be organized in a manner so that participants can openly discuss and, as required, practice and rehearse skills relevant to sexual interests.

By ensuring that sexual functioning discussions occur throughout treatment, we are actively attempting to assist the offender to 'normalize' these discussions and to prevent the defensiveness that can occur when an offender is only asked about his sexual thoughts and behaviours during particular treatment components. We are also intending to minimize the risk of offenders simply telling therapists what they think the therapist wants to hear when they need to hear it. We have noted that, when sexual functioning is segmented into its own treatment module, participants who were progressing well in treatment can quickly resort to discussing sexual interests in a manner designed to appease the therapist, as opposed to a genuine attempt to greater psychological insight into his sexual functioning. Waldram (2007, 2008) refers to the telling of the life story as 'a performance', where the narrator frequently 'surrenders' to the dominating expectations of how he should tell his story. In support of our treatment philosophy we note that long term retention of learning, and subsequent behaviour change, best occurs when learning is spaced out over time (see Marshall et al., 2011 for a brief summary of the evidence). For this reason, we emphasize the continued discussion of sexual issues throughout our preparatory, treatment, and maintenance programmes.

While we ensure that sexual functioning discussions occur frequently, we also ascribe to the philosophy that detailed discussions of *past* sexual thoughts, fantasies, or arousal is not always necessary. Indeed, a focus on this can lead to defensiveness and non-engagement (Ware & Blagden, 2017). Instead, we focus on assisting the participant to prepare for the future. In doing so, we are replicating Ware and Mann's (2012) approach to acceptance of responsibility. Ware and Mann built upon earlier work by Maruna and Mann (2006) and attempted to clarify what acceptance of responsibility should look like within sex offender treatment. Their argument is that *passive* responsibility, or seeing oneself as responsible for past actions (e.g. 'I did it') is not a necessary condition for change and should be de-prioritized as a treatment goal. Instead they argued that there should be an increased focus on *active* responsibility, whereby the therapist focuses the offender toward seeing themselves as responsible for changing their future behaviour for the better ('What do I need to do to make sure it is not done again?').

We also focus on the use of approach strategies and plans specific to sexual functioning rather than having offenders generate lists of situations, persons, and thoughts that they must avoid. Our experience is consistent with that described by Mann, Webster, Schofield, and Marshall (2004) who found that sex offenders in programmes that focused on individualized approach goals were more likely to be fully engaged in treatment and to complete within-sessions practice. In our view, if we are taking something rewarding away from individuals convicted of a sexual offence (e.g. their sexual fantasies) we must then replace this with something as, or as close to, rewarding. This forms the basis of their approach goals and is particularly important for offenders who are sexually preoccupied. Importantly, we note that significantly higher proportions of individuals convicted of a sexual offence have been assessed as sexually preoccupied when compared to matched community controls (43% versus 15%; Marshall & O'Brien, 2009) and that sexual preoccupation is an important predictor of recidivism (Hanson & Morton-Bourgon, 2005).

Specific to sexual functioning, we use the model of human sexual responding outlined by Kaplan (1979) to help structure our interventions in a way that is meaningful for offenders. As we will outline in a following section, we utilize a consistent and well-practiced range of generalized techniques and strategies to assist offenders to manage their sexual desire, excitement, orgasm, and resolution. Anecdotally, we have found that individuals are able to easily identify which treatment techniques could be used in each or all of these phases of sexual functioning.

Finally, within our broader treatment focus, our philosophy is that individuals convicted of a sexual offence should be assisted to recognize, monitor, understand, and appropriately manage situations, thoughts, physiological arousal, feelings, and behaviours *in general* and that these skills are taught to be generalizable across risk factors and situations and context including sexual functioning. In practice this means that an offender will use the same technique, for example employing various distraction techniques, to cope with issues relating to a range of dynamic risk factors rather than having discrete techniques for different risk factors or issues. We also expect that offenders will be able to demonstrate attitudinal and behavioural change across time and across context. For this reason, we are particularly interested in assessment tools such as the Violence Risk Scale: Sexual Offending (VRS: SO) where an offender can only move through stages of action and maintenance when changes in behaviour that are relevant to the risk behaviour are documented over time and over different contexts. The evidence shows that change scores on the VRS: SO were associated with reductions in sexual recidivism after controlling for static risk (Beggs & Grace, 2011; Olver, Wong, Nicholaichuk, & Gordon, 2007). Within treatment, offenders are encouraged to practice skills regularly in everyday situations that occur in the therapeutic unit, when experiencing less intense emotions or when they feel they are generally in control.

The aim is for individuals to rehearse and master the skills so they become better equipped to deal when stressors arise, when they experience strong emotions and when they experience situations in which they perceive they have limited control. These skills are then applied to deficits in sexual regulation, using sex as a coping strategy, sexual preoccupation and deviant sexual interests. Campitelli and Gobet (2011), in their review of expertise acquisition, note that repetition of a new skill alone is not enough and that deliberate practice is necessary for this to occur. Deliberate practice requires attention to, and rehearsal of, new skills across time and context

Importance of process issues

When considering the treatment of sexual issues, the environmental context is particularly important. We have described elsewhere (Frost & Ware, 2018; Ware & Galouzis, 2019; Ware, Galouzis, Hart, & Allen, 2012) that positive prison climate will provide individuals convicted of a sexual offence with the opportunity to practice and rehearse their new learning (*content*), acquired within treatment sessions, within a therapeutic context where they are exposed to a myriad of supportive relationships and therefore receive consistent feedback and challenge (*process*). In the all-day–everyday context of the prison, this means not just 'talking the talk' in the therapy group specific to modifying sexual interests but 'walking the walk' by practicing and rehearsing in the prison unit during and after treatment. This is particularly relevant to sexual deviance. Our challenge, as we have seen it, is how to provide each offender with the opportunities to practice and rehearse, not just talk about, their sexual thinking and arousal.

Although the evidence remains under-developed, it appears that the characteristics of the therapist, therapeutic relationship or alliance, and group climate positively influence sex offender treatment engagement and pre to post-treatment changes (Kozar & Day, 2012; Marshall & Burton, 2010). We believe a number of these characteristics are particularly important to modifying sexual interests. It is our experience that therapists who approach sexual deviance discussions in a manner perceived as confrontational, judgemental, or rigid had less effective outcomes with participants. In these instances, participants typically responded by withholding information relating to sexual discussions or engaging in positive impression management (acquiescing, or lying for self-preservation or through fear of judgement) or were even openly hostile. Conversely, therapists who were confident in discussing sexual issues, who demonstrated genuineness, empathy, directed discussions, and who explored issues through open ended questions generally experienced offenders as engaged in group discussions, less judgemental of each other's sexual issues, and appeared more focused on promoting and supporting change in themselves and others.

In practice we have adopted two approaches to introducing the treatment of sexual issues to group members. Firstly, we aim to introduce the participant as early as possible to the expectation of talking about sex and sexual issues. This is commonly started in the pre-treatment assessment interviews or preparatory programmes where, specific to sexual functioning, we explicitly provide treatment-related information including examples of treatment assignments. Secondly, we ensure that that sexual functioning is explored throughout every stage of treatment. While it is tempting for each therapist to ignore discussion of sexual issues, for example, when exploring the individual's life history, offence pathways, or when developing plans for their future, we will expect the individual to relate each treatment area to sexual functioning.

To assist our therapists to develop and enhance their therapeutic relationship with individuals, we focus the majority of these sexual discussions around establishing a healthy and fulfilling sex life. It is our experience that process-focused group sessions, rather than manualized or scripted session plans promote open discussions which allow individuals to direct the discussions. Our treatment groups are facilitated using a rolling format model which we believe has significant advantages specific to the discussion of sexual issues (see Ware, Mann, & Wakeling, 2009). Rolling groups greatly enhance the opportunity for new group members to learn vicariously from other group members who have been in treatment for longer who can model trust and openness. Our preference is to address sexual topics in the moment and as they arise (*process*); however throughout the duration of the programme, we facilitate psycho-education and process sessions focused specifically on sex and sexual issues, with the aim being to promote healthy sexuality.

We also recognize that attempting to change sexual preferences for some individuals is futile. There needs to be an acceptance from both participant and therapist that their sexual interests (e.g. in children) may never dissipate (Blagden, Mann, Webster, Lee, & Williams, 2017). Accepting this, may assist the individual (and therapist) to focus on their efforts on managing their sexual thoughts, feelings and behaviours and to develop enhanced risk management strategies.

Description of strategies and exercises

Having described our treatment philosophy and the importance of context and process issues to our efforts to modify sexual interests, we now illustrate treatment strategies used for sexual functioning with reference to specific exercises or concepts organized under physiological arousal, cognitions, and behavioural. Within treatment sessions we do not use these terms but instead use simple concepts to describe what type of skill or exercise is being used (e.g. thoughts, being sexually aroused, and making good decisions) and remind individuals repeatedly of the availability of each of these exercises for use with other psychological issues. We hope to demonstrate the effective use of general techniques for sexual deviance. We have also borrowed from the sexual dysfunction literature as we see these treatment strategies as inter-changeable with sexual deviance treatment.

One of the key philosophies underpinning our approach to sexual devi-ance is that individuals have often told us that they were not 'thinking' at the time leading up to their offending and instead were focused on their feelings of sexual arousal. Rather than attempting to refute this, we have considered this issue important and have used the theoretical construct of cognitive decon-struction (Baumeister, 1990; Ward, Hudson, & Marshall, 1995) to structure our treatment response. Essentially, we assist individuals to recognize that, at those times, they are choosing to focus on the immediate short term, focusing on movements and sensations (physiological arousal), and thinking only of proximal, immediate tasks and goals. In effect, we assist them to understand that they are using a problematic form of mindfulness (see next section and structured touching as an example) and need to focus, at those times, on rais-ing their level of cognitive awareness (cognitions). For these reasons, we aim to assist individuals convicted of a sexual offence master their management of physiological arousal before cognitions.

Physiological arousal

Throughout treatment individuals are introduced to a range of de-arousal techniques aimed at decreasing and regulating physiological arousal, including relaxation strategies (deep breathing techniques, use of imagery, progressive muscle relaxation), mindfulness techniques, and 'urge surfing' (Marlatt & Gordon, 1985). These techniques, once learnt and rehearsed by individuals, can assist with general emotional regulation such as managing anger or anxi-ety. However, these techniques can also assist when sex is used as a coping strategy to ameliorate emotions or tension or to reduce sexual preoccupation.

Individuals are taught a range of mindfulness strategies and are encour-aged to identify the strategy that is most effective for them. Mindfulness skill building typically commences with present-moment experiences such as breathing and mindful observation of thoughts and builds to more sensory-focused mindfulness strategies such as mindful eating or drinking, or using all five senses. Some individuals experience difficulty with the abstract aspects of imagery (such as 'leaves on a stream') and benefit from the more sensory or tactile strategies. The underlying skill in all of the mindfulness techniques is for the participant to learn to stay present (in the here and now) and manage intrusive thoughts or strong emotional experiences through developing the skills to observe and describe without judgement and without acting on thoughts or emotions. These techniques are then generalized to sexual thoughts and managing sexual arousal.

Principles of mindfulness can be found in early sexual therapy techniques such as Sensate Focus (Masters & Johnson, 1970). Sensate focus is a set of structured touching suggestions aimed to reduce the pressures associated with sex and to assist the individual to learn about their physical responses by tuning into sensations and refocusing away from evaluation of the experience (Weiner & Avery-Clarke, 2014). This is achieved through non-demand touching where the focus is on one's own tactile experience or sensations, for their own interest, rather than trying to make themselves (or their partners) aroused. When an individual diverts focus from his own body to either his partner or environmental features, he subsequently diminishes his control over his sexual arousal (Metz & Pryor, 2000). Applying techniques from the sexual dysfunction research, the ability to shift the focus from external stimuli, to one's own experiences is important in the management of sexual deviance. Sensate focus is mindful, silent and non-evaluative touching. Traditionally, sensate focus techniques focus on couples; however, these techniques increase body awareness and self-control in individuals. Within a custodial therapeutic programme, these techniques can be applied by those who are hypersexual, learning to touch and focus on sensations without becoming sexually aroused or for the need to engage in sexual intercourse or orgasm; and can also be applied by those who experience anxiety and unhelpful cognitions around sexual underperformance.

Consistent with early behavioural strategies from the sexual dysfunction literature (i.e., stop-start technique, Semans, 1956; or squeeze technique, Masters & Johnson, 1970), as well as de-arousal techniques prominent in the current self-regulation literature, the current behavioural trends focus on the sensations experienced by self, re-direction of attention and non-judgemental evaluations. Mindful masturbation may be another effective technique for individuals who experience negative appraisals or anxiety regarding their sexual interests. The aim of mindful masturbation is for an individual to focus on the sensations he experiences without using sexual stimuli, thoughts or fantasies. Focusing on senses, a participant may notice the water temperature while showering, or the rhythm and pressure of his movements while masturbating.

Drawing on mindfulness techniques and relapse prevention research (Marlatt & Gordon, 1985) participants are typically taught 'urge surfing' skills to manage strong emotions and cravings associated with substances use. Urge surfing skills can also be applied to manage sexual arousal and sexual urges. The main learning point for participants is they do not have to act on an urge when they experience it. Education is provided to students to increase their understanding that (sexual) urges pass by themselves. Often the person focuses on the urge growing stronger and feels the need to act; alternatively, they attempt to distract themselves from the urge but later giving in. Urges are described like ocean waves that build and then eventually dissipate. It is important participants understand that the urge will increase until it peaks and then dissipates. The discomfort they are likely to experience is normalized as a natural experience and offenders are encouraged to know what their triggers are for experiencing urges. These may be external factors, such as stimuli they experience as sexually arousing or internal factors such as an emotion, thought or sexual fantasy. By naming the experience as an urge, the participant can view the urge as a natural occurrence, something that they can maintain control over and something that is temporary. The outcome for the individual is to learn to wait out the urge, endure the moment in time when the urge and discomfort is peaking, and to look forward to the downside.

Online or internet sex offenders have typically paired sexual arousal with internet access/use (see de Almeida Neto, Eyland, Ware, Galouzis, & Kevin, 2013). Our approach to assist those who have offended online or via the Internet, in practice, is to manage their physiological and sexual arousal, practicing the techniques identified above, with behaviours such as sitting in front of the computer, clicking through programmes, and using the intranet available to offenders. Once the use of the computer or internet is no longer paired with sex or heightened arousal, computer stimuli are less likely to trigger sexual arousal, making it easier for the individuals to resist sexual impulses and urges.

Cognitions

We use a sexual urges log for offenders to better identify and understand their sexually deviant thoughts and urges, when they occur and in what situations. Thought stopping and 'changing the channel' exercises, used in managing their thoughts and emotions more generally, are specifically used to assist participants to gain some control over their sexual thoughts and to replace the problematic thinking with alternative more appropriate thoughts.

However, we note that attempting to simply suppress or replace intrusive or risky thoughts can be ineffective and that changing the meaning of the thoughts, so the intrusive thoughts no longer have any personal significance, is often more useful (Jennings & Deming, 2013; Shingler, 2009). Therefore, one of the skills we assist with is replacing the higher-level meanings to the participants awareness using cognitive restructuring techniques. One strategy we use, based on Marshall et al. (2011), is to ask offenders to identify as many sexual behaviours as they can; ask the group to identify which behaviours are appropriate, alternative/unusual or deviant/illegal; and provide a rationale for their decisions. From here, we explore attitudes and beliefs about the sexual behaviours identified and how to establish a healthy sex life now and in the future.

A simpler strategy, which is particularly useful for Aboriginal individuals convicted of a sexual offence, is a 'camp fire' discussion centred on the letters 'SEX'. The therapist prompts for their immediate thoughts, attitudes, or emotional experience when the letters are placed on the ground or when talking about sex, and what experience they may have had which contributed to this response. Common responses include fear around forming new sexual relationships in the future, particularly disclosing their offence history or being accused of further sexual offences because of their offence histories; and the occasional comment regarding the forced abstinence of sex in custody (e.g. 'Sex, what's that?'). Discussions frequently emerge around what healthy/unhealthy sex is, the message the media sends about sex, and how social norms have changed over time. This is an opportunity to identify and then constructively challenge myths or exaggerated stories from other males, about masturbation, the use and role of pornography, and consent.

To promote healthy sexual functioning, we ask participants to write down an appropriate sexual fantasy that they can attribute new meaning to and feels sexually exciting. We outline the elements of an appropriate fantasy in that it must involve a consenting adult able to provide consent and a willing participant in the fantasy; no power imbalance; and no unhealthy or deviant aspects to the fantasy.

Behavioural

In what is perhaps a distinct shift away from the norm we use specific behavioural approaches to address sexual deviance sparingly due to their limitations which we now outline. Initial behavioural strategies were used primarily, although not exclusively, with those who have molested children (see Marshall et al., 2009 for a review of these techniques). Treatment was based on aversive procedures pairing deviant sexual interest with aversive stimuli (e.g. olfactory aversion) and/or masturbatory strategies to enhance normality and reduce sexual interest. The aversive procedure still recently used in over half of the sex offender treatment programmes within the United States, and also by our programme, is covert sensitization (also called minimal arousal conditioning; McGrath, Cumming, Burchard, Zeoli, & Ellerby, 2010). Within this technique, an individual pairs an aversive thought within a behavioural chain of events leading to an offence with a negative consequence (Cautela, 1967). Apart from case studies there remains limited evidence of its effectiveness. Masturbatory techniques appear to be used more frequently, at least in part, due to the fact that masturbation is a common and non-invasive behaviour. It has been considered an initial cause of deviant sexual interests (McGuire, Carlisle, & Young, 1965) and therefore a key treatment target. Masturbatory techniques generally involve individuals either simply pairing appropriate sexual fantasies with masturbation and orgasm (Maletsky, 1991), or masturbating to deviant sexual fantasies before switching to appropriate sexual fantasies prior to orgasm (e.g. directed masturbation; Laws & Marshall, 1991). This is usually followed immediately by satiation techniques where the offender then verbalizes deviant sexual fantasies during the refractory period when he is sexually unresponsive (Laws, 1995).

Notwithstanding the limited evidence regarding their effectiveness, we will use these techniques in an individualized manner if we believe it to be warranted. A small number of individuals, particularly those who are sexually preoccupied and who are seeking our assistance, report these techniques to be beneficial, at least in the immediate short term. We note that, in the absence of compelling evidence, there are published case studies (e.g. Marshall, 2007) that are very useful for therapists. When using these techniques, in keeping with an overarching philosophy of our programme where participants need to take active responsibility for their treatment (see Ware & Mann, 2012), we will provide each individual with an overview of each of these techniques and will assist the offender to choose. For the most part, these techniques and their use are discussed within individual treatment sessions.

Case study

John was a 50-year-old male who reported a sexual attraction to pre- and post-pubescent children since his late teens. His sexual offending history consisted of contact offences against pubescent males when he was in his twenties and a contact offence against a pre-pubescent female when he was in his forties. John had otherwise lived a prosocial lifestyle with stable supports and employment. He had previously engaged in long-term psychotherapy with a psychiatrist. John reported establishing intimate relationships with adult women throughout his life; however, during sexual interactions with his partners, he described visualizing sexual behaviours with children to assist him to maintain an erection and achieve an orgasm. He believed masturbating to the fantasies he experienced would minimize his chances of his acting out the behaviour. In our view this resulted in his sexual interests in children strengthening over time.

While John reported an adequate intellectual understanding of his sexual interests and ability to manage his fantasies (he was proactive in his own research into the treatment of deviant sexual interests towards children), it was still considered important to assist John to appreciate in greater detail the context, triggers, and processes involved and to identify how his coping strategies were poorly conceived. Early in treatment, while the focus was on the development of better coping strategies, John was assisted to complete sexual urges logs. John reported becoming more aware of his arousal to images of children on television or in newspapers. Of note, he also reflected that his monitoring for his deviant sexual thoughts actually inadvertently increased his sexual preoccupation.

Within initial group treatment sessions, John stated that he was hopeful there was a 'cure' to his sexual interests while at the same time acknowledging how entrenched his sexual interests indeed were. He accepted that these interests may not be amenable to intervention but instead needed to be managed appropriately. For these reasons, it was considered appropriate to use directed masturbation techniques. John struggled to use these successfully. He searched television programmes for adult nudity and fiction literature for sexual content as a means to develop and pair appropriate sexual fantasy with masturbation and orgasm. John was ultimately unable to achieve an erection or orgasm using these procedures and their continued use was considered to be problematic.

By this stage in treatment, John was demonstrating significantly enhanced emotional coping strategies. He reported getting considerable benefits from distraction and mindfulness techniques. At this point, John's therapist focused John towards the use of these techniques for managing his sexual fantasies and arousal. John had been implementing mindfulness techniques into his everyday living, particularly through his art, and he was therefore encouraged to practice mindful masturbation as a strategy. John continued to explore this technique throughout treatment as a means to develop arousal without needing to resort to thoughts about children. John was also assisted to use a series of distraction techniques that he had found helpful for managing his emotions at times when he needed to reduce his sexual thoughts or arousal.

Simultaneously in treatment, John had identified a lack of emotional awareness and expression as a treatment need. Through other treatment modules (such as emotional regulation) John learnt skills in distress tolerance, radical acceptance and urge surfing and had rehearsed theses skills in the context of frustration tolerance. John applied urge surfing techniques at times he woke aroused after a sexual dream, increasingly noticing that his erection abated, and reported a preference for this technique in managing his sexual urges and deviant sexual arousal.

Together with his other treatment goals of improving the quality of his relationships, his ability to communication with others, and his view of himself, while John did not change his sexual interests in children, he gained confidence in his ability to manage his sexual arousal and implement strategies to assist with risk management in the future.

Summary

The specific treatment of sexually deviant thoughts, feelings, and arousal remains an important objective for treatment programmes. We have argued for a treatment philosophy that moves away from the sole use of behavioural techniques towards an approach using more generic and simpler techniques derived, in part, from the sexual dysfunctions and relationships areas. In our view, the treatment of sexual deviance within a therapeutic setting also requires careful consideration of a number of important contextual or process issues in order to create optimal therapeutic environments. Specifically, we described the therapeutic settings and therapist characteristics that we believe are essential to assisting individuals convicted of a sexual offence with their sexual functioning. We also articulated a small number of techniques we use specific to sexual deviance, organized under physiological arousal, cognitions, and behavioural headings. We are not able demonstrate the effectiveness of this broader approach to the treatment of sexual deviance but note that, due to the absence of any strong evidence about the effectiveness of specific behavioural techniques used, much is still to be learnt about how best to approach sexual deviance within therapeutic settings. We therefore encourage treatment providers and researchers to give greater attention to this area. To this end we hope that our descriptions of our treatment approach may inspire greater empirical and conceptual consideration of these issues in the future.

References

Baumeister, R. F. (1990). Suicide as escape from self. *Psychological Review, 97*, 90–113.

Beggs, S. M., & Grace, R. C. (2011). Treatment gain for sexual offenders against children predicts reduced recidivism: A comparative validity study. *Journal of Consulting and Clinical Psychology, 79*, 182–192.

Blagden, N. J., Mann, R., Webster, S., Lee, R., & Williams, F. (2017). It's not something I chose you know: Making sense of pedophiles' sexual interest in children and the impact on their psychosexual identity. *Sexual Abuse: A Journal of Research and Treatment, 6*, 1–27.

Campitelli, G., & Gobet, F. (2011). Deliberate practice: Necessary but not sufficient. *Current Directions in Psychological Science, 20*, 280–285.

Cautela, J. R. (1967). Covert sensitization. *Psychological Reports, 20*, 459–468.

de Almeida Neto, A. C., Eyland, S., Ware, J., Galouzis, J., & Kevin, M. (2013). Brief interventions: Solving the 'internet sex offender paradox'. *Psychiatry, Psychology, and Law, 20,* 182–188.

Frost, A., & Ware, J. (2018). The heart and soul of the transforming environment: How values driven ethos sustains a therapeutic community for sexual offenders'. In G. Akerman, A. Needs, & C. Bainbridge (Eds.), *Transforming environments and rehabilitation: A guide for practitioners in forensic settings and criminal justice* (pp. 289–305). New York, NY: Routledge.

Hanson, R. K., & Morton-Bourgon, K. E. (2005). The characteristics of persistent sexual offenders: A meta-analysis of recidivism studies. *Journal of Consulting and Clinical Psychology, 73,* 1154–1163.

Jennings, J. L., & Deming, A. (2013). Effectively utilizing the 'behavioral' in cognitive-behavioral group therapy of sex offenders. *International Journal of Behavioral Consultation and Therapy, 8*(2), 7–13.

Kaplan, H. S. (1979). *Disorders of sexual desire.* New York, NY: Brunner Mazel.

Kozar, C. J., & Day, A. (2012). The therapeutic alliance in offending behavior programs: A necessary and sufficient condition for change? *Aggression and Violent Behavior, 17,* 482–487. doi:10.1016/j.avb.2012.07.004

Laws, D. R. (1995). Verbal satiation: Notes on procedure with speculations on its mechanism of effect. *Sexual Abuse: A Journal of Research and Treatment, 7,* 155–166.

Laws, D. R., & Marshall, W. L. (1991). Masturbatory reconditioning with sexual deviates: An evaluative review. *Advances in Behaviour Research and Therapy, 13,* 13–25.

Maletsky, B. M. (1991). *Treating the sexual offender.* Newbury Park, CA: Sage.

Mann, R. E., Hanson, R. K., & Thornton, D. (2010). Assessing risk for sexual recidivism: Some proposals on the nature of psychologically meaningful risk factors. *Sexual Abuse: A Journal of Research and Treatment, 22,* 191–217.

Mann, R. E., & Marshall, W. L. (2009). Advances in eth treatment of incarcerated sex offenders. In A. R. Beech, L. A. Craig, & K. D. Browne (Eds.), *Assessment and treatment of sex offenders: A handbook* (pp. 329–347). Chichester, UK: Wiley.

Mann, R. E., Webster, S. D., Schofield, C., & Marshall, W. L. (2004). Approach versus avoidance goals in relapse prevention with sexual offenders. *Sexual Abuse, 16,* 65–75.

Marlatt, G. A., & Gordon, J. R. (1985). *Relapse prevention: Maintenance strategies in the treatment of addictive behaviors.* New York, NY: Guilford Press.

Marshall, L. E., & O'Brien, M. D. (2009). Assessment of sexual addiction. In A. R. Beech, L. A. Craig, & K. D. Browne (Eds.), *Assessment and treatment of sex offenders: A handbook* (pp. 163–177). Chichester, UK: Wiley.

Marshall, W. L. (1997). The relationship between self-esteem and deviant sexual arousal in nonfamilial child molesters. *Behavior Modifications, 21,* 86–96.

Marshall, W. L. (2007). Covert association: A case demonstration with a child molester. *Clinical Case Studies, 6,* 218–231.

Marshall, W. L., & Burton, D. (2010). The importance of group processes in offender treatment. *Aggression and Violent Behavior, 15,* 141–149.

Marshall, W. L., & Fernandez, Y. M. (2003). *Phallometric testing with sexual offender: Theory, research, and practice.* Brandon, VT: Safer Society Press.

Marshall, W. L., Hall, K. S., & Woo, C. (2017). Sexual functioning in the treatment of sex offenders. In W. L. Marshall & L. E. Marshall (Eds.), *Handbook on the assessment, treatment and theories of sexual offending* (Vol. 3, pp. 1369–1384). West Sussex, UK: Wiley-Blackwell.

Marshall, W. L., Marshall, L. E., Serran, G. A., & O'Brien, M. D. (2011). *Rehabilitating sexual offenders: A strength-based approach.* Washington, DC: American Psychological Association.

Marshall, W. L., O'Brien, M. D., & Marshall, L. E. (2009). Modifying sexual preferences. In A. R. Beech, L. A. Craig, & K. D. Browne (Eds.), *Assessment and treatment of sex offenders: A handbook* (pp. 311–327). Chichester, UK: Wiley.

Maruna, S., & Mann, R. E. (2006). A fundamental attribution error? Rethinking cognitivedistortions. *Legal and Criminological Psychology, 11*, 155–177.

Masters, W. H., & Johnson, V. E. (1970). *Human sexual inadequacy*. London: Churchill.

McGrath, R. J., Cumming, G., Burchard, B., Zeoli, S., & Ellerby, L. (2010). *Current practices and emerging trends in sexual abuser management: The Safer Society 2009 North American Survey*. Brandon, VT: Safer Society Press.

McGuire, R. J., Carlisle, J. M., & Young, B. G. (1965). Sexual deviations as aconditioned behaviour: A hypothesis. *Behaviour Research and Therapy, 2*, 185–190.

Metz, M. E., & Pryor, J. L. (2000). Premature ejaculation: A psychophysiological approach for assessment and management. *Journal of Sex & Marital Therapy, 26*, 293–320.

Olver, M. E., Wong, S. C. P., Nicholaichuk, T., & Gordon, A. (2007). The validity and reliability of the violence risk scale – sexual offender version: Assessing sex offender risk and evaluating therapeutic change. *Psychological Assessment, 19*, 318–329.

Semans, J. H. (1956). Premature ejaculation: A new approach. *Behavior Therapy, 2*, 307–320.

Shingler, J. (2009). Managing intrusive risky thoughts: What works? *Journal of Sexual Aggression, 15*(1), 39–53.

Waldram, J. B. (2007). Narrative and the construction of 'truth' in a prison-based treatment program for sexual offenders. *Ethnography, 8*, 145–169.

Waldram, J. B. (2008). The narrative challenge to cognitive-behavioral treatment of sexual offenders. *Culture, Medicine and Psychiatry, 32*, 421–439.

Ward, T., Hudson, S. M., & Marshall, W. L. (1995). Cognitive distortions and affective deficits in sex offenders: A cognitive deconstructionist interpretation. *Sexual Abuse: A Journal of Research and Treatment, 7*, 67–83.

Ware, J., & Allnutt, S. (2010). The use of antilibidinal medications in the treatment of sexual offenders. *Australian Journal of Correctional Staff Development,7*, 1–12.

Ware, J., & Blagden, N. (2017). Responding to denial, treatment refusers, and drop outs. In W. L. Marshall & L. E. Marshall (Eds.), *Handbook on the assessment, treatment and theories of sexual offending* (Vol. 3, pp. 1559–1574). West Sussex, UK: Wiley-Blackwell.

Ware, J., & Galouzis, J. (2019). Impact of prison climate on sexual offenders: Desistance and rehabilitation. In N. Blagden, B. Winder, K. Hocken, R. Lievesley, P. Banyard, & H. Elliot (Eds.), *Sexual crime and the experience of imprisonment* (pp. 35–60). Switzerland: Palgrave Macmillan, Springer.

Ware, J., Galouzis, J., Hart, R., & Allen, R. (2012). Training correctional staff in the management of sexual offenders: Increasing knowledge and positive attitudes. *Sexual Abuse in Australia and New Zealand, 4*, 23–30.

Ware, J., & Mann, R. E. (2012). How should 'acceptance of responsibility' be addressed in sexual offending treatment programs? *Aggression and Violent Behavior, 17*, 279–288.

Ware, J., Mann, R. E., & Wakeling, H. (2009). What is the best modality for treating sexual offenders. *Sexual Abuse in Australia and New Zealand, 2*, 2–13.

Weiner, L., & Avery-Clarke, C. (2014). Sensate focus: Clarifying the Masters and Johnson's model. *Sexual and Relationships Therapy, 29*, 307–319.

Compassion and acceptance as interventions for paraphilic disorders and sexual offending behaviour

9

Jamie S. Walton and
Kerensa Hocken

The term 'paraphilia' first appeared in the *Diagnostic and Statistical Manual of Mental Disorders*, third edition (DSM-III, American Psychiatric Association, 1980) for the diagnosis of disorders of sexual preference. It originates from the Greek term *philos* (friend, loved) and *para* (besides). The current DSM-V (American Psychiatric Association, 2013), use the term 'Paraphilic Disorder', to discriminate atypical arousal (paraphilia), from disorders causing distress, harm or impairment or involvement of non-consenting others. The field is yet to agree on the prognosis of paraphilic disorders, and much of this is captured in the controversy of the DSM-V (e.g. Briken, Fedoroff, & Bradford, 2014). Clinicians have nevertheless persisted for several decades with therapies aimed at modifying paraphilic arousal and associated thinking. Alongside these therapies there is a small body of anecdotal literature existing since the mid-1990s that outlines therapies promoting change, not necessarily to the nature of paraphilic thoughts but the way individuals relate to them (e.g. LoPiccolo, 1994). Therapies with this aim have been more widely summarized as 'third wave' therapies in general clinical practice (Hayes, 2004).

The term 'wave' represents a set of assumptions, methods and goals that organize research, theory and practice (Hayes, 2004). Used as a metaphor, the term has attracted controversy (e.g. Hofmann & Asmundson, 2008). Hayes' original claim was that cognitive-behavioural therapy (CBT) was based on particular philosophical assumptions about matters of truth and evidence, and that new therapies grounded in a contextual understanding of behaviour had emerged. These therapies focused not on the content of thoughts, but on how people relate to thoughts, often with use of mindfulness and acceptance techniques. Hayes tracked the first and second waves, laying out their pre-analytic assumptions and methods, and so a 'third wave', was taken to suggest that previous generations of CBT would be eroded. This is not what has happened.

14 years on from Hayes's assertion, and similar to the way in which an actual wave assimilates the energy of waves gone before it, the third wave has led to an integration rather than a segregation of practice. The emerging emphasis is on core processes of change that cut across diagnostic classifications, and of which are linked to evidence-based procedures that intend not to merely relieve symptoms, but improve human prosperity itself (Hayes & Hofmann, 2017, 2018). Such procedures are open to a range of influences, including those from our spiritual traditions.

Our aim in this chapter is threefold. Firstly, we chart the first and second waves of therapy for paraphilic disorders and sexual offending as a way of organizing a timeline of clinical practice in this field. We then discuss two therapies illustrative of the third wave; Compassion Focused Therapy (CFT; Gilbert, 2010) and Acceptance and Commitment Therapy (said as one word – ACT; Hayes, Stroshl, & Wilson, 2012), and briefly review their outcomes in general healthcare. Thirdly, we discuss how CFT and ACT dovetail with the prevailing good-lives model for rehabilitation (Ward & Laws, 2010). Our intention is not to suggest shunning first and second wave practices. Rather our intention is to communicate therapies that have gathered traction in neighboring fields of health and which could supplement rehabilitative interventions.

First wave

First wave therapies developed in the 1950s, in part rebelling against Freudian psychoanalysis. Behaviourists believed that theory should be based on objectively established principles and that associated methods should be rigorously tested. *Contingency learning*; namely, respondent conditioning – that of learning by association and B.F. Skinner's operant conditioning – that of learning based on behaviour that is contingent (i.e. reliant) on the function of it consequence were among the key principles verified through experimentation. Mental processes were not beyond behaviourism, but they were rarely studied because it was argued they emerged from the same contingencies as observable behaviour. For example, the fear of a novel stimulus could arise due to its association with a natural fear evoking event (respondent conditioning); the consequence of avoiding the novel stimulus would be a decrease in fear (operant conditioning), but nothing new beyond this functional understanding would come from analysing 'fear' itself. Early accounts of paraphilic disorders harnessed the assertion of behavioural principles, and much like other problematic behaviours such as phobias, contingency learning was heralded as the cause (McGuire, Carlisle, & Young, 1965).

The contingency learning account specified that when the natural, unlearnt response of arousal (unconditioned response) elicited by genital stimulation

Biological/unlearned-'unconditional' response		Learnt by association – 'conditional' response	
Unconditioned Stimulus	Unconditioned Response	Conditioned Response	Conditioned Stimulus
(genital stimulation)	(arousal)	(arousal)	
			(child)
Neutral Stimulus			
(child)			

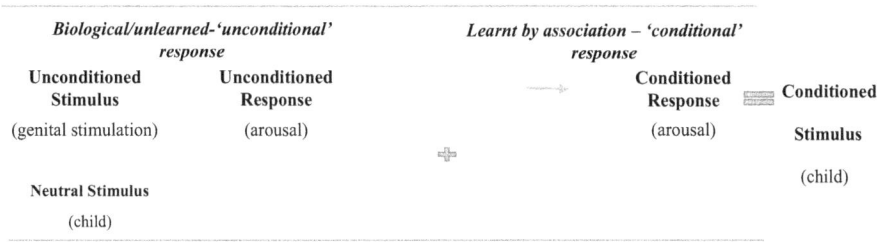

Figure 9.1 Stimulus-Response contingency: transfer of stimulus function.

(unconditional stimulus) is paired with a neutral stimulus (e.g. a child), the neutral stimulus acquires the function of eliciting arousal (Figure 9.1). It in turn then serves as a discriminative stimulus for the operant contingency of positive reinforcement; that is, where the rewarding consequence of pleasure/orgasm increases the frequency and intensity of sexual responses that occur in its presence (Figure 9.1). Generalization then enables the contingency to include similar discriminative stimuli (e.g. other children). So prevailing was the account that therapy operating from London's Institute of Psychiatry in the 1960s extended no further than attempting to change paraphilic responses by changing the contingency.

Two methods were used; aversion therapy and masturbatory reconditioning (see Marshall, O'Brien, & Marshall, 2009 for a review). Aversion therapy used a positive punishment contingency by applying consequences such as foul odours or off-putting images to paraphilic responses, the function being to reduce the rate of the responses. Masturbatory reconditioning used a positive reinforcement contingency by rewarding healthy fantasy with masturbatory induced arousal, the function being to increase the rate and appeal of the fantasy. Masturbatory reconditioning has also been used to produce a state of non-arousal after ejaculation in which paraphilic responses are then rehearsed. This technique called 'verbal satiation', uses the contingency of extinction. Extinction refers to the way behaviour that reoccurs in the absence of consequences that function to reinforce it, decreases and becomes extinct. As shown in Figure 9.2, the recurrence of paraphilic behaviour is maintained

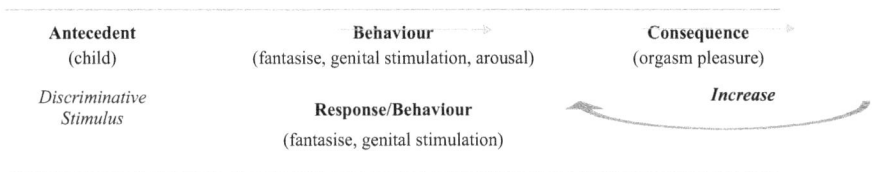

Antecedent	Behaviour	Consequence
(child)	(fantasise, genital stimulation, arousal)	(orgasm pleasure)
Discriminative Stimulus	Response/Behaviour	Increase
	(fantasise, genital stimulation)	

Figure 9.2 Positive reinforcement contingency: increase frequency and intensity of sexual response.

by the rewarding consequence of orgasmic pleasure. Having individuals promptly repeat this behaviour during a non-arousing state post-orgasm, should therefore lead to its extinction.

Earlier reviewers reported that paraphilic arousal can be manipulated by behavioural techniques, but that long-term effects were not demonstrated (Barbaree & Seto, 1997). Two decades on, clinical trials remain meagre, many have methodological problems and most are now outdated (see Barnett & Fitzalan-Howard, 2018; Dennis, Khan, Farriter, Husband, Powney & Duggan, 2012). Camilleri and Quinsey (2008) have outlined why the first wave techniques are unlikely to lead to change based on the extinction process that explains the effect of verbal satiation. That is, if there is a removal of the consequences on which behaviour (in this case reduced paraphilic fantasy and/or increased healthy fantasy) is contingent, its extinction and the re-emergence of prior behaviour will likely follow. In practice, the prompt effect of some techniques can lead participants to assume their paraphilic responses have diminished, and so cease the contingency that governs their changed frequency. First wave techniques remain in use but are incorporated with second wave interventions (McGrath, Cummings, Burchard, Zeoli, & Ellerby, 2010).

Second wave

Second wave interventions developed in response to the limitations of behaviourism in dealing with cognition. At its root was a philosophy of science known as 'mechanism', using as its metaphor, the 'commonsense machine' (Pepper, 1942). From this perspective, humans were like machines, comprising parts and processes, and the goal of science would be to model them. Mechanism is clearest in models emergent from the 1960s onwards that literally appealed to the information processing of a computer as a working metaphor for human cognition. The mental parts were modelled as constructs for example, 'schema' and 'conditional beliefs', each conceptualized to be a distinct unit of analysis. Applied clinically, the computer model thrived. Patients with comparable symptoms seemed to share similar faulty information processing, and so the 'cognitive errors' became modelled as the cause. Research preceded quickly to defining their nature and techniques were swiftly developed to correct them, in much the same way as a technician might re-programme a computer. Cognitive therapy had arrived (e.g. Beck, 1976). The movement permeated therapy for paraphilic disorders, notably for individuals who had sexually offended, with shifts in theory and practice owed to landmark contributions.

Among the contributions was the role of cognitive errors or *distortions* in theories of offending (e.g. Finkelhor, 1984), Anna Salter's (1988) therapy

guide for targeting such distortions and the introduction of a relapse prevention (RP) model (Pithers, Marques, Gilbat, & Marlatt, 1983). The aim would
be to correct distorted thoughts directly by undermining and challenging
them. Behavioural principles faded, both in terms of the attention given to the
contingencies that shape client-therapist behaviour, as well as the contextual
nature of all human behaviour, including thinking. The clearest illustration of
this was the conflation of thoughts that endorse offending with processes such
as denial (Maruna & Mann, 2006). In short, Salter's guide led to a focus on
the elimination of denial. Individuals were pressured to confess to offending
and agree with official statements. Confrontation often featured, yet the focus
on denial remained for decades. In this sense second wave CBT was far adrift
of its presence in general psychotherapy where therapeutic alliance was the
bedrock of clinical practice. Some years later, a then state-of-the-art RP programme in California had been rigorously evaluated showing no impact on
sexual recidivism (Marques, Wiederanders, Day, Nelson, & Ommeren, 2005).

By the early 2000s, experts had noted the discord and recommended
shifts toward enhancing individuals' wellbeing with a focus on their values
and capacities for the pro-social attainment of human needs – a 'Good Lives
Model' (GLM; Ward & Stewart, 2003). Some clinicians asked for 'Behavior'
to be put back into CBT (Fernandez, Shingler, & Marshall, 2006), while others differentiated between a 'cognitive distortion model' that had led to the
emphasis on denial and the 'information-processing model' on which a focus
on dysfunctional schema could progress (Mann & Shingler, 2006). Contemporary programmes stemming from these humanistic shifts are underpinned
by a strengths-based ethos that is far removed from the confessional approach.
Recently developed programmes in Her Majesty's Prison and Probation
(HMPPS) service in the UK for example aim to harness an individual's
strength and expand their repertoire of skills (Walton, Ramsay, Cunningham, & Henfrey, 2017). The interventions remain experimental. In general,
CBT programmes have been found to reduce recidivism (Schmucker & Lösel,
2017), although effects are heterogeneous and based on weak-inferential
studies (see Walton, 2018).

The third wave: principles of relational frame theory and an evolutionary functional perspective

Third wave therapies are rooted in an evolutionary model and contextual
behavioural science (CBS). CBS does not treat cognition as mechanical like in
the information processing model, and unlike the early behavioural accounts,
it suggests that it is vital to analyse cognition in order to understand behaviour. This is because CBS suggests thinking is not only influenced by direct

contingency learning (e.g., antecedent–behaviour–consequence), but also by 'relational learning' (Levin, Twohig, & Smith, 2016). Relational learning exists through language. It is the learnt ability that enables humans to relate events in a symbolic fashion, rather than according to their physical properties. Once learnt, language allows humans to imbue stimuli with meaning that is not intrinsic, and in doing so they profoundly transform their experience of the world. Third wave approaches focus on altering the function (or 'meaning') of the symbolic relations people build with language. Said another way, these approaches focus on changing how people *relate* to their thinking. We briefly expand on CFT because it makes explicit an evolutionary functional analysis (EFA) of the human mind, and ACT because of how it is grounded in CBS. Both approaches in a dissimilar but congruent way, converge on a compelling account of how behavioural problems are caused by the normal processes of an evolved human capacity for thinking and language.

CFT (Gilbert, 2010) in particular uses the notion of a 'tricky brain', where ancient neural networks common to most nonhuman mammals interact with new systems for verbal cognition that have evolved within the niche selection of our human ancestry. CFT suggests that we have an 'old brain' possessing tribal and territorial biases, competitive and caring mentalities and primal emotional functions (see Figure 9.3).[1] Like all mammals, humans have an autonomic threat system. It governs us exhibiting emotions like anger, fear and anxiety. Simply put, for our ancestral species, false positive errors were fine, but false negative decisions could be fatal, and evolution has in turn guaranteed we operate a 'better safe than sorry' policy. On the other hand, emotions like excitement and lust, activate us to peruse resources such as food, sex and shelter. Without this reward seeking function, our ancestral line would also have perished. We also have abilities for affiliation and caring. These functions are central to attachment – a vital adaptive mechanism in all mammals. Recently co-opting these systems have been 'new brain' abilities for language which selectively evolved to extend our cooperation in groups (Hayes & Sanford, 2014). The pairing of ancient emotional systems with language abilities that allow for abstract thought is a young adaptation and it contains glitches. In particular, verbal abilities activate the archetypal functions for survival and social ranking that have existed in species for millennia, leading to unique difficulties for humans, most profoundly, shame and self-criticism.

ACT is based on similar foundations, albeit with more nuanced theory on the contextual control of language on human behaviour, which while creating adaptive advantages, entails inadvertent functional problems. In short our capability to relate stimuli symbolically enables enormous generation and variation of meaning, such is the basis of our massive communicative advantage over all other species. However, this advantage is newly evolved

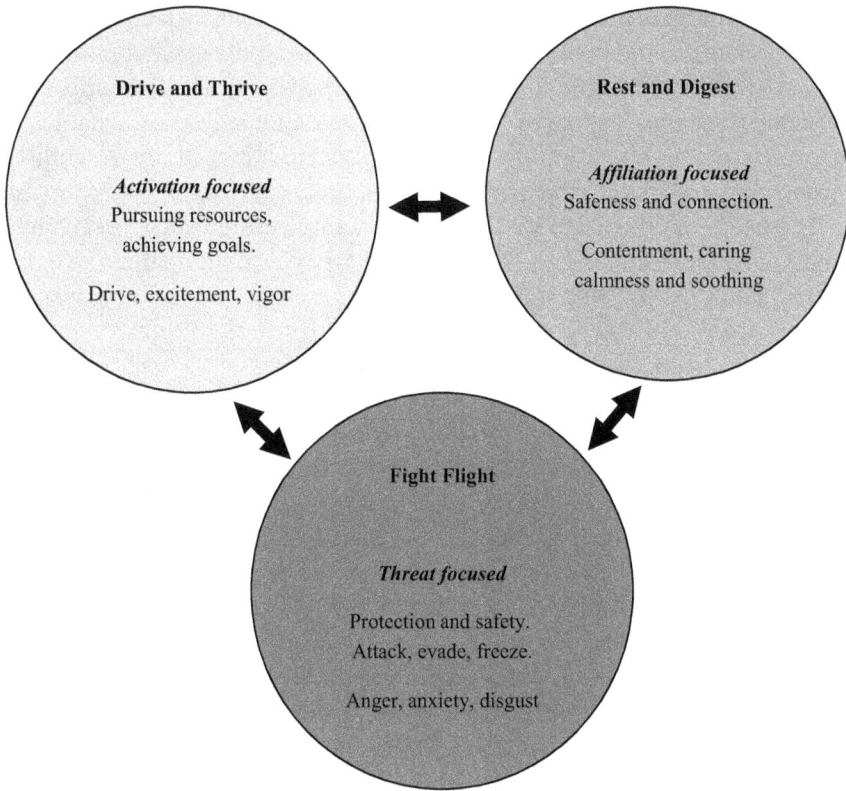

Figure 9.3 Three primitive emotional systems.

Source: adapted from Kolts and Gilbert (2018)

and humans are not yet adept at maintaining control over the new functions that stimuli acquire as a result. A branch of CBS research known as Relational Frame Theory (RFT; Hayes, Barnes-Holmes, & Roach, 2001), has established the process of relational learning at length. For brevity, RFT underpinning ACT will be outlined here without citation of the supporting data. It is however a profoundly active field of behavioral science (see Dymond & Roche, 2013).

The key claim in RFT is that language allows humans to relate any stimuli in a symbolic ('non-actual') way enabling freedom from contingency learning. Using a relevant example, consider the auditory property of the noun 'child'. It is just a stimulus sound. If this seems obscure, then consider 'hàizi', the Chinese translation for child. Until now, it was a sound with a non-specific function. It had no relevant meaning. There is no physical similarity between the properties of a sound like 'child' and an actual, real 'child'. Only under the control of a socially agreed context (language) can the two stimuli relate.

Under the contextual control of language, one symbolically names the other, and the other has the symbolic name. This is an example of what is known in RFT as a 'relational frame'. It is the most simple frame, called 'coordination' – the meaning of '*is*' (or 'same'). In this way, a relational frame is a contextual cue which defines how stimuli are to be related. Humans acquire the ability to derive relational frames; that is, one relation is taught to us and we spontaneously derive what is mutually entailed. For example, readers have been taught 'hàizi' *is* Chinese for 'child'. They will however have automatically derived without being taught, that the Chinese word for child *is* 'hàizi'. This seems so obvious because it is so specialized in humans. However, the ability to derive relations has been shown to be absent in animals, including language trained chimpanzees (Dugdale & Lowe, 2000).

Once acquired, the ability to derive relations is free to apply in combination, and in many types of relational frames, for example, opposition (a *is not* b entails b *is not* a); comparison (a *is better than* b, entails b *is worse than* a) and temporal (a *is before* b, entails b *is after* a), in an entirely arbitrary way, endlessly changing the meaning (i.e. functions) of the stimuli (e.g. others, self, objects, places, memories etc.) that are related in the process. This phenomenon is called '*arbitrarily applicable derived relational responding*'. 'Arbitrarily applicable' means symbolic, having nothing to do with actual relations between stimuli or their intrinsic properties. 'Derived relational responding', means responding to relations that are derived, and therefore not the result of contingency learning. The fundamental implication of this is the unlimited freedom of language. Unlike non-language able animals, humans can at any time, symbolically relate any stimulus to any other stimulus in any way, and in so doing the functions of those stimuli can be changed to evoke an associated changed response.

Using paraphilic arousal as an example, Figure 9 4 offers a small sample of the relational network problem that humans face. Suppose an individual for whom children elicit arousal is also told that 'hàizi' is Chinese for the noun 'child'. The noun 'child' was in a frame of coordination with an 'actual child', and now all three relate in combination. Western medicine determines that arousal to actual children or thoughts about a child (and 'hàizi') *is* 'paedophilic'. Western culture enables a 'paedophile' to be arbitrarily framed in opposition with 'normality' and by comparison with 'different paraphilia'. Self can be arbitrarily framed in coordination with a 'paedophile', and other people can be arbitrarily framed in coordination with 'normality'. There is no intrinsic relation between the actual sounds of the nouns and an actual child, self or others. Rather, it is the arbitrary use of the context; that is, the relational frames ('*is*', '*is not*', '*better/worse*') that relates them and so changes their function. The network is limitless. As shown, more stimuli (thoughts, images, events) can be arbitrarily related to each stimulus in focus. With this, the individual builds a

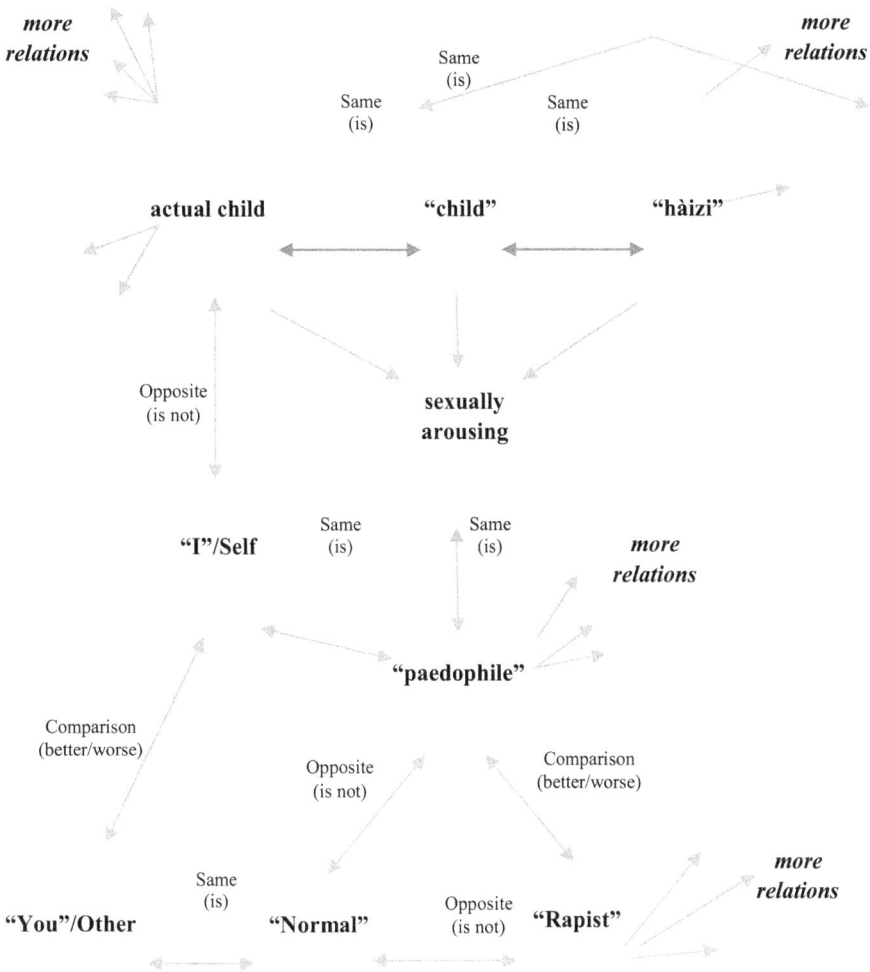

more
relations

Same
(is)

more
relations

Same
(is)

Same
(is)

actual child   **"child"**   **"hàizi"**

Opposite
(is not)

**sexually
arousing**

"I"/Self   Same
(is)   Same
(is)   *more*
relations

Comparison
(better/worse)

"paedophile"

Opposite
(is not)   Comparison
(better/worse)

more
relations

Same
(is)

"You"/Other   **"Normal"**   Opposite
(is not)   **"Rapist"**

Figure 9.4 Small relational network of paraphilic responses.

capacity to 'bring in' at any point, more antecedents that through being relationally framed evoke paraphilic responses, and maybe other experiences (e.g. shame). 'Hàizi' (and anything the individual arbitrarily relates in any way to its sound or meaning) has just acquired this function, despite having no formal relation to an actual child and never having preceded genital stimulation and arousal or been reinforced such as in Figures 9.1 and 9.2. This is how fast language is. Relational networks emerge in seconds.

To summarize, the evolved ability for thinking and language ensures humans confer themselves supreme adaptive benefits, but with it humans must also absorb unparalleled potential for pain. CFT approaches this as the result of a pairing of ancient motives and systems that direct whole-organism behaviour with verbal abilities that are unlimited in how they activate them. ACT and RFT offer a contextual account of the unlimited freedom of language, particularly in how humans relate stimuli using relational frames applied arbitrarily, thereby allowing for relations to arise without reference to the actual properties of things. Humans often respond to symbolic relations in terms of the change in meaning about the world that they produce. In other words humans fail to distinguish between the content of their thoughts and the process of having them. This is called '*cognitive fusion*'. The implication is that thoughts themselves have vast potential to be threatening and painful. There is a further destructive effect to this, which is that humans try to avoid unwanted thoughts. This is called '*experiential avoidance*' (Hayes, Wilson, Gifford, Follete, & Strosahl, 1996). It is ineffective because avoidance occurs through relational framing, leading rather ironically, to an increased opportunity to contact what is being avoided. Third wave therapy is attuned to these destructive, yet normal effects of thinking and language, particularly that of inflexible, unworkable and avoidant human behaviour.

ACT and CFT and their potential usefulness as therapies for paraphilia and offending

The foundations of ACT and CFT may provide a basis for understanding processes embedded in evolved capacities for thinking and language that contribute to paraphilic responding, including sexual offending (e.g. Roche & Quayle, 2007). The application of ACT to paraphilia is confined to a hand full of case studies and there are no published applications of CFT in this area. Therefore, the discussion here is speculative. We now examine the therapeutic processes of ACT and CFT and their potential use in this field. In following, we briefly summarize the outcome evidence for ACT and CFT in the general healthcare literature.

ACT

Because of the endless paths to psychological pain brought by language (in particular cognitive fusion and experiential avoidance), the aim of ACT is to increase 'psychological flexibility'. Psychological flexibility is defined as: '*the ability to contact the present moment more fully as a conscious human being, and to change or persist in behaviour when doing so serves valued ends*' (Hayes, Luoma, Bond, Masuda, & Lillis, 2006, p. 8). The relationship between psychological flexibility and sexual offending is yet to be explored, and we make no

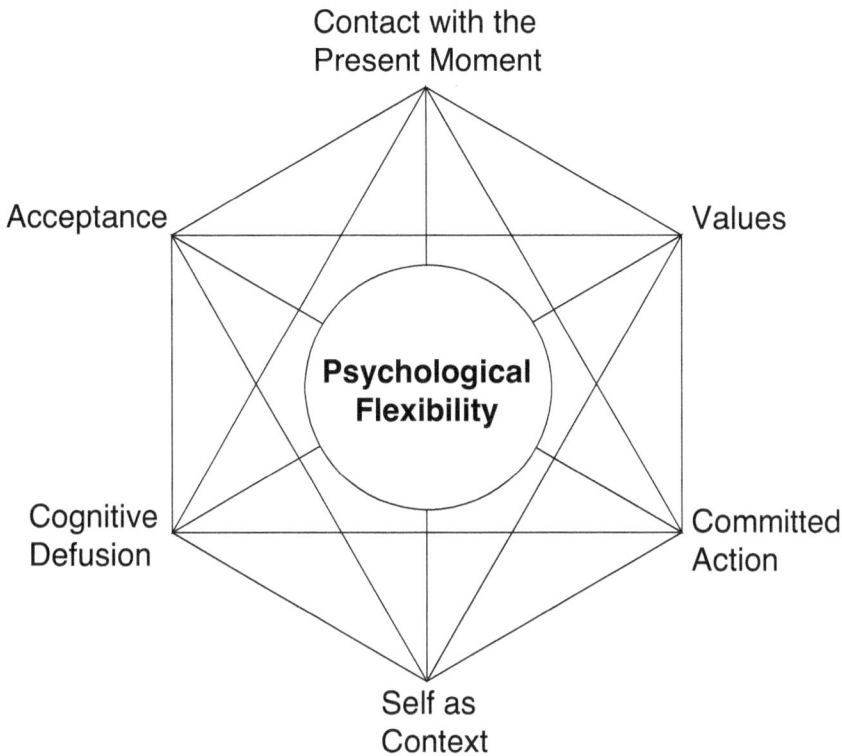

Figure 9.5 The six core processes of psychological flexibility.

premature claims. We merely note that ACT's emphasis on value-consistent living, skills development and the thriving of whole persons are of obvious appeal as others have recognized (e.g. Quayle, Vaughan, & Taylor, 2006). There are six processes in ACT that constitute psychological flexibility (see Figure 9.5). Below we have suggested how each core process might be applied in practice to individuals with paraphilic disorders and histories of sexual offending.

Contact with the present-moment refers to shifting attention to the here-and-now, being aware of the present-moment both internally and externally – a position of awareness that is routinely lost within our normal, yet nonstop temporal relational framing. Sexual recidivism is associated with increased levels of characteristics opposite to this skill, particularly grievingly ruminating over alleged wrongs (Mann, Hanson, & Thornton, 2010). In ACT, present-moment awareness is trained using mindfulness practice or experiential exercises which reinforce connection with the present and bodily control, such as pushing one's feet into the floor, movement and noticing what in one's visual space (see Harris, 2009).

Acceptance refers to the skill of opening up to all private events evoked in the present-moment without needless attempts to avoid them. Avoidance of what painful internal experiences are arbitrarily contacted is a normal, yet destructive process (Hayes et al., 1996). Indeed, animals can avoid external threats, as can humans; but how can humans avoid threats accessible at any time with lightning speed through the vehicle of their own language? The rebound effect of suppressing exciting and sexually arousal thoughts has been shown (Wegner, Shortt, Blake, & Page, 1990; Winters, Christoff, & Gorzalka, 2009), and the use of sex to avoid unwanted feelings is a familiar characteristic of people who have sexually offended. Acceptance is not a passive giving into 'how things are', but an active willingness to experience events as they are, in the service of moving in ways that are consistent with one's values. Therefore, acceptance is not synonymous with condoning (accepting) thoughts towards sexual abuse.

Acceptance is intended to be judgment free, meaning internal experiences are taught to be accepted as they are rather than categorized as 'positive' or 'negative'. This allows individuals to respond functionally in the presence of any internal experiences whether that be gratifying or threatening. This has obvious use in clinical practice with paraphilic disorders and offending, where antecedents can be a complex mix of emotions. Acceptance training can be achieved via an exposure process (Salande & Hawkins, 2017) and when applied to paraphilic thoughts (and also associated shame), may open up the way for people to respond differently in their presence, particularly where clients mindfully explore and make room for them. A component of helping clients to accept is to compassionately draw their attention to the struggles associated with their avoidance agenda. This is in the service of recognizing that trying to eliminate painful thoughts and feelings is futile and in itself a barrier to wellbeing (Hayes et al., 2012). Simple questions to achieve this include asking the client what methods they have tried to deal with the problem, if these improved or aggravated the problem, and the costs associated with these efforts (Harris, 2009). The intended outcome is for clients to begin to consider that acceptance, rather than avoidance, could be an alternative means to respond to the problem.

Cognitive defusion is the skill of being able to experience thoughts '*as thoughts*' rather than as their literal referents. The skill aims to change the context of language in order to change its automatic functions. There are many methods that enable cognitive defusion (see Harris, 2009), but it is regularly achieved by noticing an internal experience: '*I notice I'm having the thought that...*' Another technique is the 'milk, milk, milk' exercise explained by Hayes (2004). First, the response evoked by the frame of coordination (the word 'milk' ↔ 'actual milk') is explored, for example, 'actual milk' is creamy, white and frothy, and readers, by thinking of 'milk', may now be salivating, while others if opposed to consuming milk or disliking of its taste may be repulsed (*all of which is the result of cognitive fusion*.) The word 'milk' is then rapidly spoken without stopping, and in-the-moment loses its function (i.e. meaning) becoming a mere non-specific sound, like 'hàizi' was before. Words central to the clinical problem are then used and in the case of paraphilia, this could be an antecedent to arousal or a shaming word. For example, in her clinic the second author has used this technique with a client for who the word 'baby' had strong stimulus control over arousal. After frequent rapid repetition he reported the word losing its 'power'. The experiential point is that thoughts do not mean what they say they mean, and while in the case of paraphilic thoughts it is unhealthy to respond to their literal referents, it seems possible to experience thoughts as a non-permanent process if the normal context in which they occur (cognitive fusion) is changed.

Self-as-context is the ability to adopt the awareness part of self that notices. Unlike thoughts and feelings which constantly change, the noticing part of the mind naturally feels unchanged. The opposite of self-as-context is 'self-as-content'. Self-as-content covers all the beliefs, ideas, images and memories that make ones' self-story. Fusing with this story leads to inflexibility, and a sense that '*I am my thoughts and history*'. Critically then, this skill encourages people to gather their sense of self from their awareness of thoughts and feelings, not thoughts and feelings themselves – '*my thoughts change, but "I" who notices them does not*'. We suggest that this skill is important for those who sexually offend because a failure to notice internal and external experiences will result in a failure to notice antecedents to offending. Furthermore, fusing with a self-story, particularly a paraphilic self-story, may present a barrier to desistance from offending. Indeed, that desistance from crime requires a shift in self-identity is a well-documented finding. Training self-as-context requires helping an individual to notice both their internal and external experiences. This can be achieved through mindfulness practice. In ACT this is also achieved through use of metaphor (see Harris, 2009).

Values are the guiding principles for what we want to stand for in life. A value is not achieved. It is always ongoing because it is a way of being (e.g. caring, health, fun, honesty etc.) An understanding of ones values is central to the success of ACT, as they provide the motivator for the commitment required to open up to the challenging experiences that come with developing psychological flexibility. Therapeutic exercises should go beyond the generation of goals and encourage clients to explore the values that underpin them. For some, values will be an unfamiliar and a threatening concept, so coaching will be necessary.

Committed action is the skill of taking effective action in the service of values. Decisions about acting on internal experiences are down to the workability of the action in relation to values; that is, '*does an action take me away from or towards my values?'* Cognitive fusion and experiential avoidance can create a tendency for unworkable action, such as using substances to cope and socially withdrawing. Offending will also be unworkable as it likely constitutes a move away from valued-based living. Even where people hold values that seem achievable through offending, there will likely be others such as agency or caring that would be breached by it. Emphasis is kept on the act of living according to flexible habits that embody chosen values, otherwise equating goal-attainment with aspirations like 'happiness', simply creates a context in which what is important is always missing and in pursuit.

CFT

The aim of CFT is to ensure that there is equilibrium between the functions of emotions with particular focus on activating the soothing and affiliation system (see Figure 9.3 above) through the training of soothing skills and cultivation of compassion in a safe, nurturing environment (known as Compassionate Mind Training; CMT Gilbert, 2010). The most well-known definition of compassion is that of the Dalai Lama, which is: *'a sensitivity to the suffering of self and others, with a deep commitment to try to relieve it'* (Gilbert, 2010, p. 3). Capacities for acting in compassionate or damaging ways are related to evolved phenotypes; that is, characteristics emerging in response to interaction between genetic predispositions and environmental pressures (Belsky & Pluess, 2009). Typically, phenotypic adaptation will emerge to fit social niches in responsive ways.

For example, in an inconsistent, unsafe social niche, such as that where child abuse is occurring, a child may distance themselves from adults. The reduction in likelihood of abuse reinforces the distancing, adaptively so in that distress is reduced. Long term continuation of this strategy however may inhibit development of secure intimacy patterns – a characteristic associated with sexual recidivism (Mann et al., 2010). Therefore, conceptualized using CFT, certain characteristics associated with offending can be understood as natural phenotypes, originally emerging as self-protecting strategies in exploitative environments. Framed this way, individuals are enabled to re-story their history and their response to it as adaptive (i.e. normal, understandable), thereby facilitating a basis for a compassionate self-view. In the example above the individual would recognize their distrust of others and difficulties with intimate relationships as stemming from the safety strategy of avoidance of childhood abuse. This has obvious benefits for those who commit sexual offences – a group for which elevated levels of childhood adversity and shame are increasingly documented (e.g. Levenson & Grady, 2016; Levenson, Willis, & Prescott, 2016; Proeve, & Howells, 2006).

Self-soothing skills

Within CFT, addressing physiology is crucial to enable the mind to respond functionally. This can occur by developing skills that activate the parasympathetic nervous system (PNS) which counteracts the autonomic threat system through promoting physiological states associated with safeness and calm, for example by reducing heart rate. Mindfulness is one such skill able to activate the PNS, but CFT also uses a soothing breathing rhythm and safe place imagery (see Gilbert, 2010). With soothing breathing rhythm, individuals slow their breathing until they reach approximately five to six breaths per minute. The safe place technique on the other hand asks individuals to create an imagined place where they feel safe and calm.

Compassion for self and others

Compassion is a motive to guide behaviour, not an emotion in itself, and it can be attained by training in skills that facilitate it. There are three flows of compassion; that directed to the self, and those from and towards others. Before compassionate skills can be taught, blocks to compassion should be clarified and addressed. For some, compassion is misunderstood and has associations of vulnerability. A fear of compassion may be an adaptive response for those who have experienced mistreatment from people who are supposed to protect them, and compassion or its derivations, including kindness, may trigger the threat system. Therefore, addressing blocks to compassion benefits the therapeutic relationship by enabling individuals to accept care from the therapist. Adopting a warm voice tone, friendly facial expression and open body posture are all acts of compassion by the therapist. Compassion towards the self can be shaped by using self-talk, such as 'It's understandable I feel this way because ...' as well as writing oneself a compassionate letter. Compassion for others is trained by practicing kindness or directing compassionate feelings toward others through imagery exercises. Receiving compassion can be trained by recalling memories of receiving compassion and developing an image of someone or something which is compassionate.

In summary, there is considerable overlap between the therapeutic techniques used by ACT and CFT and it is increasingly recognized that used together, these approaches could improve outcomes (e.g. Tirch, Schoendorff, & Silberstein, 2014). As transdiagnostic approaches, both therapies are designed to ameliorate ubiquitous forms of human suffering, and we propose that the emphasis they place on building compassion and psychological flexibility, mean they are worthwhile interventions to integrate experimentally into therapy for paraphilic disorder and sexual offending.

A brief summary of ACT and CFT outcomes in mental health

There is an extensive body of high quality outcome evidence for ACT (https://contextualscience.org/ACT_Randomized_Controlled_Trials). Meta-analytic reviews offer qualified support for the efficacy of ACT compared to a no intervention control (A-Tjak et al., 2015; Hacker, Stone, & MacBeth, 2015). Outcome data with regards to ACT in comparison to active controls is more equivocal, in that it has been found to perform equivalently to traditional CBT methods, but does not outperform them (e.g. Lee, An, Levin, & Twohig, 2015; A-Tjak et al., 2015; Hacker et al., 2015). Owing to this extant evidence, ACT is listed on the American Psychological Association (APA) Division 12 website as having strong support for chronic pain and modest support for depression, mixed anxiety and obsessive compulsive disorder (www.div12.org/?s=Accept ance+and+Commitment++Therapy). Set apart from this, Öst (2014) has suggested that the efficacy of ACT has been overestimated by the APA. However, this is not without controversy (Atkins et al., 2017; Öst, 2017). CFT is newer than ACT and the outcome evidence are less extensive and rigorous. There is insufficient evidence to show that CFT outperforms traditional interventions, and more randomized controlled trials (RCTs) are required before CFT can be considered evidence-based practice (see Leaviss & Uttley, 2015 for a review).

The application of ACT and CFT with forensic populations is gaining momentum, with several authors having staked out the territory (Amrod & Hayes, 2014; Gilbert, 2017; Kolts & Gilbert, 2018). However, despite authors advocating a therapeutic approach that focuses on acceptance rather than change (e.g. Quayle et al., 2006) such approaches are absent in the sexual offending programme literature. There are no applications of CFT and those using ACT for paraphilic disorders amount to little more than historic, single-case studies (e.g. LoPiccolo, 1994). ACT has been applied to related problems, for example problematic internet pornography use (see Crosby & Twohig, 2016). This RCT suffers from methodological limitations including an over reliance on self-reporting, although at present it offers a rare insight into how ACT may perform in this area.

Compassion and acceptance integrated into contemporary rehabilitation practice

In this final section we examine four reasons for why ACT and CFT appear highly compatible with prevailing rehabilitation efforts. Firstly, contingency and relational learning afford little scope to suggest people have a choice in what they find erotic. Furthermore, there is converging evidence of a prenatal vulnerability for age-specific interests (see Fazio, 2018) and early onset and life-course stability are well-surveyed reports in samples of people with paraphilia (e.g. Bailey, Hsu, & Bernhard, 2016; Grundmann, Krupp, Scherner, Amelung, & Beier, 2016). While not choosing their sexual interests, individuals are however responsible for how they express them. This suggests psychotherapy must support individuals to change their functional relationship with their paraphilic thoughts, such that they do not bear down so heavily on life impeding the safety and prosperity of self and others. This goal is consistent with ACT's core objective – psychological flexibility, and CFT's CMT.

Secondly, people who find themselves saddled with paraphilic interests expect social rejection (Blagden, Mann, Webster, Lee, & Williams, 2017; Jahnke, Schmidt, Geradt, & Hoyer, 2015; Walton & Duff, 2017), to the extent that paraphilia are profoundly stigmatized (see Jahnke, 2018). Those with paraphilic interests and/or who sexually offend, can expect little acceptance once their interests and actions are known, and researchers have begun to turn their attention to the deleterious effects of this on characteristics associated with recidivism (Jahnke, 2018; Jahnke & Hoyer, 2013; Jahnke et al., 2015). Self-attacking thoughts, shame and internal avoidance of these painful experiences are of obvious clinical applicability, and in turn it would seem to us that a cornerstone of therapy, if individuals are to prosper safely with improved conditions, is to empower them with skills to construct acceptable identities. This task can be abundantly supported with the compassion and acceptance techniques described above.

The GLM is a well-popularized model for programmes (McGrath et al., 2010). The philosophy of the GLM is consistent with the third wave and as such, the third reason is that ACT and CFT provide a therapeutic modality that is aligned with current directions. In particular, the GLM adopts a humanistic view of individuals who offend, conceptualizing offending as an unhelpful means of attaining basic human needs. This connects with the evolutionary functional analysis central to CFT, particularly the de-pathologizing view that normal brains are tricky, lest we recognize harmful acts as something unfamiliar to ordinary human potential. The GLM also emphasizes the importance of expansion over elimination; that is, the importance of developing capabilities rather than an exclusive focus on risk reduction. This is consistent with ACT, particularly in how the goal of psychological flexibility centers on expanding capabilities for action that is guided by values in order that individuals can better respond to challenges in life.

Fourth and finally, there is a growing consensus that rehabilitative interventions should strengthen an individual's biological, psychological and social resources for crime-free living (Carter & Mann, 2016; Walton et al., 2017). This view supports a call for trauma-informed approaches to rehabilitation (e.g. Williams & Carter, 2018). Such approaches acknowledge and respond accordingly to the individual's traumatic experiences and the impact of this on their neurodevelopment and functioning. Psychological flexibility and CMT, are both viable in this regard, on the whole because their intent is to shape an individual's resources for responding functionally in the presence of unwanted feelings and thoughts, with a range of soothing, meditative and grounding techniques.

Conclusion

Third wave techniques may enhance current methods available to assist individuals in gaining capacities for healthier living. Their use does not require a rejection of the popularized practice of working on characteristics associated with sexual offending. In the interests of reducing the harm caused to the individual and to society as a result of offending, there is a necessary burden on practitioners to test out new approaches, and to evaluate these rigorously. We suggest the emergent empirical basis for CMT and acceptance techniques in healthcare is sufficient to increase trialling and testing them in forensic rehabilitation. Third wave theory including EFA, CBS and RFT enhance our understanding of the evolutionary and contextual nature of all human behaviour and by extrapolation, paraphilic arousal and sexual offending. CFT and ACT celebrate a person's existing workable strategies and build skills for flexibility and change – for greater agency and compassion and as such offer a non-aversive intervention; one which is ethically grounded and of likely to appeal to the individual.

Note

1. There are a number of different emotional systems and CFT focuses on a three system model. The model is simplified. For example, although oxytocin promotes pair-bonding, affiliation and calming effects, it does not indiscriminately support caring behavior. As a direct consequence of its role in promoting social attachment, oxytocin can promote preferential action toward specific individuals, such as one's children or partner (Donaldson & Young, 2008). These effects are also extended to more distantly perceived in-group members, but not those perceived as 'out-group' members (e.g. De Dreu, Greer, van Kleef, Shalvi & Handgraaf, 2011). Therefore, the effects are contextually specific.

References

American Psychiatric Association (APA). (1980). *Diagnostic and statistical manual of mental disorders* (3rd ed.). Washington, DC: American Psychiatric Association.
American Psychiatric Association (APA). (2013). *Diagnostic and statistical manual of mental disorders* (5th ed.). Arlington, VA: American Psychiatric Publishing.

Amrod, J., & Hayes, S. C. (2014). ACT for the incarcerated. In R. Tafrate & D. Mitchell (Eds.), *Forensic CBT. A handbook for clinical practice* (pp. 43–65). New York: Wiley-Blackwell.

A-Tjak, J. G. L., Davis, M. L., Morina, N., Powers, M. B., Smits, J. A. J., & Emmelkamp, P. M. G. (2015). A meta-analysis of the efficacy of Acceptance and Commitment Therapy for clinically relevant mental and physical health problems. *Psychotherapy and Psychosomatics, 84*, 30–36.

Atkins, P. W. B., Ciarrochi, J., Gaudiano, B. A., Bricker, J. B., Donald, J., Rovner, G., et al. (2017). Departing from the essential features of a high quality systematic review of psychotherapy: A response to Ost (2014) and recommendations for improvement. *Behaviour Research and Therapy* (in press).

Bailey, J. M., Hsu, K. J., & Bernhard, P. A. (2016). An Internet study of men sexually attracted to children: Sexual attraction patterns. *Journal of Abnormal Psychology, 125*, 976–988.

Barbaree, H. E., & Seto, M. C. (1997). Pedophilia: Assessment and treatment. In D. R. Laws, & W. T. O'Donohue (Eds.), *Sexual deviance: Theory, assesssment, and treatment* (pp. 175–193). New York: Guilford Press.

Barnett, G. B., & Fitzalan-Howard, F. (2018). What doesn't work to reduce reoffending? *European Psychologist, 23*, 111–129.

Beck, A. T. (1976). *Cognitive therapy and the emotional disorders*. New York: International Universities Press.

Belsky, J., & Pluess, M. (2009). Beyond diathesis-stress: Differential susceptibility to environmental influences. *Psychological Bulletin, 135*, 885–908.

Blagden, N. J., Mann, R., Webster, S., Lee, R., & Williams, F. (2017) '*It's not something i chose you know*': Making sense of pedophiles' sexual interest in children and the impact on their psychosexual identity. *Sexual Abuse: A Journal of Research and Treatment*, 1–27.

Briken, P., Fedoroff, J. P., & Bradford, J. W. (2014). Why can't pedophilic disorder remit? *Archives of Sexual Behavior, 43*, 1237–1239.

Camilleri, J. A., & Quinsey, V. L. (2008). Pedophilia: Assessment and treatment. In D. R. Laws & W. T. O'Donohue (Eds.), *Sexual deviance: Theory, assessment and treatment, section edition* (pp. 183–212). New York: Guilford.

Carter, A., & Mann, R. E. (2016). Organizing principles for an integrated model of change for the treatment of sexual offending. In D. P. Boer (Ed.), *The Wiley handbook on the theories, assessment, and treatment of sexual offending* (pp. 359–382). Oxford: Wiley-Blackwell.

Crosby, J., & Twohig, M. P. (2016). Acceptance and commitment therapy for problematic internet pornography use: A randomized trial. *Behavior Therapy, 47*, 355–366.

De Dreu, C. K. W., Greer, L. L., Van Kleef, G. A., Shalvi, S., & Handgraaf, M. J. J. (2011). Oxytocin promotes human ethnocentrism. *Proceedings of the National Academy of Sciences of the USA, 108*, 1262–1266.

Dennis, J. A., Khan, O., Ferriter, M., Huband, N., Powney, M. J., & Duggan, C. (2012). Psychological interventions for adults who have sexually offended or are at risk of offending. (CD007507; Cochrane Database of Systematic Reviews Issue 12). Chichester: John Wiley & Sons.

Donaldson, Z. R., & Young, L. J. (2008). Oxytocin, vasopressin, and the neurogenetics of sociality. *Science, 7322*(5903), 900–904.

Dugdale, N. A., & Lowe, C. F. (2000). Testing for symmetry in the conditional discriminations of language-trained chimpanzees. *Journal of the Experimental Analysis of Behavior, 73*, 5–22.

Dymond, S., & Roche, B. (Eds.). (2013). *Advances in relational frame theory: Research and application*. Oakland, CA: New Harbinge.

Fazio, R. L. (2018). Toward a neurodevelopmental understanding of pedophilia. *Journal of Sexual Medicine, 15*, 1205–1207.

Fernandez, Y. M., Shingler, J., & Marshall, L. M. (2006). Putting 'behavior' back into cognitive-behavioral treatment with sexual offenders. In W. L. Marshall, Y. M. Fernsandez, L. E. Marshall, & G. A. Serran (Eds.), *Sexual offender treatment: Controversial issues* (pp. 211–224). Chichester: John Wiley & Sons.

Finkelhor, D. (1984). *Child sexual abuse: New theory and research.* New York: The Free Press.

Gilbert, P. (2010). *Compassion focused therapy: Distinctive features.* London: Routledge.

Gilbert, P. (2017). Exploring compassion focused therapy in forensic settings: An evolutionary and social-contextual approach. In J. Davies & C. Nagi (Eds.), *Individual psychological therapies in forensic settings.* London: Routledge.

Grundmann, D., Krupp, J., Scherner, G., Amelung, T., & Beier, K. M. (2016). Stability of self-reported arousal to sexual fantasies involving children in a clinical sample of pedophiles and hebephiles. *Archives of Sexual Behavior, 45,* 1153–1162.

Harris, R. (2009). *ACT made simple: An easy-to-read primer on acceptance and commitment therapy.* Oakland, CA: New Harbinger Publications.

Hayes, S. C. (2004). Acceptance and commitment therapy, relational frame theory, and the third wave of behavioral and cognitive therapies. *Behavior Therapy, 35,* 639–665.

Hayes, S. C., & Hofmann, S. G. (2017). The third wave of cognitive behavioral therapy and the rise of process-based care. *World Psychiatry, 16,* 245–246.

Hayes, S. C., & Hofmann, S. G. (2018). *Process-based CBT: The science and core clinical competencies of cognitive behavioral therapy.* Oakland, CA: New Harbinger.

Hayes, S. C., Luoma, J., Bond, F., Masuda, A., & Lillis, J. (2006). Acceptance and commitment therapy: Model, processes, and outcomes. *Behaviour Research and Therapy, 44,* 1–25.

Hayes, S. C., & Sanford, B. (2014). Cooperation came first: Evolution and human cognition. *Journal of the Experimental Analysis of Behavior, 101,* 112–129.

Hayes, S. C., Stroshl, K. D., & Wilson, K. G. (2012). *Acceptance and commitment therapy: The process and practice of mindful change* (2nd ed.). New York: Guilford.

Hayes, S. C., Wilson, K. G., Gifford, E. V., Follette, V. M., & Strosahl, K. (1996). Emotional avoidance and behavioral disorders: A functional dimensional approach to diagnosis and treatment. *Journal of Consulting and Clinical Psychology, 64,* 1152–1168.

Hayes, S. C., Barnes-Holmes, D., & Roche, B. (Eds.). (2001). *Relational Frame Theory: A Post-Skinnerian account of human language and cognition.* New York: Plenum Press.

Hacker, T., Stone, P., & MacBeth, A. (2015). Acceptance and commitment therapy-Do we know enough? Cumulative and sequential meta-analyses of randomized controlled trials. *Journal of Affect Dosorder, 190,* 551–565.

Hofmann, S. G., & Asmundson, G. J. (2008). Acceptance and mindfulness-based therapy: New wave or old hat? *Clinical Psychology Review, 28,* 1–16.

Jahnke, S. (2018). The stigma of pedophilia clinical and forensic implications. *European Psychologist, 23,* 144–153.

Jahnke, S., & Hoyer, J. (2013). Stigmatization of people with pedophilia: A blind spot in stigma research. *International Journal of Sexual Health, 25,* 169–184.

Jahnke, S., Schmidt, A. F., Geradt, M., & Hoyer, J. (2015). Stigma related stress and its correlates among men with pedophilic sexual interests. *Archives of Sexual Behavior, 44,* 2173–2187.

Kolts, R., & Gilbert, P. (2018). Understanding and using compassion focused therapy in forensic settings. In A. Beech, A. J. Carter, R. E. Mann, & P. Rotshtein (Eds.), *Handbook of forensic neuroscience* (pp. 725–754). Chichester: Wiley-Blackwell.

Leaviss, J., & Uttley, L. (2015). Psychotherapeutic benefits of compassion-focused therapy: An early systematic review. *Psychological Medication, 45,* 927–945.

Lee, E. B., An, W., Levin, M. E., & Twohig, M. P. (2015). An initial meta-analysis of Acceptance and Commitment Therapy for treating substance use disorders. *Drug and Alcohol Dependence, 155,* 1–7.

Levenson, J. S., & Grady, M. D. (2016). The influence of childhood trauma on sexual violence and sexual deviance in adulthood. *Traumatology, 22*, 94–103.

Levenson, J. S., Willis, G. M., & Prescott, D. S. (2016). Adverse childhood experiences in the lives of male sex offenders: Implications for trauma-informed care. *Sexual Abuse: A Journal of Research and Treatment, 28*, 340–359.

Levin, M. E., Twohig, M. P., & Smith, B. M. (2016). Contextual behavioral science: An overview. In R. Zettle, S. C. Hayes, D. Barnes-Holmes, & A. Biglan (Eds.), *Handbook of contextual behavioral science* (pp. 17–36). Chichester: John Wiley & Sons.

LoPiccolo, J. (1994). Acceptance and change: Content and context in psychotherapy. In S. C. Hayes, N. S. Jacobson, V. M. Follete, & M. J. Dougher (Eds.), *Acceptance and change: Content and context in psychotherapy* (pp. 149–170). Reno, NV: Context Press.

Mann, R. E., Hanson, R. K., & Thornton, D. (2010). Assessing risk for sexual recidivism: Some proposals on the nature of psychologically meaningful risk factors. Sexual Abuse. *A Journal of Research and Treatment, 22*, 191–217.

Mann, R. E., & Shingler, J. (2006). Schema-driven cognition in sexual offenders: Theory, assessment and treatment. In W. L. Marshall, Y. M. Fernandez, L. E. Marshall, & G. A. Serran (Eds.), *Sexual offender treatment: Controversial issues* (pp. 173–185). Chichester: Wiley.

Marques, J. K., Wiederanders, M., Day, D. M., Nelson, C., & Van Ommeren, A. (2005). Effects of a relapse prevention program on sexual recidivism: Final results from California's sex offender treatment and evaluation project (SOTEP). *Sexual Abuse: A Journal of Research and Treatment, 17*, 79–107.

Marshall, W. L., O'Brien, M. D., & Marshall, L. E. (2009). Modifying sexual preferences. In A. Beech, L. Craig, & K. Browne (Eds.), *Assessment and treatment of sexual offenders: A handbook* (pp. 311–327). Chichester: John Wiley & Sons.

Maruna, S., & Mann, R. E. (2006). A fundamental attribution error? Rethinking cognitive distortions. *Legal and Criminological Psychology, 11*, 155–177.

McGrath, R., Cumming, G., Burchard, B., Zeoli, S., & Ellerby, L. (2010). *Current practices and emerging trends in sexual abuser management: The Safer Society 2009 North American Survey.* Brandon, VT: Safer Society Press.

McGuire, R. J., Carlisle, J. M., & Young, B. G. (1965). Sexual deviation as conditional behaviour: A hypothesis. *Behaviour Research and Therapy, 2*, 185–190.

Öst, L.-G. (2014). The efficacy of Acceptance and Commitment Therapy: An updated systematic review and meta-analysis. *Behaviour Research and Therapy, 61*, 105–121.

Öst, L.-G. (2017). Rebuttal of Atkins et al. (2017) critique of the Ost (2014) meta-analysis of ACT. *Behaviour Research and Therapy, 97*, 273–281.

Pepper, S. C. (1942). *World hypotheses: A study in evidence.* Berkeley, CA: University of California Press.

Pithers, W. D., Marques, J. K., Gibat, C. C., & Marlatt, G. A. (1983). Relapse prevention with sexual aggressives: A self-control model of treatment and maintenance change. In J. G. Greer & I. R. Stuart (Eds.), *The sexual aggressor: Current perspectives on treatment* (pp. 214–239). New York: Van Nostrand Reinhold.

Proeve, M., & Howells, K. (2006). Shame and guilt in child molesters. In W. Marshall, Y. Fernandez, L. Marshall, & G. Serran (Eds.), *Sexual offender treatment* (pp. 125–139). New Jersey: John Wiley & Sons.

Quayle, E., Vaughan, M., & Taylor, M. (2006). Sex offenders, Internet child abuse images and emotional avoidance: The importance of values. *Aggression and Violent Behavior, 11*, 111.

Roche, B., & Quayle, E. (2007). Sexual disorders. In J. Wood & J. Kanter (Eds.), *Understanding behavior disorders: A contemporary behavioral perspective* (pp. 341–368). Reno, NV: Context Press.

Salande, J. D., & Hawkins, R. C. I. I. (2017). Psychological flexibility, attachment style, and personality organization: Correlations between constructs of differing approaches. *Journal of Psychotherapy Integration, 27*(3), 365–380.

Salter, A. C. (1988). *Treating child sex offenders and victims.* Newbury Park, CA: Sage.

Schmucker, M., & Lösel, F. (2017), Sexual offender treatment for reducing recidivism among convicted sex offenders: A systematic review and meta-analysis. Campbell Systematic Reviews, No. 8.

Tirch, D., Schoendorff, B., & Silberstein, L. R. (2014). *The ACT practitioner's guide to the science of compassion: Tools for fostering psychological flexibility.* Oakland, CA: New Harbinger.

Walton, J. S. (2018). Random assignment in sexual offending programme evaluation: The missing method. *Journal of Forensic Practice, 20,* 1–9.

Walton, J. S., & Duff, S. (2017). I'm not homosexual or heterosexual, I'm paedosexual: Exploring sexual preference for children using interpretive phenomenology. *Journal of Forensic Practice, 19,* 151–161.

Walton, J. S., Ramsay, L., Cunningham, C., & Henfrey, S. (2017). New directions: Integrating a biopsychosocial approach in the design and delivery of programs for high risk services users in Her Majesty's Prison and Probation Service. *Advancing Corrections: Journal of the International Corrections and Prison Association, 3,* 21–47.

Ward, T. and Stewart, C.A. (2003) The treatment of sex offenders risk management and good lives. *Professional Psychology Research and Practice, 34,* 353–360.

Ward, T., & Laws, D. R. (2010). Desistance from sex offending: Motivating change, enriching practice. *International Journal of Forensic Mental Health, 9,* 11–23.

Wegner, D.M., Shortt,J.W., Blake,A.W., & Page, M.S. (1990). The suppression of exciting thoughts. *Journal of Personality and Social Psychology, 58,* 409–418.

Williams, F., & Carter, A. J. (2018). Engaging with offenders: A biologically informed approach. In A. Beech, A. J. Carter, R. E. Mann, & P. Rotshtein (Eds.), *Handbook of forensic neuroscience* (pp. 577–599). Chichester: Wiley-Blackwell.

Winters, J., Christoff, K., & Gorzalka, B. B. (2009). Conscious regulation of sexual arousal in men. *Journal of Sex Research, 46,* 330–343.

A psychoanalytic approach to paraphilic disorders, perversions and other problematic sexual behaviours

10

Jessica Yakeley

Introduction

Since Freud's seminal work *Three Essays on the Theory of Sexuality* (Freud, 1905), in which he explored the nature and infantile roots of what he termed 'perversion', psychoanalytic writers have written extensively about unusual sexual fantasies, and practices that have been characterized as perverse. However, significant societal and cultural changes over the past decades, particularly within the Western world, have resulted in a growing acceptance of sexual orientations and behaviours that would previously have been classified as deviant. The term perversion is now often viewed as pejorative and stigmatizing of people whose sexual preferences do not conform to the traditional norm.

In this chapter I will argue that the psychoanalytic concept of perversion and related ideas may still be useful in understanding the origins and meanings of sexual fantasies, arousal patterns and behaviours that cause distress or actual bodily harm to the individual concerned and/or to other people that he or she[1] is involved with. I will review historical and contemporary psychoanalytic theories regarding the aetiology, nature and function of problematic sexual fantasies and behaviours, some of which are now classified as paraphilic disorders, focussing on their unconscious meaning and function within the person's interpersonal relationships. The sexual act may be understood as a perverse defence against primitive anxieties within intimate relationships, which may stem from disturbed attachment experiences in infancy as well as adolescence, in which the child's body has been abused or used for perverse purposes. Exploring the impact of such adverse experiences on the person's psychosexual development and relationship with their own body informs the understanding of the disturbed ways in which the person relates to others, which includes in some cases using their own and others' bodies for perverse pleasure. Such ideas inform a psychoanalytic approach to the assessment, management and treatment of paraphilic disorders and other problematic sexual fantasies and behaviours, particularly in consideration of how they emerge, in overt or subtle ways, within the transference and countertransference dynamics of the therapeutic relationship. These psychoanalytic theories and their clinical applications are embedded within the discipline of forensic psychotherapy, which has gained increasing prominence over the past few decades within forensic mental health.

Forensic psychotherapy

Forensic psychotherapy has been described as the offspring of forensic psychiatry and psychoanalysis (Welldon, 2011), a child whose parents may not always agree, but one who benefits from hybrid vigour. Although psychoanalysis has traditionally been thought to be contraindicated as a treatment for those who have engaged in offending behaviours, a few early notable psychoanalysts in both the United States and the United Kingdom such as Karl Menninger and Edward Glover respectively were interested in pushing the boundaries of classical psychoanalysis by treating violent and delinquent patients. The Portman Clinic in London was founded in 1931 as an outpatient clinic treating violent, antisocial, delinquent and perverse patients with psychoanalytic psychotherapy and had on its staff notable psychoanalysts such as Edward Glover, John Bowlby, and Wilfred Bion. Meanwhile other British psychoanalysts such as Murray Cox (Cordess & Cox, 1996) and Arthur Hyatt-Williams (1998) chose to treat the most disturbed violent patients and inmates held within high secure psychiatric institutions and prisons, often working in relative isolation and without the understanding or support of their colleagues. These pioneering psychoanalysts laid the foundations for the new discipline of forensic psychotherapy, a field that has expanded over the last 40 years to include clinicians from many different core professional backgrounds such as psychiatry, psychology, social work, nursing and probation and who offer psychoanalytically informed management and treatment to patients and individuals who offend in health and criminal justice settings in different countries.

Forensic psychotherapy can be broadly defined as the use of psychoanalytic expertise to understanding the dynamic relationship between people who offend and society, and more specifically as the application of such expertise to the management and treatment of those who have committed offences and are diagnosed with mental disorder. Although only a minority of antisocial individuals or forensic patients will be suitable for psychoanalytic psychotherapy, a psychoanalytic or psychodynamic approach may be useful both in the understanding and conceptualization of antisocial and offending behaviour, as well as assisting in the management of forensic patients by the multidisciplinary team. One of the fundamental principles of forensic psychotherapy is that of psychoanalytic understanding: understanding the reasons why the individual committed his offence; understanding why some individuals relate to others by predominantly violent means; understanding the workings of the antisocial person mind and how it has been shaped by early, often adverse, experiences; understanding the unconscious meaning of person's current antisocial behaviour and how this may represent a repetition of such early experiences; understanding how this behaviour may be the manifestation of a mind in which negative emotions such as anxiety or shame are impossible to tolerate and are expressed instead by violent action towards others; and understanding how such behaviour will evoke powerful emotional responses in those around them, including the professionals involved in the their client's management and care (Yakeley & Adshead, 2013). Moreover, psychoanalytic understanding focuses on unconscious processes and motivations, using the tools of transference and countertransference[2] to gain access to the internal world of the individual who offends, a world of powerful unconscious impulses, affects and fantasies that underlie and determine his behaviour. The ultimate aim of such understanding is to enable him to accept responsibility for his acts and thereby to save him and society from the perpetuation of further crimes (Welldon, 2011).

Paraphilias, paraphilic disorders and perversions – diagnostic controversy and confusion

Individuals who develop paraphilic disorders, however, do not all go on to commit offences, and this highlights one of the problems in attempting to classify sexual orientations, fantasies and behaviours which deviate from the statistical norm. Unusual manifestations of sexuality have been documented since biblical times, and what has been deemed acceptable has varied enormously within different historical periods and different cultures. Thus, paedophilia was considered normal in Ancient Greece, but transvestism and homosexuality were prohibited by the Christian Church since the Old Testament (Gordon, 2008). Sexual deviancy was mostly judged within a religious or moral context until the 19th century with the publication of Krafft Ebbing's *Psychopathia Sexualis* in (1886), which reframed aberrant sexualities as pathological disorders that could be classified and potentially treated. This medicalization of the concept of sexual deviancy was taken up by Freud in his early theory of the developmental origins of sexuality (Freud, 1905) which ushered in the extensive body of work by the psychoanalytic community over the next century on perversion.

Clinical interest in sexual deviancy, however, was not restricted to psychoanalysis, as the wider psychiatric community became more invested in understanding and treating people who suffered or made others suffer from their sexual interests. Classification of such interests as mental disorders, however, proved problematic, as is illustrated by reviewing their iterations within successive versions of the mostly widely used contemporary psychiatric diagnostic classification system, the American Psychiatric Association's *Diagnostic and Statistical Manual of Mental Disorders* (DSM).

In the first version of the DSM (American Psychiatric Association, 1952) such disorders were termed sexual deviations, which at the time included the diagnosis of homosexuality as 'sexual orientation disturbance'. Sexual deviations were assumed to be the result of character pathology and were classified under the wider personality disorder category as 'sociopathic personality disturbance'. However, by DSM-II (American Psychiatric Association, 1968), sexual deviations were separated from personality disorders, and homosexuality was removed from a revision of this diagnostic manual in 1973. By the third edition (American Psychiatric Association, 1980), the term 'paraphilia' replaced that of 'sexual deviation' and was now put under the category of 'psychosexual disorders'. In DSM-IV (American Psychiatric Association, 1994) paraphilias were included in the broader category of 'sexual and gender identity disorders'.

The word 'paraphilia' first appeared in English in 1925 in a translation of Stekel's *Sexual Aberrations* (Stekel, 1930) as a less pejorative word than perversion. The etymology of paraphilia stems from the Ancient Greek – 'para' meaning beside or beyond, and 'philia' meaning 'friendship or love'. However, denoting paraphilias as diagnostic entities rooted in psychopathology provoked objections regarding the medicalization of sexual activities that many considered to be a choice between consenting adults as part of a spectrum encompassing myriad variations in human sexuality where 'normality' is not defined by statistics, culture or temporality.

The latest version of the DSM, DSM-5 (American Psychiatric Association, 2013), partially readdresses these criticisms in seeking to more clearly differentiate between atypical human behaviour that is not pathological, and behaviour that constitutes a mental disorder. In the case of paraphilias a new distinction is made between a paraphilia (atypical sexual interest or behaviour), and a paraphilic disorder (a mental disorder stemming from the atypical behaviour). DSM-5 defines a paraphilia as any intense and persistent sexual interest other than sexual interest in genital stimulation or preparatory fondling with phenotypically normal, physically mature, consenting human partners. To be diagnosed with a paraphilic disorder, the DSM-5 requires that people with these interests, over a period of at least 6 months feel personal distress about their interest, not merely distress resulting from society's disapproval, or have a sexual desire or behavior that involves another person's psychological distress, injury, or death, or a desire for sexual behaviours involving unwilling persons or persons unable to give legal consent.

Nevertheless, problems with the current diagnostic criteria for paraphilic disorders persist. There is confusion regarding their relationship with sexual offending and criminality, in that many people who commit sexual offences have paraphilias and most people with paraphilic disorders do not commit offences (Federoff, 2009). Certain paraphilias, such as paedophilia, are illegal if enacted, but it is not illegal to have fantasies or urges to enact. But many other forms of sexual behaviour that would be classified as paraphilic disorders, such as fetishistic disorder or transvestic disorder, or those involving more bizarre or disturbed behaviours such as coprophilia, are not illegal, though may evoke incredulity or disgust, and cause immense distress and shame to the individual who may be reluctant to seek treatment or find it difficult access help.

From a psychoanalytic perspective, one of the most significant limitations of the taxonomy of paraphilias and paraphilic disorders is its classification on the basis of manifest symptoms and behaviours rather than underlying psychopathological mechanisms or aetiology. The DSM diagnostic classification has been criticized for its poor reliability and validity (Zander, 2008), and patients often fulfil diagnostic criteria for several different paraphilic disorders concurrently. Although eight different paraphilias and their associated disorders are specified in DSM-5, more than 100 unique paraphilias have been described in the literature (Federoff, 2009). Moreover, paraphilic disorders show high rates of co-morbidity with other mental disorders, especially mood and anxiety disorders, alcohol and substance misuse and personality disorders.

These findings give weight to alternative models of paraphilic disorders in which the sexually problematic behaviours are seen as manifestations of a range of other disorders, such as the obsessive-compulsive disorder spectrum, mood disorders, and personality disorders, based on common underlying features such as poor impulse control, emotional dysregulation and difficulties in interpersonal relationships (Grubin, 2008). It therefore seems unlikely that paraphilic disorders are encapsulated illnesses but are in contrast the symptomatic expression of underlying common psychological processes, which in some cases may comprise more longstanding and pervasive personality pathology. One might argue that the original classification of sexual deviancy in DSM-I under the category of personality disorder is more accurate than in its current place within DSM-5. This is compatible with a psychoanalytic perspective of perversion, in which the person's overt sexual fantasies and behaviours are motivated by unconscious psychological mechanisms, and where psychoanalytic concepts of fantasy, conflict and defence are central to the understanding of paraphilias and perverse sexual activities.

Psychoanalytic theories of perversion

Freud (1905) proposed that all of us start out in life perverse and that a person's character is built up from defences against perverse infantile sexual impulses and dispositions that operate in the first few years of life. He described the normal child as 'polymorphously perverse', and it is not until the Oedipal period at around the age of four or five years that the child's sexual drives abate due to the influence of several unconscious factors such as shame and disgust, the development of a sense of guilt, and more mature ego defences such as sublimation and repression. In Freud's early theorizing, he believed adult perversity was the result of infantile sexual impulses that had escaped integration, repression and sublimation due to a combination of biological and developmental factors including child sexual trauma.

Freud started to conceive of perversion as a defence with his theory of fetishism as a defence against castration anxiety (Freud, 1927). He proposed that the young boy, despite correctly observing that his mother does not have a penis, does not want to believe this, as this means he may lose his too. He therefore denies or 'disavows' this fact and maintains a contradictory belief that she still possesses one. Freud proposed that in adult fetishists this belief persists with the fetish item, such as the shoe, being a symbolic substitute for the woman's missing penis, and that fetishistic activity was both a token of triumph over the threat of castration and a protection against it.

Subsequent psychoanalysts extended Freud's theory of perversion as a defence against castration anxiety, to representing a defence against much earlier and more primitive anxieties that the child experiences in the very early relationship with the mother. Here the role of aggression in the aetiology of perversion becomes more prominent. Stoller (1975) defined perversion as 'the erotic form of hatred'. He believed that hostility was the primary, albeit unconscious, motivation in perversions. This hostility and aggression are hidden behind the overt sexualization and represent a fantasy of revengeful triumph over trauma experienced in childhood, particularly in relation to the mother. Such trauma may not be overt abuse but represents the dangerousness of the early attachment to the mother who is narcissistically over-involved with her child and does not allow normal separation and development.

The core complex

Glasser's (1996) notion of the 'core complex' is central to a psychoanalytic understanding of the aetiology of perversion. The core complex is a particular constellation of interrelated feelings, ideas and attitudes, that marks a universal developmental step which deals with a child's anxieties of abandonment and engulfment during early separation and individuation from their mother. The core complex represents a primitive struggle between the wish to be close to the mother, and the fear of being overwhelmed and obliterated by her. Faced with this conflict, the individual either withdraws from the mother, experiencing isolation and feelings of abandonment, or reacts aggressively in fantasy or reality against her in an effort to preserve the self. This aggression, however, cannot be aimed directly at the mother as this would destroy the very person the child is dependent on, so instead propels him to withdraw into a narcissistic state, but which soon becomes suffused with feelings or rejection again. The core complex is to some degree present in all of us, and may be apparent in our adult intimate relationships in transient or mild fears of dependence and rejection, but where there has been an early pathological relationship to the mother, these conflicts become much more intense and persist in an unmodified form in relationships with others in adulthood.

Glasser proposed that people with perversions who have experienced an early relationship with a narcissistic mother, resort to a particular solution in an attempt to escape from the vicious circle of the core complex. This is the sexualization of hostility towards the needed maternal object, that is, the conversion of aggression, which was originally defensive, into sadism. The object – originally the mother – is now made to suffer and its suffering becomes a source of pleasure for the pervert, but at the same time, the relationship with the other person is preserved and no longer needs to be destroyed completely, but can be dominated and controlled. In adult relationships the acting out of perverse fantasies function to keep the other person enthralled in an excited interchange yet kept at a distance to avoid any genuine intimate emotional contact. Such interpersonal dynamics operate within a paradigm of power and control, which may be overtly manifest, as in sadistic sexual practices involving dominance and submission, or more covertly, as in voyeurism or exhibitionism, where aggression towards the other person is hidden behind a carapace of sexual excitement.

Corruption of the superego

These perverse relationships with others in the person's external world may be thought of as reflecting the perverse dynamics of his mind or internal world, in particular in relation to the superego. Freud's (1923) concept of the superego was an internal structure of the mind representing the individual's moral conscience, created by the internalization by the child of parental standards and goals, and acceptance of the fundamental prohibition of incest as the resolution of the Oedipal complex. Failure to achieve these moral standards gives rise to feelings of guilt. For the boy, Freud proposed that the internalization and identification with the authority of the father enables him to sublimate his incestuous longings. However, for some patients with perversions this developmental process may become thwarted and distorted where the father fails to embody the healthy Oedipal authority towards the child, but instead is abusive or corrupt, a stance and way of relating with which the superego then becomes identified (Wood, 2014).

Such a corrupt superego implies a lack of moral conscience, however, other psychoanalysts, such as Glasser (1986) proposed that this represents just one side of a sado-masochistic struggle with a severely harsh and critical superego. Here, the perverse patient experiences the superego's moral prohibitions and ethical restrictions as sadistic and a threat to his autonomy, and its high ideals and standards as impossible to achieve. This causes feelings of guilt, shame, and inadequacy, which are defended against via sexualization, and converted into masochism and secret rebellion, where the patient's self-criticism and submission secretly defies and taunts the superego to punish him again.

Such internal dynamics between the different structures of the patient's mind are inevitably projected and played out within their relationships. For example, one homosexual man sought treatment for his 'addiction' to promiscuity and sadomasochistic practices, in which he was repeatedly unfaithful to his long-term partner, an older man, secretly frequenting sex clubs where he allowed himself to be beaten and whipped by married men. His father had been distant and disapproving, particularly regarding his homosexuality, instilling in the patient a chronic sense of low self-worth and guilt about not being able to be the son that his father wanted. In his adult relationships, one might understand his sexual encounters with other men as attempts to both prove to himself that he was lovable, as he was not to his father, and at the same time a rebellion against the authority and ideals of his father, now located in his long-term older partner, in his clandestine sexual encounters with other men. Being physically abused fulfils his wish for punishment for not living up to his father's ideals, but also represents his secret defiance and triumph over the power of his father, now internalized as a critical, harsh attitude towards himself. Here he assumes the role of the masochist, taking sexual pleasure in pain and punishment in a sadomasochistic encounter where he seduces and controls the other.

Confusion of boundaries

Chasseguet-Smirgel (1985) described the world of perversion as one of perverse 'pseudocreativity', in which the inevitable traumas of discovering differences between individuals and generations are denied. This may be exemplified by the paedophile, who negates generational differences by taking a child as his sexual partner, or the sadomasochist who gains sexual gratification from pain and control rather than experiencing sexual contact as a creative and intimate union between two separate people. The Internet provides an ideal medium in which perverse fantasies can be elaborated and perpetuated in the two-dimensional world of internet pornography, where the viewer has complete control over the objects of his fantasies. Intimacy with a real person who might have their own wishes and demands is completely bypassed.

The confusion of boundaries that occurs in the development of perversion is expanded in Wood's (2014) ideas in linking the patient's perverse desires and practices to a regression to and confusion between the classical Freudian developmental stages and erotogenic zones (Freud, 1905). Thus, in normal development the child progresses through oral, urethral, anal, phallic phases, to eventually achieve full genital function. However, perversions are often centred around activities arising at these earlier stages of psychosexual development, for example sexual excitement about smearing or eating faeces, or being urinated on, reflecting a blurring of the boundaries between oral, urethral and anal development. Preoccupation with bodily products is normal for a young child, and in the context of secure maternal care, cultural norms and the realities of hygiene, the child will learn to distinguish between what is clean and what is dirty, and his pleasure in bodily excretory functions is repressed and replaced by contempt and shame. One might therefore conceptualize such paraphilic fantasies and behaviours as evidence of a fixation at an early stage of psychosexual development, the course of which has been impeded by a lack of containment and facilitation by neglectful parental figures.

Case example

The following case example illustrates these psychoanalytic theories that propose paraphilic and perverse behaviours to be sexualized defences against castration anxieties, trauma, aggression, and hostility towards a dominant maternal figure, and how in extreme cases, where these defences are breached, murderous rage may emerge, with fatal consequences.

At the age of twenty-three, Mr A received a life sentence for murder. According to the patient's account of his history, although there was no overt history of parental abuse, little affection or emotion was expressed in the family. His mother was overbearing and strict, and his father went along with his wife's decisions regarding the discipline and upbringing of the children. Mr A described himself as a 'bad' child from birth, 'breaking all the boundaries' by shoplifting from the age of five, playing truant from school and becoming involved in increasingly delinquent activities such as stealing cars and breaking into people's houses as a teenager. At the age of eleven Mr A started to engage in sexual activity with his younger sister, during which he would coerce her into what he described as 'putting willies together'. When he was thirteen, Mr A's sexual preoccupation with his sister was replaced with his mother after he saw her naked in the shower. Thereafter, his mind was filled with sexual fantasies about her and he started to steal her underwear and could only achieve orgasm on masturbation while dressed in his mother's bra and panties. At school, Mr A was bullied for a stammer and became a bully himself. From the age of fourteen he started to abuse drugs and alcohol, and by the time he was sixteen he was visiting prostitutes on a regular basis. These prostitutes were older women who reminded him of his mother. Prior to his index offence, Mr A had no convictions for violence, and by his own account did not consider himself to be a violent person.

On the night of the murder, Mr A had visited a prostitute but had failed to ejaculate due to alcohol inebriation. Discovering he had no money for a taxi, he decided to mug a passer-by for their wallet. He accosted a man and led him into a blind alley. Mr A recounted how the man appeared to have thought that Mr A wanted sex and dropped his trousers. Mr A, fearing sexual assault, attacked him with a piece of wood lying on the ground. He fled the scene but returned five minutes later with the conscious decision to 'finish him off so that he could not tell', attacked him again so that the man sustained severe head injuries and died. Post-mortem examination of the body revealed that he had also been attacked by Mr A in his groin.

Although we can only speculate about the psychodynamics of such a complex case, it is clear in Mr A's perverse behaviour as a child and adolescent how sexual and generational differences are erased. His belief that his sister had the same anatomy as himself – they both possess 'willies' – defends against castration anxieties, and his unconscious desire to have his mother as his sexual partner denies the fact that she is of a separate generation and in a couple with his father. We could hypothesize that Mr A's aggression towards his overbearing and controlling mother is sexualized at an early age in his perverse behaviour of cross-dressing in his mother's underwear, which enables him to evade the prison of the core complex. We might also suspect that Mr A's aggression was more overt in his early boundary breaking in his stealing and truancy, which was perhaps an unconscious attempt to gain the attention of his emotionally absent parents. The index offence can be understood as an enactment of his rage towards both his parents – his unobtainable mother and his ineffectual father. His initial violent attack on the man appears to be motivated by self-defence to the fear that he is being sexually assaulted. At the same time, Mr A feels rejected and humiliated by his sexual encounter with the prostitute, evidence that he cannot achieve potency with the maternal object. We can see how Mr A's initial self-defensive aggression is converted or sexualized into sadistic violence when he made a conscious and planned decision to kill the man, involving sexual assault on his genitals. The murder of this man by Mr A may be thought of as a displaced matricide, where his homicidal actions stem from unconscious murderous aggression towards his mother. The killing can also be seen as an identification with the aggressor – the bullied boy becomes the bully, and the murdered man represents a hated image of Mr A as a passive feminized figure who has to be destroyed.

Perversion and paraphilic disorders: a contemporary clinical theory

The work of these psychoanalytic thinkers highlights how the perverse person's sexual fantasies and behaviours do not reflect mature sexuality but are about the use of sexualization to defend against primitive anxieties concerning separation, abandonment and helplessness in relationships, and the aggression and anger that such experiences provoke, but which cannot be acted upon without risk of destroying the relationship on which the child depends. The experience of the early relationship with the mother and other primary caregivers becomes a template upon which adult relationships are unconsciously based: a template in which emotional closeness towards and dependence on another person is experienced as obliterating and impeding individual expression, development and creativity, and in which core complex anxieties predominate.

Although Stoller's (Stoller, 1975) and Glasser's (Glasser, 1986, 1996) theories appear to focus on the putative role of the mother in the development of perversion, this is inevitably an oversimplification of the multifactorial aetiological nature of paraphilic disorders. Nevertheless, their emphasis on the function of perverse fantasies and behaviours as defences against anxiety and aggression within relationships is invaluable in working clinically with such patients. Many have histories of childhood trauma, abuse or rejection by parents or carers who showed excessive aggression or neglect. Such patients may have been prematurely exposed to adult sexuality via experiences of overt childhood sexual abuse or exposed to disturbing pornography in early adolescence. The person may have had an experience of sexual overstimulation while still a child or have learned from abusers or significant adults about a sexualized mode of relating to exert control and defend against vulnerability. Such premature sexualization interferes with the young person's normal sexual developmental trajectory, and sexual impulses may become confused with aggressive impulses arising from prior experiences of maltreatment or neglect.

Paraphilic behaviours and fantasies which present in adulthood may be thought of as symptoms of a struggle with destructiveness and cruelty that the individual experienced in childhood that has been pivotal in character formation and in influencing their relationships with others. Paraphilic fantasies, which often start in adolescence and are utilized as an escape from painful feelings and traumatic experiences, may progress to being enacted in paraphilic behaviours which may eventually become habitual and dominate the person's social and interpersonal relationships. The paraphilic act bestows a powerful sense of excitement, control and triumph, and creates a scenario in which the dreaded situation – that of being overwhelmed or completely controlled by another, as in the original childhood experience – is reversed. Activities that appear to be primarily sexually motivated – as in fetishism, exhibitionism or voyeurism – may conceal hidden destructiveness and violence. Hostility, secrecy self-deception, and collusion are characteristic of the concrete paraphilic act, but also are features which frequently pervade the paraphilic person's relationships to self and others in general.

The patient's problematic behaviours are understood to be the bodily manifestations of fantasies, anxieties and impulses that cannot be represented in the mind and reflected upon, so are discharged in sexual excitation. We may therefore think about the person with a paraphilic disorder as using sexualization as a form of defence against anxieties aroused by intimacy. These anxieties might include fears about being overwhelmed by the other person, fears that closeness will result in loss of self or identity, fears of their own or the other's aggression, fears of humiliation, and anxieties about adequacy and potency. Many of the patients who seek treatment for their paraphilic behaviours or fantasies exhibit pervasive sexualization of their interpersonal relationships; sexualization, which provides a sense of excitement and empowerment, may be seen as an antidote to feelings of helplessness, powerless or inadequacy. Also, frequently evident is a hostile type of attachment to others based on a relationship paradigm of domination and submission, in which one person is always in control and the other defeated and humiliated. The sexual behaviour, enacted in fantasy or in reality, creates a situation where another person is often made to feel helpless or inadequate, while the individual assumes the role of the one in control and invulnerable. However, such feelings of excitement and omnipotence are often short-lived and only provide temporary relief from underlying anxieties. Individuals suffering from paraphilic disorders frequently describe a very disturbed sense of self in which feelings of self-disgust, shame and humiliation predominate.

Psychoanalytically informed treatment of paraphilic disorders and perversions

There is a lack of empirical evidence for the efficacy of any form of psychological therapy for paraphilic disorders, and the provision of treatment is mostly limited to those convicted of sexual offences in the form of treatment programmes based on cognitive behavioural principles and delivered in the criminal justice system (Ministry of Justice, 2019). Some patients with legal paraphilic disorders may be treated within psychosexual clinics, but many find it difficult to access treatment, often due to their shame in revealing their sexual preferences and actions. Psychoanalytically-informed treatment for paraphilic disorders is not widely available in the UK, the only specialized clinic offering such treatment within the National Health Service (NHS) being the Portman Clinic,[3] although there is a growing number of trained forensic psychotherapists working within a variety of health and criminal justice settings offering psychoanalytically oriented individual or group therapy. Moreover, the recent increase in the development in prisons in England of therapeutic communities and psychologically informed planned environments (PIPEs) for those who are in custody and deemed to be at high risk of re-offending with personality disorders, some of which draw on the psychoanalytic principles of unconscious individual, group and organizational dynamics, containment, and transference and countertransference communications is testament to a growing acceptance of the utility of psychoanalytic ideas in informing interventions for people who offend, some of whom may have paraphilic disorders.

Psychoanalytic psychotherapy, which is usually once weekly, explores the patient's unconscious wishes, fantasies, defences and motivations that influence the intrapsychic and interpersonal dynamics driving their paraphilic behaviours. These are seen as the symptoms of underlying personality disturbance which become manifest in the patient's relationships, including that with the therapist. An important aspect of psychoanalytic psychotherapy is in examining the patient's developmental history to understand the relational influences, particularly their early experiences with parental figures, siblings and peers, on their psychosexual development. This provides an explanatory narrative that grounds and contains the patient and facilitates the gradual emergence of the patient's unconscious internal world and interpersonal difficulties in the relationship with the therapist, which become crystallized in the transference-countertransference dynamics. Identification and interpretation of the transference, that is how the patient experiences the therapist, and understanding how this may be the result of unconscious re-enactments of previous significant relationships, enables the patient to enhance his growing intellectual insight regarding the nature and meaning of his problems by lived emotional experiences with the therapist, enabling shifts in his defensive structures within the immediacy of the therapeutic session. Therapy is aimed at enabling the patient, within the relationship with the therapist, to better tolerate distressing thoughts and emotions, such as fears of being overwhelmed or abandoned by another person, within the mind without acting these out via the body; facilitating the person in having greater control over their impulses; and understanding and relating to others as whole people rather than via isolated body parts.

Group therapy may be more effective than individual therapy for some patients, particularly those whose activities involve secrecy and deception, such as perpetrators of sexual abuse. A group of patients with similar perverse patterns of behaving and relating to others may more effectively challenge each other, and penetrate the pervasive patterns of deception, which may not be conscious, that characterize their relationships. In individual therapy, the therapist is more likely to be fooled by or unconsciously collude with the patient in his denial of his problems without a third perspective provided by other participants in the therapeutic setting. This also underscores the necessity of regular supervision of any treatment of patients with perverse interests (Yakeley, 2018).

Challenges of treatment

Whatever the setting, and indeed modality of psychological therapy, the therapist embarking on the psychotherapeutic treatment of patients with paraphilic disorders and perversions may encounter specific challenges, especially around issues of transference, countertransference and the patient's engagement in the therapeutic process. Patients often initially report an exacerbation in the frequency of their problematic sexual behaviours or intensity of their fantasies as disturbing memories, emotions and experiences from childhood are explored, although this should subside as the patient begins to develop a sense of being contained and understood by the therapist.

Simulation

However, the therapist should be alert to the existence of a false compliance in the patient within treatment, which is easy to collude with. Because deception and duplicity are often so integral to the patient's modes of relating to others, which is not just manifest in the behaviours acted out in secret, but also in their evasion of acknowledging the true pain and suffering they cause to themselves or others, their relationship to therapy and to the therapist may be based on superficiality and pretence. This may be conscious on the part of the patient, for example in the case of those who commit sexual offences who secretly deny or minimize the impact of their offences, and participate in offence related treatment programmes with the primary aim of being released from custody rather than any real wish to change their attitudes or behaviours. However, therapeutic progress of other patients or individuals, who consciously wish to address their problematic behaviours and appear to show some insight into the seriousness of their difficulties or remorse in relation to harm caused to others, may be impeded by their unconscious resistance to any real shifts in their relationships to themselves and others that might threaten their psychic equilibrium. The patient may be punctual to sessions and attend regularly, may intellectually grasp explanations about the childhood origins of his sexual interests and seem able to explore conflicts in his relationships, but these apparent insights are not internalized nor experienced at a deeper emotional level.

Psychoanalytic writers such as Sandler (1960), Gaddini (1969) and Glasser (1986) have suggested that the perverse patient's unconscious resistance to internal change results from the fragility of his character structure which has been built on the basis of 'simulations' or 'pseudo-identifications' with others, initially the patient's primary caregivers who did not offer the possibility of secure attachment. In early experiences of parental unreliability, neglect or frank abuse, the child is unable to identify with a maternal figure experienced as loving and enriching, and unable to escape from the person(s) he is dependent upon, instead develops a type of false-self, as described by Winnicott (1960), through compliance with a narcissistic mother who does not recognize the infant's needs, but substitutes her own, which the infant identifies with at the expense of development of independence and autonomy.

These patients develop a 'pseudo-attachment' to the therapist, seeming to quickly embrace and respond to the treatment model but the therapeutic relationship lacks emotional valency, and the therapist feels as if he or she could be interchangeable with any other. Attempts to get beyond this carapace of ostensible therapeutic engagement are experienced as intrusive and threatening, activating the patient's core-complex anxieties, so that he responds with anger and aggression or withdrawal by missing sessions or dropping out of treatment to defend against and escape unconscious fears of being overwhelmed by the therapist.

These dynamics are illustrated in the treatment of a young man who sought help for sadomasochism and fetishism, which involved the patient enveloping himself in a plastic bin-bag and obsessively masturbating to the point of ulcerating his penis to sexual fantasies of older women. He also liked wearing a plastic nappy, in which he would urinate and enjoy the feel of his warm urine held within the manifestation of an unconscious fantasy of returning to the womb.

He was the only child of a single mother. In his early childhood, his father was physically violent to his mother and left her altogether when the patient was three years old. Thereafter he slept in the same bed with his mother until the age of fourteen. Although she did not actively sexually abuse him, he can remember around puberty beginning to feel sexually aroused by her and his erect penis pressing against her sleeping body. His fetishistic interests developed in later adolescence and as an adult he had difficulty establishing intimate relationships with women, preferring to masturbate on his own.

In treatment, with an older female therapist, the patient rapidly reported progress as evidenced by a diminution in the frequency of his masturbatory activities, which he attributed to the expertise and skills of his therapist. He agreed with her interpretations of how the plastic bags in which he wrapped himself, and the nappies in which he urinated, symbolized a protective skin that allowed him to separate from his mother and provide comfort that she was unable to give. She suggested that at the same time his masturbation to the point of self-injury represented his wish to punish himself in a sadomasochistic way for his forbidden Oedipal longings towards his mother and hatred towards his identification with an abusive and neglectful father. Although the patient reported that these explanations for his sexual fantasies and behaviours made sense to him, the therapist experienced him as emotionally distant. Over time, his demeanour changed from submissive to contemptuous, and he began to reject her insights, deriding them as 'psychobabble' and admitting he would rather sleep with her than be subject to her facile explanations of his difficulties.

We might understand what has happened in therapy as the patient initially developing an idealized transference towards the therapist, in which she is experienced as the mother who fully understands him and fulfils all his needs. Soon, however, her interpretations as to the origins and meanings of his sexual perversions, even if these have some validity, are experienced as intrusive and humiliating, and he defends against these intolerable feelings by first simulating a compliant attitude which acts as an impermeable membrane, like the plastic bags he wraps himself in, to shield himself from emotional contact with the therapist. When her comments become more explicit regarding his unconscious sexual longings for his mother, his protective skin weakens and he is at risk of feeling engulfed and emasculated by an omniscient and omnipotent other, activating the vicious circle of the core complex. Feelings of aggression emerge, which are quickly eroticized into feelings of contempt and sexual fantasies for the therapist, ensuring that he remains in control and his sexual defences intact.

The perverse transference

The above example illustrates the risks of prematurely interpreting what is going on at a deeper unconscious level within the therapeutic relationship. Patients suffering from paraphilic disorders whose primary mode of relating to others is via bodily contact, may benefit initially from a more supportive therapeutic approach in which the patient's capacity to mentalize, tolerate and reflect upon their conscious thoughts and emotions before more exploratory therapy is possible.

Although one might argue that transference phenomena exists in all therapeutic modalities, and indeed in all relationships with others, one of the hallmarks of psychoanalytic psychotherapy is in its focus on interpretation of the transference as one of the key mechanisms of therapeutic change. By elucidating the unconscious dynamics in the encounters between therapist and patient, the latter gradually attains awareness of how these are not specific to his relationship with the therapist but are a reflection of his difficulties in relationships in general.

Patients will bring unconscious anxieties in relation to emotional inti-macy with others into their experience of the therapist. Feelings of closeness and understanding may quickly shift into feeling persecuted, taken over and controlled by the therapist, while at the same time, the therapist's breaks may trigger feelings of rejection, abandonment and desolation. The patient with perverse interests, as in his external relationships, deals with these unbearable conflicts by establishing a sadomasochistic relationship, or perverse transfer-ence, to the therapist in which he, the patient, is in control. The transference may be overtly sexualized, as in the above example, or may be more subtly perverse in the patient's thinly veiled contempt, passive-aggressiveness or masochistic submission towards the therapist. Moreover, the patient's casting of the roles of masochist and sadist oscillate between himself and the therapist, who is experienced respectively as either a passive and willing partner in a therapeutic game of seduction and corruption, or a prohibitive and punitive authority figure who forbids any sexual pleasure and to whom the patient must submit.

Exploration of the perverse transference by bringing to the patient's atten-tion, via interpretation and encouraging the patients reflections, what appears to be going on in his attitudes and feelings towards therapists and linking these to the patient's previous experiences of relationships and unconscious anxieties, may be experienced as humiliating by the patient, as this exposes underlying fears of dependence and desertion, and the aggression bound up in the patient's sadomasochistic defences becomes more evident. To defend against these intolerable feelings, the patient again may become increasingly sexualized, which may result in self-destructive behaviours which become particularly evident in patients with illegal paraphilic disorders and sexual behaviours such as voyeurism, exhibitionism or accessing access illegal images of children, with a risk of being arrested and convicted. Here the law may be seen as representing the patient's harsh superego which is flouted and disobeyed, then submitted to. For other patients, the aggression of the core complex becomes more prominently directed towards the self in overtly suicidal feelings and behaviours, and where the risk of suicide becomes real, the patient may need urgent intervention and psychiatric support to sustain him in therapy.

Countertransference

As described earlier, another central tenet of psychoanalytic psychotherapeutic technique is in the use of the therapist's countertransference. Countertransference describes the emotional reactions that the therapist has towards the patient, which stem from both unresolved conflicts in the therapist, as well as the projections of the patient. Countertransference is used as a therapeutic tool as a source of useful information about the patient, in that the therapist's responses to the patient might reflect how other people respond to the patient and provide an insight into his internal world, unconscious conflicts and modes of relating to himself and others.

Patients with perversions and paraphilic disorders often evoke powerful negative or disturbing attitudes and feelings in those who are involved in their care. Thus, feelings of shock, outrage and condemnation regarding the patient's offences are common, particularly if these are of an overtly violent sexual nature such as rape; other more bodily feelings of nausea and disgust may be provoked by paedophilic acts or legal paraphilic disorders involving bodily parts or functions such as coprophilia, urophilia or klismaphilia (deriving sexual pleasure from enemas). Such activities which involve very primitive bodily impulses and urges activate primitive somatic responses of revulsion and disgust in ourselves, which mirror the patient's own feelings of self-repugnance and shame, and provide a window into his very regressed internal world where a fixation on infantile oral, anal and urethral bodily desires impedes the development of more mature genital and emotional relationships.

Other negative responses of the clinician or therapist treating such patients where therapeutic progress is limited include feelings of hopelessness, devaluation of professional identity and expertise, lack of confidence and shame. Although such feelings may already be present in the therapist, these are enhanced by the unconscious projection of the patient's own feelings of low self-worth. By contrast, other, perhaps more unsettling and rarely admitted reactions may occur in the clinician or others managing the patient or person who offends, such as feelings of excitement or sexual attraction, reflecting an unconscious seductive and collusive union between the two, which may be particularly dangerous if acted out in sexual boundary violations. If professionals are able to talk about and reflect on such feelings in safe forums such as clinical supervision or reflective practice, the risk of acting on them inappropriately may diminish.

All of these potential counter-transferential affective and somatic responses of the therapist, or other professionals in contact with the patient, are not always consciously acknowledged or reflected upon, with the risk that they may adversely influence their interactions with him. If the countertransference is one of revulsion or moral outrage, this may result in excessively punitive responses on the part of the clinician, for example denying the patient treatment on the basis that he is 'untreatable'; on the other hand, staff may collude with the patient's narcissism, sense of victimhood and denial of responsibility for his actions and offer therapy which the patient is unable to engage with at any meaningful and mutative level.

Such unconscious subjective experiences of the perverse patient or person who offends have been empirically demonstrated to influence clinicians' ability to conduct risk assessments. Blumenthal, Huckle, Czornyj, Craissati, and Richardson (2010) conducted a study looking at the relative contribution of actuarial and emotive information in determining risk ratings of violence by experienced forensic mental health professionals. These clinicians were given vignettes of individuals who had committed violent offences and were asked to rate their risk of future violence. Despite being well trained in the use of actuarial risk assessment tools, they were found to unwittingly disregard actuarial information about the patient and were disproportionately influenced by their emotive responses to the clinical information given to them about the patient, leading them to make significant mistakes in risk prediction, for example rating the risk of violent recidivism as high for a person who had committed a one-off paedophilic violent contact offence; and as low for one with more low-level but prolific non-violent and violent offences who presented as engaging and remorseful.

These errors in clinical judgement, and other deleterious responses to the patient such as boundary violations or therapeutic nihilism, may be to some extent mitigated by staff engaging in reflective practice and supervision. Here the disturbing feelings that inevitably occur in staff in relation to their clients may be safely recognized and understood as a reflection of their psychopathology and the workings of their internal world, and reduces the risk that they will be acted upon in unprofessional attitudes and behaviours.

Conclusion

Although very few empirical studies have examined the efficacy of psycho-analytic or insight-oriented psychotherapy for individuals presenting with paraphilic disorders and other distressing sexual behaviours, both legal and illegal, this lack of evidence does not mean that psychoanalytic approaches are inappropriate or ineffective. Psychoanalytic psychotherapy may be suitable for patients who have benefitted from a more structured, goal-oriented approach who wish to explore in more depth the historical roots of their difficulties and how the ensuing unconscious anxieties, conflicts, wishes and fantasies that have emerged and been shaped by their relationships in infancy, childhood and adolescence with significant others, influence their current psychosocial functioning, especially in the realm of intimate relationships. Conversely, people who have experienced psychotherapy may then became motivated to complement with more CBT type interventions

A psychoanalytic perspective is not intended to replace other explanatory theories which inform mental health or forensic practice, but to complement other prevailing paradigms and frameworks in the field, notably those based on cognitive-behavioural, systemic or sociological models. Key psychoanalytic principles, such as the existence of a dynamic unconscious life; the operation of defence mechanisms, both conscious and unconscious, to defend against underlying conflicts and anxieties; and the use of transference and counter-transference in providing key information about the patient's interpersonal relationships, are not only integral to psychoanalytic psychotherapy as a direct treatment, but may also be helpful in the assessment and formulation of cases, the supervision of staff and to provide a conceptual framework in which other treatment modalities such as cognitive-behavioural therapy may be delivered.

Although the term 'perversion' is less accepted today in describing unusual or distressing sexual fantasies and practices due to the impression that it implies that all forms of sexuality that deviate from the norm as pathologi-cal, nevertheless, its continued use in the psychoanalytic literature in relation to behaviours which are now classified as paraphilic disorders, should not be seen as pejorative or judgemental, but as a way of highlighting the deceit, destructiveness and perniciousness, albeit often unconscious, that character-ize the relationships, to themselves and others, of the individuals suffering from paraphilic disorders. The aim is not to punish, shame or humiliate people whose sexual behaviours may appear bizarre or abhorrent, but to recognize and address with understanding and compassion the underlying anxieties and aggression that drive them to compulsively enact behaviours that cause such distress to themselves and those around them.

The growth of psychoanalytic approaches to the assessment, management and treatment of paraphilic disorders, perversions and other problematic sexual behaviours will be certainly enhanced by much needed empirical research regarding their efficacy and most appropriate deployment. At the same time, however, the voices of the many individuals suffering from these difficulties and who have benefitted from psychoanalytic treatment should also be heard.

Notes

1. I will refer to the individual with paraphilic disorders or other problematic sexual behaviours as male, reflecting the increased prevalence of these difficulties in men. I will also limit my discussion of psychoanalytic theories of perversion to those pertaining to the male gender, omitting discussion of the rich literature on female perversion which warrants a separate chapter in itself.
2. Transference is the displacement by the patient of early wishes and feelings towards people from the past, particularly the patient's parents, onto the figure of the therapist, and its interpretation by the latter in psychoanalytic therapy is important in effecting therapeutic change.Countertransference describes the unconscious emotional reactions that the therapist has towards the patient and is a result of both unresolved conflicts in the therapist and contributions or projections from the patient. It is used in psychoanalytic psychotherapy as a source of useful information about the patient and his pattern of relating to others.
3. The Portman Clinic, part of the Tavistock and Portman NHS Foundation Trust in North London, UK, is an outpatient forensic psychotherapy clinic that offers psychoanalytically informed consultations, assessments and treatment for children, adolescents and adults presenting with violent and/or problematic sexual behaviours.

References

American Psychiatric Association. (1952). *Diagnostic and statistical manual of mental disorders* (1st ed.). Washington, DC: American Psychiatric Association.

American Psychiatric Association. (1968). *Diagnostic and statistical manual of mental disorders* (2nd ed.). Washington, DC: American Psychiatric Association.

American Psychiatric Association. (1980). *Diagnostic and statistical manual of mental disorders* (3rd ed.). Washington, DC: American Psychiatric Association.

American Psychiatric Association. (1994). *Diagnostic and statistical manual of mental disorders* (4th ed.). Washington, DC: American Psychiatric Association.

American Psychiatric Association. (2013). *Diagnostic and statistical manual of mental disorders* (5th ed.). Washington, DC: American Psychiatric Association.

Blumenthal, S., Huckle, C., Czornyj, R., Craissati, J., & Richardson, P. (2010). The role of affect in the estimation of risk. *Journal of Mental Health*, *19*, 444–451.

Chasseguet-Smirgel, J. (1985). *Creativity and perversion*. New York: Free Association Books.

Cordess, C., & Cox, M. (eds.) (1996). *Forensic psychotherapy: Crime, psychodynamics and the offender patient*. London: Jessica Kingsley.

Federoff, J. P. (2009). The paraphilias. In M. G. Gelder, N. C. Andreasen, J. L. Lopez-Ibor et al. Eds., *New Oxford textbook of psychiatry* (2nd ed., pp. 832–842). Oxford: Oxford University Press.

Freud, S. (1905). Three essays on the theory of sexuality (1905). *The standard edition of the complete psychological works of Sigmund Freud, Volume VII (1901–1905): A case of Hysteria, three essays on sexuality and other works*, 123–246.

Freud, S. (1923). The ego and the id. In J. Strachey (Ed.), *The standard edition of the complete psychological works of Sigmund Freud* (Vol. *19*, pp. 3–66). London: Hogarth Press and the Institute of Psychoanalysis.

Freud, S. (1927). Fetishism. In J. Strachey (Ed.), *The standard edition of the complete psychological works of Sigmund Freud* (Vol. *21*, pp. 149–157). London: Hogarth Press and the Institute of Psychoanalysis.

Gaddini, E. (1969). On imitation. *International Journal of Psycho-Analysis, 50*, 475–484.

Glasser, M. (1986). Identification and its vicissitudes as observed in the perversions. *International Journal of Psycho-Analysis, 67*, 9–17.

Glasser, M. (1996). Aggression and sadism in the perversions. In I. Rosen (Ed.), *Sexual deviation* (5th ed., pp. 278–305). Oxford: Oxford University Press.

Gordon, H. (2008). The treatment of paraphilias: An historical perspective. *Criminal Behaviour and Mental Health, 18*, 79–87.

Grubin, D. (2008). Medical models and interventions in sexual deviance. In R. Laws & W. T. O'Donohue (Eds.), *Sexual deviance: Theory, assessment and treatment* (pp. 594–610). Guilford, CT: Guilford Press.

Hyatt-Williams, A. (1998). *Cruelty, violence and murder: Understanding the criminal mind*. London: Jason Aronson.

Krafft Ebbing, R. (1886). *Psychopathia sexualis*. trans. FS Klaf, 1965. London: Staples Press.

Ministry of Justice. (2019). Correctional services accreditation and advice panel (CSAAP) Currently Accredited Programmes. https://assets.publishing.service.gov.uk/government/uploads/system/uploads/attachment_data/file/832658/descriptions-accredited-programmes.pdf

Sandler, J. (1960). On the concept of the superego. *Psychoanalytic Study of the Child, 15*, 128–162.

Stekel, W. (1930). *Sexual aberrations: The phenomenon of fetishism in relation to sex*. New York, NY: Liveright.

Stoller, R. J. (1975). *Perversion*. New York, NY: Pantheon.

Welldon, E. V. (2011). *Playing with dynamite: A personal approach to the psychoanalytic understanding of perversions, violence and criminality*. London: Karnac.

Winnicott, D. W. (1960). Ego distortion in terms of true and false self In M M. R. Khan Reprinted London: Karnac Books, 1990 Ed., *The maturational processes and the facilitating environment* (pp. 140–152). London: Hogarth Press.

Wood, H. (2014). Working with problems of perversion. *British Journal of Psychotherapy, 30*, 422–437.

Yakeley, J. (2018). Psychoanalytic perspectives on paraphilias and perversions. *European Journal of Psychotherapy and Counselling, 20*, 164–183.

Yakeley, J., & Adshead, G. (2013). Locks, keys and security of mind: Psychodynamic approaches to forensic psychiatry. *Journal of the American Academy of Psychiatry and the Law, 41*, 38–45.

Zander, T. (2008). Commentary: Inventing diagnosis for civil commitment of rapists. *Journal of the American Academy of Psychiatry and the Law, 36*, 459–469.

Medication to manage problematic sexual arousal

11

Emma Marshall,
Belinda Winder,
Christine Norman and
Nicholas Blagden

Introduction

Problematic sexual arousal can be separated into two categories; problematic sexual interests and problematic levels of arousal. Problematic sexual interests cover a wide range of sexual interests and behaviours, many of which are classed as paraphilic. The Diagnostic and Statistical Manual of Mental Disorders (DSM-5) (American Psychiatric Association, 2013) outlines that the term paraphilia refers to sexual interests and behaviours that go beyond that of activity between consenting, physically mature, sexual partners. Paraphilic interests are often persistent and intense, however some more specific paraphilias may be better understood as sexual preferences. Paraphilias can focus on erotic activities, such as whipping, spanking and strangulation, or on erotic targets, such as sexual interests in animals, children and corpses (American Psychiatric Association, 2013). The DSM-5 distinguishes between paraphilias and paraphilic disorders. In order for a paraphilia to become a paraphilic disorder, the paraphilia must cause distress to the individual, or cause harm to the self or others through satisfaction of the paraphilia. The DSM-5 also indicates that a paraphilia alone would not cause a need for clinical intervention until it is recognized as a paraphilic disorder (American Psychiatric Association, 2013). Current paraphilic disorders recognized by the DSM-5 include Voyeuristic Disorder, Exhibitionist Disorder, Frotteuristic Disorder, Sexual Masochism Disorder, Sexual Sadism Disorder, Paedophilic Disorder, Fetishistic Disorder, Transvestic Disorder and other Specified Paraphilic Disorder (American Psychiatric Association, 2013).

The International Statistical Classification of Diseases and Health Related Problems (ICD-11) (WHO, 2018) has slightly different categories of paraphilic disorders which came into effect on May 2019. Following recommendations of the Working Group on the Classification of Sexual Disorders and Sexual Health (WGSDSH), Fetishism, Sadomasochism and Fetishistic Transvestism were removed. These behaviours are consensual or performed alone and do not cause harm or distress to the individuals and therefore no longer qualify as paraphilic disorders in the ICD-11 (Krueger et al., 2017). Exhibitionistic, Voyeuristic, Paedophilic, Frotteuristic and Coercive Sexual Sadism Disorder have all been included along with Other Paraphilic Disorder involving non-consenting individuals, and Paraphilic Disorder involving solitary behaviour or consenting individuals (WHO, 2018). The classification of paraphilic disorders is essential when treating individuals in America as clinicians need to use the ICD in order to gain insurance to deliver treatment (Reed, 2010). It is recognized that it is predominately males who are diagnosed with paraphilias (Kafka, 1997; Thibaut, Barra, Gordon, Cosyns, & Bradford, 2010; Dawson, Bannerman & Lalumiere, 2016) and for the purpose of this chapter it will be the sexual behaviour of males that will be addressed. The authors acknowledge however that greater understanding of female problematic sexual arousal is also required, but it is outside the scope of this chapter.

Problematic sexual arousal is not always paraphilic. One aspect of problematic sexual arousal which is non-paraphilic in nature is that of problematic levels of sexual arousal. Problematic levels of sexual arousal can be divided into two categories. Hyposexual desire concerns those who have low levels of arousal and interest in sex, leading to problems in relationships, maintaining healthy sexual functioning and distress (Kafka, 2003). In contrast to this, some individuals may consider their levels of arousal to be too high. For these individuals, so long as their needs are met through consenting adult relationships, they may not consider their arousal to be problematic as it does not impact on their daily functioning. For some, however, problematic levels of arousal can be so intense that the individual concerned is unable to concentrate on daily life activities, as a result of their sexual thoughts and feelings (Marshall, Marshall, & Serran, 2006). This 'abnormally intense interest in sex that dominates psychological functioning' was defined by Mann, Hanson and Thornton (2010, p. 198) as sexual preoccupation. Kafka (2003) classifies sexual preoccupation as spending more than one hour every day indulging in sexual thoughts and fantasies. Fantasies are classed as imagining scenarios which the individual finds sexually arousing and erotic (Leitenberg & Henning, 1995). Sexually preoccupied individuals often have unrealistic expectations of sexual relationships as a result of engaging in fantasies of impersonal and casual sex (Snell, Fisher, & Schuh, 1992).

Sexual preoccupation has been identified as being strongly associated with recidivism in individuals convicted with sexual offences (Hanson & Harris, 2000; Hanson & Morton-Bourgon, 2005). This means that when it is present, risk of offending is raised as sexual preoccupation (or high sex drive) acts as an intrinsic motivator for sexual behaviour (Seto, 2019). Seto (2019) points out that the focus of high sex drive is usually conventional sexual behaviour, but preoccupation can become a motivation for sexual offending if the person's desire for sex overcomes any inhibitions they have about coercing someone into sex or having sex with an individual who someone who cannot consent (for example a child). There is a link between sexual preoccupation and illicit behaviour, including child pornography (Seto & Eke, 2015; Seto, Reeves, & Jung, 2010). Indeed, the intrusive thoughts, fantasies and urges experienced by the individual as a result of their preoccupation, may result in them engaging in socially deviant and sometimes paraphilic behaviours in order to satisfy these sexual needs (Saleh & Berlin, 2003). It is also apparent that although paraphilias are often driven by problematic and anti-social interests, they are also typically driven by excessive levels of sexual arousal (Kafka, 2003).

In order to satisfy their intrusive sexual thoughts, individuals with sexual preoccupation often need to engage in high levels of sexual activity, known as hypersexuality and hypersexual desire (Kafka, 1997). This frequent engagement in sexual activities may be so excessive as to cause some individuals to injure their own genitals as a result of frequent masturbation (Winder, Lievesley, Elliott, Norman & Kaul, 2014a). Individuals may also experience levels of distress and detrimental consequences in relation to their occupational and social settings (Kafka, 2010; Kaplan & Krueger, 2010). While there is overlap between sexual preoccupation and excessive engagement in sexual activity it is possible that sexual preoccupation could be seen as 'sexual thoughts', and hypersexuality as the resulting behaviour (Winder et al., 2014a). This high engagement in sexual activity, to the extent it becomes problematic and anti-social, is referred to in the literature by a number of different terms. Early literature referred to the issue as nymphomania and satyriasis (Rinehart & McCabe, 1997). Other terms include: sexual compulsivity (Kalichman et al., 1994), compulsive sexual behaviour (Miner, Coleman, Center, Ross, & Rosser, 2007; Morgenstern et al., 2011; Muench et al., 2007), hypersexuality (Kaplan & Krueger, 2010) and hypersexual desire (Kafka, 2003). There have been numerous attempts over the years to clarify terms and produce a uniform definition; however, to date, the various terms are still used interchangeably in the literature. For the purpose of this chapter, excessive arousal shall mainly be referred to as problematic sexual arousal unless quoting directly from studies by other researchers. This term has been chosen in an attempt to capture both levels of arousal and interests. For some individuals, typical levels of arousal may be problematic due to their sexual interests and it is hoped that this term captures both aspects.

Measurements of problematic sexual arousal

Kafka (1997) was the first to attempt to provide an operational measure of problematic levels of sexual arousal which he labels hypersexual desire. Using empirical data from a large sample of sexual surveys, he suggested that to receive a diagnosis of hypersexual desire the individual must be over 15 years of age and will have participated in at least seven or more total sexual outlets (TSO), or methods to achieve orgasm, per week. Kafka (1997) indicates that this high frequency engagement in sexual activity must be over a consecutive period of at least six months. The high frequency of sexual behaviours must also occur independently of any medical condition and cause distress to the individual (Kafka, 2010). Wakefield (2012) suggests that Kafka's estimates on seven sexual outlets per week is relatively conservative when considering consenting adults with high sex drives, who do not resort to social deviant behaviours to fulfil their needs. Kafka (1997, 2003) has postulated that hypersexual desire does not necessarily mean that the individual is classed as having a pathological condition. He explains that it is the persistent engagement in a high frequency of sexual activities which increases the likelihood of risk of developing a disorder and uses the example of daily consumption of alcohol to increase the risk of alcoholism. Should the high levels of arousal cause distress, this can become problematic for the individual concerned and lead to them seeking help (Winters, Christoff, & Gorzalka, 2010).

Kafka (2003) suggests that a diagnosis of hyperactive sexual desire disorder (HSDD) could be given if the individual with hypersexual desire is also diagnosed with sexual preoccupation. Kafka (2003) suggests that Hypersexual Desire Disorder can be understood and defined through consideration of three behaviour aspects of sexual behaviour; sexual preoccupation (the amount of time spent engaged in sexual fantasies each day), repetitive engagement in sexual acts, and adverse consequences caused by the high frequency of engagement in sexual behaviour. Individuals who meet the criteria for HSDD typically report having experienced numerous failed attempts in controlling their problematic sexual urges, behaviours and fantasies (Womack, Hook, Ramos, Davis, & Penberthy, 2013). Despite efforts by the Work Group on Sexual and Gender Identity Disorders for excessively high levels of sexual arousal to be included in the DSM-5 (Kafka, 2010), currently hypersexuality is not classed as a mental disorder.

A range of measurement tools have been developed by researchers in order to assess problematic sexual arousal. The need for the effective measurement of problematic sexual arousal is important as it identifies a need for treatment and also assists in measuring the effectiveness of the treatment (Akerman, 2008, 2010; Akerman & Beech, 2012). Womack et al. (2013)

asserted that the tools developed for measuring problematic levels of sexual arousal can be placed in three main categories: self-report measures of symptoms, self-report measures of associated consequences of problematic sexual arousal and clinical interviews. For a thorough assessment, researchers should use a combination of all three categories of measures (Womack et al., 2013).

Clinical interviews

One example of a clinical interview developed to measure problematic sexual arousal was designed by Reid et al. (2012a). Reid et al. (2012a) developed the HD Diagnostic Clinical Interview (HDDCI) to specifically coincide with the diagnostic criteria created by Kafka (2010). Due to the nature of the design, Womack et al. (2013) identify the HDDCI as the closest measure to Kafka (2010) diagnostic criteria as it contained items to meet all seven aspects of the criteria. Womack et al. (2013) identify that clinical interviews are useful in gaining a wide understanding of problematic sexual arousal as they allow for further probing on answers and clarification on confusing questions to be given. However, clinical interviews may not be the best measure in order to gain the most detail on each of the criterion. Womack et al. (2013) identify that participants may feel uncomfortable verbally discussing personal, distressing and sensitive information with another individual, which may lead to less information being obtained.

Self-report measures of symptoms

Self-report measures of symptoms are a useful tool in measuring problematic sexual arousal and providing an overview of the symptoms associated with it (Womack et al., 2013; see also Chapter 2, this volume). Kalichman et al. (1994) developed the sexual compulsivity scale in one of the earliest attempts at measuring hypersexual behaviour and sexual preoccupation. The self-report scale contains ten items whereby participants rate their level of agreement to each statement on a four-point Likert scale, with a score of 4 being 'very much like me' and 1 'not at all like me'. Using a sample of 106 homosexual, sexually active men, Kalichman et al. (1994) were able to establish reliability of the scale. Kalichman and Rompa (2001) tested the scale further using a sample of males and females who tested positive for HIV and found reliability for men (Cronbach's alpha = .89) and woman (Cronbach's alpha = .92). Winder et al. (2014b) also established reliability of the scale in a sample of males who had been convicted of sexual offences with a Cronbach alpha score of .83.

Self-report measures of consequences

An example of a self-report measure of consequences is the Hypersexual Behaviour Consequences Scale (HBCS) developed by Reid, Garos, and Fong (2012b). Using a combination of self-report measures and interviews the authors developed the HBCS in order to best coincide with the Kafka (2010) diagnostic criteria. Reid et al. (2012b) recognize that there are a wide range of consequences that may be experienced by an individual with problematic sexual arousal, as a result of their sexual activities. The scale has been developed to take into consideration consequences associated with physical and mental health, emotional wellbeing, relationships, employment, finances and criminal activities. Reid et al. (2012b) demonstrated that the scale captures the consequences of problematic sexual arousal and demonstrates reliability and internal validity.

Comorbidity and wellbeing

Problematic sexual arousal and sexual preoccupation have high levels of comorbidity with a number of psychiatric disorders with an obsessional component. This perhaps demonstrates that problematic sexual arousal should be seen as part of the impulsive/compulsive spectrum of behaviours (Raymond, Coleman & Miner, 2003). Black, Kehrberg, Flumerfelt, and Schlosser (1997) reported that, in a sample of 36 participants with self-reported sexual compulsivity, seven (19%) were diagnosed as having a paraphilic disorder. In addition to this, 64% had substance misuse disorders, 42% were diagnosed with phobic disorders and 39% of the sample had a history of depression. Kafka and Hennen (2002) reported similar results in their study of 120 males with paraphilia related disorder and paraphilia. Their sample showed comorbidity in that 18% had attention deficit hyperactivity disorder (ADHD), 37.5% anxiety disorder, 37.5% substance misuse disorder and 71.5% had a history of mood disorders.

Not only can hypersexual disorder be comorbid to other psychiatric disorders, but it can be detrimental to wellbeing as a result of the impact of associated behaviours. The individual may contract sexually transmitted infections as a result of engagement in risky sexual activity (Yoon, Houang, Hirshfield, & Downing, 2016). They may experience problems in their relationships (Paunovic & Hallberg, 2014) and interpersonal problems (Lievesley, Elliott, Winder, & Norman, 2014; Winder et al., 2014b). They also may experience loss of employment (Paunovic & Hallberg, 2014) and financial loss (Reid et al., 2012). It can also have an impact on and individual's self-identity. One's sexuality and sexual identity is an integral component of how an individual construes self and their self-identity. It is also the component of identity that is the most difficult to express, explore, and to have positively validated (McKenna, Green, & Smith, 2001). Thus, for someone with high sexual pre-occupation it may bring about feelings of shame, fear of rejection or even disgust. As it affects how someone can relate to another, it may also emphasize difference from others through the experience of stability and intensity of the sexual preoccupation (Blagden, Mann, Webster, Lee and Williams, 2018). This 'othering' can be linked to feelings of being 'doomed to deviance'. For example if someone has the narrative script 'I'm a deviant person consumed by sex and different to others', this could be criminogenic as it is akin to a condemnation script (see Maruna, 2001), in that they feel they are unable to change who they are and so destined to act on it (Maruna, 2001; Crank, 2018).

It is recognized that there are individuals with problematic sexual arousal who do not act on their interests (Akerman & Beech, 2012). However, for some individuals, their problematic sexual arousal may cause them to become engaged in socially unacceptable behaviours which can lead to them com-mitting sexual offences. The effective management of wellbeing is important when considering risk of future recidivism. Research suggests that offences are often committed after the individual has been in a negative emotional state and it is suggested that sexual activity may be used as a mechanism to improve the individual's mood (Cortoni & Marshall, 2001). Bancroft and Vukadinovic (2004) studied a sample of 29 males and two females recruited from Sex Addicts Anonymous (SAA). Nineteen of the 31 participants stated that they were more likely to engage in sexual activity when under stress, anxious or depressed. Looman (1995) postulated that child molesters were more likely to engage in fantasies about children when in a negative frame of mind. Looman suggested that this use of sexual activity may be an ineffective coping mecha-nism in order to deal with negative emotions, which would lead to further inappropriate fantasies through reinforcement. Cortoni and Marshall (2001) also highlighted evidence that sex was used as a coping mechanism by indi-viduals with sexual convictions and that the use of sex to cope with negative emotions was reinforced over time. Their results showed that adult rapists and child molesters were significantly more likely than non-sexual offenders to use sex as a coping strategy. Cortoni and Marshall (2001) also asserted that individuals who had sexually offended were more likely to have been sexually preoccupied as an adolescent. Given these findings, it is apparent that effective treatment for sexually preoccupied individuals with sexual convictions should address a range of issues, including such individuals' sexual preoccupation, any comorbidities, poor wellbeing and should also teach appropriate coping mechanisms for negative emotional states in order to reduce the risk of reof-fending in such individuals.

Psychological treatment of individuals convicted of sexual offences

Most treatment of individuals convicted of sexual offences is achieved through psychological interventions delivered in the form of programmes by the Prison and Probation Service. Previously, treatment was delivered in the form of the Core Sex Offender Treatment Programme (SOTP) which is a cognitive behavioural intervention (Mews, Bella & Purver, 2017). Cognitive behavioural interventions have been identified as the most effective and robust of psychological programmes (Hanson et al., 2002; Losel & Schmucker, 2005). The effectiveness of psychological treatment interventions has been assessed. Hanson et al. (2002) reviewed 43 studies and found that the rate of recidivism was lower for individuals who had received treatment (12.3%) than the untreated comparison group (16.8%). Mandeville-Norden, Beech, and Hayes (2008) undertook a study in the UK to assess the effectiveness of the community based SOTP. The authors showed that all participants who received treatment via the programmes, showed significant, positive treatment effects (Mandeville-Norden et al., 2008). A recent meta-analysis into the effectiveness of offence specific, psychological treatment programmes was performed by Gannon, Olver, Mallion, and James (2019). The authors found evidence of treatment effectiveness with a reduction in recidivism for all treatment programmes. In relation to sexual offence treatment programmes, recidivism of a sexual nature was reduced by 32.6%, non-offence specific recidivism was also significantly reduced (Gannon et al., 2019). The authors indicated that treatment programmes were most effective when input was provided by qualified psychologists and the facilitators received regular clinical supervision (Gannon et al., 2019).

The current programmes delivered in the UK include Horizon and Kaizen which were introduced to replace the previous SOTP (Nacro, 2018). Individuals who have received convictions for sexual offences are allocated to one of these programmes according to their risk of reoffending. Individuals assessed as medium risk of reoffending are allocated to Horizon, with individuals at high and very high risk of reoffending being treated via Kaizen (McCartan, Hoggett & Kemshall, 2018). As Horizon and Kaizen are relatively new, research into the effectiveness of these programmes is ongoing.

Medication to manage problematic sexual arousal

Evidence suggests that those diagnosed with sexual preoccupation may be unable to concentrate on the psychological interventions effectively as a result of their inability to control their sexual urges and intrusive thoughts (Akerman, 2008; Marshall et al., 2006; Winder et al., 2017, 2014b). It is important that individuals with sexual preoccupation receive appropriate treatment interventions as Hanson and Harris (2000) identify that sexual preoccupation is strongly associated with recidivism. This conclusion is backed up by Hanson and Morton-Bourgon (2005) who identified that sexual deviancy and sexual preoccupation were major predictors of sexual recidivism in both adult and adolescent individuals. Beech, Fisher, and Ward (2005) also suggest that problematic sexual arousal is associated with the likelihood of the individual committing a sexual offence. The authors performed a qualitative study with 28 participants all of whom had been convicted of murder with a sexual element. A number of participants identified that their sexual arousal and associated fantasies were overwhelming and out of their control, prior to committing the offence. Beech et al. (2005) proposed an implicit theory of sexual offending which they labelled 'male sex drive is uncontrollable'. This implicit theory covers three strands, such that (i) sexual behaviour is not under the control of the individual, (ii) the emotions are so powerful that they overwhelm the individual and (iii) the individual is overcome by sexual urges and fantasies. Beech et al. (2005) found that this implicit theory was present in 71% of the sample. In order to improve the effectiveness of treatment in those identified as sexually preoccupied and/or hypersexual, medication to manage problematic sexual arousal (MMPSA) can be a useful addition to treatment. Pharmacological treatment assists in controlling sexual behaviours and urges, relieving the individual of the burden of intrusive thoughts and making the individual more susceptible to treatment (Winder et al., 2014a). Lievesley et al. (2014) asserted that medicated individuals reported being more able to deal with feelings of anger and distress and found an increased ability to manage their emotions. The headspace offered to them as a result of the reduction of sexual thoughts enabled the individual to process thoughts and emotions that they had previously been unable to do. For individuals with sexual preoccupation and hypersexuality, a combination of pharmacological and psychological treatment has been shown to be effective (Guay, 2009).

The use of pharmacological treatment has increased in recent years. In 2007, England and Wales introduced voluntary pharmacological treatment as an addition to the psychological treatment available for individuals convicted of sexual offences (Home Office, 2007). The effectiveness of this treatment has since received more attention and there has been a steady growth of positive evidence in the literature to indicate the effectiveness of this treatment method. Ultimately, the aim of pharmacological treatment is to achieve a balance between targeting problematic sexual arousal while maintaining healthy sexual functioning, without adverse side effects (Hill, Briken, Kraus, Strohm, & Berner, 2003). It is this aspect which makes the combination of pharmacological intervention and psychological intervention so important. Previously, the use of medication to treat individuals with sexual convictions has been criticized in that it has been suggested that for some individuals the medication will diminish all arousal, leaving them unable to achieve healthy sexual relationships (Harrison, 2008). In addition to this, for individuals who do not possess appropriate sexual arousal, the diminishment in arousal would lead to an absence of sexual thoughts (Winder et al., 2014a). This goes against the Good Lives Model proposed by Ward and Stewart (2003) which indicates that healthy relationships are a primary human good. However, through using MMPSA to lower problematic levels of arousal, this potentially leaves the individual in a position to develop future healthy sexual relationships through building on the skills they learn in psychological treatment which accompanies the pharmacological treatment (Home Office, 2007).

Types of medication

The forms of pharmacological medications currently used in UK Prison establishments to treat sexual preoccupation and hypersexual disorders can be categorized into two main classes: Hormonal therapy medications and Selective Serotonin Reuptake Inhibitors (SSRIs).

Hormonal therapy medications

Hormonal therapy medications include two main types: anti-androgens (for example Cyproterone Acetate (CPA)) and gonadotropin-releasing hormone agonists (GnRH) such as Triptorelin. These are both recognized in the NICE guidelines as pharmacological treatment for problematic sexual arousal (NICE, 2015). Anti-androgens and GnRH are antilibidinal in nature in that they have an effect on reducing testosterone (an androgen) which in turn leads to a reduction in arousal. Testosterone is an androgen and is the sex hormone predominantly responsible for sexual thoughts and desires and enabling erection, sperm production and ejaculation (Jordan, Fromberger, Stolpmann, & Muller, 2011). It is recognized that a reduction of testosterone of 30–40% of typical levels, leads to a substantial decrease in sexual arousal (Bancroft, 1989). Anti-androgens reduce sexual arousal by reducing testosterone to this threshold level. While anti-androgens have a direct effect on blocking androgen receptors, GnRH agonists work by stimulating the pituitary gland to release luteinising hormone (LH) resulting in a temporary 'flare' in testosterone levels but once the release of LH reduces then testosterone deprivation occurs by about week 3 or 4 (Van Poppel et al., 2008). Unfortunately, there are often adverse side effects associated with antilibidinal medications, such as weight gain, depression and gynaecomastia (Grubin, 2008).

Selective serotonin reuptake inhibitors

The second category of medication used to manage arousal is non-hormonal treatment comes in the form of SSRIs which have their effect by increasing the availability of serotonin in the synapse by blocking the serotonin reuptake transporters in the pre-synaptic membrane. Currently, SSRIs are not included in the NICE (2015) guidelines as treatment for problematic sexual arousal however effects on sexuality are recognized side effects of taking SSRIs, with 60% to 70% reporting delayed ejaculation and reduced libido (Montejo, Llorca, Izquierdo, & Rico-Villademoros, 2001). Theories concerning how serotonin manipulation produces these effects include both physiological (serotonin induces sexual satiety and inhibits erection and ejaculation, Jordan et al., 2011) and psychological aspects (reduced arousal perhaps via testosterone mediated dopamine release that controls motivation and reinforcement; Frohlich & Meston, 2000; Jordan et al., 2011). A further theory which characterizes sexual pre-occupation in terms of obsession and compulsion suggests that SSRIs work on this psychological aspect of desire (Bradford, 1995) given that SSRIs are used successfully to treat compulsive behaviours (Coleman, Gratzer, Nesvacil, & Raymond, 2000).

In addition to the effects of SSRIs on problematic sexual arousal they are effective in addressing comorbidities that are often associated with paraphilias or problematic sexual arousal such as depression (Adi et al., 2002). The effectiveness of treating the co-morbidities may also reduce the likelihood of reoffending as they act as risk factors in recidivism (Hill et al., 2003).

Side effects of medication

While not currently accepted through the NICE (2015) guidelines, there is a promising role for the future use of SSRIs in the treatment of individuals with sexual convictions. Anti-androgens for example, have been shown to be effective in reducing paraphilic fantasies and suppressing urges (Greenberg, Bradford, Curry, & O'Rourke, 1996). Unfortunately, the adverse side effects may mean individuals are less likely to want to volunteer to use the medication. While SSRIs do have side effects but these are often less extreme and are likely to be more manageable than those associated with anti-androgens, including things such as tiredness and nausea (Winder et al., 2014a). SSRIs are also considerably cheaper than hormonal therapy drugs anti-androgens and GnRH agonists. A twelve-month supply of the SSRI fluoxetine costs approximately £289, whereas a twelve-month supply of anti-androgens costs £376, and GnRH agonists may cost £992 for a twelve-month supply (NICE, 2015). It is thus important to know if each type of medication achieves

Table 11.1 Guidelines for prescribing medication when treating individuals with problematic sexual arousal.

- Level 1 – Psychological intervention should be provided for all.
- Level 2 – For individuals who pose a low risk of sexual violence, treatment can be increased by including pharmacological interventions with the use of SSRIs at a dose of 40 mg/day.
- Level 3 – For individuals who may have committed offences with sexual contact, but without penetration, or for those who have failed to respond to the SSRI treatment, a low dose of anti-androgen, 50–100 mg/day, may be added to the SSRI dosage.
- Level 4 – This level is for individuals who pose a moderate to high risk of sexual violence and those who failed to respond to the level 3 treatment. For these individuals the anti-androgen medication can be increased to the full dosage, 200–300 mg/day.
- Level 5 – Individuals who are at high risk of committing sexual violence to others, or those who have failed to respond to treatment at level 4, are to be treated at this level. For these individuals, treatment with GnRH agonists is suggested at 3 mg/month.
- Level 6 – The final level of treatment is intended for individuals who have failed to respond to treatment at level 5 and those with severe paraphilias. In cases such as this, it is recommended that anti-androgen medication is given at the rate of 50–200 mg/day, in addition to treatment with GnRH agonists. The use of SSRIs may also be added is necessary.

Thibaut et al. (2010)

similar results in terms of treating problematic sexual arousal, or indeed which type of medication is most suitable for whom, and what types of side effects each medication brings.

Medication guidelines

Thibaut et al. (2010) and the World Federation of Societies of Biological Psychiatry (WFSBP) created the guidelines for prescribing medication when treating individuals with problematic sexual arousal. The guidelines offered cover six levels of treatment which are outlined in Table 11.1.

Evidence of effectiveness

Treatment with anti-androgens

Khan et al. (2015) performed the most recent Cochrane Review assessing the effectiveness of pharmacological interventions in treating individuals who have offended or may be at risk of committing sexual offences. In their review, the authors were only able to review seven studies all of which were published over 20 years ago. The studies reviewed used predominantly Canadian samples, with only two of the studies being performed in the UK and one in Australia. Six of the studies reviewed used anti-androgen medications (Bancroft, Tennett, Loucas, & Cass, 1974; Cooper, 1981; Bradford & Pawlack, 1993; Langevin et al., 1979; Hucker, Lagevin & Bain, 1988;; McConaghy, Blaszczynski, & Kidson, 1988). While one of the studies, Tennant, Bancroft, and Cass (1974) compared two antipsychotic medications; benperidol and chlorpromazine. A summary of the studies reviewed is shown in Table 11.2. Although there were some positive findings, Khan et al. (2015) were unable to conclude

Table 11.2 Cochrane Review of the effectiveness of pharmacological interventions.

Authors	Medication Type	Results
Bancroft et al. (1974)	Compared CPA and ethinyl oestradiol, both of which are testosterone reducing medications, with a placebo.	Significant reductions in sexual activity were shown with both medications compared to the placebo. There was no significant difference between medications.
Cooper (1981)	The use of CPA was compared with a placebo.	A significant reduction in arousal and sexual outlets was shown following treatment with CPA.
Bradford and Pawlack (1993)	Compared CPA with a placebo.	Sexual activity and fantasies were significantly reduced following treatment with CPA.
Langevin et al. (1979)	Compared a combination of Medroxyprogesterone. (MPA) and assertiveness training with assertiveness training without medication.	All participants who received MPA ceased medication at the beginning of the study. The authors indicated that the side effects of MPA were considerable.
Hucker, Lagevin and Bain, (1988)	Compared MPA with a placebo.	Compliance was problematic in this study with every participant who had received MPA ceasing medication shortly after commencement. This was despite medication being ordered by the Courts.
McConaghy et al. (1988)	Compared the use of MPA and imaginal desensitization with imaginal desensitization alone.	Participants who had received MPA showed a significant reduction in testosterone. Participants were followed up after two years and no individual that had received both the MPA treatment and imaginal desensitization therapy had been charged for a further offence.
Tennant et al. (1974)	The study looked at comparisons between two types of antipsychotic medication; benperidol and chlorpromazine.	Results showed that benperidol had a weak effect on reducing libido and that chlorpromazine was not effective.

that pharmacological intervention was an appropriate treatment method for reducing sexual offending. The authors highlighted the importance of further research, larger sample sizes and a need for a randomized control trial.

Treatment with SSRIs

A number of studies have looked at the effectiveness of SSRIs in treating problematic arousal. Kafka (1994) treated a sample of 24 males with paraphilia related disorder and paraphilias, using the SSRIs sertraline and/or fluoxetine. Kafka (1994) reported that 70.8% of the participants showed a significant reduction in the amount of time they spent each day in unconventional sexual activities and the number of sexual outlets and that this was sustained for up to a year. Similar results were provided by Greenberg et al. (1996) who performed a retrospective study utilizing 58 participants with paraphilias. All participants were treated with SSRIs (fluoxetine, sertraline or fluvoxamine). Greenberg et al. (1996) found that SSRIs reduced the severity of fantasies but reported no significant difference between the type of SSRIs in terms of effectiveness.

Adi et al. (2002) performed a systematic review of nine studies in order to establish the effectiveness of SSRIs in treating those convicted of sexual offences. In addition to the studies outlined above, Adi et al. (2002) also reviewed; Kafka and Prentky (1992), Stein et al. (1992), Perilstein, Lipper, and Friedman (1991), Coleman, Cesnick, Moore, and Dwyer (1992), Bradford (1995), Fedoroff (1995) and Kafka and Hennan (2000). Adi et al. (2002) concluded that although there was evidence from each of the studies for the use of SSRIs in reducing problematic arousal, the evidence base was limited, subject to bias and further research was required.

Recent UK-based research

Medication for problematic sexual arousal was not introduced into prisons in England and Wales until 2007 (Home Office, 2007). Following the introduction of MMPSA, Professor Belinda Winder and team from the Sexual Offences, Crime and Misconduct Research Unit (SOCAMRU) at Nottingham Trent University have been running a mixed method longitudinal evaluation of the use of both SSRIs and anti-androgens in managing problematic sexual arousal of individuals who have committed sexual offences. The results to date are promising. Winder et al. (2014b) initially reported a preliminary investigation of the effectiveness of pharmacological treatment with a sample of 64 medicated individuals using both SSRIs and anti-androgens. Their findings were encouraging in that, at three months post medication, levels of sexual compulsivity were statistically significantly lower than pre-medication. This was also true for levels of hypersexuality and sexual preoccupation. The authors indicate that the results of SSRIs and anti-androgens are similar in reducing arousal and postulate that SSRIs could thus be deemed to be antilibidinal.

Winder et al. (2014a) also published a number of case studies illustrating the various treatment journeys of four individual medicated with antilibidinal medication. From their research, it was evident that the medication journey was not a simple one, and patients may change between medication types (SSRIS to anti-androgens and back again, for example) or stop and start medication for various reasons (not being able to deal with shame, 'missing' their sexual preoccupation, having too much 'headspace'); where individuals continued their medication, levels of sexual arousal were reduced in each of the case studies.

Lievesley et al. (2014) conducted qualitative studies on (i) prisoners taking medication and (ii) therapists working with prisoners in order to gain an understanding of the personal experiences of those involved in the treatment. Findings from the service user study highlighted the effectiveness of the medication, but there were concerns about side effects and whether or not they would be able to have sexual relationships in the future. Findings from the therapist study highlighted cynicism around service users taking medication, and whether they would continue to do so on post-parole (for example). Therapists reported that they felt the individual may be unaware of the importance of continuing medication in terms of reducing their risk of reoffending and that also they may cease medication as they may fear the side effects associated with it.

Another study by the SOCAMRU team (Elliott, Winder, Manby, Edwards, Norman & Lievesley, 2017) involved interviewing probation staff managing prisoners taking this medication. The findings highlighted that probation staff felt they did not know enough about the impact and effectiveness of the medication, and that they would like to be more involved in the referral process. Some staff indicated that they were not aware their service users had been prescribed medication until they disclosed this themselves leading them to feel embarrassed that they were unaware they had been referred.

Conclusion

The growing evidence base for MMPSA is promising and suggests that this is an effective addition to the treatment of individuals who have been convicted of sexual offences. Clearly, the use of MMPSA is not intended to replace psychological interventions. Pharmacological interventions have been shown to achieve the best results when combined with psychological interventions (Guay, 2009; Home Office, 2007). Recent findings by Gannon et al. (2019) indicate that psychological treatment programmes are more effective at reducing recidivism when problematic sexual arousal has been appropriately managed. MMPSA is intended to be used as an addition to treatment, in order to lower levels of arousal to the extent that meaningful work can be undertaken with the individual concerned through psychological interventions. The evidence above illustrates promising findings apropos the effectiveness of the medication currently used in the UK Prison Service; a forthcoming study by Winder et al. (submitted) with a control group will add to this evidence base. However, it is also clear that an RCT is much needed in this area. The introduction of medication into UK prisons is still relatively new, there are number of improvements that could be made in terms of communication between departments and increasing awareness of all involved in the risk management process.

In addition to this, the majority of research has focused on medicated individuals in a custodial setting. Research is currently being undertaken in order to ascertain the effectiveness of MMPSA once the individual is released from custody. There is a need to assess the effectiveness of MMPSA in terms of reducing problematic sexual arousal and rates of reoffending in a community setting. It is anticipated that this research will be a valuable contribution to the evidence base.

References

Adi, Y., Ashcroft, D., Browne, K., Beech, A., Fry-Smith, A., & Hyde, C. (2002). Clinical effectiveness and cost-consequences of selective serotonin reuptake inhibitors in the treatment of sex offenders. *Health Technology Assessment, 6*, 1–66).

Akerman, G. (2008). The development of a fantasy modification programme for a prison-based therapeutic community. *International Journal of Therapeutic Communities*, 108–188.

Akerman, G. (2010). Undertaking therapy at HMP Grendon with men who have committed sexual offences. In E. Sullivan & R. Shuker (Eds.), *Grendon and the emergence of forensic therapeutic communities: Developments in research and practice* (pp. 171–182). Chichester, UK: Wiley.

Akerman, G., & Beech, A. (2012). A systematic review of measures of deviant sexual interest and arousal. *Psychiatry, Psychology and Law, 19*, 118–143.

American Psychiatric Association. (2013). *Diagnostic and statistical manual of mental disorders: DSM – 5* (5th ed.). Arlington, VA: American Psychiatric Publishing.

Bancroft, J. (1989). *Human sexuality and its problems* (2nd ed.). Edinburgh: Churchill Livingstone.

Bancroft, J., Tennett, G., Loucas, K., & Cass, J. (1974). The control of deviant sexual behaviour by drugs. 1. Behavioural changes following oestrogens and anti-androgens. *British Journal of Psychiatry, 125*, 310–315.

Bancroft, J., & Vukadinovic, Z. (2004). Sexual addiction, sexual compulsivity, sexual impulsivity, or what? Toward a theoretical model. *The Journal of Sex Research, 41*, 225–234.

Beech, A., Fisher, D., & Ward, T. (2005). Sexual murderers' implicit theories. *Journal of Interpersonal Violence, 20*, 1366–1389.

Black, D., Kehrberg, L., Flumerfelt, D., & Schlosser, S. (1997). Characteristics of 36 subjects reporting compulsive sexual behaviour. *American Journal of Psychiatry, 154*(2), 243–249.

Blagden, N. J., Mann, R., Webster, S., Lee, R., & Williams, F. (2018). 'It's not something I chose you know': Making sense of pedophiles' sexual interest in children and the impact on their psychosexual identity. *Sexual Abuse, 30*, 728–754.

Bradford, J. (1995). An open pilot study of sertraline in the treatment of outpatients with paedophilia. Paper presented at the 1995 American Psychiatric Association, Miami, FL.

Bradford, J., & Pawlack, A. (1993). Effects of cyproterone acetate on sexual arousal patterns of paedophiles. *Archives of Sexual Behaviour, 22*, 629–641.

Coleman, E., Cesnick, J., Moore, A., & Dwyer, S. (1992). An exploratory study of the role of psychotropic medications in the treatment of sex offenders. *Journal of Offender Rehabilitation, 18*, 75–88.

Coleman, E., Gratzer, T., Nesvacil, L., & Raymond, N. C. (2000). Nefazodone and the treatment of nonparaphilic compulsive sexual behavior: A retrospective study. *The Journal of Clinical Psychiatry, 61*, 282–284.

Cooper, A. (1981). A placebo-controlled trial of the anti-androgen cyproterone acetate in deviant hypersexuality. *Comprehensive Psychiatry, 22*, 458–465.

Cortoni, F., & Marshall, W. (2001). Sex as a coping strategy and its relationship to juvenile sexual history and intimacy in sexual offenders. *Sexual Abuse: A Journal of Research and Treatment, 13*, 27–43.

Crank, B. R. (2018). Accepting deviant identities: The impact of self-labelling on intentions to desist from crime. *Journal of Crime and Justice, 41*, 155–172.

Dawson, S., Bannerman, B., & Lalumiere, M. (2016). Paraphilic Interests: An examination of sex differences in nonclinical samples. *Sexual Abuse: A Journal of Research and Treatment, 28*, 20–45.

Elliott, H., Winder, B., Manby, E., Edwards, H., & Lievesley, R. (2017). 'I kind of found out by accident': Probation staff experiences of pharmacological treatment for sexual preoccupation and hypersexuality. *The Journal of Forensic Practice, 20*, 20–31.

Fedoroff, J. (1995). Anti-androgen vs serotonergic medications in the treatment of sex offenders: A preliminary compliance study. *Canadian Journal of Human Sexuality, 4*, 111–123.

Frohlich, P., & Meston, C. (2000). Evidence that serotonin affects female sexual functioning via peripheral mechanisms. *Physiology and Behaviour, 71*, 383–393.

Gannon, T., Olver, M., Mallion, J., & James, M. (2019). *Does specialised psychological treatment for offending reduce recidivism? A meta-analysis examining staff and programme variables as predictors of treatment effectiveness.* Manuscript submitted for publication.

Greenberg, D. M., Bradford, J. M., Curry, S., & O'Rourke, A. (1996). A comparison of treatment of paraphilias with three serotonin reuptake inhibitors: A retrospective study. *Journal of the American Academy of Psychiatry and the Law Online, 24*, 525–532.

Grubin, D. (2008). Medical models and interventions in sexual deviance. In D. Laws & W. O'Donohue (Eds.), *Sexual deviancy: Theory, assessment and treatment* (2nd ed.). New York: The Guildford Press.

Guay, D. (2009). Drug treatment of paraphilic and nonparaphilic sexual disorders. *Clinical Therapeutics, 31*, 1–31.

Hanson, K., & Harris, A. (2000). Where should we intervene? Dynamic predictors of sexual offence recidivism. *Criminal Justice and Behaviour, 27*, 6–35.

Hanson, K., & Harris, A. (2001). A structured approach to evaluating change among sex offenders. *Sexual Abuse: A Journal of Research and Treatment, 13*, 105–122.

Hanson, K., Gordon, A., Harris, A., Marques, J., Murphy, W., Quinsey, V., & Seto, M. (2002). First report of the collaborative outcome data project on the effectiveness of psychological treatment for sex offenders. *Sexual Abuse: A Journal of Research and Treatment, 14*, 169–194.

Hanson, K., & Morton-Bourgon, K. E.. (2005). The characteristics of persistent sexual offenders: A meta-analysis of recidivism studies. *Journal of Consulting and Clinical Psychology, 73*, 1154–1163.

Harrison, K. (2008). Legal and ethical issues when using anti-androgenic pharmacotherapy with sex offenders. *Sexual Offender Treatment, 3*, 1–11. Retrieved 01/ 05/2019 From www. sexual-offender-treatment.org/index.php?id=70&type=123&type__=

Hill, A., Briken, P., Kraus, C., Strohm, K., & Berner, W. (2003). Differential pharmacological treatment of paraphilias and sex offenders. *International Journal of Offender Therapy and Comparative Criminology, 47*, 407–421.

Home Office. (2007). *Review for the protection of children from sex offenders.* London: Author.

Hucker, S., Lagevin, R., & Bain, J. (1988). A double-blind trial of sex drive reducing medication in paedophiles. *Sexual Abuse: A Journal of Research and Treatment, 1*, 227–242.

Jordan, K., Fromberger, P., Stolpmann, G., & Muller, J. L. (2011). The role of testosterone in sexuality and paraphilia: A neurobiological approach. Part I. Testosterone and sexuality. *The Journal of Sexual Medicine, 8*, 2993–3007.

Kafka, M. (1994). Sertraline pharmacotherapy for paraphilias and paraphilia related disorders: An open trial. *Annals of Clinical Psychiatry, 6*, 189–195.

Kafka, M. (2010). Hypersexual Disorder: A proposed diagnosis for DSM-V. *Archives of Sexual Behaviour, 39*, 377–400.

Kafka, M., & Hennan, J. (2000). Psychostimulant augmentation during treatment with selective serotonin reuptake inhibitors in men with paraphilias and paraphilia related disorders. *The Journal of Clinical Psychiatry, 61*, 664–670.

Kafka, M., & Hennen, J. (2002). A DSM-IV Axis 1 comorbidity study of males (n = 120) with paraphilias and paraphilia-related disorders. *Sexual Abuse: A Journal of Research and Treatment, 14*, 349–366.

Kafka, M., & Prentky, R. (1992). Fluoxetine treatment of nonparaphilic sexual addictions and paraphilias in men. *Journal of Clinical Psychiatry, 53*, 351–358.

Kafka, M. P. (1997). Hypersexual desire in males: An operational definition and clinical implications for males with paraphilias and paraphilia-related disorders. *Archives of Sexual Behaviour, 25*, 505–526.

Kafka, M. P. (2003). Sex offending and sexual appetite: The clinical and theoretical relevance of hypersexual desire. *International Journal of Offender Therapy and Comparative Criminology, 47*, 439–451.

Kalichman, S., Johnson, J., Adair, V., Rompa, D., Multhauf, K., & Kelly, J. (1994). Sexual sensation seeking: Scale development and predicting AIDS-risk behaviour among homosexually active men. *Journal of Personality Assessment, 62*, 385–397.

Kalichman, S., & Rompa, D. (2001). The sexual compulsivity scale: Further development and use with HIV-positive persons. *Journal of Personality Assessment, 76*, 379–395.

Kaplan, M., & Krueger, R. (2010). Diagnosis, assessment and treatment of hypersexuality. *Journal of Sex Research, 47*, 181–198.

Khan, O., Ferriter, M., Huband, N., Powney, M., Dennis, J., & Duggan, C. (2015). Pharmacological interventions for those who have sexually offended or are at risk of offending. *Cochrane Database of Systematic Reviews, 2*.

Krueger, R., Reed, G., First, M., Marais, A., Kismodi, E., & Briken, P. (2017). Proposals for para-philic disorders in the International Classification of Diseases and Related Health Problems, eleventh revision (ICD-11). *Archives of Sexual Behaviour, 46*, 1529–1545.

Langevin, R., Paitich, D., Hucker, S., Newman, S., Ramsay, G., & Pope, S. (1979). The effect of assertiveness training, Provera and sex of therapist in the treatment of genital exhibitionism. *Journal of Behaviour Therapy and Experimental Psychiatry, 10*, 275–282.

Leitenberg, H., & Henning, K. (1995). Sexual fantasy. *Psychology Bulletin, 3*, 469–496.

Lievesley, R., Elliott, H., Winder, B., & Norman, C. (2014). Understanding service users' and therapists' experiences of pharmacological treatment for sexual preoccupation and/or hypersexuality in incarcerated sex offenders. *The Journal of Forensic Psychiatry and Psychology, 25*, 262–287.

Looman, J. (1995). Sexual fantasies of child molesters. *Canadian Journal of Behavioural Science, 27*, 321–332.

Losel, F., & Schmucker, M. (2005). The effectiveness of treatment for sexual offenders: A com-prehensive meta-analysis. *Journal of Experimental Criminology, 1*, 117–146.

Mandeville-Norden, R., Beech, A., & Hayes, E. (2008). Examining the effectiveness of a UK community-based sexual offender treatment programme for child abusers. *Psychology, Crime and Law, 14*, 493–512.

Mann, R. E., Hanson, R. K., & Thornton, D. (2010). Assessing risk for sexual recidivism: Some proposals on the nature of psychologically meaningful risk factors. *Sexual Abuse: A Journal of Research and Treatment, 22*, 191–217.

Marshall, W. L., Marshall, L. E., & Serran, G. A. (2006). Strategies in the treatment of paraphil-ias: A critical review. *Annual Review of Sex Research, 17*, 162–182.

Maruna, S. (2001). *Making good: how ex-convicts reform and rebuild their lives* (1st ed.). Wash-ington, D. C.: American Psychological Association.

McCartan, K., Hoggett, J., & Kemshall, H. (2018). Risk assessment and management of indi-viduals convicted of a sexual offence in the UK. *Sexual Offender Treatment, 13*, 1–8.

McConaghy, N., Blaszczynski, A., & Kidson, W. (1988). Treatment of sex offenders with imaginal desensitisation and/or medroxyprogesterone. *Acta Psychiatrica Scandinavica, 77*, 199–206.

McKenna, K. Y., Green, A. S., & Smith, P. K. (2001). Demarginalizing the sexual self. *Journal of Sex Research, 38*, 302–311.

Mews, A., Bella, L Di, & Purver, M. (2017). Impact evaluation of the prison-based Core Sex Offender Treatment Programme. *Ministry of Justice Analytical Series*, Retrieved 18.02.2019 from https://assets.publishing.service.gov.uk/government/uploads/system/uploads/attachment_data/file/623876/sotp-report-web-.pdf

Miner, M., Coleman, E., Center, B., Ross, M., & Rosser, S. (2007). The compulsive sexual behav-iour inventory: Psychometric properties. *Archives of Sexual Behaviour, 36*(4), 579–587.

Montejo, A., Llorca, G., Izquierdo, J., & Rico-Villademoros, F. (2001). Incidence of sexual dysfunction associated with antidepressant agents: A prospective multicentre study of 1022 outpatients. *Journal of Clinical Psychiatry, 62*, 10–21.

Morgenstern, J., Muench, F., O'Leary, A., Wainberg, M., Parson, J., Hollander, E., … Irwin, T. (2011). Non-paraphilic compulsive sexual behaviour and psychiatric co-morbidities in gay and bi-sexual men. *Sexual Addiction and Compulsivity, 18*, 114–134.

Muench, F., Morgenstern, J., Hollander, E., Irwin, T., O'Leary, A., Parsons, J., … Lai, B. (2007). The consequences of compulsive sexual behaviour: The preliminary reliability and validity of the compulsive sexual behaviour consequences scale. *Sexual Addiction and Compulsivity, 14*, 207–220.

Nacro (2018). *Interventions for Perpertrators of Child Sexual Exploitation*. Retrived 18/02/2019 from https://www.csacentre.org.uk/csa-centre-prod/assets/File/CSE%20perpetrators%20 4%20-%20Interventions%20for%20perpetrators%20of%20CSE.pdf

NICE. (2015). *Hypersexuality: Fluoxetine*. Retrieved 25/ 10/2018from www.nice.org.uk/advice/ esuom46/chapter/Key-points-from-the-evidence

Paunovic, N., & Hallberg, J. (2014). Conceptualisation of hypersexual disorder with the behavioural-cognitive inhibition theory. *Psychology, 5*, 151–159.

Perilstein, R., Lipper, S., & Friedman, L. (1991). Three cases of paraphilias responsive to fluoxetine treatment. *The Journal of Clinical Psychiatry, 52*, 169–170.

Raymond, N., Coleman, E., & Miner, M. (2003). Psychiatric comorbidity and compulsive/ impulsive traits in compulsive sexual behaviour. *Comprehensive Psychiatry, 44*, 370–380.

Raymond, N., Coleman, E., Ohlerking, F., Christeson, G., & Miner, M. (1999). Psychiatric comorbidity in pedophilic sex offenders. *American Journal of Psychiatry, 156*, 786–788.

Reed, G. (2010). Toward ICD-11: Improving the clinical utility of WHO's International Classification of Mental Health Disorders. *Professional Psychology, Research and Practice, 41*, 457–464.

Reid, R., Carpenter, B., Hook, J., Garos, S., Manning, J., Gilliand, R., ... Fong, T. (2012a). Report of findings in a DSM-5 field trial for hypersexual disorder. *The Journal of Sexual Medicine, 9*, 2868–2877.

Reid, R., Garos, S., & Fong, T. (2012b). Psychometric development of the Hypersexual Behaviour Consequences Scale. *Journal of Behavioural Addictions, 1*, 115–122.

Rinehart, N., & McCabe, M. (1997). Hypersexuality: Psychopathology or normal variant of sexuality. *Sexual and Marital Therapy, 12*, 45–60.

Saleh, F., & Berlin, F. (2003). Sex hormones, neurotransmitters, and psychopharmacological treatments in men with paraphilic disorders. *Journal of Child Sexual Abuse, 12*, 233–253.

Seto, M. C. (2019). The motivation-facilitation model of sexual offending. *Sexual Abuse, 31*, 3–24.

Seto, M. C., & Eke, A. W. (2015). Predicting recidivism among adult male child pornography offenders: Development of the Child Pornography Offender Risk Tool (CPORT). *Law and Human Behavior, 39*, 416.

Seto, M. C., Reeves, L., & Jung, S. (2010). Explanations given by child pornography offenders for their crimes. *Journal of Sexual Aggression, 16*, 169–180.

Snell, W., Fisher, T., & Schuh, T. (1992). Reliability and validity of the sexuality scale: A measure of self-esteem, sexual-depression and sexual-preoccupation. *The Journal of Sex Research, 29*, 261–273.

Stein, D., Hollander, E., Anthony, D., Schneier, F., Fallon, B., Liebowitz, M., & Klein, D. (1992). Serotonergic medications for sexual obsessions, sexual addictions and paraphilias. *The Journal of Clinical Psychiatry, 53*, 267–271.

Tennant, G., Bancroft, J., & Cass, J. (1974). The control of deviant sexual behaviour by drugs: A double blind controlled study of benperidol, chlorpromazine and placebo. *Archives of Sexual Behaviour, 3*, 261–271.

Thibaut, F., Barra, F., Gordon, H., Cosyns, P., & Bradford, J. (2010). The World Federation of Societies of Biological Psychiatry (WFSBP) Guidelines for the biological treatment of paraphilias. *World Journal of Biological Psychiatry, 11*, 604–655.

Van Poppel, H., Tombal, B., de la Rosette, J., Persson, B., Jensen, J., & Olesen, T. (2008). Degarelix: A novel Gonadotropin- Releasing Hormone (GnRH) receptor blocker – Results from a 1 year, multicentre, randomised, phase 2 dosage finding study in the treatment of prostate cancer. *European Urology, 54*, 805–815.

Wakefield, J. (2012). The DSM-5's proposed new categories of sexual disorder: The problem of false positives in sexual diagnosis. *Clinical Social Work Journal, 40*, 213–223.

Ward, T., & Stewart, C. (2003). The treatment of sex offenders: Risk management and good lives. *Professional Psychology: Research and Practice, 34*, 353–360.

WHO. (2018). International classification of diseases, 11th Revision. Retrieved 23/ 04/2019 from https://icd.who.int/en/

Winder, B., Lievesley, R., Elliott, H., Hocken, K., Faulkner, J., Norman, C., & Kaul, A. (2017). Evaluation of the use of pharmacological treatment with prisoners experiencing high levels of hypersexual disorder. *The Journal of Forensic Psychiatry and Psychology, 29*(8), 53–71.

Winder, B., Lievesley, R., Elliott, H. J., Norman, C., & Kaul, A. (2014a). Understanding the journeys of high-risk male sex offenders voluntarily receiving medication to reduce their sexual preoccupation and/or hypersexuality. In D. T. Wilcox, T. Garrett, & L. Harkin (Eds.), *Sex offender treatment: A case study approach to issues and interventions* (pp. 342–370). Chichester: Wiley.

Winder, B., Lievesley, R., Kaul, A., Elliott, H. J., Thorne, K., & Hocken, K. (2014b). Preliminary evaluation of the use of pharmacological treatment with convicted sexual offenders experiencing high levels of sexual preoccupation, hypersexuality and/or sexual compulsivity. *The Journal of Forensic Psychiatry & Psychology, 25*, 176–194.

Winder, B., Norman, C., Hamilton, J., Tovey, L., Hocken, K., Lievesley, R., & Kaul, A. (submitted). Evaluation of the use of selective serotonin reuptake inhibitors and anti-androgens to manage problematic sexual arousal with individuals who have been convicted of a sexual offence and who demonstrate high levels of sexual compulsivity.

Winters, J., Christoff, K., & Gorzalka, B. (2010). Dysregulated sexuality and high sexual desire: Distinct constructs? *Archives of Sexual Behaviour, 39*, 1029–1043.

Womack, S., Hook, J., Ramos, M., Davis, D., & Penberthy, J. K. (2013). Measuring hypersexual behaviour. *Sexual Addiction and Compulsivity, 20*, 65–78.

Yoon, I., Houang, S., Hirshfield, S., & Downing, M. (2016). Compulsive sexual behaviour and HIV/STI risk: A review of current literature. *Current Addiction Reports, 3*, 387–399.

Part III

Approaches to assessment and management

Introducing the multi-component framework of female sexual offending

12

Rachel Worthington

This chapter will summarize the research in relation to the prevalance of female sexual offending and examine current theories and approaches towards the assessment and treatment for sexual violence where the perpetrator is female. The constraints of these approaches are discussed and an alternative multi-component framework will be proposed for working with females who commit sexual offences. This takes into account the biopsychosocial factors which contribute to the behaviour as well as practical strategies for reducing the behaviour. The benefits of adopting this approach are discussed and a case study example is provided to demonstrate how this may work in practice.

The extent of the problem – female perpetrators and their victims

The National Incident-Based Reporting System (NIBRS) data estimated that approximately 5% of the 800,000 sexual offences committed between 1991 and 2011 involved female perpetrators (Williams & Bierie, 2015). Other estimates suggest that women are arrested for and convicted of between 1% and 6% of the sex offences in the United States, but rates vary regionally (Sandler & Freeman, 2007). Differences are also noted to exist between conviction and self-report data. For example, Peter (2009) noted that estimates of female-perpetrated child sexual abuse from child services were more than 10 times higher than estimates of cases that had been criminally charged when self-report data was used. McLeod (2015) also estimated that females perpetrated 15–21% of child sexual abuse, with male children being more likely to report female-perpetrated sexual abuse than female children (Cortoni, Babchishin & Rat, 2017) but that this was not reflected in the arrest or conviction data. Vandiver, Braithwaite and Stafford (2017) estimated that females who sexually offend comprise less than 10% of all males who sexually offend. Thus, it would seem that the reported frequency of female sexual offending is lower than for males. However, the question remains as to who are the victims of females who sexually offend.

A meta-analysis of eight sexual assault victimization surveys found that 3% of female victims and 21% of male victims reported female perpetrators (Fergusson & Mullen, 1999). In terms of victims, 6.7% of men reported being 'made to penetrate' someone (also a form of non-consensual sex) in their life-time and 79.2% of victimized men reported female perpetrators. In addition, Basile, Smith, Breiding, Black, and Mahendra (2014) found that heterosexual male victims were much more likely to report abuse by a female perpetrator in their lifetime (71.4%) than were bisexual men (34.2%) or gay men (21.4%). Gay female victims were more likely to report such abuse by a female perpetrator in their lifetime (14.8%) than were bisexual (12.5%) or heterosexual women victims (5.3%). The Centers for Disease Control and Prevention (CDC) also estimated the rates of male and female sexual offending to be more equal than did other researchers. They found that males and females reported a nearly equal prevalence of perpetrating non-consensual sex in a 12-month period (Stemple & Meyer, 2014). However, it is also noted that despite this female perpetrators are less likely to proceed through the criminal justice system than males (Gorman-Smith & Vivolo, 2012) and reasons for this will be explored subsequently.

It is argued that the prevalance of sexual violence perpetrated by women has been impacted upon by gender biases in legal definitions. For example, rape had historically been defined as 'penetration of the victim'; however, Bre-iding (2014) found that only 1.7% of men reported experiencing unwanted penetration while 6.7% reported being 'made to penetrate' someone else. Thus it is important to ensure gender-inclusive definitions of rape (Basile et al., 2014) as well as other forms of sexual offending such as sexual coercion and unwanted sexual contact when analysing the frequency of female sexual offending. For example, Girshick (2002) noted that victims who reported being sexually abused by gay and bisexual women were de-legitimized both due to heterosexual assumptions about the definition of penetration and stig-matization associated with social attitudes about same sex relationships. In addition, Davies and Rogers (2006) also noted that historic attitudes towards masculinity and sexual activity resulted in reduced reporting and convic-tions of perpetration against males by females. They viewed this to be due to social attitudes historically taking the view that males were more sexually preoccupied and would be in some way grateful for sexual activity and would not thus experience any sexual contact as unwanted. However, this research is somewhat dated and it would be expected that social attitudes towards sexual behaviour have changed since then. Although there is limited modern research in this area, Twenge, Sherman, and Wells (2015) tracked differences in attitudes towards sex between the 1970s and 2012. They found that adults in 2000–2012 had more sexual partners, were more likely to have had sex with a casual date or an acquaintance, and were more accepting of most non-marital sex (premarital sex, teen sex, and same-sex sexual activity) than people in the 1970s and 1980s. The authors argued this was due to cultural individualism thus noting that cultural and societal influences attitudes over time. However, it is unclear how cultural and societal changes would account for the differences in female perpetration against children and this will be discussed subsequently.

Cortoni et al. (2017) found that boys reported female-perpetrated child sexual abuse more often than girls although the reasons for this are unclear. McLeod (2015) also noted that victims of female-perpetrated child sexual abuse were younger with a mean age of approximately 6 years old compared to victims of male perpetrated sexual abuse who had an approximate mean age of 9 years. In their study, 92% of victims in female-perpetrated cases were under 9 years old, compared to 57% in the male-perpetrated sample. This led researchers to consider that the conviction data may be influenced by the concealed perpetration of child sexual abuse in caregiving settings that disproportionately involves women (Burgess-Proctor, Comartin, & Kubiak, 2017). This is consistent with the literature that suggests that females tend to sexually offend against victims who are related or known to them and who are younger than 18 (Bourke et al., 2014), and that females are more likely to sexually offend against their biological children than children unknown to them or non-relatives (Williams & Bierie, 2015). It is also noted that they are more likely to co-offend with a male perpetrator (Comartin, Burgess-Proctor, Kubiak, & Kernsmith, 2018) but they are less likely to cause physical injuries to their victims (Williams & Bierie, 2015). Thus, it would seem that some differences exist in the victims of female sexual offending compared to males; however, it is unclear if this is due to the methods of data collection and difficulties with conviction and self-report data (Beech, Elliott, Birgden, & Findlater, 2008). Thus, they suggested that a way to overcome this would be to explore internet offending which may provide a more reliable source of data collection.

Females who offend using the Internet

In the UK it is thought that around one-third of male sex offences are now internet-related (Middleton, 2009). However, females who sexually offend using the internet appear to be rare in the criminal justice system. Lambert and O'Halloran (2008) were able to study this group and their study found that females who sexually offend using the internet largely replicated the pattern adopted by males whereby the majority of females openly admitted to having a sexual interest in children, they had cognitive distortions and the internet provided a forum which provided acceptance for these. It was also noted that the females in the sample discussed how being female provided them with increased opportunities for offending due to societal naivety about females being potential perpetrators of sexual abuse.

Thus, what is known is that capturing data in relation to female perpetrators of sexual violence has been made more difficult due to: lowered rates of reporting by victims; legal and societal attitudes in relation to females; and a lower frequency of this behaviour in comparison to males. Hence, attempts have been made to explore why this may be the case and to explain what risk factors and theories may account for sexual violence perpetrated by females.

Theories of female sexual offending

In an attempt to explore why females may engage in sexual offending, Gannon, Rose, and Ward (2008) developed the Descriptive Model of Female Sexual Offending (DMFSO) based on the accounts of an initial sample of 20 females who sexually offended. This consisted of three main sections: Background Factors; Pre-Offence Period; Offence and Post Offence period. This was followed by the Pathways model (Gannon, Rose, & Ward, 2010) using a slightly larger sample of females. This found that females who sexually offended followed three main 'pathways' or trajectories to offending:

1) Explicit Approach Child or Adult ($n = 9$) – wished to offend and with evidence of planning.
2) Directed Avoidant ($n = 5$) – explicitly directed to commit the offence by a coercive male.
3) Implicit Disorganized ($n = 4$) – impulsive and disorganized planning or did not appear to set out specifically to sexually offend but, upon making contact with a victim and experiencing sexual arousal or emotional loneliness, offended impulsively.

However, as Gannon et al. (2014) noted, 4 of the participants in their sample did not provide enough information to categorize their offence pathway, resulting in the model being based on a sample of 18 females. Thus, it would seem that while this was a useful attempt to consider pathways that females who sexual offended adopted, the small sample size and variability in behaviour made this difficult to generalize across the sample. Furthermore, the model provides little information in terms of methods by which harmful sexual behaviour in females should be addressed.

Wijkman, Bijleveld and Hendriks (2010) also subsequently attempted to understand the typologies of female sexual offender in order to develop pathways to offending. These consisted of the following:

1) Solo offenders who abuse adolescent children (the euphemistic 'teacher/lover' group).
2) Solo offenders who abuse pre-pubescent children.
3) Psychiatrically disordered offenders who have a variety of victim types, and whose behaviour is the result of a psychiatric disorder.
4) Offenders motivated by commercial profit by providing victims for child molesters in return for money.
5) Male-associated offenders, incorporating:
   (a) male-coerced – those who participate under the explicit threat of emotional abuse or physical violence;
   (b) active male accompanied – those who play an interested and active role
   (c) passive male-accompanied – those who provide opportunities for abuse or do not act to prevent abuse, but do not take an active role.

However, the deficit of this typology is that it only pertains to females who sexual offended against children and does not apply, for example, to females who perpetrate against adult males or adult females. Thus, in terms of understanding the functions of female sexual offending and factors that contribute to this, it is evident that unlike theories of male sexual offending the research has some significant deficits.

A common theme across theories of female sexual offending has been to place emphasis on how female sexual perpetrators have been victims of sexual abuse. This is because females who sexually offended were more likely to report a history of exposure to trauma than females in the general population and males who sexual offended (Fazel, Sjöstedt, Grann, & Långström, 2010). For example, female perpetrators report earlier sexual abuse whereby 64% were first victimized before age six, as opposed to 26% of males who sexually offended; females who sexually offended were more likely to be victims of incest (33%) than males who offended (13%) and females were also more likely to report having been raped (39%) as compared to males (4%) (Mathews, Hunter, & Vuz, 1997). Sandler and Freeman (2007) also found that females who perpetrated sexual offences reported experiencing greater childhood trauma than those convicted of non-sexual offences, including more physical violence, emotional abuse, and neglect. It is also noted that females who sexually offended may report experiencing emotional abuse during childhood. For example, Fazel et al. (2010) evaluated 61 studies with a total of 6,293 females who sexually offended. They found that females who sexually offended grew up in underprivileged homes with a lack of parental affection and that 49.2% of the females who sexually offended in the sample suffered from a psychiatric disorder and/or proven learning difficulty, compared to around 11.4% in the general population (Fazel et al., 2010). As a result, Miller and Najavits (2012) argued that trauma should be specifically attended to in treatment.

However, it should be noted that many women report a history of trauma but do not go on to sexually offend. In addition, as Plummer and Cossins (2018) note, the belief that child sexual abuse (CSA) is a predisposing factor for the transition from victim to offender is not upheld given most victims of CSA are female and yet most perpetrators of CSA are male. The authors note that if child sexual abuse predisposed perpetration of sexual abuse then on this basis it would be expected that most perpetrators of child sexual abuse would be female. This was also confirmed by Ogloff et al. (2012) who explored the link between victimization and sexual offending in a 45 year follow up study comparing offence rates of people exposed to child sexual abuse compared to those who had not been exposed to child sexual abuse. They found that 5% of male child sexual abuse victims were subsequently convicted of a sex offence, which was significantly greater than for men who had not been sexually abused as children (0.6%). However, female victims of child sexual abuse were no more likely than female non-victims to be convicted of a sex offence in adulthood. This led Ogloff et al. (2012) to argue that it was not the sexual abuse itself which contributed to sexual offending per se but other social psychological factors relating to the individual and their processing of the abuse which may be of relevance. Thus, the notion of trauma being the primary driving factor for female sexual offending should be carefully considered, not only because this may not accurately reflect reality but because this may also influence attitudes about responsibility for behaviour and risk whereby females who sexually offend are viewed as victims of trauma rather than being encouraged to take accountability for their own behaviour.

Gender equivalence

There was no evidence of gender inequivalence in the study conducted by Christensen (2018) who noted that females who sexually offended were sentenced by judges equally whether they were male or female, and that females were portrayed in the media as being both dangerous and accountable for their actions. Christensen (2018) noted how this had shifted from historical descriptions in society of females who sexually offend as 'seducing' adolescent males and 'teaching' them sexual behaviours and that society now recognizes this as sexual abuse (Hayes & Baker, 2014) and that advances in attitudes towards gender-equivalence have adjusted public attitudes towards females who sexually offended.

In terms of gender-equivalence it has also been noted that, similar to research on general criminality (Van Voorhis, Wright, Salisbury, & Bauman, 2010), male and females who sexually offended share some common characteristics such as histories of adverse childhood experiences, difficulties with relationships, antisocial attitudes, antisocial associates and substance abuse problems (Cortoni, Hanson, & Coache, 2010; Cortoni & Gannon, 2011; Pflugradt, Allen, & Zintsmaster, 2018). Thus, in much the same way that attitudes, beliefs, relationships and sexual arousal have been identified as risk factors for males who sexually offended, research has also demonstrated this to be the case for females who sexually offended. For example, Cortoni, Hanson and Coache (2010) found that females who sexually offended have treatment needs in relation to developing and maintaining healthy relationships. This was noted to be specifically the case for solo females who sexually offended perpetrating sexual violence against adolescents whereby the function of their behaviour was to obtain emotional closeness, and was motivated by increased feelings of power and control (Eldridge & Saradjian, 2000). For females who sexually offended, perpetrating with a male associate, the function of the behaviour appeared to be linked to increasing intimacy with either the victim or a co-offending partner (Gannon et al., 2008). Lambert and O'Halloran (2008) also found that women in pro-paedophile web forums show a clear focus on a sexual attraction to children, desire for sexual contact with a child and the encouragement of children into sexual behaviour. Gannon and Rose (2009) also found evidence that females who sexually offended held offence support cognitions and post hoc rationalizations that supported offending. Beech et al. (2009) also found that females who sexually offended held four out five motivational schema for offending (Uncontrollability; Dangerous World; Children seen as sexual objects; and Nature of harm) compared to males. Hence, it would seem that similarities exist between males and females who sexually offended and attending to gender as a factor of difference should be carefully considered. As a result, it is argued that females who sexually offend may be better understood by adopting a gendered perspective which takes into account the role of gender in terms of social norms, identities, history, culture, context, societal attitudes, biological and reproductive differences (Steffensmeier & Allan, 1996).

Gendered perspectives – what does it mean to be female?

Steffensmeier and Allan (1996) considered the role of gender in relation to criminal behaviour and suggested this could be understood by three main theoretical perspectives:

1) Gender-neutral: whereby traditional theories are derived from samples of males who offend and are applied to females who offend. They do not explain how gender affects the type, frequency, or context of criminal behaviour.
2) Gender-specific: which do not assume that the dynamic factors associated with male offending are the same as female.
3) Gendered: these are different from gender-neutral and gender-specific approaches in that they do not assume that causal patterns for female criminality are either the same or completely distinct from those for males.

Thus, in order to understand how gendered perspectives may apply to females who sexually offend it is perhaps pertinent to consider what does gender mean and what does it mean to be female? According to Jäncke (2018) the idea of psychological gender differences as being both large and biologically determined is based on animal research where it is much easier than it is in humans to study genetic differences in terms of sex/gender, including at the molecular, hormonal, and neurophysiological levels. While in the literature the terms sex and gender differences are often used interchangeably, the term sex is used mostly to group people into females and males on the basis of an individual's reproductive system and of secondary sexual characteristics. Gender refers to the social roles based on the sex of the person or personal identification of a person's own gender.

In terms of brain anatomy Jäncke (2018) argues that while there may be significant differences in parts of the brain between males and females it is not possible to identify these consistently. For example, the intermediate nucleus (InM) of the hypothalamus, is on average twice as large in males as it is in females. However, in about a third of the cases, males and females demonstrate InMs of the same size. Thus, it is not possible to identify a 'female' or 'male' brain because it is difficult or even impossible to identify typical and dimorphic features that justify a clear sex/gender classification. Hence, there is no such thing as a 'female' brain and furthermore the enormity of the neural network is so plastic that any individual brain can also be significantly influenced by an individual's experience and practice effects. For example, research undertaken with older adults demonstrates that hemispheric asymmetry reduces with age and is less lateral. However, asymmetry reduction is often interpreted as a typical feature of a 'female brain' thought to indicate advantageous 'female' bilateral processing. Jäncke (2018) concluded that while there are moderate to strong brain anatomical gender differences, these differences are not compelling enough to support the hypothesis of an existing sexual dimorphism in brain anatomy. Besides the fact of strong overlaps between male and female distribution, it has to be considered that brain anatomy is substantially affected by environmental influences (Jäncke, 2018).

Hyde (2005) also undertook a large meta-analytic study analysing gender differences across 124 psychological variables exploring mathematical, verbal, perceptual and motor abilities. The study also included effect sizes for personality, aggression, sexual behaviour, leadership, social behaviour, life satisfaction, moral reasoning, delay of gratification, cheating behaviour, and job factors. The results of the study indicated that 78% of the effect sizes were in the close-to-zero range or small ($0 < d > 0.35$). The only areas where there were noted exceptions related to: motor performance (e.g. throwing velocity and distance); incidence of masturbation; attitudes towards sex in uncommitted relationships; and physical aggression. This led Hyde (2005) to conclude that while the differences model (which argues that males and females are vastly different psychologically) dominates the popular media, this is not the case and that males and females are similar on most, but not all, psychological variables. This is known as the gender similarities hypothesis which notes that differences attributed to gender are largely based on social factors (Lightdale & Prentice, 1994). For example, gender differences in mathematics and science are smaller in countries with higher gender equality and less gender-restricted educational opportunities (Weber, Skirbekk, Freund & Herlitz, 2013; Hyde, 2014).

However, it should also be noted that the gender similarities hypothesis has been criticized for not observing the vast way in which the 'exceptions' (including sexual attitudes) may be perceived as vastly different. For example, in terms of sexuality, Hyde (2014) noted that stereotypical views of male and female sexuality exist but that some differences are also notable. For example, Petersen and Hyde (2010) measured 14 different types of sexual behaviours and 16 sexual attitudes. None of the 30 areas had large effect sizes and 4 were in the moderate range: males were more likely to masturbate, to use pornography, and to have more sexual partners, and males had more favourable attitudes towards casual sex. Gender similarities were found for oral sex, attitudes about extra-marital sex, attitudes about masturbation, attitudes about condom use, and attitudes about gay women (but attitudes toward gay men showed somewhat more favourable attitudes among women). The moderator analyses indicated that some gender gaps have narrowed over time, including attitudes about casual sex. Thus it is argued that as the gap in gender inequalities narrows it would be expected that differences in sexual behaviours and attitudes would also narrow and that differences are largely based on societal factors. For example, Kreager, Staff, Gauthier, Lefkowitz and Feinberg (2016) argued that differences in sexual behaviours may be explained by sexual script theory whereby sexual scripts are socially constructed cognitive schema that define normative sexual behaviours and inform individual actions in sexual situations (Simon & Gagnon, 2003). At the cultural level, traditional sexual scripts are gendered prescriptions for appropriate sexual conduct (Masters, Casey, Wells, & Morrison, 2013). Thus, it is proposed that sexual behaviours are modified by societal gender inequality whereby the internalization and deployment of distinct and potentially harmful gender scripts occurs in childhood (Martin & Ruble, 2010) and the application of differential gender expectations around sexuality begins in adolescence. Furthermore, it is argued that peers stigmatize male and female adolescents perceived as gender non-conformists (Bordini & Sperb, 2013) thus suggesting that social factors influence sexual behavioural differences between males and females.

Hence, what can be seen is that a variety of factors may influence a person's behaviour and while gender may be one of these, precisely what it means to be female may depend on the person's internal and external world. Furthermore, sexual behaviours can be influenced by a range of factors such as age, culture, religion, education, etc. Thus, to assume that gender per se is a differentiating factor for sexual violence is presumptuous in that while females may represent a minority group of people who sexually offended, there are many other minority groups of people who sexually offend for whom generalized theories are not proposed to explain their offending. For example, the British Crime Survey for England and Wales (2012) noted that 2% of people convicted for sexual offences were 60 or over; however, theories for elderly people who sexual offend highlight the need for an individualized approach in the assessment and management of people who offend (Booth, 2016) rather than seeking a generalized theory of this minority group. Thus, it would seem that attempting to find common factors to assess and treat a client group that is so small is inherently plagued with difficulties and these are worsened if the primary attention is given to the notion of being 'female', which is inherently a social and fluid construct. Hence, like males who sexually offend, females are not a homogenous group.

Pflugradt and Cortoni (2014) also supported this approach noting that female sexual offending is directly related to all other areas of the female's life and that treatment should attend to the contextual nature of the person's social functioning and the individual manifestations of sexually assaultive behaviours. Thus, it would seem that individualized and person-centred approaches which consider the biopsychosocial nature of offending should be considered as a method for exploring the assessment and treatment of females who engage in sexual violence. Current approaches to treatment will be explored subsequently alongside suggestions for how these approaches could be improved.

Treatment

Pflugradt and Cortoni (2014) suggested that interventions for females who sexually offend should seek to:

1) Reduce or eliminate antisocial attitudes and behaviours while increasing prosocial skills.
2) Empower clients to overcome both past traumas and socio-cultural barriers to rehabilitation.
3) Build and enhance coping skills and abilities, especially emotional regulation.
4) Develop relational strengths (e.g. healthy relationships with intimate partners, peers and other social supports).

Table 12.1 Four-phase model of interventions for females who sexually offend.

Phase 1:	Assessment	• intimacy/relationship issues
		• cognitive processes
		• personality characteristics
		• social functioning
		• individual or unique characteristics
		• treatment recommendations.
Phase 2:	Engagement	• overview of treatment
		• establish confidentiality requirements
		• background factors
		• enhancement of self-esteem/reduction of shame
		• improving coping and mood management
		• broaden empathy
		• reduction of treatment interfering factors
Phase 3:	Modifying Criminogenic Targets	• trauma and past abuse
		• attitudes and cognitions
		• self-regulation issues (mental health needs and emotional regulation skills)
		• relationship issues (boundaries and healthy relationships)
		• sexual issues (sexual deviancy and healthy sexuality)

(continued)

Table 12.1 *(continued)*

Phase 4:	Self-Management	• Modified Good Lives Model • generalization of skills outside of group/institution • parenting skills • release/discharge plans • connecting with various resources (e.g. economic, educational, vocational); Circles of Support • Integrating the primary positive psychology models (i.e. Good Lives Model, Circles of Support and Accountability model) .the therapeutic interventions employed within each treatment phase are individually specific and dictated by the idiosyncratic needs of each individual female.

Pflugradt and Allen (2015) extended this further to consider the sequencing in which interventions for females who sexually offend should take place in their four-phase model (Table 12.1).

In the model, Pflugradt and Allen (2015) highlight that there is no 'one size fits all' treatment program for females who sexually offend and that group treatments should be supplemented with individual sessions in order to attend to the individualized treatment targets of this client group. Thus, the benefit of this model is that it attends to the multi-factors which contribute towards female sexual offending and highlights that treatment interventions for females who sexually offend need to be individualized with a focus on improving quality of life and addressing reintegration into the community which fits with phase 3 of desistance theories of sexual offending. This also matches current thinking on effective treatment plans for males who sexually offend. For example, Göbbels, Ward and Willis (2012) suggest a four-phase model of desistance which they emphasize is gradual and bi-directional.

Phase 1 – Decisive momentum (initial desistance).
Phase 2 – Rehabilitation (promoting desistance).
Phase 3 – Re-entry (maintaining desistance).
Phase 4 – Normalcy/reintegration (successful desistance over a period time).

Hence, it is positive that the self-management part of the model emphasizes the importance of positive psychology and reintegration into the community. However, there are also several flaws to the treatment approach proposed by Pflugradt and Allen (2015). Firstly, given the current position in terms of the frequency of conviction females who sexually offend it would seem unlikely that many services would be in a position to deliver a group based intervention. Secondly, it would be difficult to match females who sexually offend in a group according to risk categorization given no risk assessment tools for females who sexually offend currently exist (such as the RM2000 for males). For example, as Eldridge et al. (2018) note, using risk assessments based on male risk of sexual offence recidivism results in overestimation of the recidivism risk for females who sexually offend. Thirdly, if the treatment needs of females who sexually offend are highly individualized then it is unclear of the utility of a group based intervention. Hence, while the model may provide some basic guidance and structure to the approach to treatment for females who sexually offend it would seem there are difficulties with this in practice.

Female sexual offending – where are we now?

We know that sexual offending is not typically the result of one individual factor, but rather, a number of interrelated factors that cross subtypes (Marshall, Anderson, Fernandez, & Mulloy, 1999) and this appears to apply to both males and females. In the male sex offender literature, sexual offending is understood with the context of the Integrated Theory of Sexual Offending – Revised (Ward & Beech, 2016) which notes that clinical symptoms (or state factors) lead to the commission of an offence, which in turn, results in particular 'ecological niche' factors which then lead to changes in neuropsychological functioning. In this way, sexual offending itself can strengthen the variables that led to the initial offending, making a re-offence more likely. In addition, the revised ITSO attends to the role of neuropsychological reinforcers and conditioning of behaviour (such as the way in which sexual gratification can reinforce deviant arousal).

In addition, theories in relation to the effective rehabilitation of those who offend have included the Risk–Need–Responsivity (RNR) model (Bonta & Andrews, 2012) which has emerged as the primary evidence based framework for the application of research into practice (Ward, Melser, & Yates, 2007). Put simply, the model proposes that rehabilitative interventions should target specific offender risk factors that are both dynamic (amenable to change) and criminogenic (directly related to recidivism outcomes). Thus, the model proposes that certain dynamic factors should be prioritized for intervention over others because of the nature and magnitude of their relationship with recidivism. However, determining what dynamic factors are related to recidivism has presented challenges in itself even for males who sexually offend with large sample sizes. In addition, despite the development of third and fourth generation risk assessments (designed to both predict recidivism risk and measure dynamic risk factors) the predictive validity of dynamic risk factors for males remains unclear (Morgan, Kroner, Mills, Serna, & McDonald, 2013).

Thus, due to the small sample sizes of females who sexually offend no reliable risk assessment tool exists for this client group both in terms of predicting recidivism and identifying dynamic risk factors.

Eldridge, Elliott, Gillespie, Bailey, and Beech (2018), in conjunction with the Lucy Faithful Foundation, have attempted to overcome this with the Assessment Framework for Female Sexual Abusers (AFFSA 2) which the authors state is 'a tool to aid the identification of deficits and strengths presented by women who sexually offend' (p. 134). The tool comprises a list of:

A) Developmental factors.
B) Psychological dispositions and historical markers.
C) Environmental niche factors.
D) Offence preceding [acute] factors.
E) Positive protective factors.

Thus, the tool presents a significant step forward in guiding practitioners to consider factors that may take the person closer towards offending and protect them from future offending. In addition, it has the benefit of considering environmental factors and including information using a method of triangulation. However, the tool provides no information on the motivation or function of offending and has been developed for women who have sexually abused children (Eldridge et al., 2018). Thus, it does not apply to females who have sexually offended against adults. Nor does it provide guidance on how the person should be supported to reduce their risk or desist from offending in the future.

Thus, alternative approaches to understanding female sexual offending are required which attend to not only the risk the person poses (against adults and children) but how they can desist from offending in the future. However, the question remains as to how this can be undertaken with a client group of small size and overall low rates of recidivism (Eldridge et al., 2018). The Women's Risk Need Assessment (WRNA) developed by Van Voorhis, Salisbury, Wright, and Bauman (2008) began to consider ways in which the assessment for females who offend should include gender neutral and gender responsive factors when formulating risk. However, this tool was not specifically designed for females who sexually offend and was based on general offending behaviour. In addition, neither does it provide a method for establishing the function of sexual offending or how this risk could be reduced. Thus, while it is a useful tool there remain gaps in its application to females who sexually offend. Ways for overcoming these deficits will be discussed subsequently.

According to Ward (2014) when research concentrates on identifying dynamic and static risk factors through statistical and psychometric approaches this can result in the neglect of modelling causal processes in the sexual offending field. Thus, a lack of assessment tools for females who sexually offend could facilitate an opportunity for adopting alternative approaches for understanding behaviour. DeMatteo, Batastini, Foster, and Hunt (2010) also suggest that a psychological assessment should go beyond the structured risk assessment and that any assessment should be used as a basis for an individualized formulation (Shingler & Needs, 2018). Ward (2014) also noted that because human beings are embedded in multiple systems (constituted by biological, psychological and social/cultural processes) explanations of complex phenomena such as sexual offending need to be multifactorial, inter-level and non-reductionist in nature. Ward (2014) also suggested that a 'preoccupation with measurement may trap us into surface level explanations' whereby qualitative methodologies may provide an opportunity for the generation of inter-level theories for the explanation of offending which refer to different levels of human functioning. Ward (2014) described this approach as integrative pluralism and methods of achieving this will be discussed subsequently.

Introducing the multi-component framework of female sexual offending

As Skinner (1953) noted 'the analysis of individual behaviour is a problem in scientific demonstration'. However Applied Behaviour Analysis (ABA) provides a scientific method to achieving this using a single participant experimental approach (Association of Behaviour Analysis). ABA seeks to develop empirically based treatments and interventions that can he demonstrated to work at the individual level whereby behaviour analysts seek to understand a specific human behaviour rather than making statements about general populations (Bailey & Burch, 2017). Furthermore, ABA seeks to use this knowledge to generate effective interventions to reduce the behaviour. As a result there is a strong evidence base for the efficacy of ABA. It has been empirically shown to be effective in a wide variety of areas with over 19,000 papers demonstrating its efficacy including parent training, substance abuse treatment, dementia management, brain injury rehabilitation, occupational safety intervention and the management of challenging behaviour in people with autism and/or intellectual disabilities (Anderson & Romanczyk, 1999). Furthermore, Baer, Wolf, and Risley (1987) highlight the following strengths of ABA interventions in that they are:

- Applied – meaning they address behaviours that are important to the client and his/her significant others.

- Behavioural – focuses on the client behaviour(s) in need of improvement and direct measurement of those behaviours (as opposed to measuring the behaviour of others who interact with the client, measuring client behaviour indirectly by asking others about it, etc.).
- Analytical – consistently produces change in a measured aspect of the target behaviour(s) when the intervention is in place in comparison to when it is not.
- Technological – described with sufficient detail and clarity that a reader has a reasonable chance of replicating the intervention.
- Conceptually systematic – grounded in the conceptualization that behaviour is a function of environmental events and described in terms of behaviour analytic principles.
- Effective – improves target behaviours to a practical degree.
- Generalized – produces changes in target behaviours that last over time, occur in situations other than those in which the interventions were implemented initially, and/or spread to behaviours that were not treated.

Thus, the benefit of the ABA approach is that 'it works well for clients where there is no large population to draw upon, it is scientifically driven and it uses methods derived from the principles of behaviour analysis to systematically improve behaviour and … to identify the variables responsible for behaviour change' (Cooper, Heron, & Heward, 2007, p. 20). ABA also adopts functional behavioural assessment and functional analysis to record the frequency, duration, latency and topography of behaviour (which can be public or private) using methods of triangulation of data collection as well as attending to environmental events. Thus, ABA provides an analysis of the function of the behaviour and provides socially valid methods of modifying behaviour through all aspects of the factors that contribute towards the behaviour. That is, it is multi-factorial in both the method of assessment and intervention.

From a practical perspective, one method of achieving ABA is through using a technique called Positive Behavioural Support (PBS) which is defined as a multi-component framework for developing an understanding of behaviour that challenges rather than a single therapeutic approach, treatment or philosophy (Gore et al., 2013). Positive Behavioural Support (PBS) is based on the principles of ABA and functional assessment which assists to identify the contingent relationship between target behaviours and environmental antecedents and consequences (Sturmey, 1996). In addition, the assessment may specify the quality and duration of specific reinforcers, and the behaviours to be targeted (Linscheid, Iwata, Ricketts, Williams, & Griffin, 1990). The results of functional assessment can be used by clinicians to develop a functionally appropriate treatment package (Sprague & Horner, 1995). In addition, the primary goal of PBS is to support the person to meet their needs in ways that improve their quality of life. In order to do this the functional assessment defines the topography of the behaviour, its frequency and duration, the antecedent events that may trigger the behaviour, and the consequences that may maintain the behaviour. From this PBS then makes recommendations for appropriate treatment interventions which may decrease the behaviour in the future (Sprague & Horner, 1995). Current best practice requires a functional analysis of biological and social variables prior to treatment implementation (Van Houten et al, 1988). Thus, it can be said that PBS maps well onto the revised ITSO model because it takes account of all the factors which may contribute to a behaviour, as well as identifying the fundamental human need which the behaviour is achieving. In addition, using this method, the treatment of problem behaviours focuses on two issues: (1) weakening the relationship between the target response and its maintaining reinforcer and (2) strengthening the response-reinforcement relationship of a substitute adaptive behaviour through teaching functional replacement behaviours and making modifications to the environment (Sprague & Horner, 1995). Thus, it is evident that these principles mirror directly onto the ITSO, and PBS also maps well onto the principles of the 'Good Lives Model' (Yates, Prescott, & Ward, 2010) in terms of offender rehabilitation focussing on the quality of life and human need fulfilment.

In addition, PBS identifies the motivation for the behaviour attending to both content theories of motivation (e.g. what motivates the person's behaviour in terms of human needs) and process theories (on how the behaviour is motivated in terms of reinforcement theory). PBS also acknowledges that behaviour and behavioural change is dependent on a person's abilities, needs (including their physical and mental health), circumstances and aspects of the social and physical environment within which the behaviour occurs. As a result, PBS plans consist of the following:

1) An in-depth assessment involving combinations of informant interviews, direct observations, structured record keeping, questionnaires and reviews of case material and whenever possible, the person themselves. The assessment should therefore be multi-disciplinary.
2) Assessment should also involve an analysis of the strengths and needs of the person (for example, the resources they have available, their existing knowledge, attitudes, their current beliefs about the behaviour, and any significant health or personal concerns).
3) The assessment should also include the strengths and needs of the people who will be supporting that person in the future (for example, the resources they have available, their existing knowledge, attitudes

towards the person, their current beliefs about the behaviour, and any significant health or personal concerns).

4) An appropriate risk assessment should be completed.
5) The formulation should integrate findings about the person, their environment and behaviour into a coherent and dynamic whole.
6) Assessment should always include a baseline measure of current behavioural rate and intensity so that repeated measurements can be taken post-intervention to gauge change.
7) Assessment should also involve baseline measures of quality of life and current usage of restrictive practices (e.g. imprisonment or lack of access to children etc).
8) Assessment should be a dynamic rather than static process because precipitating and maintaining variables may change over time.
9) Repeat assessments should always follow any change in presentation of a person's behavioural challenges.

The aim should always be to produce a functional assessment and accompanying Behaviour Support Plan (BSP) for challenging behaviour. A thorough PBS plan should include each of the 18 sections identified in the template provided in the case study. A brief example of a PBS plan has been provided in Table 12.2 to demonstrate what this may look like in practice. This is based on an example case study for the purposes of assisting the reader to see how PBS may look in practice. It is not based on any individual and is a shortened version of how a PBS plan would look in reality.

What can be seen from this example is that PBS provides a multicomponent framework for the assessment of female sexual offending which takes into account the biopsychosocial factors which contribute to the behaviour as well as practical strategies for reducing the behaviour. Furthermore, these strategies attend to both internal and external factors to the individual and PBS plans reflect biopsychosocial models of human behaviour. Furthermore, this approach also has the benefit of addressing the function and risk factors associated with offending using case formulation. It also takes into account a wide range of contributory factors to generate person specific theories as to why the behaviour exists and may persist. This approach also identifies distal and proximal causes for offending and what maintains behaviour and takes into account wide ranging theories of motivation for behaviour (such as instinct, incentive, drive, arousal, humanistic and expectancy theories of motivation). Furthermore, the PBS approach attends to the factors identified by Ward (2014) as contributing to sexual offending, namely: genetic; neurological; psychological; social/cultural; environment; and historic. PBS also takes into account the intrinsic variability of sexual offending and adopts the integrative pluralism that Ward (2014) suggests should be used to guide

Table 12.2 Example behavioural support plan.

1) Authors of the report and sources of information	This report was completed by; Dr Rachel Worthington (Consultant Psychologist) Linda Stewart (Social Worker) Janice Taylor (Support Worker) Paul Smith (Deputy Manager) Sian Mason (Offender Manager) Jane White (Clare's Mum) Clare The following sources of information were used: Staff interviews Interview with Clare's mother Functional Assessment Interview SCID Motivation Assessment Scale Contextual Assessment Inventory Medical records File information Semi-structured direct observation Momentary time sampling Mediator Analysis
2) Personal history (background information)	Clare is a 19-year-old female living in supported housing in the community. She was adopted at the age of 2 and does not recall her biological parents although it is believed that they had mental health problems and exposed Clare to aggression. Clare recalls her adoptive father being 'strict' and engaging in controlling behaviours towards her adoptive mother. At times she witnessed him engaging in physical aggression towards her adoptive mother which made her feel angry towards him and protective towards her adoptive mother. She recalls trying to please her adoptive father as a means by which to appease his anger and inhibiting her

(continued)

Table 12.2 (*continued*)

	emotions for fear her father would be angry. As she grew older her adoptive father was also controlling of her behaviour, preventing her from seeing her friends and having boyfriends. Clare left school at the age of 16 with some GCSEs. While she was at college her adoptive father died suddenly of a heart attack and her adoptive mother suffered a mental breakdown. Clare moved out to live with a boyfriend at the age of 17. She has had 3 partners and these relationships all involved violence.
3) **Current Environment**	Clare is living in a supported accommodation with 24 hours staff support after being arrested and deemed vulnerable. She has her own room but there are 6 other women living there. The home has support from psychology staff, support staff, social services, a consultant psychiatrist and a community mental health support team.
4) **Health and Medical Needs**	Clare has been diagnosed with anxiety and depression by her GP. She is prescribed citalopram but reports that she does not feel this helps with her mood. She has attempted suicide in the past by overdosing.
5) **Strengths and Needs**	Strengths: • Clare is able to attend to all of her skills of daily living and can cook meals, maintain her personal hygiene and her house is clean and tidy. • She likes to socialize and chat with other people. • Clare has a good relationship with her social worker and the staff in the accommodation. • Clare has maintained employment prior to being arrested, working in a shop for over 2 years. • Clare is warm and caring towards other people. Needs: • Clare needs a lot of reassurance in relation to her self-esteem. • She finds it difficult to cope with saying goodbye to other people and when she feels alone. • Clare needs support to assist her to plan for living on her own as she has not done this previously and is worried she will not know what to do.

6) Motivation Analysis

Clare enjoys:

- Seeing her mum.
- Thinking about the future and planning how she will decorate her own flat.
- Animals.
- Drawing and art.
- Swimming.
- Chatting to her friends on the phone and on Facebook.
- Cooking – especially trying new recipes.
- Being praised and given encouragement.

7) Behaviours of Concern

The following tools were used in identifying Clare's key behaviours, triggers and reinforcing consequences:

- Functional Assessment Interview.
- Motivation Assessment Scale.
- Context Assessment Interview.
- Observational Assessment (Momentary Time Sampling).
- ABC recordings.

Clare can display the following behaviours in isolation or as part of a behavioural chain. The functional analysis indicates that, when behaviours are displayed within a behavioural chain, verbal aggression can occur in isolation but verbal aggression always precedes physical aggression. Most of these behaviours occur in relation to Clare attempting to avoid something (such as feeling abandoned). However, the behaviour can also occur when Clare feels controlled. The functional analysis was completed with the support of Clare, her file information, the staff who support Clare and Clare's mother. Tools such as the Functional Assessment Interview (FAI), Motivation Assessment Scale (MAS) and CAI were also used to gather data alongside observational assessment to write the behavioural assessment report which they commented on and gave feedback.

1) Verbal aggression

Clare can make threats to assault partners. She can swear and shout at them saying unkind things about them. This behaviour only occurs after 4–6 weeks of being in an intimate relationship. It has spanned throughout the duration of her relationships and varies from once a week to once or twice a day. The shouting can be frightening for the victim and neighbours living near her. This behaviour only occurs in her home and Clare has not engaged in this in public. This behaviour ends when the relationship/attachment ends.

(continued)

Table 12.2 (*continued*)

2) Physical aggression

Clare can hit partners with a closed fist and this is usually to their body rather than their face although Clare also slaps people on the face with an open hand. Clare may also push people if they are in her way and throw objects. Clare can also grab partners if they attempt to leave.

In summary verbal aggression can occur in isolation but verbal aggression always precedes physical aggression. Throwing objects only occurs after physical aggression and when Clare feels controlled. Physical aggression has occurred after 8–10 weeks of being in a relationship and has spanned throughout the duration of her relationships. This behaviour ends when the relationship ends.

3) Sexual aggression

Clare has engaged in one act of rape against a male partner. Verbal and physical aggression preceded this behaviour consisting of grabbing the partner and threatening to kill herself if he did not have sex with her to 'show' her he 'loved her'.

4) Self-injury/suicide attempts

Clare can engage in cutting her arms and taking overdoses of paracetamol. Cutting has occurred on a monthly basis when she is not in a relationship and 1–2 a week when she is in a relationship. This has not required medical intervention. It can occur privately in the bathroom. Threats to injure herself without acting on these occur more publicly in the bedroom or kitchen in the presence of her partner. Clare has taken two overdoses of paracetamol when partners have ended the relationship. Cutting can occur in isolation but cutting always preceded overdosing.

8) Early indicators

When Clare is moving away from baseline, it is likely that she will:

- Become argumentative./confrontational.
- Ignore family members' text messages.
- Clare's facial expression changes- her eyes become dark, furrowed brow, lips turn down at the corners and nose becomes 'screwed up'.
- Clare may begin to shout or become louder in her verbal communication.
- Slam doors.

- Accuse partners of being unfaithful.
- Ask partners to see their phone messages.
- Waking up feeling 'grumpy' due to changes in her sleep pattern.
- Drink more alcohol than normal.
- Forget to take her medication.
- Make an increased effort in her physical appearance to appear more attractive to her partner.
- Move around the home more erratically, bumping into things and banging things in her bedroom.
- Clare may also 'mutter' under her breath.
- Clare may make accusations.

9) **Risk factors**

Clare has difficulty regulating her emotions. Her psychiatrist has indicated that she may have an emerging personality disorder but due to her age she has not had a diagnosis. Clare has expressed having attachment difficulties whereby she has a desperate need to be in a relationship but then becomes frightened they will leave her as she is not good enough. She becomes overwhelmed with anxiety and then engages in controlling and aggressive behaviour to attempt to prevent her partners from leaving. Clare can struggle to tolerate anxiety and worry thoughts which can impact upon her sleep. She can also be hyper attentive to threat stimuli such as raised voices which makes her over-react. All of Clare's relationships have been characterized by mutual violence. Clare has also expressed feeling confused over the death of her father whom she both loved and hated.

10) **Slow triggers for challenging behaviour**

Slow triggers are background factors that can set the scene for challenging behaviour to occur. That is, they make challenging behaviour more likely. If they do occur the behaviour still depends on what happens immediately prior to a behaviour. These are known as fast triggers. So for example, if you wake up tired and with a headache and then trip over the cat causing you to shout 'blimmin' cat'. Then the slow trigger would be having a headache and being tired and the fast trigger would be tripping over the cat.Slow triggers for Clare include:

- When Clare feels she has a lack of control.
- When Claire is tired.
- When a partner changes their routine as she becomes suspicious.
- When Clare feels unattractive.

(continued)

Table 12.2 (*continued*)

11) Fast triggers for challenging behaviour	• When Clare can't explain how she feels.
	• Clare's partner working away.
	• Clare has attachment and emotional difficulties and can struggle being on her own.
	• When Clare is not working as she ruminates more.
	<u>Verbal aggression</u>
	• When Clare feels jealous.
	• If her partner is late and does not reassure her as to their whereabouts.
	• If her partner refuses to show her their phone.
	• Being told 'no'.
	• Being asked to do something she does not want to do.
	• Being bored.
	• Being lonely.
	• Being given corrective feedback (for example being told by a partner they do not like the way she has done something).
	• When Clare sees her partner interacting with another female.
	<u>Physical aggression</u>
	• Verbal aggression (and all of the fast triggers listed above in relation to verbal aggression).
	• Feeling angry and being in a small space with a partner.
	• Partner calling her names (e.g. telling her she is crazy).
	• Partner attempting to leave.
	• Partner threatening to leave.
	<u>Sexual aggression</u>
	• Verbal and physical aggression (and all of the fast triggers listed above).
	• Feeling desperate.
	• Feeling 'in love' and abandoned as opposed to angry and let down.
	• Feeling 'scrry'.

- Being in close proximity to the partner in a bedroom with few clothes on.
- Having access to something to cut herself with as this can make her partner feel her threat of hurting herself is imminent and they need to comply.

Self-injury/suicide attempts
- Feeling empty inside.
- Partner stating they will leave her.
- Partner ending the relationship.
- Feeling guilty following acts of physical and sexual aggression.

12) **Maintaining functions**	Maintaining functions are the consequences that happen after a behaviour which make it more likely the behaviour will happen again in the future. Many of Clare's behaviours result in her preventing her partners from leaving her and them reassuring her that they love her. Clare's verbal aggression also enables Clare to control her partner's behaviour making it less likely they will ask her to do things she does not want to do or want them to do (e.g. see their friends instead of staying with her). Her verbal aggression also helps her to explain to other people how she is feeling.
	The maintaining functions for her physical aggression are very similar but physical aggression results in other people being physically unable to leave.
	The maintaining function for her sexual aggression is to obtain reassurance that she is loved and that the relationship has not ended. Self-injury and suicide serves to both regulate her emotions and as a means of expression of emotions. Threats of self-injury can also serve to prevent partners from leaving her.
13) **Behavioural Summary Statements**	Clare can display the verbal aggression in isolation or as part of a behavioural chain that leads to physical aggression. The functional analysis revealed that physical aggression is always preceded by verbal aggression but verbal aggression does not always lead to physical aggression. Both of these behaviours occur in an attempt by Clare to control her partners, to prevent them from leaving her and as a means by which to express and regulate her emotions. Sexual aggression is preceded by verbal and physical aggression and threats of self-injury with the function of seeking reassurance that she is lovable and the relationship is not ending. Self-injury and suicide attempts serve as a means by which to cope with overwhelming emotions.

(continued)

Table 12.2 *(continued)*

14) **Mediator analysis**	• Clare does not believe that verbal, physical or sexual aggression is acceptable.
	• Clare has empathy for others.
	• Clare's support team are currently able to meet her emotional needs.
	• Clare is not in a relationship currently.
	• There is a key worker system in place, and Clare has designated keyworkers who she gets along with.
	• 9 of the staff where she lives have been trained in PBS and emotional regulation skills.
	• Clare is compliant with her medication.
	• Clare's mother is very supportive and does not condone the use of aggression and instead encourages Clare to use alternative skills.
15) **Primary prevention (proactive strategies)**	Primary Prevention involves managing aspects of the person's living, working and recreational environments to reduce the possibility of challenging behaviour occurring.
	How to interact with Clare
	• Staff should be taught in supervision that when Clare is emotional they should prompt her to use her DBT skills.
	• Staff should ask Clare to look at the 'DBT Deck' of cards or to look at the DBT app on her phone to assist her to familiarize herself with the skills and decide which skill to use when she is in a crisis.
	• Staff should remember to praise Clare to assist in developing her self-esteem.
	• If Clare is lonely staff should ensure that they remind her of the benefits of being on her own and prompt her to use her skills so she maintains independence and does not become dependent on them.
	• Clare's team would benefit from receiving training on personality disorders and how they can best support Clare.
	• The staff working with Clare should have regular reflective practice. Clare's formulation should be discussed as part of this so that staff can be aware of how Clare may present and what her risk factors and warning signs are.

Environment

- Clare should remain living in the supported accommodation where her risk can be managed. If she moves from the accommodation then an urgent reassessment of her risk should be undertaken.
- Clare should not be permitted to have male partners visiting the accommodation.
- Clare should have to notify the Local Authority if she plans to engage in a relationship in the future.
- Clare should replace razors in her flat with an electric lady shave to reduce her risk of cutting.
- Clare should throw out any paracetamol that she has in the flat
- Clare should keep her medication for anxiety in the bathroom cupboard next to her toothpaste so she remembers to take them in the morning and evening and does not forget.
- Clare should have regular alcohol testing.

People

- Clare should engage in an exercise to map out the qualities of partners that may place herself and them at risk. This could include generating Cognitive Analytic Therapy (CAT) maps of the reciprocal roles that she enters into in unhealthy relationships and how to exit these traps.
- Clare should be encouraged to develop her friendship group so that she can improve her self-esteem and increase the number of people that she depends on for affirmation of her self-worth. For example, she enjoys cooking new meals so she could attend cookery classes as well as art.
- Clare could volunteer in the local charity shop to offset feelings of guilt she experiences for sexually assaulting her partner and to give something back to the local community which would fit with the notion of 'reparation' in DBT and criminological theories.
- If Clare engages in a relationship in the future she should be required to declare this to the Local authority and to share her risk management plan with that person.
- Clare could attend the mindfulness group run in the local community to assist her to make friends and generalize her learning from the DBT skills.
- Clare should share her PBS and relapse prevention plan with her mother so that she knows how best to support Clare in a crisis.

(continued)

Table 12.2 *(continued)*

Teaching skills

- Clare would benefit from learning alternative skills to regulate her emotions. She could engage in DBT sessions with her therapist to explore alternative coping skills for managing loneliness and jealousy. This should also include distress tolerance skills for managing distressing situations over which she has no control, emotional regulation skills for managing shifting emotions and interpersonal effectiveness skills for communicating her needs in relationships.

- Clare should engage in the partner violence programme run in the local area to develop her insight into what constitutes healthy and unhealthy relationships.

- Clare would benefit from receiving psycho-education about the effects of exposure to aggression in childhood so she can understand her emotions in relation to her father as well as using this knowledge to protect her own child from exposing her own child to violence.

- It would be helpful for Clare to engage in psycho-education in relation to sleep hygiene and how to manage worry thoughts to improve her sleep at night.

- Clare could engage in progressive counting techniques to enhance her overall feeling of safety to reduce physiological arousal.

16) Secondary prevention (active strategies)

Secondary prevention involves strategies that are brought into play once a person's behaviour begins to move away from baseline conditions. The aim of secondary prevention is to stop incidents progressing into full-blown episodes of challenging behaviour by intervening early.

- If Clare begins to use verbal aggression she should be prompted to use her DBT Skills to express her emotions more effectively (e.g. using DEARMAN).

- Staff should talk in a calm manner to validate the emotion she is experiencing.

- Clare should be reminded of the consequences of shouting.

- Clare should be prompted to use her deep breathing techniques.

- Clare should be encouraged to go for a swim to think things through. This would reduce her risk because she does not engage in aggression in public places.

- If Clare is expressing the emotion of jealousy she should be referred to her CAT map to remind her how to exit the traps of unhealthy relationships (e.g. weighing up what evidence she has that her partner likes her as opposed to liking other people).

- Clare should refer to her relapse prevention strategies (e.g. ensuring she is not alone with a partner, ensuring she is clothed, removing herself from a room where there are objects to hurt herself, taking a deep breath and getting some fresh air – either practically or mentally using her mindfulness skills).

17) Reactive Strategies

Reactive strategies provide those supporting Clare with clear instructions on how to respond safely and efficiently to behaviours that cannot be prevented:

- Staff will maintain their distance.
- Other people living in the accommodation should be encouraged to stay in their room and not to get involved.
- When Clare is shouting or throwing things staff should ask her to stop and remind her they will phone the police if she does not stop.
- If Clare is attempting to hurt herself staff should not try to stop her as they may become injured. They should ask her to stop and phone the emergency services.
- If Clare is shouting at a partner on her phone Clare should be instructed to end the call using her script ('I'm sorry I am feeling emotional at the moment so I am going to end the call and I will phone you back once I have calmed down').

18) Post-incident support

Staff will ensure that effective post-incident support is offered to Clare, other service users, her family/partner and staff following any behavioural incident. In respect of Clare, the immediate response is to try to calm her, encouraging her to return to her normal baseline levels of behaviour. This support can be offered in the following ways:

- If a member of staff has been offended/hurt by the incident and does not feel they can provide effective support to Clare a different member of staff should provide the support to her.
- Encourage Clare to have some space in her room before having a chat. Clare usually responds well to this.
- Other service users will be supported/distracted to ensure they don't try to speak to Clare until she has calmed.
- Remain calm and non-judgemental.
- Employ active listening skills.
- Clare should complete a chain analysis of what happened in the build up to the incident and what skill she could have used to cope with it differently.
- Clare should be encourage to evaluate what the effects were of her behaviour and how she can repair this damage.

theory construction in relation to sexual offending. Finally, and most importantly the PBS framework provides not only a multicomponent framework for the assessment of female sexual offending but it also provides a multicomponent treatment strategy which takes into account multi-layered strategies for the reduction of sexual violence in line with current theories of desistance. In addition, the proactive strategies are regarded as a 'menu' of options which can be implemented in the order which best suits the client based on their immediate needs, motivation and risk. That is, not all the proactive strategies need to be implemented at the same time, they can be selected for prioritization with the client and their case manager. As such PBS also adheres to the principles proposed by Livesley (2012) which notes that therapy should be undertaken using an integrated treatment model with a structured framework so they can be delivered in a co-ordinated way. It also attends to the principles identified in the Motivational-Facilitation Model of Sexual Offending (Seto, 2019) which recognizes the individual differences associated with a risk of sexual offending as it recognizes motivation, trait and state factors which would also need to be present to take a person closer to offending.

Hence, the identified PBS treatment plan and the fluid implementation of the proactive strategies means that it can be implemented at a rate and sequence that suits the client and it can also be added to and developed when internal and external factors change making it a dynamic tool for managing risk and guiding treatment.

Conclusion

Capturing data in relation to female perpetrators of sexual violence has been made more difficult due to the low rates of reporting by victims, legal and societal attitudes in relation to females and a lower frequency of this behaviour in comparison to males. In addition, both similarities and differences exist between males and females who sexually offend but the precise role gender plays in this is unclear. Hence, attempting to find common factors to assess and treat a client group that is so small is inherently plagued with difficulties and these are worsened if the primary attention is given to the notion of being 'female' which is inherently a social and fluid construct influenced by social norms, identities, history, culture, context, societal attitudes, biological and reproductive differences (Steffensmeier & Allan, 1996). Thus, adopting a qualitative but scientific method of hypothesis generation using a single participant approach may overcome these constraints. Furthermore, PBS offers a multi-component framework for developing an understanding female sexual offending which takes into account the biopsychosocial factors. Furthermore, the PBS approach adopts the integrative pluralism that Ward (2014) suggests should be used to guide theory construction in relation to sexual offending. Finally, and most importantly the PBS framework provides multi-layered strategies for the reduction of sexual violence in line with current theories of desistance and the use of an integrated treatment model with a structured framework which can be delivered in a co-ordinated way (Livesley, 2012).

References

Anderson, S. R., & Romanczyk, R. G. (1999). Early intervention for young children with autism: Continuum-based behavioral models. *Journal of the Association for Persons with Severe Handicaps, 24*, 162–173.

Baer, D. M., Wolf, M. M., & Risley, T. R. (1987). Some still-current dimensions of applied behavior analysis. *Journal of Applied Behavior Analysis, 20*, 313–327.

Bailey, J. S., & Burch, M. R. (2017). *Research methods in applied behavior analysis.* Abingdon: Routledge.

Basile, K. C., Smith, S. G., Breiding, M., Black, M. C., & Mahendra, R. R. (2014). Sexual violence surveillance: Uniform definitions and recommended data elements. Version 2.0.

Beech, A. R., Elliott, I. A., Birgden, A., & Findlater, D. (2008). The Internet and child sexual offending: A criminological review. *Aggression and Violent Behavior, 13*, 216–228.

Beech, A. R., Parrett, N., Ward, T., & Fisher, D. (2009). Assessing female sexual offenders' motivations and cognitions: An exploratory study. *Psychology, Crime & Law, 15*, 201–216.

Bonta, J., & Andrews, D. (2012). 2 Viewing offender assessment and rehabilitation through the lens of the risk-needs-responsivity model. In *Offender Supervision* (pp. 45–66). Willan.

Booth, B. D. (2016). Elderly sexual offenders. *Current psychiatry reports, 18*(4), 34.

Bordini, G. S., & Sperb, T. M. (2013). Sexual double standard: A review of the literature between 2001 and 2010. *Sexuality & Culture, 17*, 686–704.

Bourke, A., Doherty, S., McBride, O., Morgan, K., & McGee, H. (2014). Female perpetrators of child sexual abuse: Characteristics of the offender and victim. *Psychology, crime & law, 20*(8), 769–780.

Breiding, M. J. (2014). Prevalence and characteristics of sexual violence, stalking, and intimate partner violence victimization—National Intimate Partner and Sexual Violence Survey, United States, 2011. *Morbidity and Mortality Weekly Report. Surveillance Summaries (Washington, DC: 2002), 63*, 1.

Burgess-Proctor, A., Comartin, E. B., & Kubiak, S. P. (2017). Comparing female-and male-perpetrated child sexual abuse: A mixed-methods analysis. *Journal of Child Sexual Abuse, 26*, 657–676.

Christensen, L. S. (2018). The new portrayal of female child sexual offenders in the print media: A qualitative content analysis. *Sexuality & Culture, 22*, 176–189.

Comartin, E. B., Burgess-Proctor, A., Kubiak, S., & Kernsmith, P. (2018). Factors related to co-offending and coerced offending among female sex offenders: The role of childhood and adult trauma histories. *Violence and Victims, 33*, 53–74.

Cooper, J. O., Heron, T. E., & Heward, W. L. (2007). *Applied behavior analysis* (2nd ed.). Upper Saddle River, NJ: Pearson.

Cortoni, F., Babchishin, K. M., & Rat, C. (2017). The proportion of sexual offenders who are female is higher than thought: A meta-analysis. *Criminal Justice and Behavior, 44*, 145–162.

Cortoni, F., & Gannon, T. A. (2011). Female sexual offenders. *International perspectives on the assessment and treatment of sex offenders: Theory, practice and research*, 35–54.

Cortoni, F., Hanson, R. K., & Coache, M. È. (2010). The recidivism rates of female sexual offenders are low: A meta-analysis. *Sexual Abuse, 22*, 387–401.

Davies, M., & Rogers, P. (2006). Perceptions of male victims in depicted sexual assaults: A review of the literature. *Aggression and Violent Behavior, 11*, 367–377.

DeMatteo, D., Batastini, A., Foster, E., & Hunt, E. (2010). Individualizing risk assessment: Balancing idiographic and nomothetic data. *Journal of Forensic Psychology Practice, 10*, 360–371.

Eldridge, H. J., Elliott, I. A., Gillespie, S. M., Bailey, A., & Beech, A. R. (2018). Assessing women who sexually abuse children. In *Violent and sexual offenders* (pp. 156–178). Abingdon: Routledge.

Eldridge, H. J., & Saradjian, J. (2000). Replacing the function of abusive behaviors for the offender: Remaking relapse prevention in working with women who sexually abuse children. *Remaking relapse prevention with sex offenders: A sourcebook*, 402–426.

Fazel, S., Sjöstedt, G., Grann, M., & Långström, N. (2010). Sexual offending in women and psychiatric disorder: A national case–control study. *Archives of Sexual Behavior, 39*, 161–167.

Fergusson, D. M., & Mullen, P. E. (1999). *Childhood sexual abuse* (Vol. 40). Thousand Oaks, CA: Sage.

Gannon, T., Rose, M. R., & Ward, T. (2010). Pathways to female sexual offending: Approach or avoidance? *Psychology, Crime & Law, 16*, 359–380.

Gannon, T. A., & Rose, M. R. (2009). Offense-related interpretive bias in female child molesters: A preliminary study. *Sexual Abuse, 21*, 194–207.

Gannon, T. A., Rose, M. R., & Ward, T. (2008). A descriptive model of the offense process for female sexual offenders. *Sexual Abuse, 20*, 352–374.

Gannon, T. A., Waugh, G., Taylor, K., Blanchette, K., O'Connor, A., Blake, E., & Ó Ciardha, C. (2014). Women who sexually offend display three main offense styles: A reexamination of the descriptive model of female sexual offending. *Sexual Abuse, 26*, 207–224.

Girshick, L. B. (2002). No sugar, no spice: Reflections on research on woman-to-woman sexual violence. *Violence Against Women, 8*, 1500–1520.

Göbbels, S., Ward, T., & Willis, G. M. (2012). An integrative theory of desistance from sex offending. *Aggression and Violent Behavior, 17*, 453–462.

Gorman-Smith, D., & Vivolo, A. M. (2012). Developmental approaches in the prevention of female offending. In *The Oxford handbook of crime prevention*.

Gore, N. J., McGill, P., Toogood, S., Allen, D., Hughes, J. C., Baker, P., ... Denne, L. D. (2013). Definition and scope for positive behavioural support. *International Journal of Positive Behavioural Support, 3*, 14–23.

Hayes, S., & Baker, B. (2014). Female sex offenders and pariah femininities: Rewriting the sexual scripts. *Journal of Criminology, 2014*.

Hyde, J. S. (2005). The gender similarities hypothesis. *American Psychologist, 60*, 581.

Hyde, J. S. (2014). Gender similarities and differences. *Annual Review of Psychology, 65*, 373–398.

Jäncke, L. (2018). Sex/gender differences in cognition, neurophysiology, and neuroanatomy. *F1000Research, 7*.

Kreager, D. A., Staff, J., Gauthier, R., Lefkowitz, E. S., & Feinberg, M. E. (2016). The double standard at sexual debut: Gender, sexual behavior and adolescent peer acceptance. *Sex Roles, 75*, 377–392.

Lambert, S., & O'Halloran, E. (2008). Deductive thematic analysis of a female paedophilia. *Psychiatry, Psychology and Law, 15*, 284–300. website.

Lightdale, J. R., & Prentice, D. A. (1994). Rethinking sex differences in aggression: Aggressive behavior in the absence of social roles. *Personality and Social Psychology Bulletin, 20*, 34–44.

Linscheid, T. R., Iwata, B. A., Ricketts, R. W., Williams, D. E., & Griffin, J. C. (1990). Clinical evaluation of the self-injurious behavior inhibiting system (SIBIS). *Journal of Applied Behavior Analysis, 23*, 53–78.

Livesley, W. J. (2012). Integrated treatment: A conceptual framework for an evidence-based approach to the treatment of personality disorder. *Journal of Personality Disorders, 26*, 17–42.

Marshall, W. L., Anderson, D., Fernandez, Y., & Mulloy, R. (1999). *Cognitive behavioural treatment of sexual offenders.* Chichester, UK: Wiley.

Martin, C. L., & Ruble, D. N. (2010). Patterns of gender development. *Annual Review of Psychology, 61*, 353–381.

Masters, N. T., Casey, E., Wells, E. A., & Morrison, D. M. (2013). Sexual scripts among young heterosexually active men and women: Continuity and change. *Journal of Sex Research, 50*, 409–420.

Mathews, R., Hunter, J. A., & Vuz, J. (1997). Juvenile female sexual offenders: Clinical characteristics and treatment issues. *Sexual Abuse: A Journal of Research and Treatment, 9*, 187–199.

McLeod, D. A. (2015). Female offenders in child sexual abuse cases: A national picture. *Journal of Child Sexual Abuse, 24*, 97–114.

Middleton, D. (2009). Internet sex offenders. *Assessment and treatment of sex offenders: A handbook*, 199–216.

Miller, N. A., & Najavits, L. M. (2012). Creating trauma-informed correctional care: A balance of goals and environment. *European Journal of Psychotraumatology, 3*, 17246.

Morgan, R. D., Kroner, D. G., Mills, J. F., Serna, C., & McDonald, B. (2013). Dynamic risk assessment: A validation study. *Journal of Criminal Justice, 41*, 115–124.

Ogloff, J. R., Cutajar, M. C., Mann, E., Mullen, P., Wei, F. T. Y., Hassan, H. A. B., & Yih, T. H. (2012). Child sexual abuse and subsequent offending and victimisation: A 45 year follow-up study. *Trends and Issues in Crime and Criminal Justice, 440*, 1.

Peter, T. (2009). Exploring taboos: Comparing male-and female-perpetrated child sexual abuse. *Journal of Interpersonal Violence, 24*, 1111–1128.

Petersen, J. L., & Hyde, J. S. (2010). A meta-analytic review of research on gender differences in sexuality, 1993–2007. *Psychological Bulletin, 136*, 21.

Pflugradt, D., & Cortoni, F. (2014). Women who sexually offend: A case study. *Sex offender treatment: A case study approach to issues and interventions*, 181–198.

Pflugradt, D. M., & Allen, B. P. (2015). An exploration of differences between small samples of female sex offenders with prepubescent versus postpubescent victims. *Journal of Child Sexual Abuse, 24*, 682–697.

Pflugradt, D. M., Allen, B. P., & Zintsmaster, A. J. (2018). Adverse childhood experiences of violent female offenders: A comparison of homicide and sexual perpetrators. *International journal of offender therapy and comparative criminology, 62*(8), 2312–2328.

Plummer, M., & Cossins, A. (2018). The cycle of abuse: When victims become offenders. *Trauma, Violence, & Abuse, 19*, 286–304.

Sandler, J. C., & Freeman, N. J. (2007). Topology of female sex offenders: A test of Vandiver and Kercher. *Sexual Abuse, 19*, 73–89.

Seto, M. C. (2019). The motivation-facilitation model of sexual offending. *Sexual Abuse, 31*(1), 3–24.

Shingler, J., & Needs, A. (2018). The role of psychological risk assessment in Parole Board decision making: An exploration of the perspectives of psychologists, indeterminate sentenced prisoners and Parole Board members. *Prison Service Journal, 237*, 36–40.

Simon, W., & Gagnon, J. H. (2003). Sexual scripts: Origins, influences and changes. *Qualitative Sociology, 26*, 491–497.

Skinner, B. F. (1953). *Science and human behavior* (Vol. 92904). London: Simon and Schuster.

Sprague, J. R., & Horner, R. H. (1995). Functional assessment and intervention in community settings. *Mental Retardation and Developmental Disabilities Research Reviews, 1*, 89–93.

Steffensmeier, D., & Allan, E. (1996). Gender and crime: Toward a gendered theory of female offending. *Annual Review of Sociology, 22*, 459–487.

Stemple, L., & Meyer, I. H. (2014). The sexual victimization of men in America: New data challenge old assumptions. *American Journal of Public Health, 104*, e19–e26.

Sturmey, P. (1996). *Functional analysis in clinical psychology.* Chicheste: John Wiley & Sons.

Twenge, J. M., Sherman, R. A., & Wells, B. E. (2015). Changes in American adults' sexual behavior and attitudes, 1972–2012. *Archives of Sexual Behavior, 44*, 2273–2285.

Van Voorhis, P., Salisbury, E., Wright, E., & Bauman, A. (2008). Achieving accurate pictures of risk and identifying gender responsive needs: Two new assessments for women offenders. *University of Cincinnati Center for Criminal Justice Research, National Institute of Corrections, Washington DC.*

Van Voorhis, P., Wright, E. M., Salisbury, E., & Bauman, A. (2010). Women's risk factors and their contributions to existing risk/needs assessment: The current status of a gender-responsive supplement. *Criminal Justice and Behavior, 37*, 261–288.

Vandiver, D., Braithwaite, J., & Stafford, M. (2016). *Sex crimes and sex offenders: Research and realities.* Abingdon: Routledge.

Ward, T. (2014). The explanation of sexual offending: From single factor theories to integrative pluralism. *Journal of Sexual Aggression, 20*, 130–141.

Ward, T., & Beech, A. R. (2016). The Integrated Theory of Sexual Offending–Revised: A Multifield Perspective. *The Wiley handbook on the theories, assessment and treatment of sexual offending*, 123–137.

Ward, T., Melser, J., & Yates, P. M. (2007). Reconstructing the Risk–Need–Responsivity model: A theoretical elaboration and evaluation. *Aggression and Violent Behavior, 12*, 208–228.

Weber, D., Skirbekk, V., Freund, I., & Herlitz, A. (2014). The changing face of cognitive gender differences in Europe. *Proceedings of the National Academy of Sciences, 111*, 11673–11678.

Wijkman, M., Bijleveld, C., & Hendriks, J. (2010). Women don't do such things! Characteristics of female sex offenders and offender types. *Sexual Abuse, 22*, 135–156.

Williams, K. S., & Bierie, D. M. (2015). An incident-based comparison of female and male sexual offenders. *Sexual Abuse, 27*, 235–257.

Yates, P. M., Prescott, D., & Ward, T. (2010). *Applying the good lives and self-regulation models to sex offender treatment: A practical guide for clinicians.* Brandon: Safer Society Press.

Trauma, adverse experiences, and offence-paralleling behaviour in the assessment and management of sexual interest

13

Lawrence Jones

This chapter will start by exploring the psychological mechanisms linking different kinds of trauma and risk propensity. The developmental contexts of offence related sexual interests will be explored as a critical factor in understanding the nature of sexual interest linked with offending. Following the proposal by Ricci and Clayton (2016), consideration will then be given to how trauma triggers of different kinds can be linked with sequences of events leading up to offending and/or 'offence paralleling behaviour', defined as behaviour in the custodial setting that is driven by psychological mechanisms that were evident at the time of their offending. Offence paralleling behaviour will be examined as one approach to monitoring ongoing offence-related sexual interest.

Shine and Morris (2000) and Shuker and Jones (2007) identify the importance of thinking about the developmental and attachment background of an individual in building a formulation of both offending behaviour and offence paralleling behaviour (OPB). This model acknowledges the importance of adverse or traumatic experiences in the aetiology of much offending behaviour and OPB. Explicating the ways in which adverse early experiences can render an individual vulnerable to being triggered into self-destructive behaviour, or patterns of behaving that parallel those that lead up to their offences, in the custodial context, can offer a useful tool to aid assessment of the individual. Indeed, a richer and more nuanced understanding can emerge out of an iterative process where current crisis or distressed behaviour is used as a model for understanding what may have been going wrong at the time of the offence.

Developmental accounts of offending

A central tenet of cognitive-behavioural formulations of offending is that the individual's current ways of thinking and feeling are underpinned by early experiences. Recent thinking about how early experiences impact on later life suggest that it is not only beliefs that are impacted but also fundamental ways of orienting to the world that are derived from bodily experiences and altered states of consciousness, as well as beliefs and internal working models (Frewen & Lanius, 2015; Jones, 2019).

Developmental accounts of offending postulate a range of adverse or ultimately harmful cascades of events that culminate in the lifestyle contexts in which offending takes place (Layne, Briggs & Courtois, 2014). Key drivers for these processes can be thought of as deriving from a limited set of evolutionary 'systems'. Building on the work of evolutionary psychologists (e.g. Gilbert, 2017; Liotti, 2017; Panksepp, 1998), Jones (2016) proposed that adverse experiences impact on each of these systems in such a way that their impact on conscious experience and behaviour is, at least, partly outside of conscious control.

In addition to the three systems most often explored in the context of trauma formulations – Safety, Attachment, and Status or achievement (dominance) – Jones explored the Sexual system and the Hunting (or violence) systems (Köbach & Elbert, 2015) as being significant to making sense of offending behaviour (Table 13.1).

Each one of these systems can be impacted by adverse developmental and later life experiences. Any intense activation of a system – either intensely painful experiences or intensely pleasurable experiences – is associated with a change in the functioning of that system in the future. PTSD is familiar to most practitioners as being linked with experiences of dissociation, flashbacks, and intrusive thinking brought about by an overwhelming experience or experiences that activate the fear system. The same cognitive and affective processes are, however, associated with all the systems described above. They all, when activated, are linked with intrusive thoughts and urges, flashbacks, dissociation, myopia, and, when dysregulated, can be associated with compulsive behaviour (i.e. approach for pleasant experiences and avoidance of painful experiences).

Evolution can be thought of as conferring on the individual a process for interfering with or, in more extreme contexts, overriding conscious control in the interests of survival or consolidating 'resources'. Contexts in which experiences associated with the systems outlined above are strongly activated (i.e. mating, survival from imminent life-threatening events, attachment, resource acquisition, such as food or status, and substance misuse), which effectively

Table 13.1 Evolved systems impacted by trauma and contributing to sexual offending.

System	Activating process	Impact of trauma on system	Impact on emotion and state of consciousness when activated	Intrusive thoughts	Flashbacks	Urges to approach or avoid	Interaction with other systems
Attachment system	Forming relationships	Attachment trauma leading to: Avoidance of intimacy Switching to dominance system for sense of safety, Emotional dysregulation, Failure to mentalize	Myopia linked with feeling of 'falling in love' strong pleasurable body sensations. Feeling safe/secure	Intrusive thoughts and memories about the loved person, about how to form and maintain the relationship	Sometimes unsolicited memories of intense attachment moments	Thoughts and urges to be with the loved person	Inhibits fear system May pair up with sexual system and status system
	Maintaining relationships	Forming impersonal brief sexual relationships Failure to form and maintain relationships	Normal waking consciousness Feeling of a 'secure base'	Thoughts and concerns about what to do to prevent loss	Flashforwards experiences of fears of loss or abandonment – if some degree of attachment insecurity	Urges to control, reinforce and sustain relationships Searching behaviour in absence of object of attachment	Maintaining stability
	Ending or losses in relationships	Either avoided by:Precipitating ending or, react dramatically to threat of separation from significant others, and do not tolerate being alone.	Depression Dissociation Withdrawal symptoms Grief and grieving	Intrusive thoughts about experience of loss	Intrusive memories of loved person and experience with loved person	Searching for lost object Desperate attempts to re-establish relationship Later stages involve grieving; anger and then acceptance	Feelings of loss of status

(continued)

Table 13.1 *(continued)*

System	Activating process	Impact of trauma on system	Impact on emotion and state of consciousness when activated	Intrusive thoughts	Flashbacks	Urges to approach or avoid	Interaction with other systems
Safety system	Threat to life absence of secure attachment as protective factor	PTSD reactions, Pervasive sense of lack of safety	Myopia linked with fight or flight, depersonalization dissociation, Loss of future perspective	Intrusive thoughts about danger, hypervigilance	Intrusive memories of traumatic event, re-living	Urges to avoid and escape	Inhibited by attachment system Inhibited by dominance system
Dominance system, status and achievement system	Achieving status	Preoccupation with power, control and dominance	Hypervigilance to threats to status		Shame imagery and thoughts Grandiose manic thinking	Seeking submission cues from others	Dominance used to achieve safety/security in absence of attachment
Violence system	Exposure to extreme violence	Acquisition of appetitive violence	Not specified	Not specified	Not specified	Urges to engage in appetitive violence	Inhibits fear system
Sexual system	Sexual activity, real or imagined	Sexual compulsive behaviour or avoidance of sexual activity Sexual scripts or	Sexual Myopia,	Intrusive sexual thoughts and feelings	Compulsive and intrusive sexual memories and fantasies	Urges to act on fantasy and to replay intensely enjoyable past experiences	Inhibits other systems
Substance Abuse Hijacking other systems by artificial stimulation using substances	Exposure to substances, reward and getting rid of negative affect	Addiction Escalation in substance misuse	Altered states of consciousness induced by substances. Including dissociative states and myopia.	Intrusive thoughts linked with not having the drug of choice	Flashbacks to 'high', sometimes literally re-living experience, 'euphoric recall'	Urges to use drugs sometimes experienced as overwhelming	Used to offset experience of lack of status and relational estrangement and separation

hijack the same systems, are associated with changes in the capacity for day-to-day agency in the interests of quick and survival focussed responses. In order to achieve this shift in the face of survival-relevant situations, a number of processes are set in play.

Mills and Teeson (2019) argue that PTSD and substance misuse have been shown to be associated with changes in the cortico-limbic system; specifically, hyperactivity or hypoactivity of the amygdala, hypo-activity of the prefrontal cortex, and reduced volume of the hippocampus. These structures are involved in the mediation of stress responses, executive functioning, and memory, respectively. Together, dysregulation of these structures can 'impair an individual's ability to regulate intrusive trauma-related and craving-related thoughts and inhibit repetitive maladaptive behaviours...' (p. 183). Prefrontal cortex dysregulation is both brought about by poor or damaging attachment experiences and is involved with a range of 'addictive' processes, such as gambling addiction and sexual addiction (Katehakis, 2016).

Jones (2016) proposed that shifts in states of consciousness reflect shifts in cortico-limbic functioning. Amygdala hyperactivity is linked with intrusive thoughts/memories, as well as urges to approach (if it is a rewarding experience, such as sexual activity, substance misuse, or status) or to avoid (if it is a painful experience, such as unsafety or fear inducing situations). Prefrontal dysfunction is linked with experiences of dissociation and myopia. Using Kahneman's (2011) framework, these experiences undermine System 2's ability (i.e. deliberative decision-making) to override System 1 (automatic) thinking. Thus, System 1 thinking becomes much more dominant, which impacts on System 2 thinking through: (a) Intrusive thoughts; (b) Intrusive action urges; and (c) dissociative states in which System 2 thinking is much harder. Amygdala hypoactivity can be linked with the offence-related trauma processes such as emotional numbing, lack of interpersonal responsivity, and acquired callousness (Kerig & Becker, 2010).

Shifting states of consciousness have been described in the literature on compulsive sexual behaviour. Walton, Cantor, Bhullar, and Lykins (2017) have proposed a similar process in the context of compulsive sexual behaviour. They write: 'Hypersexual persons may have difficulty moderating their hypersexuality when in a heightened state of sexual arousal because of what we have termed 'cognitive abeyance'. Cognitive abeyance describes a state of inactivity, deferment, suspension, or diminution of logical cognitive processing. We suggest that during heightened states of sexual arousal, hypersexual persons frequently misappraise, dismiss, or fail to appropriately consider the risks, rewards, and consequences of their sexual behaviour, either past or present. Indeed, when hypersexual persons are in a state of cognitive abeyance, they are likely to operate from a euphoric or highly excited disposition, and their sexual inhibitions are substantially reduced. As such, some hypersexual persons (when highly sexually aroused) may feel unable to "put the brakes on" to stop their sexual activity and so frequently act on a sexual urge' (p. 13).

Even when there is no obvious shift in mental state, as for instance in some apparently planned offending, the individual's beliefs about what is pleasurable and what is aversive are likely to be strongly influenced by past experiences where they have experienced intense pleasure or pain associated with significant shifts in mental state. Planning is then associated with strong feelings of anticipation of reward or relief at avoiding pain.

Conceptualizing the psychological mechanisms at play in the context of offending and OPB requires, then, a formulation of shifting states of consciousness – as well as thoughts and feelings – associated with reminders of experiences associated with each of these systems. More specifically, it requires some consideration of: (a) dissociative states, (b) ways in which the individual's felt sense of agency has been compromised, albeit, sometimes only for brief periods, (c) hyperreactivity and hypo-reactivity, (d) the unique meanings given by the individual to these experiences (i.e. pleasure and pain beliefs), and (e) the social context(s) of state shifting.

Internal working models

Another significant construct related to the systems identified is the 'internal working model'. Attachment theory postulates that the individual has an 'internal working model' (IWM). This an internal representation of the relationship the individual has had with key attachment figures that has been internalized and shapes how an individual sees themselves and others in a relationship. Insecure attachment is thought to be a state where the model of the attachment figure is inconstant. This 'model' is then seen to impact in all social interactions of the individual. Each of the systems can also be seen as having their own IWM.

The sexual IWM is a representation of the individual's characteristic patterns of sexual relating. The concept of 'love-maps' (Money & Pranzarone, 1993) is a similar concept but relates to the individual's definition of what kinds of sexual activity and people they find attractive. Like the IWM for attachment (where a template based on early experiences of relating is in operation), this is a template for future sexual relationships based on the early sexual experiences that an individual has. Pfaus et al. (2012) also proposes that 'a critical period exists during an individual's early sexual experience that creates a "love map" or Gestalt of features, movements, feelings, and interpersonal interactions associated with sexual reward' (p. 31). Emotional and sexual abuse, alone or together, have been found to be significant developmental antecedents of problematic sexual behaviour (Knight & Sims-Knight, 2011), while emotional abuse from a male caregiver has been found to be a strong predictor of hypersexual thoughts and behaviour in adults (Kingston, Graham, & Knight, 2017). The concept of sexual scripts is similar to this also (Ward & Siegert, 2002).

Links between trauma and offending

Following Ricci and Clayton (2016), if we look at the Pathways Model of sexual offending developed by Ward and Siegert (2002), we can see the way in which each pathway has trauma origins. Thus, each of the specified causal mechanisms can be seen as deriving from these trauma origins

Intimacy deficits

Ward and Siegert (2002, p. 336) argue that those with a

> preoccupied attachment style were characterised by emotional neediness and profound doubts about their ability to elicit love and support from partners. Alternatively, the fearful-dismissively attached offenders tended to emotionally distance themselves in relationships because of their fear of rejection. Both groups of child molesters experience problems with intimacy and may turn to sex with children if their adult relationships are compromised or unsatisfactory … their (normal) needs for sex and closeness will be transferred to children, because of their perceived acceptance of the offender.

In this pathway, the impact of trauma on the attachment system is postulated as the central mechanism.

Deviant sexual scripts

The core causal mechanism in this pathway is a 'distorted' sexual script, Ward and Siegert (2002) write: 'These individuals may have experienced sexual abuse as children and as a consequence become prematurely sexualised' (p. 336). In this pathway, the impact of trauma on the sexual system is postulated as the central mechanism. Attachment or connection (see Needs, 2018) crises are, however, seen as setting events for triggering the enactment of the problematic sexual scripts. They write: 'The onset of sexual offending is expected to typically start in adulthood and be episodic in nature; associated with periods of rejection, disappointment or extreme loneliness' (p. 337).

Emotional dysregulation

Ward and Siegert (2002, p. 337) argue that

> individuals following this pathway offend if unable to effectively manage
> negative emotions and either become disinhibited or else use sex as a soothing
> strategy. Thus, the primary dysfunctional mechanisms might reside in defects
> in emotional and behavioural control or relate to the inappropriate utilisation
> of sex as a coping strategy.

Also, 'their base level of masturbation may be high and typically occurs in
response to periods of emotional dysphoria' (p. 338). Formulation of what
underpins emotional regulation difficulties typically link it with a combination of: a) poor attachment experiences leading to a lack of opportunity to
learn how to regulate affect (Fonagy, Target, Gergely, Allen, & Bateman, 2003);
and b) people with chronic trauma histories being repeatedly triggered by a
range of trauma reminders. Thus, the attachment system, as well as fear system
trauma, are postulated as drivers. Biologically determined emotional dysregulation can be seen as traumatic in so far as it can create the conditions for
traumatic events impacting on all the systems described above.

Antisocial cognitions

For this pathway, Ward and Siegert (2002, p. 339) write

> The major type of mechanisms for this group resides in their antisocial
> attitudes and beliefs. These cognitive distortions (for want of a better term), in
> conjunction with sexual desire and opportunity, will result in the sexual abuse
> of a child. Such individuals disregard social norms forbidding sex with children
> and are expected to exploit any opportunity for self-gratification if it presents
> itself.

Hackett and Smith (2018) argue that there is a developmental path from
'their prior experience of physical neglect and domestic violence to general
aggression and the development of *antisocial thinking* into sexual aggression
and violence' (p. 19). This pathway is largely linked with dysregulation of the
attachment system (lack of parental protection) and the dominance system.
Hilburn-Cobb (2004) argues that, in the absence of secure attachment experiences providing a secure base and a sense of safety, the individual turns to
one of the other systems, dominance primarily, to meet safety and contact
needs.

Offence paralleling behaviour, trauma and the self-regulation model

Four pathways to offending were outlined by Yates and Ward (2008); namely, avoidant passive, avoidant active, approach automatic, and approach explicit. Each one is potentially linked with different kinds of OPB and different ways in which trauma-derived processes impact on the individual. All the pathways are seen as being triggered by a 'life event' that precipitates an underlying developmentally determined psychological process. Custodial 'life events' are, thus, ideal opportunities for assessing and formulating what it is that is being triggered in an individual's offending process. Yates and Ward (2008, p. 7) write:

> For some individuals, the occurrence of a life event ….triggers a progression to sexual offending, whereas for other individuals, the same event will not trigger such a progression. The difference between these individuals lies in differences in their developmental and learning histories, and psychological, social, biological, and other factors. For example, individuals for whom a life event triggers the offence progression may have experienced histories of sexual or other abuse, modelling of violence and abuse during development, insecure attachment during development, or may be biologically predisposed to respond to the event in a sexual manner.

For the avoidant pathways, there is a 'turning point' at the moment of lapsing (Stage 6) in the lead up to the offence, which requires some kind of regulation. Trauma-derived processes contribute significantly to both the initial response to the life event and to the absence of or misapplied self-regulation strategies. Lapsing can be linked with a significant shift in state of consciousness involving a reduced capacity to self-monitor and experience potentially pro-social emotions, such as empathy and shame. For the approach pathways, the absence of an aversive emotional reaction to the offending and the absence of self-regulation is often linked with longstanding trauma derived dysregulation of the sexual, dominance, and attachment systems that do not require a significant shift in state in order for the offending process to proceed.

Trauma triggers

If we use a broad definition of trauma as outlined above, including exposure to intense experiences that are illegal, such as early sexual experiences or substance misuse (in effect a form of/consequence of neglect), then we can outline a set of trigger types that may be relevant to working with people who have offended sexually. Triggers are experiences that evoke a trauma

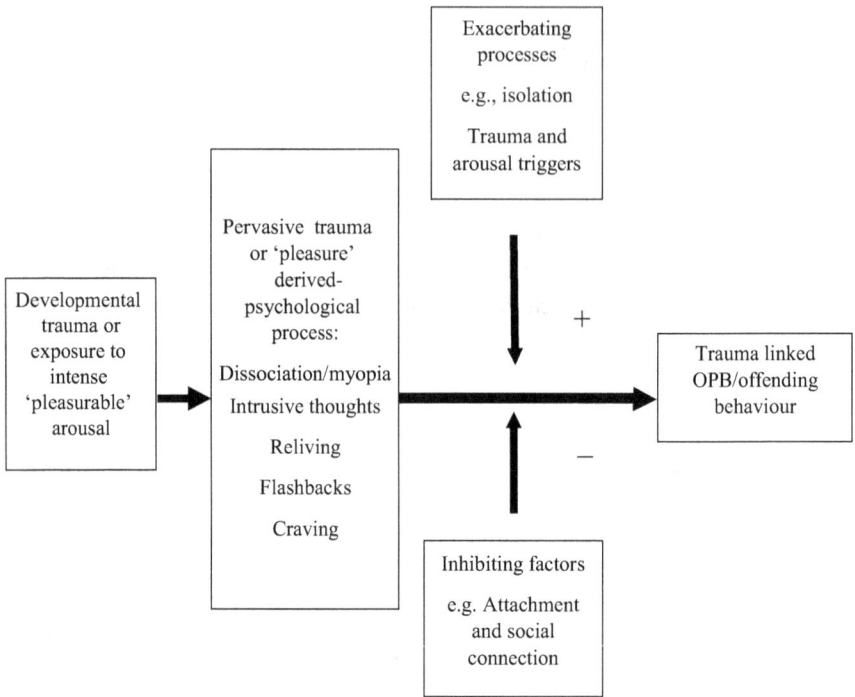

Figure 13.1 Exacerbating and inhibiting processes to trauma derived risk mechanisms.

memory-based reaction ranging from simply remembering, unintentionally thinking about, reliving or vividly recalling, feeling urges or cravings to acting in manner driven by the trauma – either approach or avoidance depending on the kind of experience.

Trauma triggers impact on behaviour in different ways. On one hand, they can directly elicit a state that the individual wants to get rid of, such as feelings of rejection or abandonment pain following real or imagined rejection or abandonment. On the other hand, they can have a more indirect impact by, for instance, triggering a state of consciousness in which – much in the same way as drink and substance misuse can increase impulsivity – the capacity to reflect is impaired or in which the propensity to be impulsive is increased. The impact of this kind of trigger is non-specific in that it is not specific to sexual offending but it is a background factor that increases the likelihood of any kind of offending or relapse to substance misuse.

Another related non-specific process is the notion of 'post traumatic risk-seeking' (e.g. Kerig, 2019)

> posttraumatic risk-seeking can be defined as the emergence in the aftermath of trauma of the active pursuit of experiences that serve the function of imparting

danger to the self or others. These behaviors are construed as intentionally motivated in that they serve distinctly posttraumatic functions, whether those involve striving for mastery, turning passive into active, masking vulnerability with fear defiance, escaping from intolerable emotions, or activation of reward centers of the brain following from surviving threat, but they do not necessarily require conscious recognition of their intention. Further, unlike more globally ascribed characteristics such as recklessness or sensation-seeking, which can be viewed as characterological in nature or related to other psychopathologies such as conduct disorder, posttraumatic risk-seeking refers specifically to the emergence of these behaviors following exposure to trauma.

Whilst Kerig is here referring to a general increase in risk-seeking following PTSD, clinical observation suggests that this phenomenon becomes more salient amongst traumatized people who have offended after further experiences of trauma or trauma reminders.

Trigger chaining also needs to be considered, Briere (2019); this is a process whereby one reaction, (e.g. shame) triggered by a current event then triggers a memory of another response (e.g. shame from an abusive experience) and this then triggers another response (e.g. memories of self-harm), which triggers a further reaction (e.g. panicky thoughts about having self-harmed). This is important as the triggers might not be directly related to the eventual reaction(s).

Sexual triggers

If we see sexual preoccupation as deriving from sexual system imprinting experiences, such as: (a) early childhood exposure to sexual experiences as a consequence of either sexual abuse or neglect linked with sexual acting out amongst peer group or exposure to pornography; and (b) exposure later in life to offence-oriented or offending pornography or information about offending that has a strong impact, then inevitably triggers for sexualized behaviour will include exposure to individuals or images that fit the individual's sexual script or 'love-map'.

Andrew

This fictional vignette illustrates a process of trauma triggering an increase in an already existent risk-seeking problem.

Andrew had been through a series of repeating and serious traumatic experiences in his childhood and adolescence (Layne et al., 2014 describe this as a cascade or risk factor caravan of traumatic experiences highlighting the complexity of multiple traumatic experiences – rather than traditional PTSD based single event conceptualizations of trauma). He was placed into care due to his mother's neglect, physical abuse and his father's sexual abuse. In care he was exposed to repeated experiences of loss and abandonment as he was moved from one foster family to another. He was also sexually abused and violently abused by peers and staff in the context of care. He reacted to this by becoming increasingly hostile and engaging in risk-seeking behaviour, such as stealing and abusive behaviour with peers and teachers. This resulted in him being moved within care, which further exacerbated the adverse impact. When he reached adolescence, he assaulted another child and was sentenced to a period in a young offenders' institution. Whilst there, he was assaulted sexually by older boys and violently assaulted also.

When he was released, he committed a series of three rape offences and was imprisoned again for a long sentence. In custody, he was involved in a dispute over a drug debt and was assaulted seriously by a group of five inmates. Following this, he began to self-harm and became extremely assaultive. It took little provocation to trigger him into strong reactions. He described enjoying the violence, saying that it made him excited. Occasionally he reported becoming sexually aroused when he was violent. He said that he had developed a survival strategy that involved 'getting in there first' if he felt threatened in terms of his 'status' or reputation.

This kind of risk-seeking can take on the form of a behavioural addiction that serves the function of regulating trauma-related affective dysregulation, particularly in the context of the absence of healthy attachment-based regulation and learning experiences (Katehakis, 2016).

The complexity of trauma accumulation as a causal process

Most practitioners think of PTSD when the concept of trauma is raised. However, more recent thinking in this area has highlighted the complexity of trauma and its cumulative impact across the life course. Layne et al. (2014) talk about 'risk factor caravans' for trauma having an impact:

> Risk factor caravans consist of constellations of causal risk factors that: a) occur, co-occur, and statistically covary; b) 'travel' with their host over time; c) each serve as a risk marker for the occurrence (whether temporally prior, concurrent, or subsequent) and adverse effects of one another; d) intersect with, and exacerbate, the adverse effects of one another in potentially complex ways; e) tend to increase their host's risk for subsequent exposure to, and vulnerability to the adverse effects of, additional risk factors; and f) accumulate in number, accrue, and 'cascade forward' in their cumulative adverse effects across development. In contrast, elements making up risk factor caravans do not necessarily: g) emanate from the same causal origin, h) occur, co-occur, or recur at the same point in

time or during the same developmental periods, i) relate in similar ways to other variables, j) carry the same risks, k) exert similar causal effects, l) operate through the same pathways of influence, m) eventuate in the same causal consequences or sequelae, or n) respond in similar ways to the same intervention components …

Jones (submitted) argues that this causal modelling framework can also usefully be used for thinking about risk factors for offending. What is clear, from clinical experience, is that there is a complex cascade of causal processes in the lives of people who offend. See Figure 13.2 for illustration of a characteristic trauma history of an individual who has offended seriously. Both the trauma impact on offending and the trauma impact on mental health is not a

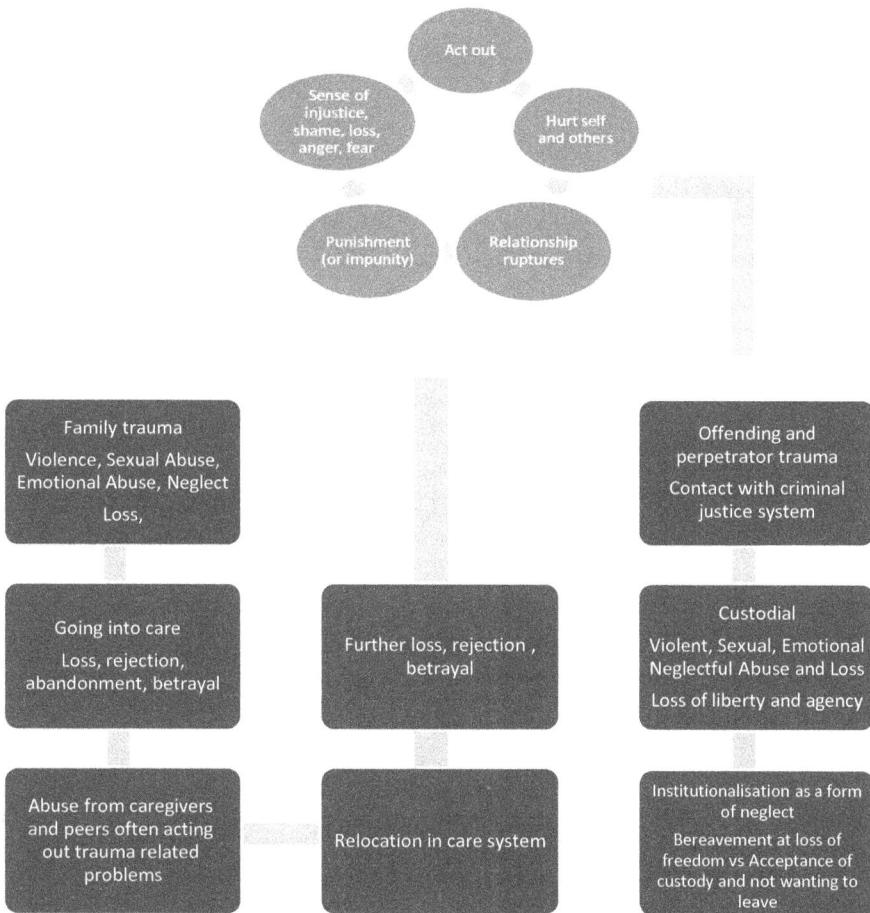

Figure 13.2 Developmental pathway frequently experienced by people who have offended repeatedly.

simple process. The Bentall et al. (2014) empirical programme attempting to identify specific kinds of psychological sequalae linked with specific kinds of trauma misses the importance of the complex interactions between multiply traumatic background factors that aggregate over time both in complexity and in their adverse impact (e.g. Farrell & Zimmerman, 2017).

Trauma triggers and OPB linked to sexual interest risk domains

Akerman and Beech (2013) identified a range of OPBs linked with empirically supported risk domains identified by Mann, Hanson, and Thornton (2010). In the following section, the sexual interest-related domains are explored in terms of the potential trauma triggers linked with each.

Sexual preoccupation

Attachment and trauma process

Sexualization developed in the context of sexual abuse is well documented in the literature on the impacts of child sexual abuse. One of the most common impacts of sexual abuse is sexualization and precocious sexual activity. Inevitably in childhood, when acted out with peers, this is offending behaviour. The impact of a poor attachment experience on this kind of acting out is not described or explored in the literature. However, seeking sexual contact as a way of meeting attachment needs has been previously hypothesized. For example, Liotti (2000) argued that, for people with traumatic attachment experiences resulting in a disorganized attachment style, there can be a propensity to *avoid* experiences where their attachment system is triggered. This is because the experiences that trigger the attachment system are associated with feelings of unsafety and distress. For this group of individuals, inhibiting the activation of the attachment system can be achieved in a number of ways; one of which is sexualizing attachment needs. Liotti (2000, p. 245) writes:

> inhibiting the activation of the attachment system implies a shift of the meaning attributed to the wish for bodily contact with another human being. Since both the attachment system (whose goal is protective proximity and comforting hug) and the sexual system imply a wish for physical closeness, borderline patients may misinterpret as sexual, both in themselves and in other

people, wishes that are instead related to attachment needs. It is because of the confusion between sexual and attachment wishes that borderline patients may appear improperly seductive within the therapeutic relationship and may get trapped into promiscuous or dangerous sexual affairs within other social relationships.

Briere (2019) also describes compulsive sexual behaviour as a response to trauma derived confusion between a need for attachment experiences and sex when an individual is experiencing distress. He construes sexual compulsivity as one of a set of Distress Reduction Behaviours (DRBs) used to manage trauma sequelae.

Associated with this is are the links between attachment trauma, sexual trauma, and sexual compulsivity highlighted by Katehakis (2016), essentially elaborating on the sex as coping model of the Ward and Siegert's (2002) emotional dysregulation pathway.

Trauma process triggers

The trauma related process here is relapse – often precipitated by an interpersonal crisis or loss resulting in negative affect – to, or reiteration of, sexually preoccupied behaviour originating in abuse related sexualization experiences. Sexual triggers such as pornography, images in magazines and television, listening to accounts of sexual offending from peers eliciting 'euphoric recall' – sometimes consciously or unwittingly inciting self or others to engage in this kind of discussion because of the 'euphoric recall'. In the absence of the possibility of having relationships individuals may increasingly take recourse to fantasy as a way of meeting sexual needs. Current interpersonal triggers such as loss or abandonment might be associated with fantasies that are about undoing this loss in some way (e.g. trapping or imprisoning somebody so that they can't get away). These fantasies can then parallel what was happening at the time of the offence.

Offence paralleling behaviour

OPB is behaviour in the current setting that is driven by the same or similar psychological mechanisms and process/processes as those that were evident in the lead up to and during the offence. Understanding the trauma origins of an individual's presentation can assist in identifying the kinds of precipitating factors for relapses.

Akerman and Beech (2013, p. 11) describes the following kinds of OPB linked with sexual preoccupation:

> Excessive discussion of sex, Sexualising female staff, stalking staff, Producing drawings of offence related images, Brushing against a female visitor, Excessive masturbation, Described having three to four sexual fantasies in a half-hour period, Sexualising non-sexual situations, Use of pornography, Seeking sex in prison.

Sexual preference for prepubescent or pubescent children

Attachment and trauma process linked with this preference

For some individuals, abuse has involved sexual contact with other children, for others abuse was modelled by perpetrators, which resulted in them believing it did no harm them (and consequently they don't believe it harms their victims). For some individuals, adults are associated with a range of abusive experiences and feelings of unsafety such as flashbacks to violent sexual or physical abuse. If, at the time of the abuse, they sought solace and support from other children then they may develop beliefs and attachment styles whereby they only feel a sense of attachment and intimacy with children; this can be associated with a sense that they themselves – as adults – are children. Alternatively, they may replay grooming experiences, developed in the context of their own abuse, whereby they feel that they are protecting or rescuing vulnerable children but then go on to abuse them. They describe seeing their victims as being like they were when they were vulnerable and abused. This may be influenced by their attachment needs for safety and security having been met by somebody who went on to abuse them. Identification with (social learning) perpetrators can develop out of this.

Trauma triggers

Being exposed to images of children, hearing, seeing or reading about vulnerable children. This triggers protective and 'rescuing' thoughts and feelings, and misinterpreting vulnerability as indicating sexual need – in a way that might parallel their own abuse. Experiences of violent abuse as an adult in the custodial context, or witnessing this in others, can trigger a return to seeking safety from children or others that they see as vulnerable.

Offence paralleling behaviour

Akerman and Beech (2013) describe the following kinds of OPB linked with sexual preference for prepubescent or pubescent children: 'Seeking images of children, Seeking sex change to a 'girl' to enable abuse, Watching children's' television. Seeking out collusive relationships with people in the custodial setting who are clearly very dependant, vulnerable and also identify with children in a similar manner can be evidence of a version of this pattern' (p. 11).

Sexualized violence

Attachment and trauma process

Some individuals who go on to develop a propensity to sexualized violence have had abusive and violent experiences from attachment figures in the past. The violence may be a generalized form of violence or may be more specifically focussed on female attachment figures. Residual feelings of anger and rage at experiences of shame or humiliation and rage linked with early violent and emotional abuse is a common theme. This is then played out in fantasy and offending. Shame can be conceptualized as loss of status, while the individual's reactions are attempts to 'turn the tables' and feel better by taking on a position of power in relation to them.

Trauma triggers

Triggers might be experiences where they are left feeling ashamed as a result of interaction with somebody that is similar to or reminds them of the early experiences of shame or humiliation. It is important to recognize that the reaction isn't just to the person now who has triggered a shame reaction, it is often a shame reaction deriving from a traumatic early experience – perhaps from a significant attachment figure – involving shame.

Offence paralleling behaviour

Akerman and Beech (2013) describe the following OPB linked to sexualized violence: 'exposing genitals to female members of staff, describing masturbating about female staff knowing it is non-consensual, describing films involving sexually violent scenes' (p. 11).

Paraphilic interest

Attachment and trauma process

Sexual behaviour influenced by unusual early sexual experiences, which in turn shape an individual's sexual script or 'love-map', can result in a range of paraphilic interests. Some of these interests can be specifically linked with offending behaviour. For example, sadistic interests can derive from experiences of being punished or abused in a violent manner (Longpré, Guay, & Knight, 2018; MacCulloch, Gray, & Watt, 2000). Also, paraphilias are often derived from early sexual experiences that are linked with the paraphilia (Pfaus et al., 2012). For example, being exposed to sexual abuse from an elderly woman may be linked to a later sexual interest in elderly women

Paraphilic interests and fantasies can also serve the functions attributed to fear-derived, trauma linked, risk seeking, as proposed by Kerig (2019). These can include 'striving for mastery, turning passive into active, masking vulnerability with fear defiance, escaping from intolerable emotions, or activation of reward centres of the brain following from surviving threat'.

Paraphilic interest does not, however, have to come out of interpersonal traumatic experiences. It can also derive from chance pairings of sexual arousal with some particular stimuli, such as experiencing arousal when rubbing against a particular object. For example, an individual who formed an attraction to stuffed animals reported:

> I've felt this way since I was 10 when I'd go to sleep cuddling a bear named Kerry. I used to rub myself against her, in quite an innocent way at first, and eventually I'd look forwards going to bed just so I could hold her. As I grew up, I tried to understand what was happening to me. I panicked that I'd developed feelings towards real animals, but after finding an online community of other plushophiles I realised these fears were unfounded.
>
> (Anonymous contributor to *The Guardian*'s
> 'My life in sex' column, 2019, p. 69)

Trauma triggers

Experiences that map onto sexual scripts are the obvious triggers for paraphilias. Reminders of abuse or of the paraphilia that evolved in the context of the abuse – for example, trauma compensation coping that involves taking on a perpetrator role – trigger the paraphilic response repertoire. Buschman and van Beek (2003) describe the development of fantasy interests in people who have offended sexually and who have personality disorder diagnoses developing out of traumatic childhood experiences being triggered by current events.

Offence paralleling behaviour

The kinds of OPB linked with paraphilia include: 'masturbating to an image of an animal, interest in particular (non-sexual) parts of a female's anatomy' (Akerman & Beech, 2013, p. 11).

Illustrative fictional case example – Chris

Attachment events

As we have seen, attachment events can trigger offence-related behaviours in the treatment setting. In the following fictional vignette, the trigger is the therapist being away for a protracted period of time. This is associated with a reaction involving a return to older ways of managing the attachment-related beliefs derived from early experiences of abandonment and neglect.

When Chris was 10 years old, his father left his mother and the family home. His father had frequently assaulted his mother and Chris witnessed this often. He sometimes tried to intervene to defend his mother, but this only served to provoke his father into assaulting him. Sadly, his father did not maintain contact with Chris. This left Chris feeling relieved – as the violence stopped – but also unloved and betrayed. He had an ongoing preoccupation with thoughts about previous traumatic events he had experienced or had witnessed in the family home. He had also learned an abusive version of what it meant 'to be a man' from these experiences and, later in his life, he acted in ways that were similar to what he had seen his father doing. He was violent both in relationships and in his offending.

Chris had also had significant experiences of separation from his mother on at least two occasions in his childhood. At the age of five, his mother was in a car accident and was seriously injured, spending six months in hospital. He was reported to have been strongly affected by his mother's absence, becoming aggressive and withdrawn at school. Soon after his father left the family home, his mother had a mental health crisis and was taken into psychiatric care. Chris was left with his maternal grandmother, eventually re-joining his mother when she was released from psychiatric care a year and a half later.

Chris's offending history was characterized by repeated episodes of violence, mainly where he experienced challenges to his status (e.g. he was in pub fights that started by perceived challenges to his status) or fears about his partner leaving him. He was more prone to violence when he had been working long hours, when he had little contact with his family, and after his partner had been away without him, when he would become increasingly preoccupied with thoughts of her being unfaithful to him, and he would withdraw and drink. His offence of rape had been committed following a row with his partner where he had left the house and had followed a woman and attacked her angrily and proceeded to rape her.

Model of offending

Reduced contact with his partner resulted in attachment fears associated with becoming withdrawn, ruminating about possible abandonment or infidelity, and a vulnerability to feeling threatened by others, or feeling that his status was being challenged. This was then triggered by arguments where these anxieties were played out and he felt a loss of control and used violence to try and force people into behaving in a manner that restored his sense of being in control. His rape offence was an instance of a range of situations where this same dynamic was played out and he used violence to offset feelings of shame and loss of power, safety or intimacy – real or imagined.

It was hypothesized that Chris would play out this kind of pattern of behaviour whilst in therapy – that if he felt insecure in relationships with staff, therapists or peers, this could trigger controlling behaviour including, but not exclusively, violence.

Offence paralleling behaviours

Chris was engaging well in his therapy attending sessions regularly and attempting to complete homework tasks and actively engaging in the therapy process. He had formed a good therapeutic relationship with his therapist. His therapist had to be away from work for a prolonged period and during this period he began to withdraw. He stopped spending time outside of his room, preferring to be alone for as much time as he could. When he explored this time after the event, he described spending a lot of time thinking about his therapist and thinking that he had been a fool to trust her and that she preferred working with other patients. He began to believe that she had gone away from work because she didn't want to work with him and that he had been too difficult for her. During this period, he was involved with an argument with another inmate and attempted to assault him violently. He was stopped by a member of staff who took him away from the situation and talked him down. He was described by staff as being preoccupied and distant at this time. When this was fed back to him, he reflected that he had been 'in a world of his own' or a 'paranoid bubble'. He reported that at this time he was having lots of intrusive thoughts about being abandoned and not being in control.

He also identified, after the event in therapy sessions exploring what had happened, having had – during this period – fantasies about being controlling and domineering and at times thinking about raping women. From an assessment perspective, it is important to use information about how the individual manages attachment ruptures in the present as a way of thinking about scenario planning for future possible relapses. In this pattern of behaviour, there is evidence of both attachment and status issues being triggered, which then link in with sexual thinking and fantasies.

There is also evidence of shifts in his social orientation to staff and state of consciousness; he reported a state of dissociation – the 'paranoid bubble' – and his preoccupation consisted of intrusive thoughts, all suggestive of a state in which his capacity to self-regulate was at least partially compromised by trauma-related state shifts. For generalist offenders, for whom sexual offending can be one of many forms of coercive behaviour that is triggered by status, attachment and safety crises, real or imagined, paralleling behaviour does not need to be sexual. It simply needs to be a pattern of behaviour that repeats the same kind of disturbed response to attachment based concerns deriving from early attachment traumas.

Conclusion

In this chapter, the critical role of psychological processes linked with early traumatic experiences impacting on the attachment system, the sexual system, the dominance system, the violence system, and substance misuse have been foregrounded as significant with regards to making sense of offending and assessing offending through working with OPB. Foregrounding trauma (see also Hasley, 2018) in this way helps the practitioner to think about a range of psychological processes that need to be actively evaluated in developing a formulation that can be used for both risk assessment and psychological intervention. Seeing psychological phenomena, such as sexual preoccupation, as being part of a complex constellation of responses to adverse developmental experiences (which includes significant shifts in states of consciousness, capacity and willingness to think, felt agency and bodily experiences) can facilitate the identification of new and more focussed interventions. Practitioners can use responses to custodial life events as a rich source of information about the kinds of response to life events at the time of the offence that lead to the sequence of events that, in turn, lead up to the offence.

Much work is required to further explore the role of trauma-derived psychological mechanisms in creating the context for the choices that people make in their offending. In this chapter, experiences of social oppression such as social stigmatization and 'othering', bullying, homophobia, racism, sexism, ageism and poverty have not been directly addressed. Future work needs to take these kinds of traumatic experience into account as a significant factor in the development of offending and explore how they interact with other kinds of trauma.

The framework developed by Becker-Blease and Kerig (2016) for exploring the developmental sequelae of trauma at different stages of the life course is a useful model to explore the range of relevant trauma processes. This highlights differential impact of trauma in infancy/toddlerhood, pre-school age, school age, early adolescence and late adolescence/adulthood on stage salient issues, cognitive development, attachment development, self-development, emotional development, moral development, social development, family relations, memory for trauma, risk outcomes, PTSD symptoms and trauma processing.

References

Akerman, G., & Beech, A. R. (2013). *Exploring offence paralleling behaviours in incarcerated offenders. Prisons and Prison Systems: Practices, types and challenges* (pp. 1–24). USA: Nova Publishers.

Anonymous contributor to Guardian's 'My life in sex' column (2019). *My life in sex, The Plushophile.* Guardian Weekend Magazine, 13th April 2019, p 69.

Becker-Blease, K., & Kerig, P. K. (2016) *Child Maltreatment: A developmental psychopathology approach.* Washington, DC. American Psychological Association.

Bentall, R. P., de Sousa, P., Varese, F., Wickham, S., Sitko, K., Haarmans, M., & Read, J. (2014). From adversity to psychosis: Pathways and mechanisms from specific adversities to specific symptoms. *Social Psychiatry and Psychiatric Epidemiology, 49*, 1011–1022.

Briere, J. (2019) *Treating risky and compulsive behavior in trauma survivors.* New York: Guilford.

Buschman, J., & van Beek, D. (2003). A clinical model for the treatment of personality disordered sexual offenders: An example of theory knitting. *Sexual Abuse, 15*, 183–199.

Farrell, C., & Zimmerman, G. (2017) Does offending intensify as exposure to violence aggregates? Reconsidering the effects of repeat victimisation, types of exposure to violence and poly-victimisation on property crime, violent offending and substance use. *Journal of Criminal Justice, 3*, 25–33.

Fonagy, P., Target, M., Gergely, G., Allen, J. G., & Bateman, A. W. (2003). The developmental roots of borderline personality disorder in early attachment relationships: A theory and some evidence. *Psychoanalytic Inquiry, 23*, 412–459. d.

Frewen, P., & Lanius, R. (2015). *Healing the traumatized self: Consciousness, neuroscience, and treatment.* New York: W. W. Norton.

Gilbert, P. (2017). Exploring compassion focused therapy in forensic settings: An Evolutionary and social-contextual approach. In J. Davies & C. Nagi (Eds.), *Individual psychological therapies in forensic settings.* London: Routledge.

Hackett, S., & Smith, S. (2018) '*Young people who engage in child sexual exploitation behaviours: An exploratory study.*', Project Report. Centre for Expertise on Child Sexual Abuse, Ilford, Essex.

Hasley, M. (2018) Child victims of adult offenders: Foregrounding the criminogenic effects of (unresolved) trauma and loss. *British Journal of Criminology, 57,* 17–36.

Hilburn-Cobb, C. (2004). Adolescent psychopathology in terms of multiple behavioral systems: The role of attachment and controlling strategies and frankly disorganized behavior. In L. Atkinson & S. Goldberg (Eds.), *Attachment issues in psychopathology and intervention* (pp. 95–135). Mahwah, NJ: Lawrence Erlbaum Associates.

Jones, L. (2016) *Conceptualising trauma and trauma informed care in forensic settings.* Paper presented at the joint Division of Forensic Psychology and Forensic Faculty of the Clinical Psychology Division of the British Psychological Society conference, Winchester.

Jones, L. (2019) New developments in interventions for working with offending behaviour. In D. L. L. Polaschek, A. Day, & C. R. Hollin (Eds.), *International handbook of correctional psychology.* Chichester: Wiley.

Jones, L. (submitted) Violence risk formulation; the move towards collaboratively produced, 'strengths based' safety planning. In S. Wormith, L. Craig, & T. Hogue (Eds) *What works in violence risk management: Theory, research and practice.* Chichester: John Wiley.

Kahneman, D. (2011). *Thinking, fast and slow.* Basingstoke: Macmillan.

Katehakis, A. (2016). *Sex addiction as affect dysregulation: A neurobiologically informed Holistic treatment.* New York and London: Norton.

Kerig, P. K. (2019). Linking childhood trauma exposure to adolescent justice involvement: The concept of posttraumatic risk-seeking. *Clinical Psychology: Science and Practice.* Doi:10.1111/cpsp.12280.

Kerig, P. K., & Becker, S. P. (2010). From internalizing to externalizing: Theoretical models of the processes linking PTSD to juvenile delinquency. In S. J. Egan (Ed.), *Posttraumatic stress disorder (PTSD): Causes, symptoms and treatment* (pp. 33–78). Hauppauge, NY: Nova Science Publishers.

Kingston, D. A., Graham, F. J., & Knight, R. A. (2017). Relations between self-reported adverse events in childhood and hypersexuality in adult male sexual offenders. *Archives of Sexual Behavior, 46,* 707–720. doi:10.1007/s10508-016-0873-5

Knight, R. A., & Sims-Knight, J. E. (2011). Risk factors for sexual violence. In J. W. White, M. P. Koss, & A. E. Kazdin (Eds.), *Violence against women and children, Volume 1: Mapping the terrain* (pp. 125–172). Washington, DC: American Psychological Association.

Köbach, A., & Elbert, T. (2015) Sensitive periods for developing a robust trait for appetitive aggression. *Frontiers in Psychiatry, 6,* 144.

Layne, C. M., Briggs, E., & Courtois, C. A. (2014). Introduction to the special section: Using the trauma history profile to unpack risk factor caravans and their developmental consequences. *Psychological Trauma: Theory, Research, Practice, and Policy, 6,* (Suppl. 1), S1–S8.

Liotti, G. (2000). Disorganized attachment, models of borderline states, and evolutionary psychotherapy. In P. Gilbert & K. Bailey (Eds.), *Genes on the couch: Essays in evolutionary psychotherapy* (pp. 232–256). Hove, UK: Psychology Press.

Liotti, G. (2017). The multimotivational approach to attachment-informed psychotherapy: A clinical illustration. *Psychoanalytic Inquiry, 37,* 319–331.

Longpré, N., Guay, J. P., & Knight, R. A. (2018). The developmental antecedents of sexual sadism. International handbook of sexual homicide. In J. Proulx, E. Beauregard, A. J. Carter, A. Mokros, R. Darjee, & J. James (Eds.), *Routledge international handbook of sexual homicide studies* (pp. 196–218). Abingdon, UK: Routledge.

MacCulloch, M., Gray, N., & Watt, A. (2000). Brittain's sadist murderer syndrome reconsidered: An associative account of the aetiology of sadistic sexual fantasy. *Journal of Forensic Psychiatry, 11,* 401–418.

Mann, R. E., Hanson, R. K., & Thornton, D. (2010). Assessing risk for sexual recidivism: Some proposals on the nature of psychologically meaningful risk factors. *Sexual Abuse, 22,* 191–217.

Mills, K., & Teeson, M. (1919). Trauma informed care in the context of alcohol and other drug use disorders. In R. Benjamin, J. Haliburn, & S. King (eds) *Humanising mental health care in Australia: A guide to trauma informed approaches.* Abingdon: Routledge.

Money, J., & Pranzarone, G. F. (1993). Development of paraphilia in childhood and adolescence. *Child and Adolescent Psychiatric Clinics of North America: Sexual and Gender Identity Disorders, 2,* 463–475.

Needs, A. (2018) Only connect: implications of social processes and contexts for understanding trauma. In Akerman, G., Needs, A. & Bainbridge, C. (Eds.) *Transforming Environments and Rehabilitation: A guide for practitioners in forensic settings and criminal justice.* Abingdon: Routledge.

Panksepp, J. (1998). *Affective neuroscience.* New York: Oxford University Press.

Parker, M. (2007) Repeating patterns, sexual abuse, sexualised internal working models and sexual offending. In M. Parker (Ed) *Dynamic security: The democratic therapeutic community in prison.* Jessica Kingsley. London.

Pfaus, J. G., Kippin, T. E., Coria-Avila, G. A., Gelez, H., Afonso, V. M., Ismail, N., & Parada, M., (2012). Who, what, where, when (and maybe even why)? How the experience of sexual reward connects sexual desire, preference, and performance. *Archives of Sexual Behavior, 41,* 31–62.

Ricci, R. J., & Clayton, C. A. (2016). EMDR with sex offenders: Using offense drivers to guide conceptualization and treatment. *Journal of EMDR Practice and Research, 10* (2), 104–118.

Shine, J., & Morris, M. (2000). Addressing criminogenic needs in a therapeutic community prison. *Therapeutic Communities, 21,* 197–219.

Shuker, R., & Jones, D. (2007). Assessing risk and need in a prison therapeutic community: An Integrative model. In M. Parker (Ed) *Dynamic security: The democratic therapeutic community in prison.* Jessica Kingsley. London.

Walton, M. T., Cantor, J. M., Bhullar, N., & Lykins, A. D. (2017). Hypersexuality: A critical review and introduction to the 'sexhavior cycle'. *Archives of Sexual Behavior, 46,* 2231–2251.

Ward, T., & Siegert, R. (2002). Toward a comprehensive theory of child sexual abuse: A theory knitting perspective. *Psychology, Crime & Law, 8,* 319–351.

Yates, P. M., & Ward, T. (2008). Good lives, self-regulation, and risk management: An integrated model of sexual offender assessment and treatment. Sexual Abuse in Australia and New Zealand: *An Interdisciplinary Journal, 1,* 3–20.

Index

AB *see* attentional blink

ABA *see* Applied Behaviour Analysis

abandonment 177, 181, 184, 187, 262, 265, 269

Abel, G. G. 6–7

acceptance 149, 159, 160

Acceptance and Commitment Therapy (ACT) 150, 154–155, 158–162, 163, 164–166

accountability 222–223

addiction 255, 262; *see also* substance abuse

Adi, Y. 206

adverse experiences 221–222, 223, 251, 252, 261, 268, 271; *see also* sexual abuse; trauma

'aesthetic response' 102

AFFSA 2 *see* Assessment Framework for Female Sexual Abusers

aggression 42–44; developmental path 258; example behavioural support plan 237–238, 240–241, 244; gender differences 225; PPG assessment 46–49; psychoanalytic approach 176, 177, 179, 180–181, 185, 186, 187–188, 190; *see also* violent offenders

Akerman, Geraldine 23–39, 264, 266, 267, 269

Allan, E. 224

Allen, B. P. 227–228

Alleyne, E. 122–123

American Psychiatric Association 174

American Psychological Association 164

amygdala 255

anger 181, 185, 201, 267

animals 6, 89–91, 269; *see also* bestiality

Antfolk, J. 91

anti-androgens 106, 202, 203, 204–207

antisociality 74, 75, 173, 195, 223, 227, 258

anxiety: emotional regulation 139; example behavioural support plan 236, 239, 243; problematic sexual arousal 199; psychoanalytic approach 173, 182, 187, 190; Rapid Serial Visual

Presentation 90, 91, 94; Sensate Focus 140

Applied Behaviour Analysis (ABA) 231–232

approach behaviours 252, 253–254, 255, 259, 260

approach goals 135–136

Arnell, K. M. 86, 94

arousal: attention-based measurement procedures 84–85; contingency learning 150–152; developmental trauma 260; emotionality of stimulus 87–88; eye-tracking 102, 104; hypersexuality 255–256; neuropsychological reinforcers 229; offence-related sexual interests 115; paraphilic sexual interests 268; PPG assessment 41, 44, 48, 50–51, 102–103; problematic 193–208; psychoanalytic approach 171; Rapid Serial Visual Presentation 88; Relational Frame Theory 156–157; risk factors for offending 223; sexual fantasizing 116; treatment 134, 139–141, 144–145

assessment: adverse experiences 251; Applied Behaviour Analysis 232; attachment issues 271; attention-based measurement procedures 84–85; Explicit and Implicit Sexual Interest Profile 59–78; eye-related measures 101–111; female sexual offending 227, 230–231; forensic contexts 57; meta-analyses of indirect latency-based measures 58; physical measures 83; Positive Behavioural Support 233–234; PPG 41–53; psychoanalytic approach 172, 190–191; psychometric tools 83–84; Rapid Serial Visual Presentation 85–96; sexual fantasy 115, 117, 118–126; *see also* questionnaires; risk assessment; self-reports

Assessment Framework for Female Sexual Abusers (AFFSA 2) 230

For Product Safety Concerns and Information please contact our EU
representative GPSR@taylorandfrancis.com
Taylor & Francis Verlag GmbH, Kaufingerstraße 24, 80331 München, Germany

www.ingramcontent.com/pod-product-compliance
Lightning Source LLC
Chambersburg PA
CBHW071839270326
41929CB00013B/2046

9 780367 254186